ERRATUM

The author, Reverend Jules A. Baisnée, S.S. is Professor of Philosophy and not Professor of Theology, as indicated on the cover.

THE COLLEGE READINGS SERIES, No. 7

Readings in
Natural Theology

Selected, with an Introduction

by JULES A. BAISNÉE, S.S.
Theological College
The Catholic University of America

THE NEWMAN PRESS • WESTMINSTER, MARYLAND

1962

Nihil obstat: EDWARD A. CERNY, S.S., S.T.D.
Censor Librorum
Imprimatur: LAWRENCE J. SHEHAN, D.D.
Archbishop of Baltimore

March 16, 1962

Copyright © 1962 by THE NEWMAN PRESS
Library of Congress Catalog Card Number: 62-16556
Printed in the United States of America

Preface

When the writer began his task of preparing a selection of Readings in Natural Theology, he was confronted with a difficult problem. Should an attempt be made to include as many authors as possible, making brief excerpts from the numerous books and articles in which the various aspects of the problem of God have been ably treated, or should the choice be restricted to the most eminent representatives of what may be called the classical tradition? The second course has been adopted. Important though many valuable articles contributed in recent years to leading Catholic philosophical reviews may be for a thorough understanding of certain fine points of theodicy, their insertion would have given undue extension to the present work.

As to the passages taken from the classical authorities, it has seemed preferable to quote these in full, so that the reader may form an adequate idea of their authors' contribution to theodicy. In most cases the texts are taken from the philosophers themselves; but because the arguments of certain authors like St. Augustine, St. Bonaventure, and John Duns Scotus, or their positions on certain important points of doctrine are found scattered throughout several of their works, it has seemed more useful to present an interpretation of their teaching by some established interpreter. When the name of a translator is not given, the article or passage has been translated by the editor.

In keeping with the more recent documents of the Church making St. Thomas the leading authority in Catholic philosophy, the plan generally followed in the arrangement of the texts quoted has been that of the First Part of the Summa Theologica. *But certain additions, especially in the introductory pages that deal with the problems of the origin of the idea of God and of the demonstrability of His existence, have been found indispensable for the proper setting forth of the Catholic solution of the problem of God against modern philosophical ideologies. Nevertheless, St. Thomas has been the guide faithfully followed, as will be evident to the reader who observes the numerous references to his works.*

The usual divisions of theodicy have been followed: in the first part the demonstrations of the existence of God have been given in a "chrono-

*logical" order; and, in the second, the various analyses of the divine at-
tributes and operations have been recorded. While he recognizes the
merits of this time-honored plan, the editor is aware that another scheme
could have been adopted, which would take into account the new trends
in philosophical thought.*

*The same arguments cannot impress in the same way minds that
have been molded after different patterns of thought. For instance, a
positivist or a Kantian will recognize the logic of the quinque viae, but
will refuse to grant the conclusion which refers to an order of reality
that he deems to be beyond the range of human reason. Materialists,
pantheists, and deists will see the force of St. Thomas' arguments from
motion and from contingency and acknowledge the existence of an ultimate reality, both immutable and necessary; but they will object to his
identification of the God of Christianity with that ultimate reality. Pantheists and deists will join with theists in rejecting the materialistic interpretation of the universe; but until the transcendence of God has been
made clear, and until the rejection of providence by the deists has been
shown to be baseless, we cannot think we have attained our goal, which
is to demonstrate the existence of the eternal, infinite spirit, creator and
ruler of the universe, the source of all truth, goodness, and beauty, endowed with what, for lack of a better word, we call personality, and
therefore worthy of adoration, praise, and love, as well as of fear; in one
word, the God whom we worship, and who revealed His name to Moses
as I AM WHO AM.*

*A progressive demonstration of God's existence may be conceived—it
has, in fact, been used to the evident satisfaction of the students to whom
it was offered—which would take into account the great variety of modern attitudes toward the religious problem.*

*Starting from the fact of the universality of religion, which is revealed
in history and ethnology, and which is a challenge to the human mind,
a way should be found to demonstrate God's existence by proving the
untenableness of various psychological or sociological theories which attempt to establish the illusory character of the idea of God by making
it the product of the tendency of the primitive mind to animism, ancestor worship, or fetishism.*

*Against all forms of Positivism and against Kantian subjectivism, epis-
temology vindicates the ability of the human mind to reach beyond the
world of experience. Upon this ability rests the validity of the metaphysical concept of cause and the corresponding principle of causality. Both*

*of these form the basis of the first step in the demonstration of God's
existence, viz., the need of admitting an ultimate principle, whatever
may be its nature, of all contingent and changing reality. All this should
be reasserted and has been at great length in Father Garrigou-Lagrange's
well-known work,* God: His Existence and His Nature.

*But at the same time, the need of moral dispositions to prepare the
mind to assent to a truth which involves such tremendous practical consequences in the life of the believer, which makes such a difference, to
use a term made popular by pragmatists, should be stressed with the
same vigor, as has been done by Léon Ollé-Laprune in his* La Certitude
Morale.

*The first step of the demonstration, in which all philosophers, mate-
rialists, and pantheists as well as deists and theists, concur, consists, as
we have said, in demonstrating the existence of some ultimate reality, or
first principle.*

*In the second step, issue is joined with the materialists. Even in its
"vitalized" form resulting from the introduction of Hegelian dialectic,
materialism makes matter the ultimate reality out of which have emerged
life, consciousness, thought, and all that gives value to human activity.
That mind rather than matter should be taken as the first principle is
clear to one who has the power of recognizing the hierarchy of beings,
and who sees the necessity of ascribing to any effect, and particularly to
orderly effects, a cause really proportionate. The more perfect cannot
originate from the less perfect except through the intervention of a cause
possessing at least the same degree of perfection as is found in the effect.
Neither life nor thought—with everything that thought implies, such as
self-consciousness, power of invention, freedom, and morality—could
have developed from matter. Nor could order have arisen from chaos
without the intervention of an intelligent cause.*

*At this point we would part company with pantheism. Stressing to
the extreme the truth that God is immanent in the world, pantheism refuses to acknowledge the divine transcendence; in other words, it makes
God the only reality, and the material and the spiritual worlds are mere
attributes of this reality. In whatever attenuated form it may be presented, such identification of mind and matter, of the infinite and finite,
runs against the principle of contradiction. God indeed lives in the
world, but He is also out of the world. He possesses the attribute of personality.*

Deism, on the contrary, stresses the divine transcendence to the point of denying God's presence and action in the world. It conceives God as living in splendid isolation from the universe which He has created and for which, as its great architect, He has established inviolable laws. Hence its denial of divine providence, and of the propriety of the worship of God, or of recourse to God by prayer. For the theist it is thus necessary to make as clear as possible to human reason the various modes of the divine action upon the universe of finite beings: creation, conservation, concurrence, and providence or government.

To crown his task, and at the same time to curb any temptation to intellectual pride which might arise in him when he forms an estimate of what he has accomplished, the student of theodicy should remind himself of the inadequacy of the concepts he has formed of God. Without taking to the letter the saying of one of the Fathers of the Church: Deus melius scitur nesciendo, *he should acknowledge that man is at best able to form only analogical concepts of the infinite being, who passes all understanding and is truly ineffable.*

It is the editor's hope that this volume, which has cost him much labor, but has also given him many hours of enjoyment, will help both teachers and students of philosophy in their search for Him who is the light of the soul. He wishes to express his deep gratitude to the Right Rev. Msgr. John K. Ryan, Dean of the School of Philosophy, The Catholic University of America, at whose suggestion he undertook this work, for his generous encouragement and his helpful suggestions, and to the Rev. John F. Smolko, M.A., for his cooperation in preparing the manuscript.

JULES A. BAISNÉE, S.S.

Theological College
The Catholic University of America
Washington, D. C.

Contents

*Section Two: Main Philosophical Demonstrations of the
Existence of God*

I. INTRODUCTION: HUMAN REASON'S APTITUDE TO DEMONSTRATE GOD'S EXISTENCE

II. GOD IN ANCIENT PHILOSOPHY

III. THE EXISTENCE OF GOD IN MEDIEVAL PHILOSOPHY

IV. THE EXISTENCE OF GOD IN MODERN PHILOSOPHY

Part Two

THE NATURE OF GOD AND DIVINE LIFE

Section One: The Analogical Character of Our Knowledge of God

Section Two: The Nature of God

I. THE METAPHYSICAL ATTRIBUTES OF GOD

II. THE ESSENCE OF GOD IS HIS EXISTENCE

III. THE TRANSCENDENCE OF GOD

Part Three

GOD AND HIS CREATURES

Section Two: God and His Co-operation with Creatures

I. DIVINE CONCURRENCE WITH CREATURES

II. PROVIDENCE AND GOVERNMENT

III. THE PROBLEM OF EVIL

READINGS IN NATURAL THEOLOGY

Introduction

1

GOD, THE OBJECT OF NATURAL THEOLOGY *

B Y THEOLOGY I simply mean the science of God, or the truths we know about God put into system; just as we have a science of the stars, and call it astronomy, or of the crust of the earth, and call it geology.

For instance, I mean, for this is the main point, that, as in the human frame, there is a living principle, acting upon it and through it by means of volition, so, behind the veil of the visible universe, there is an invisible, intelligent Being, acting on and through it, as and when He will. Further, I mean that this invisible Agent is in no sense a soul of the world, after the analogy of human nature, but, on the contrary, is absolutely distinct from the world, as being its Creator, Upholder, Governor, and Sovereign Lord. Here we are at once brought into the circle of doctrines which the idea of God embodies. I mean then by the Supreme Being, one who is simply self-dependent, and the only Being who is such; moreover, that He is without beginning or Eternal, and the only Eternal; that in consequence He has lived a whole Eternity by Himself; and hence that He is all-sufficient, sufficient for His own blessedness, and all-blessed, and ever-blessed. Further, I mean a Being who, having these prerogatives, has the Supreme Good, or rather is the Supreme Good, or has all the attributes of Good in infinite intenseness; all wisdom, all truth, all justice, all love, all holiness, all beautifulness; who is omnipotent, omniscient, omnipresent, ineffably one, absolutely perfect; and such that what we do not know and cannot even imagine of Him, is far more wonderful than what we do and can. I mean One who is sovereign over His own will and actions, though always according to the eternal Rule of right and wrong which is Himself. I mean, moreover, that He created all things out of nothing, and preserves them every moment, and could destroy them as easily as He made them; and that, in consequence, He is separated from them by an abyss, and is incommunicable in all His attributes. And further, He has stamped upon all things, in the hour of their creation, their respective natures, and has given them their work

* Cardinal John Henry Newman, *The Idea of a University Defined and Illustrated*, 3rd ed. (London: Pickering, 1873), Discourse III, "Bearing of Theology on Other Knowledge," pp. 61-66.

and mission and their length of days, greater or less, in their appointed place. I mean, too, that He is ever present with His works, one by one, and confronts everything He has made by His particular and most loving Providence, and manifests Himself to each according to its needs, and has on rational beings imprinted the moral law, and given them power to obey it, imposing on them the duty of worship and service, searching and scanning them through and through with His omniscient eye, and putting before them a present trial and a judgment to come.

Such is what Theology teaches about God, a doctrine, as the very idea of its subject-matter presupposes, so mysterious as in its fulness to lie beyond any system, and in particular aspects to be simply external to nature, and to seem in parts even to be irreconcilable with itself, the imagination being unable to embrace what the reason determines. It teaches of a Being infinite, yet personal; all-blessed, yet ever operative; absolutely separate from the creature, yet in every part of the creation of every moment; above all things, yet under everything. It teaches of a Being who, though the highest, yet in the work of creation, conservation, government, retribution, makes Himself, as it were, the minister and servant of all; who, though inhabiting eternity, allows Himself to take an interest, and to have a sympathy, in the matters of space and time. His are all beings, visible and invisible, the noblest and the vilest of them. His are the substance, and the operation, and the results of that system of physical nature into which we are born. His too are the powers and achievements of the intellectual essences, on which He has bestowed an independent action and the gift of origination. The laws of the universe, the principles of truth, and relation of one thing to another, their qualities and virtues, the order and harmony of the whole, all that exists, is from Him; and, if evil is not from Him, as assuredly it is not, this is because evil has no substance of its own, but is only the defect, excess, perversion, or corruption of that which has substance. All we see, hear, and touch, the remote sidereal firmament, as well as our own sea and land, and the elements which compose them, and the ordinances they obey, are His. The primary atoms of matter, their properties, their mutual action, their disposition and collocation, electricity, magnetism, gravitation, light, and whatever other subtle principles of operations the wit of man is detecting or shall detect, are the work of His hands. From Him has been every movement which has convulsed and re-fashioned the surface of the earth. The most insignificant or unsightly insect is from Him, and good in its kind; the ever-teeming, inexhaustible swarms of animalculae, the myriads of living motes invisible to the naked eye, the restless ever-spreading vegetation which creeps like a garment over the whole earth, the lofty cedar, the umbrageous banana, are His. His are the tribes and families of birds and beasts, their graceful forms, their wild gestures, and their passionate cries.

And so in the intellectual, moral, social, and political world. Man, with his motives and works, his language, his propagation, his diffusion, is from Him. Agriculture, medicine, and the arts of life, are His gifts. Society, laws, government, He is their sanction. The pageant of earthly royalty has the semblance and the benediction of the Eternal King. Peace and civilization, commerce and adventure, wars when just, conquest when humane and necessary, have His cooperation, and His blessing upon them. The course of events, the revolution of empires, the rise and fall of states, and the retrogressions of the world's history, not indeed the incidental sin, but the great outlines and the results of human affairs, are from His disposition. The elements and types and seminal principles and constructive powers of the moral world, in ruins though it be, are to be referred to Him. He "enlighteneth every man that cometh into this world." His are the dictates of the moral sense, and the retributive reproaches of conscience. To Him must be ascribed the rich endowments of the intellect, the irradiation of genius, the imagination of the poet, the sagacity of the politician, the wisdom (as Scripture calls it), which now rears and decorates the Temple, now manifests itself in proverb or in parable. The old saws of nations, the majestic precepts of philosophy, the luminous maxims of law, the oracles of individual wisdom, the traditionary rules of truth, justice, and religion, even though imbedded in the corruption, or alloyed with the pride, of the world, betoken His original agency and His long-suffering presence. Even where there is habitual rebellion against Him, or profound far-spreading social depravity, still the undercurrent, or the heroic outburst of natural virtue, as well as the yearnings of the heart after what it has not, and its presentiment of its true remedies, are to be ascribed to the Author of all good. Anticipations or reminiscences of His glory haunt the mind of the self-sufficient sage, and of the pagan devotee; His writing is upon the wall, whether of the Indian fane, or of the porticoes of Greece. He introduces Himself, He all but concurs, according to His good pleasure, and in His selected season, in the issues of unbelief, superstition, and false worship, and He changes the character of acts by His overruling operation. He condescends, though He gives no sanction, to the altars and shrines of imposture, and He makes His own fiat the substitute for its sorceries. He speaks amid the incantations of Balaam, raises Samuel's spirit in the witch's cavern, prophecies of the Messiah by the tongue of the Sibyl, forces Python to recognize His ministers, and baptizes by the hand of the misbeliever. He is with the heathen dramatist in the denunciations of injustice and tyranny, and his auguries of divine vengeance upon crime. Even on the unseemly legends of a popular mythology He casts His shadow, and is dimly discerned in the ode or the epic, as in troubled water or in fantastic dreams. All that is good, all that is true, all that is beautiful, all that is beneficent, be it great or small, be it perfect or fragmentary, natural as well as supernatural, moral as well as material, comes from Him.

If this be a sketch, accurate in substance and as far as it goes, of the doctrines proper to Theology, and especially of the doctrine of a particular Providence, which is the portion of it most on a level with human sciences, I cannot understand at all how, supposing to be true, it can fail, considered as knowledge, to exert a powerful influence on philosophy, literature, and every intellectual creation or discovery whatever. I cannot understand how it is possible, as the phrase goes, to blink the question of its truth or falsehood. It meets us with a profession and a proffer of the highest truths of which the human mind is capable.

2

CONTEMPORARY ATHEISM *

BENEATH the numerous surface-currents which carry contemporary thought in every direction, it seems possible to detect a deep undercurrent, by no means new—or rather a sort of immense *drift;* through the action of a large proportion of its foremost thinkers, the peoples of the West are denying their Christian past and turning away from God. This is not the everyday type of atheism which crops up in all ages, and is of no particular significance; nor is it the purely critical atheism so fashionable in the last two hundred years; for, though the effects of this are still conspicuously in evidence today, it does not represent a living force, since it is manifestly incapable of replacing what it destroys—its only function being to hollow a channel for that other atheism which is my real subject.

Contemporary atheism is increasingly positive, organic, constructive. Combining a mystical immanentism with a clear perception of the human trend, it has three principal aspects, which can be symbolised by three names: Auguste Comte, Ludwig Feuerbach (who must share the honour with his disciple, Karl Marx) and Friedrich Nietzsche. Through a number of intermediaries, and with a number of accretions, admixtures and, in many cases, distortions, the doctrines of these three nineteenth-century thinkers are, even today, the inspiration of three philosophies of life (social and political as well as individual), which all exercise a powerful attraction. Thus the immediate interest they present is only too manifest; and, whatever the vicissitudes of the causes and parties whose clashes occupy the front of the stage, there is a danger that these philosophies, perhaps in new forms, will long continue to be a matter of direct concern.

The negation which underlies Positivist humanism, Marxist humanism and Nietzschean humanism is not so much atheism, in the strict

* The Drama of Atheist Humanism by Henri de Lubac, S.J., trans. by Edith M. Riley. Copyright 1950 by Sheed and Ward, Inc. Reprinted by permission.

sense of the word, as *anti*theism, or, more precisely, antichristianism. Great as the contrast is between them, their common foundation in the rejection of God is matched by a certain similarity in results, the chief of which is the annihilation of the human person. This dual character I have tried to place in the strongest light. The reader will find in these pages hardly any theoretical discussion and little of what is commonly called, and goes by the name of "theology." What the book offers is merely a historical survey in which special emphasis has been laid upon the essential feature—often passed over too lightly.

First and foremost, then, it is suggested that Christians should take cognizance of the spiritual situation of the world in which they are involved. It is recognized that Positivism is an immense edifice of scientific philosophy and practical politics; that Marxism, which has received its Summa if not its Bible in *Das Kapital,* is a vast and powerful system of political and social economy; and that Nietzsche's ideas offer an extraordinary profusion of pedagogic resources (in the profoundest sense of the term). . . . There are many elements to be found in all three to which a Christian, as such, is not required to define his attitude; there are many others, often mutually contradictory, which he would have the right to claim as his own, after rescuing them from the synthesis which has warped them. They contain many audacities which do not frighten him. And, even at their most blasphemous, they advance criticisms whose justice he is bound to admit.

These three systems, of course, are not three cast-iron constructions. In the real life of the human mind many dissociations take place, so that not all those who call themselves Positivists, Marxists or Nietzscheans are necessarily atheists. Some, for instance, leaving the metaphysical problem open, join the Marxists only for the sake of their special programme, or, without even examining the details of that programme, because of their own aspirations for society; they are, in some cases, more Christian than those who oppose them; and often they have a clearer insight into history. Certain maxims of Comtist origin have served for the expression of what is soundest in conservative circles. Many ideas of a more or less Marxist, Nietzschean or Positivist stamp may even find a place in some blueprint for a new synthesis, and neither its orthodoxy nor its value will be called into question in that account. In the Church, the work of assimilation never ceases, and it is never too soon to undertake it. Nevertheless, all systems, as shaped and held together by their underlying inspiration, have their own internal logic; and not to see this quite clearly from the outset is to run the risk of going dangerously astray. In the threefold case engaging our attention, this inspiration and this logic are very forcibly thrusting mankind away from God, and at the same time urging it along the lines of a double bondage, social and spiritual.

Feuerbach and Marx, like Comte and Nietzsche, were convinced that faith in God was disappearing forever. The sun was sinking on our horizon never to rise again. Their atheism both believed and rejoiced in its own finality, having, it thought, this advantage over former atheisms, that it discarded everything, even to the problem which had brought God to birth in man's consciousness. They were antitheists like Proudhon, but in a still more radical way; and they did not come to his conclusion that the existence of God, like that of man, "is proved by the eternal antagonism between them." They did not share his sense of the militant return of mystery after each attempt to overcome it. Beneath the variety of its manifestations, their "humanism" seems equally lightless. Yet the sun did not cease to rise. Marx was not yet dead, and Nietzsche had not yet written his most searing books, when another man, another disturbing but more truly prophetic genius, announced the victory of God in the human soul, and his eternal resurrection.

Dostoevsky was only a novelist. He originated no system, he supplied no solution for the terrible problems with which our age is confronted in its efforts to organise social life. But he made one profoundly important truth clear; man cannot organise the world for himself without God; without God he can only organise the world *against man*. Exclusive humanism is inhuman humanism. Moreover, it is not the purpose of faith in God to install us comfortably in our earthly life that we may go to sleep in it. On the contrary, faith disturbs us and continually upsets the too beautiful balance of our mental conceptions and our social structures. Bursting into a world that perpetually tends to close in upon itself, God brings it the possibility of a harmony which is certainly superior, but is to be attained only at the cost of a series of cleavages and struggles coextensive with time itself. "I came not to bring peace, but a sword." Christ is, first and foremost, the great disturber. That certainly does not mean that the Church lacks a social doctrine, derived from the Gospel. Still less does it tend to deter Christians, who, like their brothers, are men and members of the city, from seeking to solve the city's problems in accordance with the principles of their faith; on the contrary, it is one more necessity impelling them to do so. But they know at the same time that, the destiny of man being eternal, he is not meant to find ultimate repose here below.

PART ONE

The Existence of God

Section One
Belief in God and Its Sources

I. Universal Belief in God

While the argument for the existence of God based upon the universality of religious belief and practice has lost the appeal it enjoyed when Traditionalism flourished in the early nineteenth century, the fact of such a universality continues to challenge the mind of the religious inquirer. We shall quote a few testimonies, both ancient and modern, which make the fact clear.

3

ANCIENT TESTIMONIES

Two Latin authors: Marcus Tullius Cicero (106–43 B.C.), and Marcus Aurelius Seneca (3 B.C.–A.D. 65), and one Greek author (46?–A.D. 120), are quoted in J. Donat's *Theodicea* (ed. 7a, 1936, p. 75). We give our English translations of these texts. Cicero writes in *De natura deorum*, B. II, c. 4: "Belief in gods is universal among people; it seems to be innate and, as it were, engraved on the human soul. Men may entertain different notions as to their nature, but no one denies their existence." Seneca in his Epistle 117: "Belief in gods is innate in the human soul, and there are no people so devoid of respect for law and morals as not to admit the existence of some divinity." And Plutarch in his treatise *Adversus Coleten*, c. 31: "If you go around the world, you may find towns without walls, without laws, without houses, without wealth, without money; in which there are neither gymnasiums nor theatres; but no one has ever seen a town without temples and divine worship; where no recourse is had to oaths and oracles; where no sacrifice is offered for the common weal; where no attempt is made to ward off evils by means of sacrifices."

4

MODERN TESTIMONIES

UNDER the influence of the doctrine of evolution, many histories of religion assume that the so-called "primitive" races were devoid of religion and attempt to trace the origin of belief in God to nature worship or ancestor worship. These views have been challenged by eminent authorities in the field of anthropology. We shall quote three of these: 1) Andrew Lang (1844–1912) in *The Making of Religion* (Longmans, 1898); 2) Wilhelm Schmidt, S.V.D. (1868–1954), editor of *Anthropos*, in *The Origin and Growth of Religion: Facts and Theories*, trans. by H. J. Rose (The Dial Press, 1931); 3) Alexandre Le Roy of the Congregation of the Holy Ghost (1854–1938), who started his apostolate among the Bantus of East Africa, in *Religion of the Primitives*, trans. by Newton Thompson (Macmillan, 1922).

In the conclusion of Andrew Lang's work (pp. 328–329), we read: "We turned from the subject of supernormal experiences to the admitted facts about early religion. Granting the belief in souls and ghosts and spirits, however attained, how was the idea of a Supreme Being to be evolved out of that belief? We showed that, taking creeds as found in the lowest races, the process put forward by anthropologists could not account for their evolution. The facts would not fit into, but contradicted the anthropological theory. The necessary social conditions postulated were not found in places where the belief is found. Nay, the necessary social conditions for the evolution even of ancestor-worship were confessedly not found where the supposed ultimate result of ancestor-worship, the belief in a Supreme Being, flourished abundantly."

Father Schmidt sums up the result of his researches on the Primitive High God in the following words (*op. cit.*, ch. 16, p. 282): "If now we briefly review the data, we find that while this or that form of worship may be wanting in a particular tribe, no tribe is known in which there is not some form in use. As we might expect, prayer has the widest distribution; but, even here, we may be sure that there is still much to discover, and that much will be discovered. The wide distribution of the first-fruits in this, the oldest culture, is of great importance as a matter of principle. The cult of the Supreme Being has already reached a very high level among several Pygmy races, also in the Arctic culture, among the Algonkin, and, in North Central California, in the combination of prayer and sacrifice, in a solemn expressive ceremonial. But it is to be noted that these are the areas where the best and most thoroughly trained observers have been employed. Perhaps equally competent researches in South-East Australia, for instance, might have discovered yet more; and it may be that the Pygmy races of Africa still have many surprises in store for us."

From Bishop Le Roy's *Religion of the Primitives*, ch. IV, "Belief," we quote the following lines, pp. 125–128:

In the mind of our Negrillos and Bantus, Mulungu (i.e., God) is certainly not the sky—dry or rainy—nor the light, nor the moon, nor the wind, nor the water, nor the earth, and so on. He is in all of them, he acts in and by all these elements, he is sometimes assimilated to them, but his personality is distinctly separate from them; he is something else.

God is not in their minds the "power" (totemistic or otherwise) of nature or society, in the sense that our philosophers and sociologists mean it; this refined, critical idea is altogether foreign to our poor savages. God is not conceived by them as the "Principle of Good" in opposition to a "Principle of Evil," whose effects would appear to our eyes and for which our mind would seek a cause; that too, is an idea that is not in vogue in the black country.

God is not to them a deified chief. The Negrillos have no chief, they do not claim any special ancestor; but they have a very precise idea of God. God is not to them a "spirit," neither the "spirit" of a dead man nor an independent "spirit"; he is conceived as anterior to death, as having never died himself; and he it is precisely who commands life. . . .

Among the Blacks, God does not come from an abstract union in one personality of the multitude of powers and qualities attributed to different spirits, nor from the necessity of giving a president to the assembly of inferior divinities, nor from any like conception. Once again, we repeat, these ideas proceed from speculations to which the black world is a total stranger. Whence, then, have our Bantus received the idea of God? To tell the truth, in this study we prefer to prove that this idea exists than to indicate its origin. In fact, we do not know its origin. . . .

This notion naturally suggests that of master, proprietor, and sovereign of the universe . . . God, the Master of the world, is also the Father of men. . . . He, the author of life, is also the author of death in the sense that he takes the souls of men when he wishes and as he wishes with no one able to hinder or reproach him. . . . It is God who sends the rain, warning men of its coming by the voice of the thunder, and it is he who keeps it back; it is he who makes the grass grow in the plains for the herds; it is he who makes the forest green, makes the fruits ripen and the crops prosper; it is he who feeds all—trees, beasts, and men. The entire world, in fine, is dependent on him.

5

THEISM IN POSSESSION *

A N ATHEIST is one who is not a theist. Atheists may be divided into two classes, positive and negative. Positive atheists are those who deny positively the existence of God, and profess to be able to prove that God is not; negative atheists are those who, if they do not deny positively that God is, maintain that he is unknowable, that we have, and can have no proof of his existence, no reason for asserting it, for the hypothesis of a God explains and accounts for nothing. Of this latter class of atheists are the Comtists and the Cosmists, or those who take Auguste Comte for their master and those who swear by Herbert Spencer.

False theists, or pantheists, reject the name of atheists, and yet are not essentially distinguishable from them. They are divided into several classes: 1, the emanationists, or those who hold that all things emanate, as the stream from the fountain, from the one and only being or substance which they call God, and return at length to him and are reabsorbed in him; 2, the generationists, or those who hold that the only being or substance is in itself both male and female, and generates the world from itself; 3, the formationists, or those who, like Plato and Aristotle, hold that God produces all things by giving form to a preexisting and eternal matter, as an artificer constructs a house or temple with material furnished to his hand; 4, the ontologists, or Spinozists, who assert that nothing is, or exists, but being or substance, with its attributes or modes; 5, the psychologists or egoists, or those who assert that nothing exists but the soul, the Ego, and its productions, modes, or affections, as maintained by Fichte.

There are various other shades of pantheism; but all pantheists coalesce and agree in denying the creative act of being producing all things from nothing, and all, except the formationists, represented by Plato and Aristotle, agree in maintaining that there is only one substance, and that the cosmos emanates from it, is generated by it, or is its attribute, mode, affection, or phenomenon. The characteristic of pantheism is the denial of creation from nothing and the creation of substantial existences or second causes, that is, existences capable, when sustained

* Orestes A. Brownson (1803-1876), *The Works*, collected and arranged by Henry F. Brownson (Detroit: Thorndike Nourse, 1882), "Essay in Refutation of Atheism," Vol. II, pp. 4-9.

by the first cause, of acting from their own centre, and producing effects of their own. Plato and Aristotle approach nearer to theism than any other class of pantheists, and if they had admitted creation they would not be pantheists at all, but theists.

Omitting the philosophers of the Academy and the Lyceum, all pantheists admit only one substance, which is the substance or reality of the cosmos, on which all the cosmic phenomena depend for their reality, and of which they are simply appearances or manifestations. Here pantheism and atheism coincide, and are one and the same; for whether you call this one substance God, soul, or nature, makes not the least difference in the world, since you assert nothing above or distinguishable from the cosmos. Pantheism may be the more subtle form, but is none the less a form of atheism, and pantheists are really only atheists; for they assert no God distinct from nature, above it, and its creator.

Pantheism is the earliest form of atheism, the first departure from theology, and is not regarded by those who accept it as atheism at all. It undoubtedly retains many theistical conceptions, around which the religious sentiment may linger for a time; yet it is no-theism and no-theism is atheism. Pantheism, if one pleases, is inchoate atheism, the first step in the descent from theism, as atheism is the blossom of the ripe fruit. Pantheism is a misconception of the relation of cause and effect, and the beginning of the corruption of the ideal; atheism is its total corruption and loss. It is implicit not explicit atheism, as every heresy is implicitly though not explicitly the total denial of Christianity, since Christianity is an indivisible whole. In this sense, and in this sense only, are pantheism and atheism indistinguishable.

Pantheism in some of its forms underlies all the ancient and modern mythologies; and nothing is more absurd than to suppose that these mythologies were primitive, and that Christianity has been gradually developed from them. Men could not deny God before his existence had been asserted, nor could they identify him with the substance or reality manifested in cosmic phenomena if they had no notion of his existence. Pantheism and atheism presuppose theism; for the denial cannot precede the affirmation, and either is unintelligible without it, as Protestantism is unintelligible without the church in communion with the See of Rome against which it protests. The assertion of the papal supremacy necessarily preceded its denial. Dr. Draper, Sir John Lubbock, as well as a host of others, maintain that the most perfect forms of religion have been developed from the less perfect, as Professor Huxley maintains that life is developed from protoplasm, and Charles Darwin that the higher species of animals have been developed from the lower, man from the ape or some one of the monkey tribe, by the gradual operation for ages of what he calls "natural selection."

It has almost passed into an axiom that the human race began, as religion, in fetichism, and passed progressively through the various forms of polytheism up to the sublime monotheism of the Jews and Christians;

yet the only authority for it is that it chimes in with the general theory of progress held by a class of antichristian theorists and socialists, but which has itself no basis in science, history, or philosophy. So far as history goes, the monotheism of the Jews and Christians is older than polytheism, older than fetichism, and in fact, as held by the patriarchs, was the primitive religion of mankind. There is no earlier historical record extant than *Genesis,* and in that we find the recognition and worship of only one God, Creator of the heavens and the earth, as well established as subsequently with the Jews and Christians. The oldest of the Vedas are the least corrupt and superstitious of the sacred books of the Hindoos, but the theology even of the oldest and purest is decidedly pantheistic, which, as we have said, presupposes theism, and never could have preceded the theistical theology. Pantheism may be developed by way of corruption from theism, but theism can never be developed in any sense from pantheism.

All the Gentile religions or superstitions, if carefully examined and scientifically analysed, are seen to have their type in the patriarchal religion—the type, be it understood from which they have receded, but not the ideal which they are approaching and struggling to realize. They all have their ideal in the past, and each points to a perfection once possessed, but now lost. Over them all hovers the memory of a departed glory. The *genii, deus,* or *dii,* the good and the bad demons of the heathen mythologies, are evidently travesties of the Biblical doctrine of good and bad angels. The doctrines of the fall, expiation, and reparation by the suffering and death of a God or Divine Person, which meet us under various forms in all the Indo-Germanic or Aryan mythologies and indeed in all the known mythologies of the world, are evidently derived from the teachings of the patriarchal or primitive religion of the race—not the Christian doctrine of original sin, redemption, and reparation by the passion and death of Our Lord, from them. The heathen doctrines on all these points are mingled with too many silly fables, too many superstitious details and revolting and indecent incidents, to have been primitive, and clearly prove that they are a primitive doctrine corrupted. The purest and simplest forms are always the earliest.

We see also, in all these heathen mythologies, traces or reminiscences of an original belief in the unity of God. Above all the *Dii Majores* and the *Dii Minores* there hovers, so to speak, dimly and indistinctly it may be, one supreme and ever-living God to whom Saturn, Jupiter, Juno, Venus, Vulcan, Mars, Dis, and all the other gods and goddesses to whom temples were erected and sacrifices were offered, were inferior and subject. It is true the heathen regarded him as inaccessible and inexorable; paid him no distinct worship, and denominated him Fate or Destiny; yet it is clear that in the *to en* of the Alexandrians, the Eternity of the Persians, above both Ormuzd and Ahriman, the heathen retained at least an obscure and fading reminiscence of the unity and supremacy of the one God of tradition. They knew him, but they did not, when they knew him, worship him as God, but gave his glory unto creatures or empty idols.

We deny, then, that fetichism or any other form of heathenism is or can be the primitive or earliest religion of mankind. The primitive or earliest religion of mankind was a purely theistical religion. Monotheism is, historically as well as logically, older than polytheism; the worship of God preceded the worship of nature, the elements, the sun, moon, and stars of heaven, or the demons swarming in the air. Christian faith is in substance older than pantheism, as pantheism is older than undisguised atheism. Christian theism is the oldest creed, as well as the oldest philosophy of mankind, and has been from the first and still is the creed of the living and progressive portion of the human race.

Christianity claims, as everybody knows, to be the primitive and universal religion, and to be based on absolutely catholic principles, always and everywhere held, though not held by all individuals, or even nations, free from all admixture of error and superstition. Yet analyse all the heathen religions, eliminate all their differences, as Mr. Herbert Spencer proposes, take what is positive or affirmative, permanent, universal, in them, as distinguished from what in them is negative, limited, local, variable, or transitory, and you will have remaining the principles of Christianity as found in the patriarchal religion, as held in the Synagogue, and taught by the Church of Christ. These principles are all absolutely catholic or universal, and hence Christianity, in its essential principles at least, is really the universal religion, and in possession as such. The presumption, as say the lawyers, is then decidedly in favor of the Christian and against the atheist.

Christianity, again, not only asserts God and his providence as its fundamental principle, but claims to be the law of God, supernaturally revealed to man, or the revelation which he had made of himself, of his providence, of his will, and of what he exacts of his rational creatures. Then, again, Christianity asserts, in principle, only the catholic or universal belief of the race. The belief in God, in providence, natural power, and in supernatural intervention in human affairs in some form, is universal. Even the atheist shudders at a ghost story, and is surprised by sudden danger into a prayer. Men and nations may in their ignorance and superstition misconceive and misrepresent the Divinity, but they could not do so, if they had no belief that God is. Prayer to God or to gods, which is universal, is full proof of the universality of the belief in Divine Providence and in supernatural intervention. Hence, again, the presumption is in favor of Christian theism and against the atheist.

Of course, this universal belief, or this *consensus hominum*, is not adduced here as full proof of the truth of Christianity, or of the catholic principles on which it rests; but it is adduced as a presumptive proof of Christianity and against atheism, while it undeniably throws the burden of proof on the atheist, or whoever questions it. It is not enough for the atheist to deny God, providence, and the supernatural; he must sustain his denial by proofs strong enough, at least, to turn the presumption against Christianity, before he can oblige or compel the Christian to plead. Till then, "So I and my fathers have always held," is all the reply he is required to make to anyone that would oust him.

II. Sources of Belief in God

6

ORIGIN OF BELIEF IN GOD *

THERE are many theories about the origin of the idea of God, and their number has increased in the last century. Most of them give no explanation of it, or, unconsciously, cause to vanish the very fact they attempt to explain. They mix up the most diverse methods of investigation and take their inspiration from the a priori assumption that belief in God is an illusion. Their starting point is atheism, which they keep on assuming through their researches: no wonder that it is their conclusion. The conclusion which, in general, they more or less explicitly reach is that we should reject the idea of God because we have found "the mechanism through which *man* has constructed that idea, and that this mechanism is a self-deception." But that is merely begging the question.

For instance, it is said that man has made heaven a god. Even if we should grant the fact, we would ask where he got the idea of divinity in order to apply it to the heavens. Why do we observe everywhere among men that spontaneous instinct? How can we account for that deification of heaven, or of any other being? Appealing to philology, some argue that the Latin word *Deus* means nothing but "the heavens made luminous by day-light." Be it so, but how did men come to see a god in this luminous heaven? Many fail to see that this involves a problem.

All those who claim that the idea of God had a genesis in the proper sense of the word—whether they conceive that genesis as ideological or sentimental, as individual or social, and hold either that it is a complete illusion, or that it has some relative basis—all of them, I say, start with denying, at least implicitly, the validity of the idea of God. They deny it by reducing it to *something which it is not*. "It is hard to see," writes Mircea Eliade in *Le Chamanisme* (1951), "how the fact, that the discovery of the first laws of geometry can be traced to the empirical requirements of the irrigation of the Nile delta, has any bearing on the validity or invalidity of those laws."

* Henri de Lubac, S.J., *Sur les chemins de Dieu* (Paris: Aubier, 1956), ch. I.

We may here use the same argument. We do not see how the fact that the first dawning of the idea of God in human consciousness may have been prompted by this or that spectacle, or linked with such or such experience of the senses, could warrant questioning the validity of that idea. In both cases we must distinguish the problem of the empirical origin from the problem of the essence and validity of the idea. They belong to different orders. No more than land-measuring was the real source of geometry, was the sight of a storm or of the luminous heaven the real source of the idea of God. That idea must be considered in itself and in its intrinsic bases, not in the occasions of its apparition.

If the idea of God is really valid, no fact of history, psychology, sociology, or any other science can be taken as the cause that brought it about. No observable process can account for it. If it is understood in this sense, it had no genesis, any more, to resume our comparison, than geometry had a genesis. This does not mean—far from it—that it cannot be "inferred"; it means that it cannot be reduced to the illusory result of some empirical transformation. Its springing in human consciousness may have depended on various conditions, been brought about by various circumstances, and determined by this or that token. Certain phenomena may have proved especially apt to awaken the mind by some warning stimulus. It is possible, for instance, that "the first idea of the Word of God as a cosmic power" should have come to our ancestors through "the natural phenomenon of a storm, for did not the pealing of thunder suggest the mighty voice of the Eternal?" (Psalm 28). Many other hypotheses can be offered with more or less probability, greater or less support, which, after all, are not necessarily opposed to each other, but often complementary. It is therefore possible and interesting to analyze certain conditions and methods that have led to the discovery of God; and here we find an abundance of useful information in the works of historians, ethnologists and psychologists, even though most of it is inadequate. Rich as may be their findings, they cannot account for the essential. We should not commit the fallacy of "looking for principles in mere beginnings."

There are ways, innumerable ways, which actually lead us to God. They may be diverse, but some are sound and universally valid, giving a rational basis to our idea of God and strength to our affirmation of His existence. For it is possible to "reach HIM WHO IS if we take as our starting point any reality of which it can be said that it is, but of which it must also be said that it is not" (Gilson, Le Thomisme). On a level very different from that of empirical processes, they are proofs of God's existence. And that is the very reason why, in the strict sense of the term, there can have been no "genesis" of the idea of God.

The words of St. Thomas (in In Polit. I, 2): "He who considers things in their first growth and origin . . . will obtain the clearest view of them," find here their application. For precisely—and St. Thomas makes it clear—it is not in our power to have such knowledge of God. The idea of God can be explained neither as the idea of an illusion of which we understand perfectly the sources, nor as that of some mental construct.

A great controversy centers around the question whether the objective affirmation of God pertains to "logical" or to "mythical" thought, to reason or imagination; or again to truth or illusion. But it may be that sufficient advertence is not had to the existence of logical illusions, to the mind's temptation to extrapolate into the field of imagination, or to the danger it runs of being too "rational" to be able to discover Him Who is above reason. . . . Is the God of rationalism really "the True God"? Is the idea of such a God truly founded on reason?

Actually, the authentic affirmation of God—which is much more than an affirmation—belongs primarily to the deepest mental operation, which is neither "mythical" nor purely "logical," even though, in its expression it must ordinarily borrow the ways of logic, while it makes use of the power of imagination to embody that expression, so that we find in its spontaneous formulations a structure analogous to the structure of myths. Perhaps we should rather use a word, in spite of its recent misuse, which would take all these elements into account, and call that affirmation "symbolical," or as the ancient fathers liked to call it, "anagogical."

Mythical or logical instinct? The first would lead us only to an illusory deity; and the second, if it were used alone, to a God who would not be holy. And yet both instincts are at work, united by a mysterious synergy, under the direction of a "divine instinct."

All the attempts at explaining the "genesis" of the idea of God, or its "reduction"—or at explaining it by "a reductive genesis"—fail in some respect. It is a distinct, a unique idea, which has run through human history like flashes of lightning upsetting the painstaking syntheses of ethnologists and historians, of all evolutionary theories, of all the learned "physiologies of religion." As soon as human intelligence reaches maturity, the idea of God springs in it spontaneously.

However, no matter how indestructible it may be henceforth, it is far from attaining at once its full brilliancy. It is far also from settling in the intelligence in peace and prevailing. On the contrary, one might believe that, like the Gospel seed falling among brambles, the germ is quickly stifled under a mad proliferation of myths. Or, if it bears fruit, that fruit gets so intermingled with luxuriant varieties of tares, that it seems impossible to get rid of the tares without uprooting the fruit. So, in proportion as religion coexists with myths, it imparts to them a new power of seduction, which turns against it. The parasites, which the gods are, feed secretly on the idea of God, and thus prevent the true God from appearing. Hence that "deluge of idolatry" over the surface of the earth. So, to reach a pure religion, we seem to be bound to sweep away rather than purify all deities, or test their title to be recognized as genuine. Man often gets rid of superstition by becoming an atheist, only to fall back into superstition. How many hypotheses he is apt to imagine!

But he cannot escape falling into a vicious circle. Every path he takes fails to satisfy his reason; new difficulties arise; new illusions have to be cleared away. Most of such men fail to reach certitude, or fall into errors. Even the monotheist who proclaims God with such rational assurance often experiences hesitations—

> O Chariot of earth, and thou who hast thy seat over earth,
> Whoever thou art, hard to be known even by conjecture,
> Jove, whether [thou art] the necessity of nature, or the
>   mind of mortals. . . .
>   (Euripides, *The Troades,* v. 884-886.)

—unless God Himself, breaking the fatal circle, choose a confidant to whom He gives the mission of making Him known to his brethren. And this, we read in the Epistle to the Hebrews (1:1) may happen "at sundry times and in divers manners."

For man, who was made after the image of God, but fell into sin, who therefore has to grope upwards, and yet is stirred by an appeal from on high as soon as his intelligence awakens, it is normal that the idea of God should ever be ready to spring forth, and ever be threatened with stifling. There are from the start two tendencies at work to stop or divert man's natural movement to the Creator. The one arises from the very conditions under which his intelligence must labor to conquer darkness; the other is, according to the teaching of Catholic faith, the immediate fruit of original sin. Both tendencies, the natural and the perverse, reinforce each other in obstructing the royal way of reason and causing it to get lost in the thousand mazes of myth and magic. There is first the tendency to identify the Author of Nature with that nature through which He gives a faint revelation of Himself and from which man must borrow the very features with which he will represent Him; there is also the tendency to abandon, in favor of subaltern deities or fictions, the God who is too incorruptible and too demanding. Under this twofold influence, mere analogies soon harden up, and the world becomes thicker. What was to be a sign becomes a screen, and the first vision fades away when it has hardly been grasped. The Divine Star disappears behind its "gross shadow." The Fire, the wind, the subtile air, the starry heaven, the wild Sea, or the heavenly luminaries, are looked upon as the masters of the world.

In the depth of consciousness, even before it has shone in its full brightness, "the glory of the incorruptible God" (Rom. 1:23) is changed into deities which are false, or are nothing. At any rate, the God who was near has become remote, and for a long time He will remain the unknown God. Even with those who keep His memory, He will be forsaken. He will have to be rediscovered gradually, in the groping of ambiguity, and even at times by those who think they are losing Him. Even in ages when the knowledge of Him seems to have made definite progress, God has been readily conceived as moved by human passions, or on the contrary, as some nebulous Force. For men who imagine they have made an exhaustive analysis of the idea of God, He turns out to be a sort of *materia prima*, a being as indefinite and as near to nothing as space, or He becomes an abstraction devoid of any power of irradiation. Each formula proves discouraging and causes a contrary formula to be conceived. Men never make for good a spiritual gain which alone could stabilize and feed the idea they have acquired. The best turns into the worst, and what ought to be the great stimulus to man's perfection (or progress) becomes a means to profane ends: Man again deifies his needs, his interests, his passions, his ignorance, his folly. . . . Progress becomes a negation. More often than the Living God, the Divine is substituted to the gods of fable. Religion and ethics fight a deadly battle. Man develops his interior life at the expense of the gods. . . . At great intervals, however, a pure ray of light breaks through the darkness. Pagans themselves have their "hidden saints," and the true God chooses prophets from all nations.

Many facts seem to support the Marxian and similar theories. The religious system is different according as man is a hunter, a tiller of the ground or a shepherd. Marxists and other unbelievers are not alone in stressing what seems to be a law. It is confirmed by all investigations, and cultural historians have made it a rigorous principle of all religious evolution outside of supernatural revelation. The religions of the "pluckers," the "shepherds," and the "hunters" are distinguished. For example, in the era of horse civilization, god-riders were worshipped, etc. It is also a fact that the gods of large cosmopolitan cities bear little resemblance to those of little self-centered communities. According as the human group, which begins as a small tribe, becomes a town, then a nation, then an empire, and as thereby cosmic consciousness develops in an orderly fashion, rites and myths undergo parallel transformations. It is true then that they reflect the social condition, which is also closely dependent on economic conditions—and that religion helps to reinforce civic authority with all its restraints. But it would be fair to remember also how religion, more than any other factor, owing to the social and spiritual cohesion which it insures, helps man to endure and to live, and therefore to progress.

Something else has to be considered, however, and this is the essential point. Marxism as well as rationalism is right, we might say quantitatively, just as determinism is right when it deals with the largest and the most obvious segment of human activity. Historical materialism is one of the basic truths which we have to accept on first evidence, but which offer no help to him who seeks to reach the heart of reality. Do not error and insignificant facts hold an infinitely larger place in matters of experience than authentic and substantial data? Counterfeits and returns to old errors, familiar and spurious concepts, wild imaginations or standardized ideas are spread in daylight and forced upon the observer. They open large vistas and encumber the stage. On the contrary, what has true value, what is just starting but is destined to transform everything, is nearly always rare and hidden, even though its diffuse influence may already be felt almost everywhere. But, if it happens to be noticed, to appreciate its real value, one ought to search inside it by a method which has nothing to gain from statistics and which goes beyond the range of empirical observation. For instance, we have the right to think that Marxian analysis applied twenty centuries ago in Palestine, most conscientiously and most intelligently, would have overlooked the humble fact which is summed up in one name—Jesus of Nazareth—as indeed it was ignored by Jewish and Roman historians. That almost imperceptible event would have slipped through the net of scholarly explanation or, if it had been held in its meshes, it would have been found empty of its explosive power.

Some features, however, are too striking to remain entirely hidden from anyone who is willing to open his eyes. For instance, we are told that the worship of an imageless God reflects a culture of widespread trade and banking transactions; that monotheism is the result of the slow unification of earthly powers. But how shall we explain the history of India, where deep philosophical systems and lofty forms of worship have flourished amidst primitive economics and a politically amorphous society? Above all, is real account given of the first precepts of the Jewish Decalogue? (The question of their precise date does not matter here.) "O Israel, listen. I am Yahweh, your God. . . . You shall have no gods but me. You shall not carve for yourselves any idol. . . . For I, Yahweh, your God, am a jealous God" (Deut. 5:1-9).

No minute examination is needed to recognize in the history of the West two kinds of "monotheistic" religions, the origins of which are different. The first is, at least in part, the outcome of a social and political evolution as well as of a progress in reflection. Pantheons arise gradually after the image of human affairs; a hierarchy of gods is arranged, as their very number and mixture suggests the unity of the divine, until the time when the chief of the society of gods becomes the supreme god, of whom the rest will be the mere manifestations or the servants. When a nation comes to know the gods of the people it has conquered, it amalgamates them to its own gods through a process of equalization both enriching and unifying. If by chance a conflict arises, the gods of the conquered people are thought to be conquered, and are eliminated, unless they are adopted by the conquerors, or turned into demons. This happened—with numerous variations in the process—in Babylon, in Egypt, among the old Indo-Europeans, in the Greek world, in Rome under the empire. Was it a gain for politics, for civilization and for thought? Most often it was, and at times in a high degree. But did it involve a specifically religious progress? Not in every case, and frequently not at all. Even in cases when anthropomorphism was abandoned, it was in favor of an abstract divinity or a deification of Nature. *"Aequum est, quidquid omnes colunt, unum putari; eadem spectamus astra, commune coelum est, idem nos mundus involvit"* (Symmachus, *Relatio,* n. 10). There was a concentration of gods; but God did not originate from them.

On the contrary, in the second kind of monotheism, the one God fiercely claims to be the only God. "There is no God but God." That God has not originated from any intellectual or political assembling or syncretism. He imposes and consecrates a new order of values. He is not a God who can be reached through the other gods, but One who demands that we should be converted to Him by breaking the idols—the handmade idols, and those that have been formed by the human heart. He is a God who challenges the Nature gods, as the young David, when he was yet unknown, challenged Goliath, the famous giant. He is a God who bids man to leave his fatherland, to follow Him—a God who leads into the unknown, a scandal for those who have not been captivated by Him. Compared to Him, "the gods of nations" are only "wood and stone"; they are "vanity," "nothing," "abomination" and "sin"; they are "unclean things," "corpses," "no gods." "Riding on a swift cloud, the Eternal reaches Egypt, and Egypt's idols shake before Him" (Is. 19:1). "A jealous God, an exclusive God, who breaks everything and allows nothing to subsist before Him." Instead of the complaisant Principle which justified the ritual practices of polytheism, while consolidating carnal domination, and remained the possession of a small elite of wise men, we have now a Being who is spiritual though not at all abstract, living and acting, though invisible, an intransigent Being who claims for Himself all worship and wants to be acknowledged by all; a transcendent Being, who in spite of His marked personality, reaches out beyond all earthly cities, even beyond the whole world; not a cosmopolitan god, but a God who will be, if He is not yet, the God of all.

This second monotheism alone is loaded with explosive power; it alone carries religious progress, because it is the source of radical transformation of human ideas and of religious life. It alone is capable of assuming moral and social progress when it is not its original promoter. Its God alone can be the object of faith, in the full sense of the word. When it meets the other monotheism it admits of no compromise; it must begin by conquering it. *Hebraeorum Deus a Romanis non receptus, quia se solum coli voluerit* (St. Augustine, *De consensu Evangelistarum,* I, ch. 18, 26). Then it will make use of it to formulate its doctrine, to grow and spread, while bringing out its full development. Now, we observe that it does not appear in large unified states nor in the wake of mighty conquests, neither after deep speculations nor broad economic transformations. As far as it is possible, in the lamentable condition of sources, to form a picture of history, the religion of Zoroaster, "the least pagan of pagan religions," that religion in which divine powers are "attributes of the one divinity," rather than gods, originated in a remote village of Iran, far from the center of culture that was Babylon at the time, and before the era of syncretism which the conquests of Cyrus opened in that city. Judaism and Islam no less contradict every theory of a religious progress based upon factors wholly alien to religion. Israel was a small people, undeveloped mentally and economically, far inferior in culture to its great neighbors which crushed it one after the other. If it took great advantage from their broadened conceptions, especially in the period of the exile, it was for its own ends and, as it were, to clothe with a more beautiful mantle the God in whom it was the only nation to believe. And it was at the very time of Israel's destruction and captivity that it extolled His triumph. As to the Arabs before the Hegira, they were hardly unified. The idea of God, in its highest manifestations and in its most humble forms, breaks and transcends all social as well as all mental frameworks. We can truly say: "The Spirit breatheth where he will" (John, 3:8).

. . . .

Every religion, if it is to last, must have roots; and its birth depends on a number of conditions which are not always of a religious character. No Christian will wonder at that, who knows what place the idea of "the fulness of time" holds even in revealed religion. Supernatural does not mean superficial. The divine does not exclude the human element, though it is not arbitrarily superposed on it. However, we should again be on our guard against the temptation of making causes out of mere conditions.

. . . .

In paganism, the progress of reflection tended to the elimination of the gods. Through Christianity belief in God has stimulated the development of conscience. Called by God, man has understood his nature by knowing his vocation. He has become forever, in his own estimation, a person.

. . . .

If *God* has the same name as *the gods*, it is not in virtue of any kinship, as though, for instance, He was the perfection, the sublimation or the unification of the others. It is to mark that the others never had any but borrowed, or rather stolen, existence and names. God is but coming into His rights, which vain phantasms or evil forces usurped when man turned his back upon Him.

Some think that the one God is the product of religious evolution. The divine, first scattered in a dust of sacred beings, gradually became organized, hierarchized, until it was centralized and sublimated into a supreme divinity, of which the other powers created by mythical imagination were from that time merely the handmaids. Henceforth it could at leisure become more pure, more spiritual, more refined—even to the point of fading away.

Others, on the contrary, maintain that the one God emerged through a sudden religious revolution and asserted himself against other divinities, either as one god who brushes others away, or as an exclusive concept of the divine which overcame older ones of which man tired, either when he recognized their emptiness, or lost a sense of their value.

Both theories rest upon exact observations and deserve consideration, though the latter contains more historical truth, if more attention is paid to the living God of religion than to the philosophical supreme Principle. The God of the Bible has a proper name: Yahweh, and He asserts His unicity by choosing a special people as His own, apart from other peoples, imposing upon it special laws, and, through the mouth of the prophets, mocking the handmade gods. The God of the Gospel is no less personal; He is the Heavenly Father, and if in the eyes of Christians the pagan gods really exist, they can be nothing but demons. However, it is true that the phase of intransigence in the course of which monolatry or monotheism was established, was soon followed by a phase in which the victorious God allowed himself to be enveloped, though not contaminated, and turned to his profit the genuine concepts and rites which had got lost in other religions. Opposition was followed by absorption, so that the two theories seem to be less contradictory than complementary.

However, neither theory goes to the bottom of the problem; neither goes back to the very source of religion. In fact, the idea of God, unique and transcendent, does not, when it appears in history, rise from any form of criticism, nor from any disappointment. It is not the fruit of any immanent dialectic, whether this be taken as leading to a revolution or some form of evolution. It is neither the result of a synthesis answering the need to unify the scattered expressions of the divine, nor of an antithesis following upon the realization of the empty character of old divinities. It can be reduced to a process of integration or of substitution. What the theories take to be the cause is actually an effect. The idea of the one God arises spontaneously in human consciousness, either from the realization of some rational necessity, or by some supernatural illumination, and it compels the assent of the mind by its own necessity. Actually, in the clearest instance, it is God Himself who reveals Himself and causes the idols to vanish, or compels him whom He visits to pluck them out of his heart. *Reverberasti infirmitatem aspectus mei, radians in me vehementer, et contremui amore et horrore* (St. Augustine, *Confessions*, VII, ch. 10, n. 16). What comes first is that "radiation," with the light and the attraction mixed with awe which rise from it. Then, through a phenomenon of "reverberation" the weakness of human conceptions reveals itself in its full light, and man, thus touched by God, is filled with horror of the phantasms he has created, and is freed from their spell by the faith which is born in him.

Therefore, at the origin of religion we find a contact, a meeting of man with God, and a certain apperception, by whatever name it may be called: a flash of intelligence, a vision, or an assent of faith. Then follow the antithesis, and in the last place the synthesis, inasmuch as we can use the term.

In truth, it is the first phase that counts: Abraham, when he answers the call to abandon his ancestors' land and worship; Moses, when he receives the Law on Mount Sinai; Isaias when he sees in the Temple the majesty of Yahweh; Jesus, when He was stirred by the Holy Spirit and conversed with His Father. In all this reversal from negation to affirmation, no relativity. In every dialectic, historical or otherwise, there is opposition and negation, and whatever be its spring, a term is brought about by another. The reversal does not imply the insertion of a new principle. Dialectic is a powerful weapon because it corresponds to one of the essential mental processes. But if it attempt, not merely to arrange logically, but to produce new ideas, it obeys a blind necessity; and it sheds no light upon the inner nature of the beings which it posits at every step; or rather it posits beings devoid of inner nature, since they are merely terms wholly relative to those with which they form a series. No doubt, once it has fallen as a germ into human consciousness— whether coming by the light of reason or by a supernatural revelation— the idea of the living God, as every other idea, will be a theme for dialectical thinking. And, in a sense, it will be a proper theme for such reasoning, because it will be the source of an undying "anxiety" in the human mind, an anxiety which will always torment the soul. But it will remain wholly substantial and positive, and that will insure its victory. Far from corresponding to a phase in human dialectic, it will, on the contrary, play the part of an intermediary which unfolds itself between a reality that has been perceived and a mystery that is felt, while in its movement it never loses the support of some Presence.

How much more strikingly this appears in the concrete dialectic of history. Religious monotheism, which we owe to Israel and to Christ and find in a weaker degree in analogous religions—was enkindled by a divine Fire. Before it was a belief, and a fortiori, before it became a tradition or a concept, it was a vocation, and it will always remain so where it retains its authentic vigor. There is no trace, in its formation, of that dialectic movement which Nietzsche calls "resentment." Abraham did not come to God because of any disgust for his ancestral gods; rather he had to struggle to abandon them, and his faith had to be a victory. Jesus does not, like Buddha, preach the vanity of the world and the gods which make it sacred because they are its mythical offspring. He announces the kingdom of heaven, in which His soul breathes, and He makes manifest in His own person the love of the Heavenly Father. Here again we find the verification of the deep words of the Apostle: "*The Son of God . . . was not 'It is' and 'it is not,' but 'It is' was in Him* (2 Cor. 1:19).

. . . .

Attempts have been made, more or less successfully, at writing a psychoanalysis of mythologies. More and more the need appears of writing a psychoanalysis of atheism. Every attempt at writing a psychoanalysis of faith is doomed to failure.

7

INTUITION OF GOD

Immediate Intuition *

Ariste: Your definition of God is the very definition He gave of Himself to Moses: *God is He Who Is.* Intelligible extension is the idea or archetype of bodies; but the idea of God is that of a being which admits of no restriction, in one word, it is Being; and this is the way in which, in this life, God becomes present to our mind in the way we see Him.

Theodore: You are right. But remember that God, the Infinite, is not apprehended by means of an idea through which He could be represented. The Infinite is His own Idea. He has no archetype. Though He can be known, He cannot be made. Only creatures, only such beings as can be made, are apprehended through ideas which express them, even before they are. There needs to exist no actual circle, or house, or sun, for you to apprehend them. For, every finite being can be apprehended in the Infinite which contains its intelligible idea. But it is only through Itself that the Infinite can be apprehended. It is necessary that God exist, for us to be able to think of Him. Even if we have an idea of a finite being, this being may be nonexistent. Its essence may be known though it may not exist; it may be conceived even though it is not seen. But it is impossible to apprehend the essence of the Infinite, without knowing that It exists; impossible to form an idea of It which would not include existence. For, existence cannot be the object of an idea; it has no archetype expressing its whole intelligible reality. It is Its own archetype, which contains the archetypes of all other beings. So, you can see that the proposition: There is a God, is, by its very nature, the most evident of all the propositions which assert the existence of anything, and that it is as certain as the proposition: I think, therefore I am. And by this you see also what God is, since God and Being, or the Infinite are identical.

But I insist, make no mistake. It is only confusedly, and only from afar that you see what God is. You do not see Him as He really is; even though you truly see Being, or the Infinite, you have a very imperfect vision of It. You do not see It in Its simplicity. In the uncreated Being's infinity you see the multitude of created things, but you have no distinct

---

* Nicholas Malebranche (1638-1715), *Entretiens sur la Métaphysique* (1688), ed. A. Cuvillier (Paris: J. Vrin), II Entretien, V-VI, pp. 87-89.

apprehension of Its unity. The reason is that you do not apprehend It so much in Its absolute reality as in Its relations to possible creatures, a number of which It can increase ad infinitum, without their ever being able to equal the reality in which they are represented. The reason for that is you do not apprehend It as the universal Reason, which enlightens intelligences to the degree in which they need light here below to live a moral life, and in order that they may discover Its perfections as participable by finite beings. But you cannot discover the essential property of the Infinite, by virtue of which It is at the same time the one and the all, made up, as it were, of an infinity of diverse perfections, and yet so simple that in It every perfection includes all other perfections, though none of them is really distinct from the others.

Appeal to the Heart *

"The heart has its reasons, which reason knows not, as we see in a thousand instances. . . . It is the heart that is conscious of God, and not the reason. This then is faith—God sensible to the heart, not to the reason" (277, 278).†

Many serious errors have been made about these well-known words from lack of agreement about the meaning of the terms used, a circumstance which is the origin of most of the misunderstandings and disputes between human beings. Pascal has been accused of fideism, and his accusers have used a superficial interpretation of these passages to affirm that, according to him, faith is a mere matter of sentiment, that God cannot be reached by the reason and cannot, where man is concerned, be the object of rational knowledge. Now, nothing is more alien to Pascal's real thought than such an interpretation. It is quite easy to convince ourselves of this, if we will but take the trouble to get rid for a moment of our own phraseology and our own method of propounding the problem to examine the aim Pascal was pursuing, and the meaning he attaches to the words *heart, feeling, knowledge, reason.*

To Pascal, the heart is not feeling; it participates in feeling but is not reduced to it.

The heart participates in feeling through its intuitive, *immediate,* spontaneous nature, and because, like feeling, "it acts in a moment, and is always ready to act." It participates in it above all because it is, as we shall see later, the organ of *love.* Now when God is in question, knowledge cannot suffice without love: "How great is the distance between knowing God and loving Him." To know God in a purely speculative manner without loving Him, is to know Him not (280).

* Jacques Chevalier, *Pascal* (London: Sheed and Ward, 1930), ch. ix, "The Heart and the Order of Charity," pp. 266-272. The author clarifies the concept of heart as understood by the author of the *Pensées.*

† Numbers are those of the *Pensées* in the Brunschvicg edition.

But the heart is something other than feeling. Pascal, rightly, is distrustful of feeling. He has explicitly banished it from the realm of natural knowledge, and if he has experienced its benefits, he does not fail to recognize its dangers, for there is no certain rule for differentiating feeling from fancy or from imagination, and by mistaking the one for the other we very often run the risk of going astray.

What, then, is the *heart* to Pascal? Let us note first of all that Pascal, differing in this from most philosophers, did not form a technical vocabulary for his own use. If, on this account, his language is apparently lacking in precision and directness, it gains astonishingly in suppleness and vividness, and it is to this fact, possibly, that Pascal owes his superiority over all other philosophers; namely, that with him the thought is never either the prisoner or the slave of the words in which it is expressed, but always dominates them. Pascal uses ordinary language, but he is a wonderful master of it, and all its terms are to be found in his works, with the rich variety of meaning bequeathed by the ages, and with all the delicate gradations which re-establish between them the continuity interrupted by too rigid conceptual thought. Now it is precisely in this way that Pascal uses the word *heart*. In his work, as in the language of the day, and in the Scripture, the heart denotes the most secret part of our being: it is not only the instrument of feeling and of morality, but one of the instruments of knowledge, and, as it were, the origin of all our intellectual operations; it is, we might say, the pinnacle of feeling and reason: "The heart naturally loves the Universal Being" (277).

Between the heart and the reason Pascal establishes, in the *Pensées*, a distinction akin to that established by the Greeks between the *nous* and the *dianoia*, pure thought and discursive thought. What is indeed this "reason" which Pascal continually contrasts with the heart, and to which he prefers it? It is not the reason that he exalted in his fragment of the *Traité du Vide*, which is created for infinity alone; it is reasoning, discourse, the faculty that takes slow, obdurate views, which would prove everything down to its very origin, which comprehends nothing of intuition (*finesse*) or feeling, because it desires to proceed in every case by demonstration (281), and which always runs the risk of being mistaken because it cannot do without the memory for all its operations (369). The heart, on the contrary, may be likened to the eye of the mind. Like the eye, it knows its object at a glance. It is a kind of intellectual instinct, and like the instinct, it coincides with its object. And it is this from which all our discourse is suspended, because it provides us with the direct principles whence all our reasoning proceeds.

This instinct, which Pascal contrasts sometimes with reason (344, 395), and sometimes with experience (396), according to the matter in hand, is the aspiration toward goodness which God has put in us, and which remains with us from our former greatness. It is that idea of truth which is as invincible for scepticism as the reason's incapability of proof is for dogmatism; it is those natural principles which in good faith we cannot doubt, and which prevent the reason from talking so wildly as to end in denying everything. The heart then, in Pascal's view, is essentially the *direct apprehension, knowledge and feeling both together, of principles.*

This interpretation is confirmed by a passage from the *Pensées,* which we must quote at length, for it is decisive, and by the light of the definitions just given, it settles the question once for all.

"We know truth, not by the reason alone, but also by the heart; it is in this way that we know first principles, and reasoning, which has nothing to do with it, tries in vain to combat them. The sceptics, whose object it is to do this, find their labours vain. We know that we are not deceived, however incapable we may be of proving it by reason, and this incapability demonstrates nothing but the feebleness of our reason; it does not prove the uncertainty of all our knowledge, as they maintain. For our knowledge of first principles, such as the existence of space, time, movement, number, [is] as certain as any knowledge that our reasoning can give us. And it is upon the knowledge gained by the heart and the instinct that [this other] knowledge must rely and must base all its arguments. . . . It is as useless and absurd for reason to demand of the heart proofs of these first principles before it will admit them as it would be for the heart to ask from reason a feeling of all the propositions demonstrated before accepting them. This inability, therefore, can but serve to belittle reason which would fain judge of all things; it does not combat our certainty, as if it were reason alone that could instruct us. Would to God, on the contrary, that we never had need of reason, but could discern all things by feeling and instinct. But Nature has refused us this boon. On the contrary, she has given us very little knowledge of this kind, and all the rest must be acquired through reasoning. This is why those to whom God has given religion by an instinctive feeling are indeed blessed, and rightly convinced. But to those who do not possess it thus, we can give it by reasoning only, waiting for God to give it them through the feeling of the heart, without which faith is but human, and unavailing for salvation" (282).

. . . Hence we may define the heart fairly precisely by saying that it is the faculty which perceives *principles* and perceives *order.* This power is not opposed to the intellect, nor is it even different from the intellect; it is its loftiest part; it discerns and it loves, and in it knowledge and feeling, far from being mutually hurtful, are mutually helpful. . . . Better indeed than the intellect, love, true love, imbued with intellect, the attachment of the whole being to the truth, is able to grasp this higher truth in its source and in its origin, and to relate all things to it according to their order.

Such is the exact part which the heart plays in belief. It is by the heart that we apprehend the truths of religion, in their origin and in their order. But it is necessary to define clearly what Pascal means by this. He certainly does not mean to say that faith is a mere matter of feeling, still less that, as to its objective, actual content, it is posited or created by feeling. The principles to which the heart is attached in respect of faith are *facts*, which are *without* and *above* us.

The Voice of Conscience *

Can I attain to any more vivid assent to the being of a God, than that which is given merely to notions of the intellect? Can I enter with a personal knowledge into the circle of truths which make up that great thought? Can I rise to what I have called an imaginative apprehension of it? Can I believe as if I saw? Since such a high assent requires a present experience and memory of the fact, at first sight it would seem as if the answer must be in the negative; for how can I assent as if I saw, unless I have seen? But no one in this life can see God. Yet I conceive a real assent to be possible, and I proceed to show how.

When it is said that we cannot see God, this is undeniable; but still in what sense have we a discernment of His creatures, of the individual beings which surround us? The evidence which we have of their presence lies in the phenomena which address our senses, and our warrant for taking these for evidence is our instinctive certitude that they are evidence. By the law of our nature we associate those sensible phenomena or impressions with certain units, individuals, substances, whatever they are to be called, which are outside and out of the reach of sense, and we picture them to ourselves in those phenomena. The phenomena are *if* pictures; but at the time they give us no exact measure or character of the unknown things beyond them—for who will say there is any uniformity between the impressions which two of us would respectively have of some third thing, supposing one of us had only the sense of touch, and the other only the sense of hearing? Therefore, when we speak of our having a picture of the things which are perceived through the senses, we mean a certain representation, true as far as it goes, but not adequate.

And so those intellectual and moral objects which are brought home to us through our senses—that they exist, we know by instinct; that they are such and such, we apprehend from the impressions which they leave upon our minds. . . .

Now certainly the thought of God, as Theists entertain it, is not gained by an instinctive association of His presence with any sensible phenomena; but the office which the senses directly fulfill as regards creation, that devolves indirectly on certain of our mental phenomena as regards the Creator. These phenomena are found in the sense of moral obligation. As from a multitude of instinctive perceptions, acting in particular instances, of something beyond the senses, we generalize the

* Cardinal John Henry Newman, *Grammar of Assent* (London: Longmans, Green, 1891), Part I, ch. 5, "Apprehension and Assent in the Matter of Religion," pp. 102-110.

notion of an external world, and picture that world in and according to those particular phenomena from which we started, so from the perceptive power which identifies the intimations of conscience with the reverberations and echoes (so to say) of an external admonition, we proceed on to the notion of a Supreme Ruler and Judge, and then again we image Him and His attributes in those recurring intimations, out of which, as mental phenomena, our recognition of His existence was originally gained. And, if the impressions which His creatures make on us through our senses oblige us to regard those creatures as *sui generis* respectively, is it not wonderful that the notices, which He indirectly gives us, through our conscience, of His own nature are such as to make us understand that He is like Himself and like nothing else.

I have already said I am not proposing here to prove the Being of a God; yet I have found it impossible to avoid saying where I look for the proof of it. For I am looking for that proof in the same quarter as that from which I would commence a proof of His attributes and character—by the same means as those by which I show how we apprehend Him, not merely as a notion but as a reality. The last indeed of these three investigations alone concerns me here, but I cannot altogether exclude the two former from my consideration. However, I repeat, what I am directly aiming at, is to explain how we gain an image of God and give a real assent to the proposition that He exists. And next, in order to do this, of course I must start from some first principle—and that first principle, which I assume and shall not attempt to prove, is that which I also use as a foundation in those other two inquiries, viz., that we have by nature a conscience.

I assume, then, that conscience has a legitimate place among our mental acts; as really so, as the action of memory, of reasoning, of imagination, or as the sense of the beautiful; that, as there are objects which, when presented to the mind, cause it to feel grief, regret, joy, or desire, so there are things which excite in us approbation or blame, and which we in consequence call right or wrong; and which, experienced in ourselves, kindle in us that specific sense of pleasure or pain, which goes by the name of a good or bad conscience. This being taken for granted, I shall attempt to show that in this special feeling, which follows on the commission of what we call right or wrong, lie the materials for the real apprehension of a Divine Sovereign and Judge.

The feeling of conscience (being, I repeat, a certain keen sensibility, pleasant or painful—self-approval and hope, or compunction and fear—attendant on certain of our actions, which in consequence we call right or wrong) is twofold—it is a moral sense, and a sense of duty; a judgement of the reason and a magisterial dictate. Of course its act is indivisible; still these two aspects are distinct from each other, and admitting of a separate consideration. Though I lost my sense of the obligation which I lie under to abstain from acts of dishonesty, I should not in consequence lose my sense that such actions were an outrage offered to my moral nature. Again; though I lost my sense of their moral deformity, I should not therefore lose my sense that they are forbidden to me. Thus conscience has both a critical and a judicial office, and though its promptings, in the breasts of the millions of human beings to whom it is given, are not in all cases correct, that does not necessarily interfere with the force of its testimony and of its sanction; its testimony that there is a right and a wrong, and its sanction to that testimony conveyed in the feelings which attend on right or wrong conduct. Here I have to speak of conscience in the latter point of view, not as supplying us, by means of its various acts, with the elements of morals, such as may be developed by the intellect into an ethical code, but simply as the dictate of an authoritative monitor bearing upon the details of conduct as they come before us, and complete in its several acts, one by one.

Let us then consider conscience, not as a rule of right conduct, but as a sanction of right conduct. This is its primary and most authoritative aspect; it is the ordinary sense of the word. Half the world would be puzzled to know what was meant by the moral sense; but every man knows what is meant by a good or bad conscience. Conscience is ever forcing on us by threats and by promises that we must follow the right and avoid the wrong; so far it is one and the same in the mind of everyone, whatever its particular errors in particular minds as to the acts which it orders to be done or to be avoided; and in this respect it corresponds to our perception of the beautiful and deformed. As we have naturally a sense of the beautiful and graceful in nature and art, though tastes proverbially differ, so we have a sense of duty and obligation, whether we all associate it with the same certain actions in particular, or not. Here, however, Taste and Conscience part company; for the sense of beautifulness, as indeed the Moral Sense, has no special relations to persons, but contemplates objects in themselves; conscience, on the other hand, is concerned with persons primarily, and with actions mainly as viewed in their doers, or rather with self alone and one's own actions, and with others only indirectly, and as if in association with self. And further, taste is its own evidence, appealing to nothing beyond its own sense of the beautiful or the ugly, and enjoying the specimens of the beautiful simply for their own sake; but conscience does not repose on itself, but vaguely reaches forward to something beyond self, and dimly discerns a sanction higher than self for its decisions, as is evidenced in that keen sense of obligation and responsibility which informs them. And hence it is that we are accustomed to speak of conscience as a voice, imperative and constraining, like no other dictate in the whole of our experience.

And again, in consequence of this prerogative of dictating and commanding, which is of its essence, Conscience has an intimate bearing on our affections and emotions, leading us to reverence and awe, hope and fear, especially fear, a feeling which is foreign for the most part, not only to Taste, but even to the Moral Sense, except in consequence of some accidental associations. No fear is felt by anyone who recognizes that this conduct has not been beautiful, though he may be mortified at himself, if perhaps he has thereby forfeited some advantage; but, if he has been betrayed into any kind of immorality, he has a lively sense of responsibility and guilt, though the act be no offence against society— of distress and apprehension, even though it may be of service to him— of compunction and regret, though in itself it may be most pleasurable— of confusion of face, though it may have no witnesses. Those various perturbations of mind which are characteristics of a bad conscience, and may be very considerable—self-reproach, poignant shame, haunting remorse, chill dismay at the prospect of the future—and their contraries, when the conscience is good, as real though less forcible, self-approval, inward peace, lightness of heart, and the like—these conditions constitute a specific difference between conscience and other intellectual senses —common sense, good sense, sense of expedience, taste, sense of honour, and the like—as indeed they would also constitute between conscience and the moral sense, supposing that these two were not aspects of one and the same feeling, exercised upon one and the same subject-matter.

So much for the characteristic phenomena, which conscience presents, nor is it difficult to determine what they imply. I refer once more to our sense of the beautiful. This sense is attended by an intellectual enjoyment, and is free from whatever is of the nature of emotion, except in one case, viz., when it is excited by personal objects; then it is that the tranquil feeling of admiration is exchanged for the excitement of affection and passion. Conscience too, considered as a moral sense, an intellectual sentiment, is a sense of admiration and disgust, of approbation and blame; but it is something more than a moral sense; it is always what the sense of the beautiful is only in certain cases; it is always emotional. No wonder then that it always implies what that sense only sometimes implies; that it always involves the recognition of a living object, towards which it is directed. Inanimate things cannot stir our affections; they are correlative with persons. If, as is the case, we feel responsibility, are ashamed, are frightened at transgressing the voice of conscience, this implies that there is One to whom we are responsible, before whom we are ashamed, whose claims upon us we fear. If, on doing wrong, we feel the same tearful, broken-hearted sorrow which overwhelms us on hurting a mother; if, on doing right, we enjoy the same serenity of mind, the same soothing, satisfactory delight, which follows on receiving praise from a father, we certainly have within us the image of some person, to whom our love and veneration look, in whose smile we feel happiness, for whom we yearn, towards whom we direct our pleadings, in whose anger we are troubled and waste away. These feelings in us are such as require for their exciting cause an intelligent being; we are not affectionate toward a stone, nor do we feel shame before a horse or a dog; we have no remorse or compunction in breaking mere human law: yet, so it is, conscience excites all these painful emotions, confusion, foreboding, self-condemnation; and on the other hand it sheds upon us a deep peace, a sense of security, a resignation, and a hope, which there is no sensible, no earthly object to elicit. "The wicked flees, when no one pursueth"; then why does he flee? when his terror? Who is it that he sees in solitude, in darkness, in the hidden chambers of his heart? If the cause of these emotions does not belong to this visible world, the Object to which his perception is directed must be Supernatural and Divine; and thus the phenomena of Conscience, as a dictate, avail to impress the imagination with the picture of a Supreme Governor, a Judge, holy, just, powerful, all-seeing, retributive, and the creative principle of religion, as the Moral Sense is the principle of Ethics.

Mystical Experience *

. . . With the origin and meaning of Aristotle's God thus traced back we can but wonder at how modern thinkers, when treating of the existence and the nature of God, hamper themselves with insoluble problems which arise only if God is studied from the Aristotelian point of view, and if they are pleased to call by that name of being whom mankind has never dreamed of invoking.

Now, is mystical experience able to solve these problems? It is easy to see the objections that such a notion will arouse. We have disposed of those which consist in asserting that no mystic is sound in the head and that all mysticism is a pathological state. The great mystics, the only ones that we are dealing with, have generally been men or women of action, endowed with superior common sense: it matters little that some of them had imitators who well deserved to be called "crazy," or that there are cases when they themselves felt the effect of extreme and prolonged strain of mind and will; many a man of genius has been in the same condition. But there is another series of objections, which it is impossible to overlook. For it is alleged that the experiences of the great mystics are individual and exceptional, that they cannot be verified by the ordinary man, that they cannot therefore be compared to a scientific experiment and cannot possibly solve problems. There is a good deal to be said on this point. In the first place, it is by no means certain that a scientific experiment, or more generally an observation recorded by science, can always be repeated or verified. In the days when Central Africa was a *terra incognita*, geography trusted to the account of one single explorer, if his honesty and competence seemed to be above suspicion. The route of Livingstone's journeys appeared for a long time on the maps and atlases. You may object that verification was potentially, if not actually, feasible, that other travellers could go and see if they liked, and

* From *The Two Sources of Morality and Religion* by Henri Bergson, pp. 233-246. Translated by R. Ashley Audra and Cloudesley Brereton. Copyright 1935 by Holt, Rinehart and Winston, Inc. Reprinted by permission of Holt, Rinehart and Winston, Inc.

that the map based on the indications of one traveller was a provisional one, waiting for subsequent exploration to make it definitive. I grant this: but the mystic too has gone on a journey that others can potentially, if not actually, undertake; and those who are actually capable of doing so are at least as many as those who possess the daring and energy of a Stanley setting out to find Livingstone. Indeed, that is an understatement. Along with the souls capable of following the mystic way to the end there are many who go at least part of the way: how numerous are those who take a few steps, either by an effort of will or from a natural disposition. William James used to say he had never experienced mystic states; but he added that if he heard them spoken of by a man who had experienced them "something within him echoed the call." Most of us are probably in the same case. It is no use invoking as evidence to the contrary the indignant protests of those who see nothing in mysticism but quackery and folly. Some people are doubtless impervious to mystical experience, incapable of feeling or imagining anything of it. But we also meet with people to whom music is nothing but noise; and some of them will express their opinions of musicians with the same anger, the same tone of personal spite. No one would think of accepting this as an argument against music. Let us leave, then, these merely negative arguments and see whether the most superficial examination of mystic experience will not incline us favourably towards it.

We must first note the fact that mystics generally agree among themselves. This is striking in the case of Christian mystics. To reach the ultimate identification with God, they go through a series of states. These may vary from mystic to mystic, but there is a strong resemblance between them. In any case, the path followed is the same, even admitting that the stopping-places by the way are at different intervals. They have in any case the same terminal point. In the description of the final state we find the same expressions, the same images, the same comparisons, although the authors were generally unknown to each other. It will be replied that in some cases they have known one another, that furthermore there is a mystical tradition, and that all mystics may have felt its influence. We grant this, but the fact must be noted that the great mystics give little thought to this tradition; each one has his own originality, which is not intentional, which he has not sought, but which we feel is of fundamental importance to him; it means that he is the object of an exceptional favour, unmerited though it be. Now it may be objected that a community of religion suffices to explain the resemblance, that all Christian mystics have lived on the Gospels, that they have all received the same theological teaching. But this would be to forget that, if the resemblance between the visions is indeed explainable by a common religion, these visions occupy but a small place in the lives of the great mystics; they are soon left behind and treated as if they had been merely symbolical. As to theological teaching in general, it is true that they seem to accept it with utter docility, and in particular to obey their confessors; but, as has been shrewdly remarked, "they obey themselves alone, and a sure instinct leads them straight to the very man who can be relied upon to guide them in the way they want to go. If he should happen to depart from it, our mystics would not hesitate to shake off his authority, and, on the strength of their direct contact with the Deity, place their own liberty above all else." *

It would indeed be interesting at this point to study closely the relations between the spiritual adviser and the soul seeking counsel. It would be found that, of the two, he that has meekly acquiesced in yielding to guidance has more than once, no less meekly, become the guide. But this is not for us the important point. All we want to make clear is that, if external resemblances between Christian mystics may be due to a common tradition or a common training, their deep-seated agreement is a sign of an identity of intuition which would find its simplest explanation in the actual existence of the Being with whom they believe themselves to hold intercourse. So much the more so, then, if we consider that the other mysticisms, ancient or modern, go more or less far, stopping at this or that stage, but all point in the same direction.

Yet we may admit that mystical experience, left to itself, cannot provide the philosopher with complete certainty. It could be absolutely convincing only if he had come by another way, such as a sensuous experience coupled with rational inference, to the conclusion of the probable existence of a privileged experience through which man could get into touch with a transcendent principle. The occurrence in mystics of just such an experience would then make it possible to add something to the results already established, whilst these established results would reflect back on to the mystical experience something of their own objectivity. Experience is the only source of knowledge. But, since the intellectual record of the fact inevitably goes further than the raw fact, all experiences are far from being equally conclusive and from justifying the same certainty. Many lead us to merely probable conclusions. Yet probabilities may accumulate, and the sum-total be practically equivalent to certainty. We have alluded elsewhere to those "lines of fact," each one indicating but the direction of truth, because it does not go far enough; truth itself, however, will be reached if two of them can be prolonged to the point where they intersect. A surveyor measures the distance to an unattainable point by taking a line on it, now from one, now from the other of two points which he *can* reach. In our opinion this method of intersection is the only one that can bring about a decisive advance in metaphysics. By this means collaboration between philosophers can be established; metaphysics, like science, will progress by the gradual accumulation of results obtained, instead of being a complete take-it-or-leave-it system, always in dispute and always doomed to start afresh. Now it so happens that a thorough study of a certain order of problems, en-

* M. de Montmorand, *Psychologie des mystiques catholiques orthodoxes.* Paris, 1920, p. 17.

tirely different from religious problems, has led us to a conclusion which makes probable the existence of a singular privileged experience, such as a mystic experience, and, on the other hand, supplies us with pointers that can be added and fitted to the knowledge obtained in an entirely different field, by an entirely different method. Let us begin with the first point.

It was by following as closely as possible the evidence of biology that we reached the conception of a vital impetus and of a creative evolution. As we set it out at the beginning of the last chapter, this conception was by no means a hypothesis, it was a condensation of fact, a summing up of summings up. Now, whence came the impetus, and what was the principle behind it? If it sufficed unto itself, what was it in itself, and what meaning were we to ascribe to its manifestations as a whole? To such questions the facts under consideration supplied no direct answer; but we saw clearly from what direction the answer might come. For the energy thrown through matter appeared to us, as it were, below or above consciousness. It had to get round many obstacles, squeeze itself through others; above all, divide itself between diverging lines of evolution; at the extremities of the two main lines we ultimately found two modes of knowledge into which it had resolved itself in order to materialize: the instinct of insects, the intelligence of man. Instinct was intuitive; intelligence reflected and reasoned. It is true that intuition had had to debase itself to become instinct; it had become intent, as though hypnotized, on the interest of the species, and what had survived of its consciousness had assumed a somnambulistic form. But just as there subsisted around animal instinct a fringe of intelligence, so human intelligence preserved a halo of intuition. The latter, in man, had remained fully disinterested and conscious, but it was only a faint flow and did not radiate very far. Yet it was from this that the light had to come, if ever the inner working of the vital impetus were to be made clear in its significance and in its object. For this intuition was turned inward; and if, in a first intensification, beyond which most of us did not go, it made us realize the continuity of our inner life, a deeper intensification might carry it to the roots of our being, and thus to the very principle of life in general. Now is not this precisely the privilege of the mystic soul?

This brings us to what we have just stated as our second point. The first question was to find out whether or no the mystics were merely "queer," if the accounts of their experience were purely fanciful or not. But the question was soon settled, at least as far as the great mystics were concerned. The next thing was to find out whether mysticism was no more than a more fervent faith, an imaginative form such as traditional religion is capable of assuming in passionate souls, or whether, while assimilating as much as it can from this religion, while turning to it for confirmation, while borrowing its language, it did not possess an original content, drawn straight from the very well-spring of religion, independent of all that religion owes to tradition, to theology, to the churches. In the first case, it would necessarily stand aloof from philosophy, for the latter ignores revelation which has a definite date, the institutions which transmitted it, the faith that accepts it: it must confine itself to experience and inference. But, in the second case, it would suffice to take mysticism unalloyed, apart from the visions, the allegories, the theological language which express it, to make it a powerful helpmeet to philosophical research. Of these two conceptions of the relation that it maintains to religion, the second seems to us indubitably the right one. We must then find out in what measure mystic experience is a continuation of the experience which led us to the doctrine of the vital impetus. All the information with which it would furnish philosophy, philosophy would repay in the shape of confirmation.

Let us first note that the mystics ignore what we have called "false problems." It may perhaps be objected that they ignore *all* problems, whether real or false, and this is true enough. It is none the less certain that they supply us with an implicit answer to questions which force themselves upon the attention of philosophers, and that difficulties that should never have perplexed philosophy are implicitly regarded by the mystic as nonexistent. We have shown elsewhere that part of metaphysics moves, consciously or not, around the question why anything exists—why matter, or spirit, or God, rather than nothing at all. But the question presupposes that reality fills a void, that underneath Being lies nothingness, that *de jure* there should be nothing, that we must therefore explain why there is *de facto* something. And this presupposition is pure illusion, for the idea of pure nothingness has not one jot more meaning than a square circle. The absence of one thing being always the presence of another—which we prefer to leave aside because it is not the thing that interests us or the thing we were expecting—suppression is never anything more than substitution, a two-sided operation which we agree to look at from one side only; so that the idea of the abolition of everything is self-destructive, inconceivable; it is a pseudo-idea, a mirage conjured up by our imagination. But, for reasons we have stated elsewhere, the illusion is natural: its source lies in the depths of the understanding. It raises questions which are the main origin of metaphysical anguish. Now, for a mystic these questions simply do not exist; they are optical illusions arising, in the inner world, from the structure of human intelligence; they recede and disappear as the mystic rises superior to the human point of view. And, for similar reasons, the mystic will not worry about the difficulties accumulated by philosophy around the "metaphysical" attributes of Deity: he has nothing to do with properties which are mere negations and can only be expressed negatively; he believes that he sees what God is; for him there is no seeing what God is not. It is therefore on the nature of God, immediately apprehended on the positive side, I mean on the side which is perceptible to the eyes of the soul, that the philosopher must question him.

The philosopher could soon define this nature, did he wish to find a formula for mysticism. God is love, and the object of love: herein lies the whole contribution of mysticism. About this twofold love the mystic will never have done talking. His description is interminable, because what he wants to describe is ineffable. But what he does state clearly is that divine love is not a thing of God: it is God Himself. It is upon this point that the philosopher must fasten, who holds God to be a person, and yet wishes to avoid anything like a gross assimilation with man. He will think, for example, of the enthusiasms that can fire a soul, consume all that is within it, and henceforth fill the whole space. The individual then becomes one with the emotion; and yet he was never so thoroughly himself; he is simplified, unified, intensified. Nor has he ever been so charged with thought, if it be true, as we have said, that there are two kinds of emotion: the one below intellect, which is mere disturbance following upon a representation; the other above intellect, which precedes the idea and is more than idea, but which would burst into ideas if, pure soul that it is, it chose to give itself a body. What is there more systematically architectonic, more reflectively elaborate, than a Beethoven symphony? But all through the labour of arranging, rearranging, selecting, carried out on the intellectual plane, the composer was turning back to a point situated outside that plane, was in search of acceptance or refusal, of a lead, an inspiration; at that point there lurked an indivisible emotion which intelligence doubtless helped to unfold into music, but which was in itself something more than music and more than intelligence. Just the opposite of infra-intellectual emotion, it remained dependent on the will. To refer to this emotion the artist had to make a constantly repeated effort, such as the eye makes to rediscover a star which, as soon as it is found, vanishes into the dark sky. An emotion of this kind doubtless resembles, though very remotely, the sublime love which is for the mystic the very essence of God. In any case, the philosopher must bear the emotion in mind when he compresses mystic intuition more and more in order to express it in terms of intelligence.

He may not write music, but he generally writes books; and the analysis of his own state of mind when he writes will help him to understand how the love in which the mystics see the very essence of divinity can be both a person and a creative power. He generally keeps, when writing, within the sphere of concepts and words. Society supplies ideas ready to hand, worked out by his predecessors and stored up in the language, ideas which he combines in a new way, after himself reshaping them to a certain extent so as to make them fit into his combination. This method will always produce some more or less satisfactory result, but still a result, and in a limited space of time. And the work produced may be original and vigorous; in many cases human thought will be enriched by it. Yet this will be but an increase of that year's income; social intelligence will continue to live on the same capital, the same stock. Now there is another method of composition, more ambitious, less certain, which cannot tell when it will succeed or even if it will succeed at all. It consists in working back from the intellectual and social plane, to a point in the soul from which there springs an imperative demand for creation. The soul within which this demand dwells may indeed have felt it fully only once in its lifetime, but it is always there, a unique emotion, an impulse, an impetus, received from the very depths of things. To obey it completely new words would have to be coined, new ideas would have to be created, but this would no longer be communicating something; it would be writing. Yet the writer will attempt to realize the unrealizable. He will revert to the simple emotion, to the form which yearns to create its matter, and will go with it to meet ideas already made, words that already exist, briefly social segments of reality. All along the way he will feel it manifesting itself in signs born of itself, I mean in fragments of its own materialization. How can these elements, each unique of its kind, be made to coincide with words already expressing things? He will be driven to strain the words, to do violence to speech. And, even so, success can never be sure; the writer wonders at every step if it will be granted to him to go on to the end; he thanks his luck for every partial success, just as a punster might thank the words he comes across for lending themselves to his fun. But if he does succeed, he will have enriched humanity with a thought that can take on a fresh aspect for each generation, with a capital yielding ever-renewed dividends, and not just with a sum down to be spent at once. These are the two methods of literary composition. They may not, indeed, utterly exclude each other, yet they are radically different. The second one, as providing the image of the creation of matter by form, is what the philosopher must have in mind in order to conceive as creative energy the love wherein the mystic sees the very essence of God.

Has this love an object? Let us bear in mind that an emotion of a superior order is self-sufficient. Imagine a piece of music that expresses love. It is not love for any particular person. Another piece of music will express another love. Here we have two distinct emotional atmospheres, two different fragrances, and in both cases the quality of love will depend upon its essence and not upon its object. Nevertheless, it is hard to conceive a love which is, so to speak, at work, and yet applies to nothing. As a matter of fact, the mystics unanimously bear witness that God needs us, just as we need God. Why should He need us unless it be to love us? And it is to this very conclusion that the philosopher who holds to the mystical experience must come. Creation will appear to him as God undertaking to create creators, that He may have, besides Himself, beings worthy of His love.

We should hesitate to admit this if it were merely a question of humdrum dwellers on this corner of the universe called Earth. But, as we have said before, it is probable that life animates all the planets round all the stars. It doubtless takes, by reason of the diversity of conditions in which it exists, the most varied forms, some very remote from what we imagine them to be; but its essence is everywhere the same, a slow accumulation of potential energy to be spent suddenly in free action. We might still hesitate to admit this, if we regarded as accidental the appearance amid the plants and animals that people the earth of a living creature such as man, capable of loving and making himself loved. But we have shown that this appearance, while not predetermined, was not accidental either. Though there were other lines of evolution running alongside the line which led to man, and though much is incomplete in man himself, we can say, while keeping closely to what experience shows, that it is man who accounts for the presence of life on our planet. Finally, we might go on hesitating if we believed that the universe is essentially raw matter, and that life has been super-added to matter. We have shown, on the contrary, that matter and life, as we define them, are coexistent and interdependent. This being the case, there is nothing to prevent the philosopher from following to its logical conclusion the idea which mysticism suggests to him of a universe which is the mere visible and tangible aspect of love and of the need of loving, together with all the consequences entailed by this creative emotion: I mean the appearance of living creatures in which this emotion finds its complement; of an infinity of other beings without which they could not have appeared, and lastly of the unfathomable depths of material substance without which life would not have been possible.

No doubt we are here going beyond the conclusions we reached in *Creative Evolution*. We wanted to keep as closely as possible to facts. We stated nothing that could not in time be confirmed by the tests of biology. Pending that confirmation, we had obtained results which the philosophic method, as we understand it, justified us in holding to be true. Here we are in the field of probabilities alone. But we cannot reiterate too often that philosophic certainty admits of degrees, that it calls for intuition as well as for reason, and that if intuition, backed by science, is to be extended, such extension can be made only by mystical intuition. In fact, the conclusions just set out complete naturally, though not necessarily, those of our former work. Granted the existence of a creative energy which is love, and which desires to produce from itself beings worthy to be loved, it might indeed sow space with worlds whose materiality, as the opposite of divine spirituality, would simply express the distinction between being created and creating, between the multifarious notes, strung like pearls, of a symphony and the indivisible emotion from which they sprang. In each of these worlds vital impetus and raw matter might thus be complementary aspects of creation: life owing to the matter it traverses, its subdivision into distinct beings, and the potentialities it bears within it being mingled as much as the spatiality of the matter which displays them permits. This interpenetration has not been possible on our planet; everything conduces to the idea that whatever matter could be secured here for the embodiment of life was ill-adapted to favour life's impetus. The original impulsion therefore split into different lines of evolutionary progress, instead of remaining undivided to the end. Even along the line on which the essential of the impulsion travelled it ended by exhausting its effect, or rather the movement which started as straight ended as circular. In that circle, humanity, the terminal point, revolves. Such was our conclusion. In order to carry it further otherwise than by mere guesswork, we should simply have to follow the lead of the mystic. That current of life which traverses matter, and which accounts for its existence, we simply took for granted. As for humanity, which stands at the extremity of the main line, we did not ask whether it had any other purpose but itself. Now, this twofold question is contained in the very answer given to it by mystical intuition. Beings have been called into existence who were destined to love and to be loved, since creative energy is to be defined as love. Distinct from God, who is this energy itself, they could spring into being only in a universe, and therefore the universe sprang into being. In that portion of the universe which is our planet—probably in our whole planetary system—such beings, in order to appear, have had to be wrought into a species, and this species involved a multitude of other species, which led up to it, or sustained it, or else formed a residue. It may be that in other systems there are only individuals radically differentiated—assuming them to be multifarious and moral—and it may be these creatures too were shaped at a single stroke, so as to be complete from the first. On Earth, in any case, the species which accounts for the existence of all the others is only partially itself. It would never for an instant have thought of becoming completely itself, if certain representatives of it had not succeeded by an individual effort, added to the general work of life, in breaking through the resistance put up by the instrument, in triumphing over materiality—in a word, in getting back to God. These men are the mystics. They have blazed the trail along which other men may pass. They have, by this very act, shown to the philosopher the whence and whither of life.

8

REVELATION AND TRADITION

The Need of Revelation to Supplement Reason *

WHILE the truth of the intelligible things of God is twofold, one
to which the inquiry of reason can attain, the other which surpasses the whole range of human reason, both are fittingly proposed by God to man as an object of belief. We must first show this with
regard to that truth which is attainable by the inquiry of reason, lest it
appear to some, that, since it can be attained by reason, it was useless
to make it an object of faith by supernatural inspiration. Now three disadvantages would result if this truth were left solely to the inquiry of
reason. One is that few men would have knowledge of God; because very
many are hindered from gathering the fruit of diligent inquiry, which is
the discovery of truth, for three reasons. Some indeed on account of an
indisposition of temperament, by reason of which many are naturally
indisposed to knowledge; so that no effort of theirs would enable them to
reach to the attainment of the highest degree of human knowledge,
which consists in knowing God. Some are hindered by the needs of
household affairs. For there must needs be among men some that devote
themselves to the conduct of temporal affairs, who would be unable to
devote so much time to the leisure of contemplative research as to reach
the summit of human inquiry, namely the knowledge of God. And some
are hindered by laziness. For, in order to acquire the knowledge of God
in those things which reason is able to investigate, it is necessary to have
a previous knowledge of many things; since almost the entire consideration of Philosophy is directed to the knowledge of God; for which reason
metaphysics, which is about divine things, is the last of the parts of
philosophy to be studied. Wherefore it is not possible to arrive at the
inquiry about the aforesaid truth except after the most laborious study;
and few are willing to take upon themselves this labour for the love of
knowledge, the natural desire for which has nevertheless been instilled
into the mind of man by God.

The second disadvantage is that those who would arrive at the discovery of the aforesaid truth would scarcely succeed in doing so after a long
time. First, because this truth is so profound, that it is only after long

* St. Thomas Aquinas (1225-1274), *Summa Contra Gentiles* (London: Burns, Oates,
1924), I, 4, pp. 7-9.

practice that the human intellect is enabled to grasp it by means of reason. Secondly, because many things are required beforehand, as stated above. Thirdly, because, at the time of youth, the mind, when tossed about by the various movements of the passions, is not fit for the knowledge of so sublime a truth, whereas *calm gives prudence and knowledge,* as stated in 7 *Phys.* III, 7. Hence mankind would remain in the deepest darkness of ignorance, if the path of reason were the only available way to the knowledge of God; because the knowledge of God which especially makes men perfect and good would be acquired only by the few, and by these after a long time.

The third disadvantage is that much falsehood is mingled with the investigations of human reason, on account of the weakness of our intellect in forming its judgments, and by reason of the admixture of phantasms. Consequently many would remain in doubt about those things even which are most truly demonstrated, through ignoring the force of the demonstration; especially when they perceive that different things are taught by the various men who are called wise. Moreover, among the many demonstrated truths, there is sometimes a mixture of falsehood that is not demonstrated, but assumed for some probable or sophistical reason which at times is mistaken for a demonstration. Therefore it was necessary that definite certainty and pure truth should be offered to man by way of faith.

The Universal Consent of Mankind and the Existence of God *

I make bold to set forth as an eminently philosophical thesis that, if the First Cause we call God, exists, It is known, and that if It is known, It exists; in other words, God cannot exist and not be known, nor can He be known unless He exists. . . .

But God is known by men, since they *have a name for Him,* according to Fontenelle's pithy expression: "A truth that is known has a name, and to *give a name* to God is to prove His existence, as to love Him means that one knows Him. For we dare all grammarians to *give a name* to what neither exists, nor can exist, and to make sense for themselves and for others. In vain would they imagine the strangest monster and give it a name; this monster will never be but made up of parts actually found in several individuals, bound up together by imagination and called a *fiction;* such a fictitious being will be a possibility, since I have an image of it and make a drawing of it. By the very fact that He has a name, and that men grasp its meaning, when they think of Him, or talk about Him, *God exists;* and here we return to Descartes' argument "God is possible, therefore God exists." In one word, if we give a name to God,

* Vicomte Ambroise de Bonald (1784-1840), *Recherches philosophiques sur les premiers objets des connaissances morales* (Paris: Adrien Le Clere, 1853), ch. x, "La Cause Première" (extracts).

that means that we know Him, for we *cannot give a name to what we know not*. Since God is known He exists, for what does not exist *cannot be known*.

. . . Every human society, then, has had an idea of God, has attempted to form an image of Him, has entertained feelings of love and of fear towards Him, since every one has evidenced its idea of God in the universal language, its image of God in external representations, its feelings about God in public actions. *"Nulla gens tam fera, cujus mentem non imbuerit deorum opinio,"* says Cicero.

. . . It is this common fund of uniform feelings about a few general truths which constitutes *common sense* and, if the world *is ruled by opinion*, society is ruled by common sense which, to quote Bossuet, *governs human affairs*. Woe to those who lay down common sense with wit and smartness. We must even note that it is precisely that rectitude of thought and feeling in most men which is the basis of the most important social actions, the framing and application of laws, since the first requisite of a deliberating body, and the indispensable condition of its operations is that the feeling of the greatest number must be regarded as law and decision. It is only in matters at most useful to society but never necessary, such as arts and physical science, that the broadest knowledge is found among the few, or at least is presumed to be found there. It is strange then that the same philosophers who would have each people exercise authority and regard its aspirations as the supreme political norm, when they come to morals, regard the whole human race as a child and call prejudices its most general beliefs. However, we must be careful to distinguish universal beliefs which of necessity are true and express a natural, or a divine law, *lex naturae*, from local opinions which are held by some peoples and may be errors and the fruit of human invention.

Everywhere then I find the idea of God, an image of God and a sense of God, and on that ground I believe in the existence of the common element of that idea, of that image, and of that sense. However, I perceive in various societies diverse expressions of this general idea of God, of this common tendency to *imagine* God, of this common attempt which is prompted by the sense of God, and, far from concluding from that variety of local opinions to the non-existence of God on the ground that He is not adored everywhere *in the same way*, I conclude on the contrary that He exists, because the knowledge of Him is *the same* everywhere. In the same way as from the innumerable varieties of judiciary customs in various countries, I infer the existence everywhere of the notion of distributive justice, and from the variety of healing methods the universality of medicine, I content myself with examining the most logical application of the idea of God, the most natural and the most rational images of God, the most pure and innocent forms of Divine worship; and, even leaving aside such an examination as is not within every man's power, I find in the beliefs and practices of civilized nations the same motives of credibility for the applications of the common belief in the existence of God, that is, for religion, as I have found for the truth itself in the universal belief of mankind. My reason is that societies could not have attained civilization, that is, a perfect code of laws (very different from the rules of the fine arts which constitute education), under the influence of a general error regarding the basic principle of every religious belief.

9

NON-PHILOSOPHICAL APPROACHES TO GOD

"The Wager" *

WE KNOW neither the existence nor the nature of God, because He has neither extension nor limit. But by faith we know that He exists; in glory we shall know Him as He is. Now I have already shown that one can perfectly well know that a thing exists without knowing its nature.

Let us now speak according to the light of nature.

If there is a God, He is infinitely incomprehensible, since, having neither parts nor limits, He has no relation to us. We are therefore incapable of knowing what He is, or whether He is. This being so, who will dare to solve the problem? Not we who have no relation to Him.

Who then will blame Christians for inability to give a reason for belief, professing as they do a religion for which they can give no reason? When they expound it, they declare it to be folly, *stultitiam*, and then you complain that they do not prove it. If they proved it they would belie themselves; their lack of proof shows that they do not lack common sense. "Agreed; but although that excuses those who present religion as they do, and clears them from blame for setting it forth without supporting reason, it does not excuse those who accept it." Let us then examine this point and say "God is or is not." But which way shall we lean? Reason can settle nothing here; there is an infinite gulf between us. A game is on, at the other end of this infinite distance, and heads or tails will turn up, What will you wager? According to reason you cannot do either; according to reason you cannot leave either undone.

Do not then condemn those who have made a choice, for you know nothing about it. "I won't, but I shall blame them for making not this

---

* Blaise Pascal (1623-1662), *Pensées*, English translation, brief notes, and introduction by H. F. Stewart (New York: Pantheon Books, 1950), pp. 117-123. It is to be noted that the "wager" is not offered by Pascal as an actual proof of God's existence, but as a challenge to freethinkers to embrace religious belief.

choice but any choice; for, although he who calls 'heads' and the other are equally wrong, they are both of them wrong; the right thing is not to wager."

Yes, but wager you must; there is no option, you have embarked on it. So which will you have? Come, since you must choose, let us see what concerns you least. You have two things to lose: truth and good, and two things to stake: your reason and your will, your knowledge and your happiness. And your nature has two things to shun: error and misery. Your reason does not suffer by choosing one more than the other, for you must choose. That is one point cleared. But your happiness? Let us weigh gain and loss in calling heads that God is. Reckon these two chances; if you win, you win all; if you lose, you lose naught. Then do not hesitate, wager that He is. "Admirable. Yes, I must wager; but I stake perhaps too much." Now, now. Since there is equal chance of gain and loss, if you had only two lives to gain for one, you might still wager; but were there three to win you would have to play (since play you must) and you would be foolish, when you are forced to play, not to risk one life to win three at a game, where the chances of loss and gain are equal. But here there is an eternity of life and happiness. And this being so, though there should be an infinity of chances and only one for you, you would still be right to stake one in order to win two, and you would be stupid, being obliged to play, did you refuse to stake one life against three at a game in which out of an infinity of chances there is one for you, if there were an infinite amount of infinitely happy life to gain. But here there *is* an infinity of infinitely happy life to gain, one chance of gain against a finite number of chances of loss, and your stake is finite. That settles it; wherever there is infinity, and not an infinity of chances of loss against the chance of gain, there can be no hesitation, you must stake all. And thus, when you are forced to play, you must renounce reason in order to keep life, rather than risk it for infinite gain which is as likely to happen as the loss of naught.

For it is no use saying that our gain is uncertain, and that the infinite distance between the *certainty* of what we stake and the *uncertainty* of what we gain, equals the finite good which is certainly staked against the uncertain infinite. Every gambler risks a certainty to gain an uncertainty; and yet he stakes a finite certainty to gain a finite uncertainty, and that without transgressing reason. There is not an infinite distance between the certain stake and the uncertain gain; that is quite wrong. There is, in truth, an infinity between certainty of gain and certainty of loss. But the uncertainty of gain is proportioned to the certainty of the stake, according to the proportion of the chances of gain and loss. Hence it comes to that, where there are as many risks on one side as on the other, the game is even; and then the certainty of the stake is equal to the uncertainty of the gain; they are far from being infinitely separated. And so our argument is of infinite force when there is the finite to stake in a game in which the chances of gain and loss are equal, and the winnings are infinite. This is demonstrable; and if men are capable of any truth, this is one.

"I confess and admit it. But still there is no way of seeing the face of the cards." Yes, Scripture and the rest, etc. "Yes, my hands are tied and my lips are closed; I am forced to wager, and I am not free; I am not released, and I am so made that I cannot believe. What am I to do?" You speak true. But at least get to understand your inability to believe, since reason leads you to belief, and yet you cannot believe. Do your best then to gain conviction, not by increase of divine proofs, but by a decrease of human passions. You would fain reach faith, but you know not the way? You would cure yourself of unbelief, and you ask for a remedy? Take a lesson from those who have been bound like you, and who now stake all they possess. These are they who know the road you would follow, who are cured of a disease of which you would be cured. Follow the way by which they began, that is by making themselves believe that they believed, by taking holy water, by hearing mass, etc. This will quite naturally bring you to believe, and will calm you . . . will stupefy you. "But that is just what I fear." Why pray? What have you to lose? But to show you that this is the way, this is what will lessen your passions which are your great stumbling block.

Now what harm will you get in following this line? You will be faithful, honest, humble, grateful, beneficent, a good friend, true. Certainly you will be freed from poisonous pleasures, such as ambition and luxury; but will you not have others? I tell you that you will gain in this life, and that at every step you take on this road you will see such certainty of gain, such nothingness in what you risk, that you will at last recognize that you have wagered on something certain and infinite, for which you have risked naught.

"Oh, your words transport me, delight me, etc."

If they please you and seem cogent, know that they are the utterance of a man who has been on his knees before and after, beseeching that Being, infinite and without parts, to whom he submits all his being, that He may likewise bring into submission all your being for your good and for His glory; that so strength may come to the help of weakness.

How Untrained Minds Arrive at Certitude of the Existence of God *

In many places Scripture declares in the most express manner that, even for those to whom God has not manifested Himself by His prophets or by His Son, there exists a revelation of God in His works and even

* Joseph Kleutgen, S.J. (1811-1883), *La Philosophie scholastique exposée et défendue* (Paris: Gaume, 1868), III⁰ᵐᵉ Dis., "De la certitude," Nos. 226-229, 231-232. Trans. and quoted by William George Ward in *The Philosophy of Theism* (London: Kegan Paul, 1884), Vol. II, Essay XV, "Explicit and Implicit Thought," pp. 216-220.

within the minds of men, whereby they can without any difficulty cognize God their Creator and Maker, as well as His sovereign law. It is not necessary to point out that Scripture does not in this speak of any [supposable] first cause; but of the Living and True God, Who has created heaven and earth, and inscribed His law in the heart of man; and that consequently it speaks also of the moral order. Now, it says in the same passages that men who do not thus cognize their God are without excuse; that they are insensate, that they deserve God's wrath and all His chastisements. It necessarily follows, then, that this manifestation of God by His works is such that man cannot fail by this means to cognize God with certitude, unless he commits a grave fault. . . .

Assuredly this idea does not mean that it is philosophical research, continued laboriously through obstacles and doubts, which can alone lead to the knowledge of God. Very few men, in fact, are capable of these laborious researches; whereas Scripture speaks of the heathens in general; and in the book of Wisdom (13:1) it is said expressly, "All men are vanity who do not possess the knowledge of God." The sacred writer even adds that this knowledge to which he gives the name of "sight" "*cognoscibiliter poterit Creator horum videri,*" to express its clearness and certitude, can be obtained with as much ease—and even more—as knowledge of this world; which certainly does not fail any one capable of the least reflection ("*Si enim tantum potuerunt scire, ut possent aestimare saeculum, quomodo hujus Dominum non facilius invenerunt?*" [Wisd. 13:9]). . . . It is easier, therefore, to know God, the Governor of the world, than to know enough of nature to admire its power and beauty.

It necessarily follows, therefore, that there is a knowledge of God different from philosophical knowledge; a knowledge so easy to acquire and so certain, that ignorance and doubt on that head cannot be explained, except either by culpable carelessness or proud obstinacy. Such is also . . . the common doctrine of the Holy Fathers. They distinguished that knowledge of God which is obtained by philosophical research from that which springs up spontaneously in every man at the very sight of creation. This latter kind of knowledge is called by them "a witness of Himself," which God gave to the soul at its creation; "an endowment of nature," "an infused knowledge," inherent in every man without preliminary instruction; a knowledge which springs up in one sense of itself in proportion as reason is developed; and which cannot fail, except in a man either deprived of the use of reason or else given up to vices which have corrupted his nature. And when the Fathers of the Church declare unanimously on this head that this knowledge is really found and established in all men, the importance of their testimony is better understood by remembering that they lived in the midst of heathen populations.

God has implanted in our reasonable nature everything which is necessary, that we may know Him and know Him with facility. Now, He does not (after creation) withdraw Himself from creatures, but always remains near them, cooperating with them, exciting them to act, supporting and directing each one to its end conformably to its nature. If this is true of all creatures, how could this concurrence be refused to the most noble of all creatures, to those whom God has created for the very purpose of their knowing and loving Him? Man indeed does not arrive at this end, except by using the powers which God has given him; but the author of those gifts lends to man His concurrence, in order that he may make due use of them. Since that moral and religious life for which man was created is founded on the knowledge of the truths whereof we speak, God watches over man, in order that reason, as it is developed, may come to know them with facility and certainty. (Observe, the question here is not of supernatural grace, but is of the natural order.)

What would not be the misery of man [if there were no reasonable certainty without philosophical argument]? It is only to show those [ordinary] men who are capable of any reflection at all, that their knowledge of the truth is not scientific; that they do not deduce it (consciously and explicitly) from the first principles of thought, and consequently they cannot defend it against the attacks of scepticism. If, then, as soon as we came to know that our knowledge is not scientific, the conviction of its truth were at once shaken, what, on that supposition, would be the lot of man?

The fact is indeed not so; that consciousness which every man can interrogate within himself attests its denial; and at every period the voice of mankind has confirmed that denial. As soon as we arrive at the use of reason, the voice of conscience awakes within us. Whether we choose or no, we must cognize the distinction between good and evil. [Again] just as it is absolutely impossible for us to doubt our own existence, [in like manner] we are absolutely compelled to regard as real the external world; [to hold] that, further, there exists a Supreme Author of our being and of all other things; and that through Him there is a certain moral order. These also are truths which we cannot refuse to admit. No doubt we can do violence to ourselves in order to produce in ourselves the contrary persuasion, just as we may use efforts to regard the moral conscience itself as an illusion. But these efforts never succeed, or, at least, never succeed perfectly; and we feel ourselves even under an obligation of condemning the very attempt as immoral. The mind of man, in fact, is under the influence of truth which has dominion over it, and which gives [man] certainty even against his own wish. Truth manifests itself to our intelligence, and engenders therein the knowledge of its reality, even before we [explicitly] know what truth is. Still truth, [I say], reigns over man and reveals itself to him, however great may be his resistance, as a sacred and sovereign authority which commands him and summons him before its tribunal. And [standing] before that tribunal, he is obliged to admit the immorality of even attempting to doubt. Just as he is bound to condemn the madness, I will not say of doubting, but of trying to doubt the reality of the external world, so he is obliged to regard as an impiety [all] doubt in God's existence and Providence. . . .

Nor can it here be objected that conscience, [in the proper sense of that word, moral conscience], gives us no certainty so long as its existence within us and its pronouncements are purely spontaneous. Of the conscience, more than anything else, it may be said that it reveals to us its own truth; that it compels us to acknowledge an absolute good and a sovereign rule over our wills and actions (even though we know not its innermost nature), not only as really existing, but as an august and sacred power which is [in authority] over us. Whatever efforts man may make to overthrow and destroy his own intimate persuasion on the truthfulness of conscience, he will never succeed in doing so. Even though he seeks by any possible means to persuade himself that nothing obliges him to regard it as truthful, nevertheless he will always feel himself compelled to acknowledge its authority, and even to condemn his resistance to it.

It is true, indeed, that, though conscience often speaks against a man's inclination [so loudly] as to confound, [by its manifestation of its own truthfulness], all pride and all sophistical dreams by which he might wish to stifle it, it does not always so speak and raise its voice as to take from man the power of turning from it and refusing to listen. If he enters into himself and chooses to observe what passes within him, he will obtain that reflex knowledge which, as we said above, is required for actual certainty; he will know that he cannot prevent himself from acknowledging the truth of what the voice of conscience dictates. But it is in his power, if not always at least often, to abstain from entering into himself and lending his ear to that voice. He has [often] the power of not hearing it, or of giving it so little attention that he withdraws himself from that influence which would make him certain. It is in this manner that, for a certain time at least, notwithstanding the habitual certainty which nature gives him, he may remain undecided on the truthfulness of conscience, supposing that he has not yet acknowledged that truthfulness by philosophical reflection, or, again, that he does not seek to know it. But even though we were not able to demonstrate by the intimate experience of every man that the doubt whereof we speak is utterly contrary to the principles of morality, we ought, nevertheless, to be persuaded of that truth by the judgment of all mankind. Among civilized nations in every time the necessity of philosophical studies has been admitted, and those have been held in high esteem who devoted themselves thereto, and who were regarded as sages. Nevertheless, though the nations, it is true, accepted at the hand of philosophers the solution of many questions, they have never ascribed to these men a decisive judgment on all truth without exception. As to these first truths on which all our convictions rest, humanity bears within itself the consciousness or intimate persuasion of knowing them with certainty. Philosophers may make these rules the subject of their speculations; but they are not allowed the right of pronouncing a definite judgment on these truths; and if their researches lead them to deny or doubt them, those very persons who would otherwise be the disciples of these philosophers, rise against them as judges and condemn them. Was there ever a nation which did not regard it as madness to doubt an external world: a nation which did not hold in horror a man so perverted as to acknowledge no truth superior to the senses, and reject all distinction between virtue and vice? Has not atheism among all nations been accounted a crime? And by the very fact of seeing culpability in denial of these truths, does not the world declare that they cannot possibly be unknown to men of good will?

The Primordial Way *

1. From Plato and Aristotle to St. Anselm and St. Thomas Aquinas, to Descartes and Leibnitz, philosophers have proposed proofs or demonstrations of the existence of God, or, as Thomas Aquinas more modestly puts it, *ways* through which the intellect is led to the certitude of His existence. All are highly conceptualized and rationalized proofs, specifically philosophic ways of approach. Kant rightly criticized the proof advanced by Descartes (what is called "the ontological argument"), but wrongly claimed to reduce all the ways of demonstration to this particular proof. That was a great error; for the five ways indicated by Thomas Aquinas are completely independent of the ontological argument, and stand firm in spite of all criticism.†

However, it is not these highly conceptualized and specifically philosophical ways of approach which I should like to consider at present. When St. Paul affirmed that:

that which is known of God is manifest in them. For God hath manifested it unto them. For the invisible things of Him, from the creation of the world, are clearly seen, being understood by the things that are made; His eternal power also, and divinity. (Rom. 1:19-20)

he was thinking not only of scientifically elaborated or specifically philosophical ways of establishing the existence of God. He had in mind also and above all the natural knowledge of the existence of God to which the vision of created things leads the reason of every man, philosopher or not. It is this doubly *natural* knowledge of God I wish to take up

* "The Primordial Way of Approach" from *Approaches to God* by Jacques Maritain. Copyright 1954 by Jacques Maritain. Reprinted by permission of Harper & Row, Publishers.

† For a discussion of the ontological argument and of the primacy unduly attributed by Kant to this argument, see our *Dream of Descartes* (New York: Philosophical Library, 1944), ch. IV.

here. It is natural not only in the sense that it belongs to the rational order rather than to the super-natural order of faith, but also in the sense that it is *prephilosophical* and proceeds by the natural or, so to speak, instinctive manner proper to the first apperceptions of the intellect prior to every philosophical or scientifically rationalized elaboration.

Before entering into the sphere of completely formed and articulated knowledge, in particular the sphere of metaphysical knowledge, the human mind is indeed capable of a prephilosophical knowledge which is *virtually metaphysical*. Therein is found the first, the primordial way of approach through which men become aware of the existence of God.

2. Here everything depends on the natural intuition of being—on the intuition of that act of existing which is the act of every act and the perfection of every perfection, in which all the intelligible structures of reality have their definite actuation, and which overflows in activity in every being and in the intercommunication of all beings.

Let us rouse ourselves, let us stop living in dreams or in the magic of images and formulas, of words, of signs and practical symbols. Once a man has been awakened to the reality of existence and of his own existence, when he has really perceived that formidable, sometimes elating, sometimes sickening or maddening fact *I exist*, he is henceforth possessed by the intuition of being and the implications it bears with it.

Precisely speaking, this primordial intuition is both the intuition of *my* existence and of the existence of *things*, but first and foremost of the existence of things. When it takes place, I suddenly realize that a given entity—man, mountain, or tree—exists and exercises this sovereign activity *to be* in its own way, in an independence *of me* which is total, self-assertive and totally implacable. And at the same time I realize not only that *I* exist, but also this other existence by which things assert themselves and in which I have positively no part, to which I am exactly as naught. And no doubt, in face of my existence others have the same feeling of being frail and threatened. As for me, confronted with others, it is my own existence that I feel to be fragile and menaced, exposed to destruction and death. Thus the primordial intuition of being is the intuition of the solidity and inexorability of existence; and, second, of the death and nothingness to which *my* existence is liable. And, third, in the same flash of intuition, which is but my becoming aware of the intelligible value of being, I realize that this solid and inexorable existence, perceived in anything whatever, implies—I do not yet know in what form, perhaps in the things themselves, perhaps separately from them—some absolute, irrefragable existence completely free from nothingness and death. These three leaps by which the intellect moves first to actual existence as asserting itself independently of me; and then from the sheer objective existence to my own threatened existence, and finally from my existence spoiled with nothingness to absolute existence

—are achieved within the same unique intuition, which philosophers would explain as the intuitive perception of the essentially analogical content of the first concept, the concept of Being.*

Next—this is the second stage—a prompt, spontaneous reasoning, as natural as this intuition (and as a matter of fact more or less involved in it), immediately springs forth as the necessary fruit of such a primordial apperception, and as enforced by and under its light. It is a reasoning without words which cannot be expressed in articulate fashion without sacrificing its vital concentration and the rapidity with which it takes place. I see, first that my being is liable to death; and, second that it is dependent on the totality of nature, on the universal whole of which I am a part. I see that Being-with-nothingness, such as my own being, implies, in order that it should be, Being-without-nothingness—that absolute existence which I confusedly perceived from the beginning as involved in my primordial intuition of existence. But then the universal whole of which I am a part is itself Being-with-nothingness, by the very fact that I am part of it. And from this it follows finally that, since this universal whole does not exist by virtue of itself, it must be that Being-without-nothingness exists apart from it. There is another Whole—a separate one—another Being, transcendent and self-sufficient and unknown in itself and activating all beings, which is Being-without-nothingness, that is, self-subsisting Being, Being existing through itself.

Thus the internal dynamism of the intuition of existence, or of the intelligible value of Being, causes me to see that absolute existence of Being-without-nothingness transcends the totality of nature. And there I am, confronted with the existence of God.

3. This is not a new approach to God; it is human reason's eternal way of approaching God. What is new is the manner in which the modern mind has become aware of the simplicity and liberating power, of the natural and in some way intuitive character, of this eternal approach. The science of the ancients was steeped in philosophy. Their scientific imagery was a pseudo-ontological imagery. Consequently, there was a kind of continuum between their knowledge of the physical world and their knowledge of God. This later knowledge was seen as the summit of the former, a summit which had to be scaled by the multiple paths of the causal connections at work in the sublunar world and the celestial spheres. And the sense of Being, which everywhere and always ruled their thought, was for them an atmosphere too habitual to be regarded as a surprising gift. At the same time, the natural intuition of existence was so strong in them that their proofs of God could take the form of the most conceptualized and the most rationalized scientific demonstrations, and be offered as a skillful unfolding of logical necessities, without losing the inner energy of that intuition. This logical ma-

---

* On the concept of Being, see our book, *Existence and the Existent* (New York: Pantheon, 1948), ch. I.

chinery was surreptitiously enlivened by the deep-seated intuition of Being.

We are in quite a different position now. In order to reach physical reality in its own enigmatic way and to conquer the world of phenomena, our science has become a kind of *Maya* (illusion or deception)—a Maya which succeeds and makes us masters of nature. But the sense of Being is absent from it. Thus when we come to experience the impact of Being upon our mind, it appears to us as a kind of revelation, and we become keenly aware both of its awakening and liberating power, and of the fact that it involves a knowledge separate from the sphere of knowledge peculiar to our science. At the same time we realize that the knowledge of God, before being developed in logical and perfectly conceptualized demonstrations, is first and foremost a natural fruit of the intuition of existence, and that it imposes itself upon our mind through the imperative force of this intuition.

In other words, we have become aware of the fact that in its primordial vitality the movement of the human reason in its approach to God is neither a pure intuition (which would be superhuman), nor the kind of philosophical reasoning of a technical type through which it will be expressed in its achieved form, and which at each of its stages is pregnant with conflicts and with problems to clarify. In its primordial vitality the movement of the human reason in its approach to God is a *natural* reasoning, that is, intuitive—like or irresistibly maintained in, and vitalized by, the intellectual flash of the intuition of existence. In this natural reasoning it is just this intuition of existence which, seizing in some existing reality Being-with-nothingness, by the same stroke makes the mind grasp the necessity of Being-without-nothingness. And nowhere is there any problem involved, because the illumining power of this intuition takes possession of the mind and obliges it to see, in such a way that the mind proceeds naturally, within a primordial intuitive flash, from imperative certainty to imperative certainty. I believe that from Descartes to Kierkegaard the effort of modern thought—to the extent that it has not completely repudiated metaphysics and if it is cleansed of the irrationalism which has gradually corrupted it—tends to such an awareness of the specific *naturalness* of man's knowledge of God, definitely more profound than any scientifically developed logical process, and an awareness of the primordial and simple intuitiveness in which this knowledge originates.[*]

4. I have just tried to describe the manner in which this natural prephilosophic knowledge spontaneously proceeds. It involves a reasoning, but a reasoning after the fashion of an intuitive grasp, bathed in the primordial intuition of existence. Let us say that this natural knowledge is a kind of *innocent* knowledge, a knowledge free of all dialectic. Such

---

[*] The preceding pages are adapted and reprinted from *The Range of Reason* (New York: Scribner, 1952), pp. 88-90.

a knowledge is rich in certitude, a certitude that is indeed compelling, although it exists in an imperfect logical state. It has not yet crossed the threshold of *scientific* demonstration, whose certitude is critical and implies that the difficulties inherent in the question have been surmounted through a scrutiny of the rational connections and necessities involved. Such natural knowledge is still in happy ignorance of these difficulties and of all the *videtur quod non's;* because scientific certitude and the objections to be met—and the replies to the objections—all come into the world together.

It appears, therefore, that the philosophic proofs of the existence of God, let us say the five ways of St. Thomas Aquinas, are a development and an unfolding of this natural knowledge, raised to the level of scientific discussion and scientific certitude. And they normally presuppose this natural knowledge, not with regard to the logical structure of the demonstration, but with regard to the existential condition of the thinking subject. If the preceding observations are true, it would be necessary, before proposing the philosophic proofs, to be assured in so far as possible (by trying, where need be, to aid in such awakening) that the minds to which one addresses oneself are alive to the primordial intuition of existence, and conscious of the natural knowledge of God involved in this intuition.

One more remark seems to be called for here. I have just used the expression "the philosophic proofs of the existence of God," and I noted above that St. Thomas Aquinas preferred to use the word *ways.* He had reasons for this.* These ways are proofs, but the word "proof" or "demonstration" may be misunderstood. To prove or to demonstrate is, in everyday usage, to render evident that which of itself was not evident. Now, on the one hand, God is not *rendered evident* by us. He does not receive from us and from our arguments an evidence which He would have lacked. For the existence of God which is not immediately evident *for us* is immediately evident *in itself*—more evident in itself than the principle of identity, since it is infinitely more than a predicate contained in the notion of the subject. It is the subject, the divine essence itself (but to know this from immediate evidence, it would be necessary to see God). On the other hand, what our arguments render evident for us is not God Himself, but the testimony of Him contained in His vestiges, His signs, or His "mirrors" here below. Our arguments do not give us evidence of the divine existence itself or of the act of existing which is in God and which is God Himself—as if one could have the evidence of His existence without having that of His essence. They give us only evidence of the fact that the divine existence must be affirmed, or of the truth of the attribution of the predicate to the subject in the assertion "God exists." †

* Cf. *Les Degrés du Savoir* (Paris: Desclée de Brouwer), pp. 445-446.

† Cf. *De Potentia,* q. 7, a. 2, ad 1; *Summa Theologica,* I, 3, 4, ad 2; *Les Degrés du Savoir,* pp. 837-839. It is regrettable that, for want of having seen this very simple dis-

In short, what we prove when we prove the existence of God is some-thing which infinitely surpasses us—us and our ideas and our proofs. "To demonstrate the existence of God is not to submit Him to our grapplings, nor to define Him, nor to take possession of Him, nor to handle anything else than ideas that are feeble indeed with regard to such an object, nor to judge anything but our own radical dependence. The procedure by which reason demonstrates that God is places reason itself in an attitude of natural adoration and of intelligent admira-tion." * And thus the words "proof" and "demonstration," in reference to the existence of God, must be understood (and in fact are so under-stood spontaneously) with resonances other than in the current usage—in a sense no less strong as to their rational efficacy but more modest in that which concerns us and more reverential in that which concerns the object. On this condition it remains perfectly legitimate to use them. It is just a matter of marking well the differences in station. This being understood, we shall not hesitate to say "proof" or "demonstration" as well as "way," for all these words are synonymous in the sense we have just specified.

As to the very word *existence,* the existentialist philosophers arbi-trarily corrupt its meaning when they say that to exist is "to stand out-side oneself." † But even in its genuine meaning—to stand "outside its causes" or "outside nothingness" (the etymological sense of the word being *"sistere ex,* that is to say, to stand or to be posited in itself, from an interior term on which it depends") ‡—the word existence, in order to apply to God, must lose the connotation which thus refers it to created things. It is clear that God does not stand "outside IIis causes" —as though He were caused; nor "outside nothingness"—as though noth-ingness preceded God; and that He is not *sistens ex*—as if He depended on some antecedently existing source. Of itself, the notion of existence is in no wise restricted to such a connotation, which in fact refers to the analogue that falls first and immediately under our apprehension; from the outset it overflows all pseudo-definitions carried over from this con-notation. Just as the notion of being, the notion of existence, is of it-self, essentially and from the first, an analogous notion, validly appli-cable to the uncreated and to the created. No doubt, the word being, in contrast to the word existence, does not need to be purified of accidental vestiges due to etymology. Truth to tell, however, the word existence has been spontaneously purified of them, all by itself, and in any event

---

tinction, theologians such as Dr. Paul Tillich, one of the most remarkable representa-tives of Protestant thought in the United States, believe that to wish to demonstrate the existence of God is to deny it. (Cf. Paul Tillich, *Systematic Theology* [University of Chicago Press, 1951], I, pp. 204-205.)

* *Les Degrés du Savoir,* p. 446.

† Cf. *Existence and the Existent,* p. 12, note 3; Michel Sora, *Du Dialogue Intérieur* (Paris: Gallimard, 1947), p. 30.

‡ Etienne Gilson, *L'Etre et l'Essence* (Paris: Vrin, 1948), p. 249.

this does not affect at all the meaning itself of the notion. Those who think that one can say "God is," but not "God exists," maintain for being its essential analogicity but refuse it to existence—the strangest of illusions, since being itself is understood only in relation to existence. To say "God is" and "God exists" is to say exactly the same thing. One speaks the language of simple truth in speaking of the ways through which it is shown that God is, or that He *exists*.

Section Two

Main Philosophical Demonstrations of the Existence of God

I. Introduction: Human Reason's Aptitude to Demonstrate God's Existence

10

DENIED *

I T APPEARS to me that the examples of mathematics and natural philosophy, which, as we have seen, were brought into their present condition by a sudden revolution, are sufficiently remarkable to fix our attention on the essential circumstances of the change which has proved so advantageous to them, and to induce us to make the experiment of imitating them, so far as the analogy which, as rational sciences, they bear to metaphysics may permit. It has hitherto been assumed that our cognition must conform to the objects; but all attempts to ascertain anything about these objects a priori, by means of conceptions, and thus to extend the range of our knowledge, have been rendered abortive by this assumption. Let us then make the experiment whether we may not be more successful in metaphysics, if we assume that the objects must conform to our cognition. This appears, at all events, to accord better with the *possibility* of our gaining the end we have in view, that is to say, of arriving at the cognition of objects a priori, of determining something with respect to these objects, before they are given to us. We here propose to do just what Copernicus did in attempting to explain the celestial movements. When he found that he could make no progress by assuming that all the heavenly bodies revolved around the spectator, he

* Immanuel Kant (1724-1804), *Critique of Pure Reason*, trans. by J. M. D. Meiklejohn and ed. by Ernest Rhys, "Everyman's Library" (New York: E. P. Dutton & Co., Inc., 1934) pp. 11-18. This excerpt of the Preface to the second edition presents a fair introduction to his views.

reversed the process, and tried the experiment of assuming that the spectator revolved, while the stars remained at rest. We may make the same experiment with regard to the intuition of objects. If the intuition must conform to the nature of the objects, I do not see how we can know anything of them *a priori*. If, on the other hand, the object conforms to the nature of our faculty of intuition, I can then easily conceive the possibility of such an *a priori* knowledge. Now I cannot rest in the mere intuitions, but—if they are to become cognitions—must refer them, as *representations*, to something, as *object*, and must determine the latter by means of the former; here again two courses are open to me. *Either*, first, I may assume that the conceptions, by which I effect this determination, conform to the object—and in this case I am reduced to the same perplexity as before, *or*, secondly, I may assume that the objects, or, which is the same thing, that *experience*, in which alone, as given objects, they are cognized, conform to my conceptions—and then I am at no loss how to proceed. For experience itself is a mode of cognition which requires understanding. Before objects are given to me, that is, *a priori*, I must presuppose in myself laws of the understanding which are expressed in conceptions *a priori*. To these conceptions, then, all the objects of experience must necessarily conform. Now there are objects which reason *thinks*, and that necessarily, but which cannot be given in experience, or, at least, cannot be given as reason thinks them. The attempt to think these objects will hereafter furnish an excellent test of the new method of thought which we have adopted, and which is based on the principle that we only cognize in things *a priori* that which we ourselves place in them.

This attempt succeeds as well as we could desire, and promises to metaphysics in its first part—that is where it is occupied with conceptions *a priori*, of which the corresponding objects may be given in experience —the certain course of science. For by this new method we are enabled perfectly to explain the possibility of *a priori* cognition and, what is more, to demonstrate satisfactorily the laws which lie *a priori* at the foundation of nature, as the sum of the objects of experience—neither of which was possible according to the procedure hitherto followed. But from this deduction of the faculty of *a priori* cognition in the first part of metaphysics, we derive a surprising result, and one which, to all appearance, militates against the great end of metaphysics, as treated in the second part. For we come to the conclusion that our faculty of cognition is unable to transcend the limits of possible experience; and yet this is precisely the most essential object of this science. The estimate of our rational cognition *a priori* at which we arrive is that it has only to do with phenomena, and that things in themselves, while possessing a real existence, lie beyond its sphere. Here we are enabled to put the justice of this estimate to the test. For that which of necessity impels us to transcend the limits of experience and of all phenomena, is the *unconditioned*, which reason absolutely requires in things as they are in themselves, in order to complete the series of conditions. Now, if it appears that when on the one hand, we assume that our cognition conforms to its objects as things in themselves, *the unconditioned cannot be thought without contradiction,* and that when, on the other hand, we assume that our representation of things as they are given to us, does not conform to these things as they are in themselves, but that these objects, as phenomena, conform to our mode of representation, *the contradiction disappears;* we shall then be convinced of the truth of that which we began by assuming for the sake of experiment; we may look upon it as established that the unconditioned does not lie in things as we know them, or as they are given to us, but in things as they are in themselves, beyond the range of our cognition.

But, after we have thus denied the power of speculative reason to make any progress in the sphere of the supersensible, it still remains for our consideration whether data do not exist in *practical* reason, which may enable us to determine the transcendent conception of the unconditioned, to rise beyond the limits of all possible experience from a *practical* point of view, and thus to satisfy the great ends of metaphysics. Speculative reason has thus, at least, made room for such an extension of our knowledge, and, if it must leave this space vacant, still it does not rob us of the liberty to fill it up, if we can, by means of practical data—nay, it even challenges us to make the attempt.

. . . What is the real value of this system of metaphysics, purified by criticism, and thereby reduced to a permanent condition? A cursory view of the present work will lead to the supposition that its use is merely *negative,* that it only serves to warn us against venturing, with speculative reason, beyond the limits of experience. This is, in fact, its primary use. But this, at once, assumes a *positive* value, when we observe the principles with which speculative reason endeavours to transcend the limits of sensibility, which is their proper sphere, over the entire realm of thought, and thus to supplant the pure (practical) use of reason. So far, then, as this criticism is occupied in confining speculative reason within its proper bounds, it is only negative; but, inasmuch as it thereby, at the same time, removes an obstacle which impedes and even threatens to destroy the use of practical reason, it possesses a positive and very important value. In order to admit this, we have only to be convinced that there is an absolutely necessary use of pure reason—the moral use—in which it inevitably transcends the limits of sensibility, without the aid of speculation, requiring only to be insured against the effects of a speculation which would involve it in contradiction with itself. . . . I cannot even make the assumption—as the practical interests of morality require—of God, Freedom and Immortality, if I do not deprive speculative reason of its pretensions to transcendent insight. For to arrive at these, it must make use of principles which, in fact, extend only to the objects of possible experience, and which cannot be applied to objects beyond this sphere without converting them into phenomena, and thus rendering the *practical extension* of pure reason impossible. I must, therefore, abolish *knowledge,* to make room for *belief.*

11

AFFIRMED *

THE same Holy Mother Church holds and teaches that God, the beginning and end of all things, may be certainly known by the natural light of human reason, by means of created things, "for the invisible things of Him from the creation of the world are clearly seen, being understood by the things that are made" (Rom. 1:20); but that it pleased His wisdom and bounty to reveal Himself and the eternal decrees of His will to mankind by another and a supernatural way: as the Apostle says, "God, having spoken on divers occasions, and many ways, in times past, to the fathers by the prophets; last of all, in these days, hath spoken to us by His Son" (Heb. 1:1-2).

12

VINDICATED †

Section I. What kind of demonstration we have in mind.

70. It is a philosophical or metaphysical demonstration, more rigorous than what are called today scientific demonstrations.
80. It will not be *a priori,* nor like the ontological argument of St. Anselm, Descartes and Leibniz.
90. It will be *a posteriori,* and to make it rigorous, we shall trace a "proper" effect to its "proper" (i.e., necessary and immediate) cause.
100. Therefore it will not look back in the past for a series or chain of effects accidentally dependent on some first cause, but look in the present for a series of effects actually and essentially dependent on some first cause.

* Vatican Council (1870), "Dogmatic Constitution of the Catholic Faith" (ch. II), translation by Archbishop Manning, quoted in *The Vatican Council* by Dom Cuthbert Butler (London: Longmans, 1930), Vol. II, p. 255.

† Reginald Garrigou-Lagrange, O.P. (1877-   ), *God: His Existence and His Nature,* trans. by Bede Rose (St. Louis: Herder, 1934-36). Owing to the length of this thorough discussion of agnosticism, we content ourselves with giving the outline of ch. II of the First Part, as found in the Analytical Index. The translation is ours, with some slight additions to the text. Numbers refer to the paragraphs of each section.

110. In this series of effects essentially dependent on some cause, we must come ultimately to the affirmation of the existence of a so-called "proper" cause.

Section II. Objections raised against the demonstrability of the existence of God. Agnosticism both in its empirical and in its idealistic forms.

120. Statement of the objection raised by the Empirics against the necessary character of the principle of causality, basis of our demonstration, and its validity, both ontological and transcendental. Both the objection and the agnosticism which results from it must be traced to Empirical Nominalism.

130. Kant's objection to the ontological and transcendental validity of the principle of causality is based on his assumption that the principle is a synthetic judgment a priori which applies only to the order of phenomena.

140. The common source of modern agnostic systems is the assumption that our knowledge is limited to the order of phenomena.

Section III. Proof of the demonstrability of God's existence.

Article I. The ontological validity of first notions and first principles.

150. How the human mind apprehends intelligible reality and grasps first principles by an act of intuition.

160. How we can vindicate the ontological character of our knowledge and of our fundamental notions.

170. First, indirectly, by showing to what absurd conclusions agnostics are led by their denial of the ontological validity of these notions and by showing how Kant's synthetic judgments a priori involve an arbitrary application of his categories to empirical data.

180. Second, directly, by showing how the ontological validity of our primary notions follows logically from the realization of the part played by "being" in our every concept, judgment and reasoning.

190. Answer to the objection of the Idealists that we cannot have concepts of anything that exists outside of our mind, and therefore are not justified in making "being" our starting point.

200. The first principles, which we grasp intuitively, are based upon the idea of Being, which is the formal object of the intellect. The supreme principle (the principle of identity) is the ultimate basis of every proof of the existence of God. By affirming this principle we come to acknowledge the existence of the transcendent God Who is absolutely identical with Himself; while every form of evolution-

ary Pantheism is bound to make contradiction the principle of all that exists.

210. The anti-intellectualistic objection to the *principle of contradiction,* first offered by Heraclitus and renewed by Bergson in our day, finds its solution in the analysis of the concept of potency, which enters into every argument for the existence of God.

220. Hegel's opposite objection to the principle of contradiction springs from his absolute intellectualism and his identification of pure being with indeterminate being.

230. The *principle of substance,* which is merely an explicit determination of the principle of identity, provides a ground for the demonstration of the existence of God.

240. The *principle of sufficient reason,* which is the proximate basis of the demonstration, is merely an explicit determination of the principle of identity.

250. The *principle of causality* is the immediate basis of the demonstration. Even though the concept of cause can be traced to the experience of becoming, it is really an intellectual concept which expresses the mode of actualization of a potential being; and that is the proof of its objectivity.

260. Hence all becoming and everything that is made up of parts require an efficient cause.

270. The *principle of finality* is derived from the principle of sufficient reason. Far from presupposing the knowledge of God's existence, it is indispensable for its demonstration.

Article II. The transcendental validity of first notions and first principles.

Have we the right to extend their application to the order of transcendental reality?

280. In the third antinomy, and above all in the fourth, Kant objects to that extension. He thus carries to its extreme limit Maimonides' teaching regarding the inadequacy of our concepts of God.

290. A *direct proof* of the transcendental validity of our primary concepts may be given as follows: By taking in their proper sense both absolute and analogical perfections, we can form an analytical idea of the absolutely perfect Being, and, if the world demands an infinite first cause endowed with such perfections, these notions will give us a true knowledge of that Being. Now, the notions of: being, unity, truth, goodness, source, end, intelligence, will, etc. denote such absolute and analogical perfections. Therefore, by taking these primary notions in their proper sense, we can form an idea of the supremely perfect Being, and, therefore, if the universe requires an infinite cause endowed with those perfections, we can have a true knowledge of Him by means of these notions.

300. An *indirect proof* can be drawn from the consequences of the denial, or from the calling into question of the transcendental validity of primary notions. These consequences are either absolute scepticism or pantheism.

310. It is in the analogical sense that we take the notion of God, first Cause of the world and distinct from the world, as middle term of our demonstration of His existence, but that does not impair the rigor of the demonstration.

320. By means of these analogical notions we ascertain the existence of God and we learn something of His essence, though we do not know that essence, viz. the very nature of the Deity quidditatively, that is in such a way that we could give a proper definition of it.

330. The chapter ends with the consideration of some objections raised against the application to God of primary notions, and particularly of the notion of cause in Kant's fourth antinomy.

II. God in Ancient Philosophy

13

ARGUMENT FROM THE ORDER OF NATURE *

. . . I will first state what I once heard him [Socrates] say about the godhead in conversation with Aristodemus the dwarf, as he was called. On learning that he was not known to sacrifice or pray or use divination, and actually made a mock of those who did so, he said: "Tell me, Aristodemus, do you admire any human beings for wisdom?"

"I do," he answered.

"Tell me their names."

"In epic poetry Homer comes first, in my opinion; in dithyramb, Melanippides; in tragedy, Sophocles; in sculpture, Polycleitus; in painting, Zeuxis."

"Which, think you, deserves the greater admiration, the creators of phantoms without sense and motion, or the creators of living, intelligent and active beings?"

"Oh, of living beings, by far, provided only they are created by design and not by mere chance."

"Suppose that it is impossible to guess the purpose of one creature's existence, and obvious that another's serves a useful end, which in your judgment, is the work of chance, and which of design?"

* Xenophon, *Memorabilia*, trans. by F. C. Marchant, "The Loeb Classical Library," (Cambridge: Harvard University Press, 1922), Bk. I, ch. IV, pp. 55-59.

"Presumably the creature that serves some useful end is the work of design."

"Do you not think then that he who created man from the beginning had some useful end in view when he endowed him with his several senses, giving eyes to see visible objects, ears to hear sounds? Would odours again be of any use to us had we not been endowed with nostrils? What perception should we have of sweet and bitter and all things pleasant to the palate had we no tongue in our mouth to discriminate between them? Besides these, are there not other contrivances that look like the result of forethought? Thus the eyeballs, being weak, are set behind eyelids, that open like doors when we want to see, and close when we sleep; on the lid grow lashes through which the very winds filter harmlessly; above the eyes is a coping of brows that lets no drop of sweat from the head hurt them. The ears catch all sounds, but are never choked with them. Again, the incisors of all creatures are adapted for cutting, the molars for receiving food from them and grinding it. And again, the mouth, through which the food they want goes in, is set near the eyes and nostrils; but since what goes out is unpleasant, the ducts through which it passes are turned away and removed so far as possible from the organs of sense. With such signs of forethought in these arrangements, can you doubt whether they are the works of chance or design?"

"No, of course not. When I regard them in this light they do look very like the handiwork of a wise and loving creator."

"What of the natural desire to beget children, the mother's desire to rear her babe, the child's strong will to live and strong fear of death?"

"Undoubtedly these, too, look like the contrivances of one who deliberately willed the existence of living creatures."

"Do you think you have any wisdom yourself?"

"Oh, ask me a question and judge from my answer."

"And do you suppose that wisdom is nowhere else to be found, although you know that you have a mere speck of all the earth in your body and a mere drop of all the water, and that of all the other mighty elements you received, I suppose, just a scrap towards the fashioning of your body? But as for mind, which alone, it seems, is without mass, do you think that you have snapped it up by a lucky accident, and that the orderly rank of all these huge masses, infinite in number, is due, forsooth, to a sort of absurdity?"

"Yes, for I don't see the master hand, whereas I see the makers of things in this world."

"Neither do you see your own soul, which has the mastery of the body; so that, as far as that goes, you may say that you do nothing by design, but everything by chance."

Here Aristodemus exclaimed: "Really, Socrates, I don't despise the godhead. But I think it is too great to need my service."

"Then the greater the power that deigns to serve you, the more honour it demands of you."

N.B. *The dialogue goes on illustrating the Providence of God to bring Aristodemus to recognize the duty of piety towards God.*

14

GOD THE INTELLIGENT CAUSE OF THE WORLD *

Tim. All men, Socrates, who have any degree of right feeling, at the beginning of every enterprise, whether small or great, always call upon God. And we, too, who are going to discourse of the nature of the universe, how created or how existing without creation, if we be not altogether out of our wits, must invoke the aid of gods and goddesses and pray that our words may be acceptable to them and consistent with themselves. Let this, then, be our invocation of the gods, to which I add an invocation of myself to speak in such manner as will be most intelligible to you, and will most accord with my own intent.

First then, in my judgment, we must make a distinction and ask, What is that which is always becoming and never is? That which is apprehended by intelligence and reason is always in the same state; but that which is conceived by opinion with the help of sensation and without reason, is always in a process of becoming and perishing and never really is. Now everything that becomes or is created must of necessity be created by some cause, for without a cause nothing can be created. The work of the creator, whenever he looks to the unchangeable and fashions the forms and nature of his work after an unchangeable pattern, must necessarily be made fair and perfect; but when he looks to the created only, and uses a created pattern, it is not fair or perfect. Was the heaven then or the world, whether called by this or by any other more appropriate name—assuming the name, I am asking a question which has to be asked at the beginning of an enquiry about anything—was the world, I say, always in existence and without beginning? or created, and had it a beginning? Created, I reply, being visible and tangible and having a body, and therefore sensible; and all sensible things are apprehended by opinion and sense and are in a process of creation and created. Now that which is created must, as we affirm, of necessity be created by a cause. But the father and maker of all this universe is past finding out; and even if we found him, to tell of him to all men would be impossible.

* Plato (427-347 B.C.), "Timaeus" (27-30) in *The Dialogues of Plato*, trans. by B. Jowett (New York: Random House, 1937). Reprinted by permission of The Clarendon Press, Oxford. This dialogue between Socrates and Timaeus deals with the problem of origin.

And there is still a question to be asked about him: Which of the patterns had the artificer in view when he made the world—the pattern of the unchangeable, or of that which is created? If the world be indeed fair and the artificer good, it is manifest that he must have looked to that which is eternal; but if what cannot be said without blasphemy is true, then to the created pattern. Everyone will see that he must have looked to the eternal; for the world is the fairest of creations and he is the best of causes. And having been created in this way, the world has been framed in the likeness of that which is apprehended by reason and mind and is unchangeable, and must therefore of necessity, if this is admitted, be a copy of something. Now it is all-important that the beginning of everything should be according to nature. And in speaking of the copy and the original we may assume that words are akin to the matter which they ascribe; when they relate to the lasting and permanent and intelligible, they ought to be lasting and unalterable, and, as far as their nature allows, irrefutable and immovable—nothing less. But when they express only the copy or likeness and not the eternal things themselves, they need only be likely and analogous to the real words. As being is to becoming, so is truth to belief. If then, Socrates, amid the many opinions about the gods and the generation of the universe, we are not able to give notions which are altogether and in every respect exact and consistent with one another, do not be surprised. Enough, if we adduce probabilities as likely as any others; for we must remember that I who am the speaker, and you who are the judges, are only mortal men, and we ought to accept the tale which is probable and enquire no further.

Soc. Excellent, Timaeus, and we will do precisely as you bid us. The prelude is charming, and is already accepted by us—may we beg of you to proceed to the strain?

Tim. Let me tell you then why the creator made this world of generation. He was good, and the good can never have any jealousy of anything. And being free from jealousy, he desired that all things should be as like himself as they could be. This is in the truest sense the origin of creation and of the world, as we shall do well in believing on the testimony of wise men; God desired that all things should be good and nothing bad, so far as this was attainable. Wherefore also finding the whole visible sphere not at rest, but moving in an irregular and disorderly fashion, out of disorder he brought order, considering that this was in every way better than the other. Now the deeds of the best could never be or have been better than the fairest; and the creator, reflecting on the things which are by nature visible, found that no unintelligent creature taken as a whole was fairer than the intelligent taken as a whole; and that intelligence could not be present in anything which was devoid of soul. For which reason, when he was framing the universe, he put intelligence in soul, and soul in body, that he might be the creator of a work which was by nature fairest and best. Wherefore, using the language of probability, we may say that the world became a living creature truly endowed with soul and intelligence by the providence of God.

This being supposed, let us proceed to the next stage: In the likeness of what animal did the Creator make the world? It would be an unworthy thing to liken it to any nature which exists as a part only; for nothing can be beautiful which is like any imperfect thing; but let us suppose the world to be the very image of that whole of which all other animals both individually and in their tribes are portions. For the original of the universe contains in itself all intelligible beings, just as this world comprehends us and all other visible creatures. For the Deity, intending to make this world like the fairest and most perfect of intelligible beings, framed one visible animal comprehending within itself all other animals of a kindred nature. Are we right in saying that there is one world, or that there are many and infinite? There must be one only, if the created copy is to accord with the original. For that which includes all other intelligible creatures cannot have a second or companion; in that case there would be need of another living being which would include both, and of which they would be parts, and the likeness would be more truly said to resemble not them, but that other which included them. In order then that the world might be solitary, like the perfect animal, the creator made not two worlds nor an infinite number of them; but there is and ever will be an only-begotten and created heaven.

15

GOD THE ETERNAL MOVER *

VI. Since there were three kinds of substances, two of them physical, and one unmovable, regarding the latter we must assert that it is necessary that there should be an eternal unmovable substance. For substances are the first of existing things, and if they are all destructible, all things are destructible. But it is impossible that movement should either have come into being or cease to be (for it must always have existed), or that time should. For there could not be a before and an after if time did not exist. Movement, therefore, is continuous in the sense in which time is; for time is either the same thing as movement or an attribute of movement. And there is no continuous movement except movement in place, and of this only that which is circular is continuous.

But if there is something which is capable of moving things or acting

* Aristotle (384-322 B.C.), "Metaphysics," Bk. XII, chs. VI-VII. This extract is taken from the Oxford translation of Aristotle found in *The Basic Works of Aristotle*, ed. by R. McKeon (New York: Random House, 1941). The same argument is found in Aristotle's "Physics," Bk. VIII, chs. V-VI.

on them but is not actually doing so, there will not necessarily be movement; for that which has a potency need not exercise it. Nothing, then, is gained even if we suppose eternal substances, as the believers in the Forms do, unless there is to be in them some principle which can cause change; nay, even this is not enough, nor is another substance besides the Forms enough; for if it is not to *act*, there will be no movement. Further, even if it acts, this will not be enough, if its essence is potency; for there will not be *eternal* movement, since that which is potentially may possibly not be. There must, then, be such a principle, whose very essence is actuality. Further, then, these substances must be without matter; for they must be eternal, if *anything* is eternal. Therefore they must be actuality.

Yet there is a difficulty; for it is thought that every thing that acts is able to act, but not that every thing that is able to act acts, so that the potency is prior. But if this is so, nothing that is need be; for it is possible for all things to be capable of existing but not yet to exist.

Yet if we follow the theologians who generate the world from night, or the natural philosophers who say that "all things are together," the same impossible result ensues. For how will there be movement if there is no actually existing cause? Wood will surely not move itself—the carpenter's act must act on it; nor will the menstrual blood nor the earth set themselves in motion, but the seed must act upon the earth and the *semen* on the menstrual blood.

This is why some suppose eternal actuality—e.g. Leucippus and Plato (in *Timaeus*); for they say there is always movement. But why and what the movement is they do not say—nor, if the world moves in this way or that, do they tell us the cause of its doing so. Now nothing is moved at random, but there must always be something present to move it; e.g. as a matter of fact a thing moves in one way by nature, and in another by force or through the influence of reason or something else. (Further, what sort of movement is primary? This makes a vast difference.) But again for Plato, at least, it is not permissible to name here that which he sometimes supposes to be the source of movement—that which moves itself; for the soul is later, or coeval with the heavens according to his account. To suppose potency prior to actuality, then, is in a sense right, and in a sense not; and we have specified these senses. That actuality is prior is testified by Anaxagoras (for this "reason" is actuality) and by Empedocles in his doctrine of love and strife, and by those who say that there is always movement, e.g. Leucippus. Therefore chaos or night did not exist for an infinite time, but the same things have always existed (either passing through a cycle of changes or obeying some other law), since actuality is prior to potency. If, then, there is a constant cycle, something must always remain, acting in the same way. And if there is to be generation and destruction, there must be something else which is always acting in different ways. This must, then, act in one way in virtue of itself, and in another in virtue of something else—either of a third agent, therefore, or of the first. For otherwise this again causes the motion both of the second agent and of the third. Therefore it is better to say "the first." For it was the cause of eternal uniformity; and something else is the cause of variety, and evidently both together are the cause of eternal variety. This, accordingly, is the character which the motions actually exhibit. What need then is there to seek for other principles?

VII. Since (1) this is a possible account of the matter, and (2), if it were not true, the world would have proceeded out of night and "all things together" and out of non-being; these difficulties may be taken as solved. There is, then, something which is always moved with an unceasing motion, which is motion in a circle; and this is plain not in theory only but in fact. Therefore the first heaven must be eternal. There is therefore also something which moves it. And, since that which is moved and moves is intermediary, there is something which moves without being moved, being eternal, substance, and actuality. And the object of desire and the object of thought move in this way; they move without being moved. The primary objects of desire and of thought are the same. For the apparent good is the object of appetite, and the real good is the primary object of rational wish. But desire is consequent on opinion rather than opinion on desire, for the thinking is the starting-point. And thought is moved by the object of thought, and one of the two columns of opposites is itself the object of thought; and in this substance is first, and in substance that which is simple and exists actually. (The one and the simple are the same, for "one" means a measure, but "simple" means that the thing itself has a certain nature.) But the beautiful, also, and that which is in itself desirable are in the same column; and the first in any class is always best, or analogous to the best.

That a final cause may exist among unchangeable entities is shown by the distinction of its meanings. For the final cause is (a) some being for whose good some action is done, and (b) something at which the action aims; and of these the latter exists among unchangeable entities though the former does not. The final cause, then, produces motion as being loved, but all other things move by being moved.

Now if something is moved it is capable of being otherwise than it is. Therefore if its actuality is the primary form of spatial motion, then, in so far as it is subject to change, in this respect it is capable of being otherwise—in place, even if not in substance. But since there is something which moves while itself unmoved, existing actually, this can in no way be otherwise than as it is. For motion in space is the first of the kinds of change, and motion in a circle the first kind of spatial motion and this the first mover produces. The first mover, then, exists of necessity; and in so far as it exists by necessity, its mode of being is good, and it is in this sense a first principle. For the necessary has all these senses

—that which is necessary perforce because it is contrary to the natural impulse, that without which the good is impossible, and that which cannot be otherwise but can exist only in a single way.

On such principles, then, depend the heavens and the world of nature. And it is life such as the best which we enjoy, and enjoy but a short time (for it is ever in this state, which we cannot be), since its actuality is also pleasure. (And for this reason are waking, perception, and thinking most pleasant, and hopes and memories are so on account of these.) And thinking in itself deals with what is best in the fullest sense. And thought thinks on itself because it shares the nature of the object of thought; for it becomes an object of thought in coming into contact with and thinking its objects, so that thought and object of thought are the same. For that which is *capable* of receiving the object of thought, i.e. the essence, is thought. But it is *active* when it *possesses* this object. Therefore the possession rather than the receptivity is the divine element which thought seems to contain, and the act of contemplation is what is most pleasant and best. If, then, God is always in that good state in which we sometimes are, this compels our wonder; and if in a better this compels it yet more. And God *is* in a better state. And life also belongs to God; for the actuality of thought is life, and God is that actuality; and God's self-dependent actuality is life most good and eternal. We say therefore that God is a living being, eternal, most good, so that life and duration continuous and eternal belong to God; for this *is* God.

Those who suppose, as the Pythagoreans and Speusippus do, that supreme beauty and goodness are not present in the beginning, because the beginnings both of plants and of animals are *causes*, but beauty and completeness are the *effects* of these, are wrong in their opinion. For the seed comes from other individuals which are prior and complete, and the first thing is not seed but the complete being; e.g. we must say that before the seed there is a man—not the man produced from the seed, but another from whom the seed comes.

It is clear then from what has been said that there is a substance which is eternal and unmovable and separate from sensible things. It has been shown also that this substance cannot have any magnitude but is without parts and indivisible (for it produces movement through infinite time, but nothing finite has infinite power; and while every magnitude is either infinite or finite, it cannot, for the above reason, have finite magnitude, and it cannot have infinite magnitude because there is no infinite magnitude at all). But it has also been shown that it is unpassive and unalterable; for all the other changes are posterior to change of place.

16

ARGUMENT FROM THE ORDER OF NATURE *

A LL nations agree that there are Gods; the opinion is innate, and as it were engraved in the minds of all men. The only point in dispute amongst us is what they are. Their existence no one denies. V. Cleanthes, one of our sect, imputes the way in which the idea of the Gods is implanted in the minds of men, to four causes. The first is that which I just now mentioned, the foreknowledge of future things. The second, the great advantages which we enjoy from the temperature of the air, the fertility of the earth, and the abundance of various benefits of other kinds. The third cause is deduced from the terror with which the mind is affected by thunder, tempests, storms, snow, hail, devastation, pestilence, earthquakes often attended with hideous noises, showers of stones, and rain like drops of blood; by rocks and sudden openings of the earth, by monstrous births of men and beasts; by meteors in the air, and blazing stars, by the Greeks called *cometae*, by us *crinitae*, the appearance of which, in the late Octavian war, were foreboders of great calamities; by two suns, which, as I have heard my father say, happened in the consulate of Tuditanus and Aquillius, and in which year also another sun (P. Africanus), was extinguished. These things terrified mankind, and raised in them a firm belief of some celestial and divine power. His fourth cause, and that the strongest, is drawn from the regularity of the motion and revolution of the heavens, the distinctness, variety, beauty, and order of the sun, moon, and all the stars, the appearance only of which is sufficient to convince us they are not the effect of chance; as when we enter into a house, or school, or court, and observe the exact order, discipline, and method of it, we cannot suppose that it is so regulated without a cause, but must conclude that there is some one who commands, and to whom obedience is paid; it is quite impossible for us to avoid thinking that the wonderful motions, revolutions and order of these many and great bodies no part of which is impaired by the countless and infinite succession of ages, must be governed and directed by some supreme intelligent being.

VI. Chrysippus, indeed, had a very penetrating genius; yet such is the doctrine which he delivers, that he seems rather to have been instructed by nature than to owe it to any discovery of his own. "If," says he, "there is anything in the universe which no human reason, ability,

* M. Tullius Cicero (106-43 B.C.), *De Natura Deorum*, Bk. II, ch. vi in *The Treatises of M. T. Cicero*, literally translated by C. D. Yonge (London: Bell and Sons, 1878).

or power can make, the being who produced it must certainly be preferable to man; now celestial bodies, and all those things which proceed in any eternal order, cannot be made by man; the being who made them is therefore preferable to man. What then is that being but a God? If there is no such being as a Deity, what is there better than man, since he only is possessed of reason, the most excellent of all things? But it is a foolish piece of vanity in man to think there is nothing preferable to him; there is therefore something preferable, consequently there is certainly a God.

When you behold a large and beautiful house, surely no one can persuade you it was built for mice and weasels, though you do not see the master; and would it not, therefore, be most manifest folly to imagine that a world so magnificently adorned, with such an immense variety of celestial bodies of such exquisite beauty, and that the vast sizes and magnitude of the sea and land, were intended as the abode of man, and not as the mansion of the immortal Gods? Do we not also plainly see this, that the most elevated regions are the best, and that the earth is the lowest region, and is surrounded with the grossest air, so that, as we perceive in some cities and countries, the capacities of men are naturally duller from the thickness of the climate, so mankind in general are affected by the heaviness of the air which surrounds the earth, the grossest region of the world.

Yet even from this inferior intelligence of man we may discover the existence of some intelligent agent that is divine, and wiser than ourselves; for, as Socrates says, in Xenophon, from whence had man his portion of understanding? And, indeed, if any one were to push his inquiries about the moisture and heat which is diffused through the human body, and the earthy kind of solidity existing in our entrails, and that soul by which we breathe, and to ask whence we derived them, it would be plain that we have received one thing from the earth, another from liquid, another from fire, and another from that air which we inhale every time we breathe.

VII. But where did we find that which excels all these things, I mean reason, or (if you please, in other terms) the mind, understanding, thought, prudence? and from whence did we receive it? Shall the world be possessed of every other perfection, and be destitute of this one, which is the most important and valuable of all? But certainly there is nothing better or more excellent, or more beautiful than the world, and not only there is nothing better, but we cannot even conceive anything superior to it and if reason and wisdom are the greatest of all perfections, they must necessarily be a part of what we all allow to be the most excellent.

Who is not compelled to admit the truth of what I assert by that agreeable, uniform and continued agreement of things in the universe? Could the earth at one season be adorned with flowers, at another be covered with snow? Or, if such a number of things regulated their own changes, could the approach and retreat of the sun in the summer and winter solstices be so regularly known and calculated? Could the flux and reflux of the sea and the height of the tides be affected by the increase or wane of the moon? Could the different courses of the stars be preserved by the uniform movement of the whole heaven? Could these things subsist, I say, in such a harmony of all the parts of the universe without the continued influence of a divine spirit?

If these points are handled in a free and copious manner, as I purpose to do, they will be less liable to the cavils of the Academics; but the narrow, confined way in which Zeno reasoned upon them, laid them more open to objections; for as running streams are seldom or never tainted, while standing waters easily grow corrupt, so a fluency of expression washes away the censures of the caviller, while the narrow limits of a discourse which is too concise are almost defenceless. . . .

III. The Existence of God in Medieval Philosophy

17

THE ARGUMENT OF ST. AUGUSTINE *

WE MUST at the outset note the role which St. Augustine assigns to faith, if we are to grasp the true import of his demonstration.

He conceives of no philosophy apart from theology, for, in his estimation, Christian wisdom, which is the only knowledge, contains all truth. This often shocks the modern thinker who is so careful to distinguish, without however separating them, the various planes of human thought. . . . St. Augustine never considers the case of the atheist, who does not acknowledge the existence of God; hence would look in vain for a strictly philosophical demonstration in any of his works. In his treatise *De libero arbitrio* (b. II, ch. 2), he himself tells us how he appeals to faith when he speculates on that truth. Evodius with whom he discusses the problem of evil stakes his position in these words: "I hold this firmly by faith; but I do not hold it on rational evidence (*quia cognitionem nondum teneo*)." To St. Augustine's question: "At least you are certain that God exists?" he replies "Yes, I am, but it is not because I see, it is because I believe (*non contemplando, sed credendo*)." St. Augustine goes

* After his conversion in 387, St. Augustine (A.D. 354-430) devoted his talent to a refutation of the scepticism of the Academicians. His arguments for the existence of God are scattered in several of his works. We present here an able synopsis of them by Pedro Descoqs, S.J., in his *Praelectiones Theologiae Naturalis* (Paris: Beauchesne, 1936), Vol. II, Sect. IV, c. 2, art. 3. Our translation is a faithful rendering of the text, though in a few instances we have condensed it for the sake of clarity.

on: "But if an unbeliever were in good faith and asked for proofs, would you leave him in his unbelief, or would you not attempt to convince him by some argument?" "Your question," replies Evodius, "suggests my answer. . . . I would offer to him that argument which, I think, anyone would accept readily, and say: 'Since you expect others to believe, without seeing, in the existence of feelings hidden in your own soul, don't you think it still more reasonable to admit the existence of God, on the testimony of great men who assure us that they lived in the company of the Son of God? The more so as they assert having witnessed things that would be impossible, if God did not exist. Why then should we not accept their authority to help us in settling our doubts?" "But have we not agreed," asks Evodius, "that we want to know and understand what we hold by faith?" St. Augustine answers: "If believing and understanding were not two different acts, and if we had not first to accept on faith the sublime truths about God we have to understand, it would have been in vain that the prophet said: 'Unless you first believe, you will not understand.' No one will be able to find God unless he first take on faith what he must know."

It is clear then that St. Augustine assumes that his hearer has faith, and that he moves on a plane that neither St. Thomas nor modern philosophers and apologists have adopted. The latter are careful to mark the distinction between the realm of faith and that of the prerequisites to belief. The proof of the existence of God and all that relates to Theodicy as such are the concern of pure reason and should, in a *scientific* synthesis of religious truths, be treated apart from Revelation. However such scientific and methodological scruples which have been sanctioned by the Vatican Council did not enter into St. Augustine's plan, as he aimed rather at concrete results than at building up a system, and relied more on a psychological, than on a scientific process of arriving at truth. Besides, even though he never denied that reason could by its own power arrive at the knowledge of God, and was never a fideist in the strict sense of the term, St. Augustine's philosophy, as Professor Gilson says, was above all a rational exploration of the revealed truths and should not be taken as an independent system of philosophy. No doubt such a position was inadequate and required to be completed as it was completed by St. Thomas; nevertheless it is quite acceptable to any man who is concerned, not with science, but with his own salvation.

To penetrate the thought of St. Augustine one must remember that for him the great problem was the problem of human destiny, a problem which is practical rather than speculative: what is the *quickest and the surest way* to God. Now St. Augustine is convinced that the way to God is through faith. Hence he urges the inquirer after God to begin with an act of faith, because it is through faith that we get hold of truth. This initial faith is not blind, it is based on rational evidence; that evidence is derived from the Holy Scriptures the testimony of which cannot be denied by any fair-minded man. Once he has taken this step the believer will see that what he believes is in perfect harmony with the truths of reason, and he will be able by the use of his reason to arrive at a deeper and more complete knowledge of the truths he believes, the more so as his intelligence will be enlightened and strengthened by the supernatural light of faith: *"Credo ut intelligam."* Reason and authority support and help each other.

In another work, *De vera Religione* (c. 24), St. Augustine writes: "Divine Providence uses two remedies . . . to cure our soul: authority and reason. The former bids us to make an act of faith and paves the way for reason. Reason gives us understanding and knowledge. And yet authority does not dispense with reason which examines what we should believe, and once a truth has been rightly demonstrated and rightly understood, it becomes itself a real authority."

2. Having cleared this point we may now examine St. Augustine's demonstration of the existence of God, or, to express it differently, his rational explanation of our belief in God.

He gives a brief statement of his argument in *De diversis quaestionibus,* qu. 45, *Adversus mathematicos:* "The human mind, which passes judgment over visible things, has the power to recognize its own superiority over them. However, it is subject to change, as it does not possess all wisdom and is capable of advancing towards it. It therefore discovers the existence above it of the immutable Truth, and by clinging to it, according to the words of the Psalmist, *'Adhaesit anima mea post te,'* it finds happiness as it discovers in itself the Creator and Lord of all visible things."

Such is the broad outline of the way the soul follows to reach God, but the treatise *De libero arbitrio* (b. II, c. 3 *et seq.*) helps us to follow it step by step and thus to grasp better the principle which gives its strength to the demonstration. St. Augustine addresses Evodius:

"To begin with the most evident truths, I ask you whether you exist yourself. Are you afraid of making a mistake in answering this question? Then you exist, for if you did not exist you could not fall into error."

Before taking up the rational demonstration of the existence of God, we must make sure that we have some certitudes; now, life and thought, which is the consciousness of life, are undeniable facts, and universal doubt rests on a play on words. Passing then to the examination of the degrees of perfection in beings, St. Augustine calls Evodius' attention to the distinction between existence, life, and thought, or, in other terms, between sensible objects, the senses, and reason. On what principle can we set up a hierarchy? "Nobody doubts that he who passes judgment belongs to a higher order than that upon which he passes judgment." Hence, according to this rule, we ascribe superiority to the senses over their objects; the eye, for instance, distinguishes colors, and appreciates their shades and differences. But each of the senses fails to perceive the objects of the other senses, and has not consciousness that it perceives. There is therefore an inner sense which has the power to pass judgment on the several senses, and to direct each of them to its proper object, as, for instance, when the eye opens and looks in a certain direction, it is not the eye that knows whether it sees or not, but that inner sense which is superior to the eye.

How in fine can we make the distinction between sensible objects, external senses, and inner sense, and assign to each one its limits and its function? It is because reason, which is the highest power of our nature, can estimate the sensible objects and the senses, and therefore is superior to them.

But has not reason something superior to itself? We see all minds understanding certain truths in the same way, although each acts independently of the others, in the same way as all eyes see the same sun. The first of these truths are the truths regarding numbers and their relations, truths which appear to be absolute and immutable: "seven and three are ten; not only now but always there has been no time when seven and three were not ten, and no time will ever be when seven and three are not ten." Such knowledge has not come to reason through the senses: "For each number draws its name from the number of times it contains unity . . . but anyone who sets his thought on the true concept of unity will easily recognize that it cannot be perceived by any corporeal sense." But there are many other truths that command the assent of our minds and are acknowledged by all men to be necessary: our appreciation of things must be based upon justice, we must prefer what is better to what is not so good, we must correlate only similar things; an immutable reality is of a higher value than a corruptible one, the eternal transcends the temporal, etc. What conclusion can we draw from that? We must conclude that this truth, since it is grasped by all in the same way, is independent from our individual minds. The question then is, whether it is lower or higher than our mind, or equal to it? "If it were lower, it would not be the norm of our judgments, but we would pass judgment over it as we do over the world of bodies . . . of these norms no one is, in any way, the judge. For when we say that eternal things are to be preferred to the temporal, or that seven and three are ten, no one says that it should be so, but everyone, realizing that it is so in fact, acts not as a judge intent on correcting these maxims, but rather as a discoverer who rejoices over his finding. Besides, if truth were of the same order as our minds it would share their changeableness. . . . Therefore, truth is neither lower than, nor on a level with, our minds, it is higher than they are, and better than they."

Have we then reached God? Not yet perhaps, for to have found something superior to our minds, does not mean that we have found the being above whom nothing exists, viz. God. But the truth we have discovered with the notes of necessity, immutability, and absoluteness, cannot be anything but God since it possesses characteristics which can be found only in God. The partial truths which are the norm of our minds have values and meaning only if there exist a total Truth of which they are participations, viz. God.

3. St. Augustine has condensed his demonstration in a chapter of his *Confessions*, VII, 17.

"I was looking for the source of my approval of the beauty of bodies, whether heavenly or earthly, and what enabled me to judge in a sound way concerning mutable things and to say: 'This should be this way; that should not.' And so, in looking for that source of my judgments, when I did judge in this way, I had discovered the immutable and true eternity of Truth, above my mutable mind.

"Thus, by a gradual process, I passed from bodies to the soul which senses through the body, and then to its interior power to which bodily sensation takes messages about exterior things (and this is as far as brutes can go), and then, further, to the reasoning power, to which what is taken from the bodily senses is brought for judgment. And this power, also finding itself mutable in me, lifted itself to its understanding and withdrew the thinking process from the customary level, taking itself away from the contradictory crowd of phantasms, so that it might discover by what light it was besprinkled when it cried out without any hesitation that the immutable is to be preferred to the mutable; that it might know from this the immutable itself (for, unless it could know it in some way, it would not put it above the mutable with such certainty). And, in the flash of a trembling glance (*in ictu trepidantis aspectus*) it reached up to THAT WHICH IS.

"Then, truly, did I see clearly Thy invisible things, that are understood through those that are made. But, I was not able to keep my gaze fixed, and, when my weakness was beaten back, I returned to the ordinary things, bringing with me nothing but the loving memory which longed, as it were, for things whose odor had been scented but which I was not yet able to eat."

But is this ascending progress, which starts from sensible objects, and passes first through the senses and then through reason to reach out to the immutable Truth, absolutely indispensable? It does not seem so, for the whole force of the argument lies in this dependence of our mind on a necessary and absolute superior Norm. The first degrees are preliminaries which can be omitted; and, actually, most of the time, St. Augustine omits them, being content with expressing his thought in a few sentences; but the reasoning is always the same whatever form it may take, whether it starts from the idea of Truth, or of Goodness, or of Beauty. We may give a few illustrations.

From the idea of Beauty (*De vera religione*, c. 30-31): "As this norm by which all arts are ruled is immutable, while the human mind, though able to grasp it, is subject to the variations of error, we must conclude that there is above our intelligence a Norm which is called Truth. . . . Nor are we allowed to doubt that this immutable nature, superior to the soul, and intelligent, is no other than God himself, and that where lies the first life, there also lie the first essence and the first wisdom."

From the idea of Goodness (*De Trinitate*, VIII, c. 3): "In all these good things, whether those which I have mentioned, or any else that are to be discerned or thought, we could not say that one was better than another, when we judge truly, unless a conception of the good itself has been impressed upon us, such that according to it we might both approve some things as good, and prefer one good to another. . . . Whenever then thou are told of this good thing and that good thing, which things can also in other respects be called not good, if thou canst put aside those things which are good by the participation of the good, and discern that good itself by the participation of which they are good (for when this or that thing is spoken of thou understandest together with them the good itself also), if then, I say thou canst remove these things, and canst discern the good in itself, then thou wilt have discerned God. And if thou shalt cleave to Him with love, thou shalt be forthwith blessed."

From the idea of Beauty (*De Trinitate*, IX, c. 6, 11): "When I call back to my mind some arch, turned beautifully and symmetrically which, let us say, I saw at Carthage; a certain reality that had been made known to the mind through the eyes, and transferred to the memory, causes the imaginary view. But I behold in my mind yet another thing, according to which that work of art pleases me, and whence also, if it displeased me, I should correct it. We judge therefore of those particular things according to that (form of eternal truth), and discern that form by the intuition of the rational mind."

4. The very quickness with which St. Augustine gives the essential points of his arguments, shows that he holds them to be evident; but we may ask whether he attempts a demonstration, if by demonstration we understand a logical deduction leading us to certitude. If the human mind is, as St. Augustine supposes it to be, always under the influence of the divine light, and if, without it, we can know nothing, every man, by the very fact that he leads a rational life, is in close contact with God, whom he always knows at least implicitly. This man therefore needs only to reflect on himself and on his intellectual activity, to become immediately conscious of his dependence on divine Truth, and therefore of the existence of that Truth without which he could not even attempt to think. It follows that the truth of the existence of God is revealed to us by a psychological analysis rather than by a true logical reasoning. All the arguments offered by St. Augustine bear on the existence of that immutable norm of Truth, Goodness, Beauty, and Justice, which we sense to rule over our soul, and without which we could offer no explanation of our knowledge: how do we know that anything is beautiful, or good, or better, or more beautiful than another, if there is not in us a criterion of beauty and of goodness, a perfect exemplar in which every imperfect beauty or goodness participates? How could we

discern the just from the unjust, except in the light of infinite Justice? How could we elicit necessary judgments, when everything around us is changing, if there did not exist somewhere an eternal, an immutable Truth, which gives that assurance to our mind? It is clear that, in the eyes of St. Augustine, the soul grasps with greater ease the eternal, the necessary, the infinite, than it does the contingent, the changeable, and the finite reality. And the reason is that, because directly enlightened by the divine light, the soul enjoys a more intimate contact with it than with sensible things: *"Noli foras exire, in teipsum redi; in interiore homine habitat Veritas."*

18

THE ONTOLOGICAL ARGUMENT *

A ND SO, Lord, do thou, who dost give understanding to faith, give me, so far as Thou knowest it to be profitable, to understand that Thou art as we believe; and that Thou art that which we believe. And, indeed, we believe that Thou art a being than which nothing greater can be conceived. Or is there no such nature, since the fool hath said in his heart, there is no God. (Ps. 13:1). But, at any rate, this very fool, when he hears of this Being of which I speak—a Being than which nothing greater can be conceived—understands what he hears, and what he understands is in his understanding; although he does not understand it to exist.

For, it is one thing for an object to be in the understanding, and another to understand that the object exists. When a painter first conceives of what he will afterwards perform, he has it in his understanding but he does not yet understand it to be, because he has not yet performed it. But after he has made the painting, he both has it in his understanding, and he understands that it exists, because he has made it.

Hence even the fool is convinced that something exists in the understanding, at least, than which nothing greater can be conceived. For, when he hears of this, he understands it. And whatever is understood exists in the understanding. And assuredly, that than which nothing greater can be conceived cannot exist in the understanding alone. For, suppose it exists in the understanding alone; then it can be conceived to exist in reality; which is greater.

Therefore, if that than which nothing greater can be conceived, exists

* St. Anselm (1033-1109), *Proslogium*, trans. by S. N. Deane (Chicago: The Open Court, 1903). In the *Monologium* St. Anselm argues for the existence of God from the degrees of perfection in creatures. His celebrated ontological argument is given in the *Proslogium*, ch. II. We offer the translation of Sidney N. Deane with the Appendix, "In Behalf of the Fool," by Gaunilon.

in the understanding alone, the very being, than which nothing greater can be conceived, is one than which a greater can be conceived. But obviously this is impossible. Hence, there is no doubt that there exists a being, than which nothing greater can be conceived, and it exists both in the understanding and in reality.

GAUNILON'S ANSWER: "IN BEHALF OF THE FOOL"

1. If one doubts or denies the existence of a being of such a nature that nothing greater than it can be conceived, he receives this answer:

The existence of this being is proved, in the first place, by the fact that he himself, in his doubt or denial regarding this being, already has it in his understanding; for in hearing it spoken he understands what is spoken of. It is proved therefore by the fact that what he understands must exist not only in his understanding but in reality also.

And the proof of this is as follows: It is a greater thing to exist both in the understanding and in reality than to be in the understanding alone. And if this being is in the understanding alone, whatever has, even in the past, existed in reality will be greater than this being. And so that which was greater than all beings will be less than some being, and will not be greater than all: which is a manifest contradiction.

And hence, that which is greater than all, already proved to be in the understanding, must exist not only in the understanding, but also in reality; for otherwise it will not be greater than all other things.

2. The fool might make this reply: This being is said to be in my understanding already, only because I understand what is said. Now could it not with equal justice be said that I have in my understanding all manner of unreal objects, having absolutely no existence in themselves, because I understand these things, if one speaks of them, whatever they may be?

Unless indeed it is shown that this being is of such a character that it cannot be held in concept like all unreal objects, or objects whose existence is uncertain; and hence I am not able to conceive of it, or to hold it in concept; but I must understand and have it in my understanding; because, it seems, I cannot conceive of it in any other way than by understanding it, that is, by comprehending in my knowledge its existence in reality.

But if this is the case, in the first place there will be no distinction between what has precedence in time—namely, the having an object in the understanding, and what is subsequent in time—namely, the understanding that an object exists; as in the example of the picture, which exists first in the mind of the painter, and afterwards in his work.

Moreover, the following assertion can hardly be accepted: that this being, when it is spoken of or heard of, cannot be conceived not to exist in the way in which even God can be conceived not to exist. For if this is impossible, what was the object of this argument against one who doubts or denies the existence of such a being?

Finally, that this being so exists that it cannot be perceived by an understanding convinced of its own indubitable existence, unless this being is afterwards conceived of—this should be proved to me by an indisputable argument, but not by that which you have advanced: namely, that what I understand, when I hear it, already is in my understanding. For thus in my understanding, as I still think, could be all sorts of things whose existence is uncertain, or which do not exist at all, if someone whose words I should understand mentioned them. And so much the more if I should be deceived, as often happens, and believe in them; though I do not yet believe the being whose existence you would prove.

3. Hence, your example of the painter who already has in his understanding what he is to paint cannot agree with this argument. For the picture, before it is made, is contained in the artificer's art itself; and any such thing, existing in the art of the artificer, is nothing but a part of his understanding itself. A joiner, St. Augustine says, when he is about to make a box, in fact, first has it in his art. This box which he made in fact is not life; but the box which exists in his art is life. For the artificer's soul lives, in which all these things are, before they are produced. Why, then, are these things life in the living soul of the artificer, unless because they are nothing else than the knowledge or understanding of the soul itself?

With the exception, however, of those facts which are known to pertain to the mental nature, whatever, on being heard and thought out by the understanding, is perceived to be real, undoubtedly that real object is one thing, and the act of understanding, itself, by which the object is grasped is another. Hence, even if it were true that there is a being than which a greater is inconceivable: yet to this being, when heard of and understood, the not yet created picture in the mind of the painter is not analogous.

4. Let us notice also the point touched on above, with regard to this being that is greater than all which can be conceived, and which, it is said, can be no other than God himself. I, so far as actual knowledge of the object, either from its specific or general character, is concerned, am as little able to conceive of this being when I hear of it, or to have it in my understanding, as I am to conceive of, or understand God himself: whom, indeed, for this very reason, I can conceive not to exist. For I do not know that reality itself which God is, nor can I form a conjecture of that reality from some other like reality. For you yourself assert that that reality is such that there can be nothing else like it.

For, suppose that I should hear something said of a man absolutely unknown to me, of whose very existence I was unaware. Through that special or general knowledge by which I know what man is, or what men are, I could conceive of him also, according to the reality itself, which man is. And yet it would be possible, if the person who told me of him deceived me, that the man himself, of whom I conceived, did not exist; since that reality according to which I conceived of him, though a no less indisputable fact, was not that man, but any man.

Hence, I am not able, in the way in which I should have this unreal being in concept or in understanding, to have that being of which you speak in concept or in understanding, when I hear the word *God* or the words, *a being greater than all other beings.* For I can conceive of the man according to a fact that is real and familiar to me: but of God, or a being greater than all others, I could not conceive at all, except merely according to the word. And an object can hardly or never be conceived according to the word alone.

For when it is so conceived, it is not so much the word itself (which is, indeed, a real thing—that is, the sound of the letters and syllables) as the signification of the word, when heard, that is conceived. But it is not conceived as by one who knows what is generally signified by the word; by whom, that is, it is conceived according to a reality and in true conception alone. It is conceived as by a man who does not know the object, and conceives of it only in accordance with the movement of his mind produced by hearing the word, the mind attempting to image for itself the signification of the word that is heard. And it would be surprising if in the reality of fact it could even attain to this.

Thus, it appears, and in no other way, this being is also in my understanding, when I hear and understand a person who says that there is a being greater than all conceivable beings.

So much for the assertion that this supreme nature already is in my understanding.

5. But that this being must exist, not only in the understanding but also in reality, is thus proved to me: If it did not so exist, whatever exists in reality would be greater than it. And so the being which has already been proved to exist in my understanding, will not be greater than all other things.

I still answer: If it should be said that a being which cannot be even conceived in terms of any fact, is in the understanding, I do not deny that this being is, accordingly, in my understanding. But, since through this fact it can in no wise attain to real existence also, I do not yet concede to it that existence also, until some certain proof of it shall be given.

For he who says that this being exists, because otherwise the being which is greater than all will not be greater than all, does not attend strictly enough to what he is saying. For I do not yet say, no, I even deny or doubt that this being is greater than any real object. Nor do I concede to it any other existence than this (if it should be called existence) which it has when the mind, according to a word merely heard, tries to form the image of an object absolutely unknown to it.

How, then, is the veritable existence of that being proved to me from the assumption, by hypothesis, that it is greater than all other beings? For I should still deny this, or doubt your demonstration of it, to this extent, that I should not admit that this being is in my understanding and concept, even in the way in which many objects whose real existence is uncertain and doubtful, are in my understanding and concept. For it should be proved first that this being itself really exists somewhere; and then, from the fact that it is greater than all, we shall not hesitate to infer that it also subsists in itself.

6. For example: It is said that somewhere in the ocean is an island, which, because of the difficulty, or rather the impossibility, of discovering what does not exist, is called the Lost Island. And they say that this island has an inestimable wealth of all manner of spices and delicacies in greater abundance than is told of the Islands of the Blessed; and that, having no owner or inhabitant, it is more excellent than all other countries, which are inhabited by mankind, in the abundance with which it is stored.

Now if someone should tell me that there is such an island, I should easily understand his words, in which there is no difficulty. But suppose that he went on to say, as if by a logical inference: "You can no longer doubt that this island which is more excellent than all lands exists somewhere, since you have no doubt that it is in your understanding. And since it is more excellent not to be in the understanding alone, but to exist both in the understanding and in reality, for this reason it must exist. For, if it does not exist, any land which really exists will be more excellent than it; and so the island already understood by you to be more excellent will not be more excellent."

If a man should try to prove to me by such reasoning that this island truly exists, and that its existence should no longer be doubted, either I should believe that he was jesting, or I know not which I ought to regard as the greater fool: myself, supposing that I should allow this proof; or him, if he should suppose that he had established with certainty the existence of this island. For he ought to show first that the hypothetical excellence of this island exists as a real and indubitable fact, and in no wise as any unreal object, or one whose existence is uncertain, in my understanding.

7. This, in the meantime, is the answer the fool could make to the arguments urged against him. When he is assured in the first place that this being is so great that its nonexistence is not even conceivable and that this in turn is proved on no other ground than the fact that otherwise it will not be greater than all things, the fool may make the same answer and say: "When did I say that any such being exists in reality, that is, a being greater than all others, that on this ground it should be proved to me that it also exists in reality to such a degree that it cannot even be conceived not to exist? Whereas in the first place it should be in some way proved that a nature which is higher, that is, greater and

better, than all other natures, exists; in order that from this we may then be able to prove all attributes which necessarily the being that is greater and better than all possesses.

Moreover, it is said that the nonexistence of this being is inconceivable. It might better be said, perhaps, that its nonexistence, or the possibility of its nonexistence, is unintelligible. For according to the true meaning of the word, unreal objects are unintelligible. Yet their existence is conceivable in the way in which the fool conceived of the nonexistence of God. I am most certainly aware of my own existence; but I know, nevertheless, that my nonexistence is possible. As to that supreme being, moreover, which God is, I understand without any doubt both his existence, and the impossibility of his nonexistence. Whether, however, so long as I am most positively aware of my existence, I can conceive of my nonexistence, I am not sure. But if I can, why can I not conceive of the nonexistence of whatever else I know with the same certainty? If, however, I cannot, God will not be the only being of which it can be said, it is impossible to conceive of its nonexistence."

8. The other parts of this book are argued with such truth, such brilliancy, such grandeur; and are so replete with usefulness, so fragrant with a certain perfume of devout and holy feeling, that though there are matters in the beginning which, however rightly sensed, are weakly presented, the rest of the work should not be rejected on this account. Then rather ought these earlier matters to be reasoned more cogently, and the whole to be received with great respect and honor.

ST. ANSELM'S ANSWER TO GAUNILON *

It was a fool against whom the argument of my *Proslogium* was directed. Seeing, however, that the author of these objections is by no means a fool, and is a Catholic, speaking in behalf of the fool, I think it sufficient that I answer the Catholic.

I. You say—whosoever you may be, who say that a fool is capable of making these statements—that a being than which a greater cannot be conceived is not in the understanding in any other sense than that in which a being that is altogether inconceivable in terms of reality, is in the understanding. You say that the inference that this being exists in reality, from the fact that it is in the understanding, is no more just that the inference that a lost island most certainly exists, from the fact that when it is described the hearer does not doubt that it is in his understanding.

But I say: if a being than which a greater is inconceivable is not understood or conceived, and is not in the understanding or in concept, certainly either God is not a being than which a greater is inconceivable, or else he is not understood or conceived, and is not in the under-

* The titles of chapters have been omitted.

standing or in concept. But I call on your faith and conscience to attest that this is most false. Hence, that than which a greater cannot be conceived is truly understood and conceived, and is in the understanding and in concept. Therefore either the grounds on which you try to con-trovert me are not true, or else the inference which you think to base logically on those grounds is not justified.

But you hold, moreover, that supposing that a being than which a greater cannot be conceived is understood, it does not follow that this being is in the understanding; nor, if it is in the understanding, does it therefore exist in reality.

In answer to this, I maintain positively: if that being can be even conceived to be, it must exist in reality. For that than which a greater is inconceivable cannot be conceived except as without beginning. But whatever can be conceived to exist, and does not exist, can be conceived to exist through a beginning. Hence what can be conceived to exist, is not the being than which a greater cannot be conceived. Therefore, if such a being can be conceived to exist, necessarily it does exist.

Furthermore: if it can be conceived at all, it must exist. For no one who denies or doubts the existence of a being than which a greater is inconceivable, denies or doubts that if it did exist, its nonexistence, either in reality or in the understanding, would be impossible. For otherwise it would not be a being than which a greater cannot be conceived. But as to whatever can be conceived, but does not exist—if there were such a being, its nonexistence, either in reality or in the understanding, would be possible. Therefore if a being than which a greater is inconceivable can be even conceived, it cannot be nonexistent.

But let us suppose that it does not exist, even if it can be conceived. Whatever can be conceived, but does not exist, if it existed, would not be a being than which a greater is inconceivable. If, then, there were a being greater than which is inconceivable, it would not be a being than which a greater is inconceivable: which is most absurd. Hence, it is false to deny that a being than which a greater cannot be conceived exists, if it can be even conceived; much the more, therefore, if it can be understood or can be in the understanding.

Moreover, I will venture to make this assertion: without doubt, whatever at any place or at any time does not exist—even if it does exist at some place and at some time—can be conceived to exist nowhere and never, as at some place and at some time it does not exist. For what did not exist yesterday, and exists today, as it is understood not to have existed yesterday, so it can be apprehended by the intelligence that it never exists. And what is not here, and is elsewhere, can be conceived to be nowhere, just as it is not here. So with regard to an object of which the individual parts do not exist at the same place or time: all its parts and therefore its very whole can be conceived to exist nowhere and never.

For, although time is said to exist always, and the world everywhere, yet time does not as a whole exist always, nor the world as a whole everywhere. And as individual parts of time do not exist when others exist, so they can be conceived never to exist. And so it can be apprehended by the intelligence that individual parts of the world exist nowhere, as they do not exist where other parts exist. Moreover, what is composed of parts can be dissolved in concept, and be nonexistent. Therefore, whatever at any place or at any time does not exist as a whole, even if it is existent, can be conceived not to exist.

But that than which a greater cannot be conceived, if it exists, cannot be conceived not to exist. Otherwise, it is not a being than which a greater cannot be conceived: which is inconsistent. By no means, then, does it at any place or at any time fail to exist as a whole: but it exists as a whole everywhere and always.

Do you believe that this being can in some way be conceived or understood, or that the being with regard to which these things are understood can be in concept or in the understanding? For if it cannot, these things cannot be understood with reference to it. But if you say that it is not understood and that it is not in the understanding, because it is not thoroughly understood; you should say that a man who cannot face the direct rays of the sun does not see the light of day, which is none other than the sunlight. Assuredly a being than which a greater cannot be conceived exists, and is in the understanding, at least to this extent— that these statements regarding it are understood.

II. I have said, then, in the argument which you dispute, that when the fool hears mentioned a being than which a greater is inconceivable, he understands what he hears. Certainly a man who does not understand when a familiar language is spoken, has no understanding at all, or a very dull one. Moreover, I have said that if this being is understood, it is in the understanding. Is that in no understanding which has been proved necessarily to exist in the reality of fact?

But you will say that although it is in the understanding, it does not follow that it is understood. But observe that the fact of its being understood does not necessitate its being in the understanding. For, as what is conceived is conceived by conception, as it is conceived, so is in conception; so what is understood, is understood by understanding, and what is understood by understanding, as it is understood, so is in the understanding. What can be more clear than this?

After this, I have said that if it is even in the understanding alone, it can be conceived also to exist in reality, which is greater. If, then, it is in the understanding alone, obviously the very being than which a greater cannot be conceived is one than which a greater can be conceived. What is more logical? For if it exists even in the understanding alone, can it not be conceived also to exist in reality? And if it can be so conceived, does not he who conceives of this conceive of a thing greater than that being, if it exists in the understanding alone? What more consistent inference, then, can be made than this: that if a being than which a greater cannot be conceived is in the understanding alone, it is not that than which a greater cannot be conceived?

But, assuredly, in no understanding is a being than which a greater is conceivable a being than which a greater is inconceivable. Does it not follow, then, that if a being than which a greater cannot be conceived is in any understanding, it does not exist in the understanding alone? For if it is in the understanding alone, it is a being than which a greater can be conceived, which is inconsistent with the hypothesis.

III. But, you say, it is as if one should suppose an island in the ocean, which surpasses all lands in its fertility, and which, because of the difficulty, or rather the impossibility, of discovering what does not exist, is called a Lost Island; and should say that there can be no doubt that this island truly exists in reality, for this reason, that one who hears it described easily understands what he hears.

Now I promise confidently that if any man shall devise anything existing either in reality or in concept alone (except that than which a greater cannot be conceived) to which he can adapt the sequence of my reasoning, I will discover that thing, and will give him his lost island, not to be lost again.

But it now appears that this being than which a greater is inconceivable cannot be conceived not to be, because it exists on so assured a ground of truth; for otherwise it would not exist at all.

Hence, if anyone says that he conceives this being not to exist, I say that, at the time when he conceives of this, either he conceives of a being than which a greater is inconceivable, or he does not conceive at all. If he does not conceive, he does not conceive of the nonexistence of that of which he does not conceive. But, if he does conceive, he certainly conceives of a being which cannot be even conceived not to exist. For if it could be conceived not to exist, it could be conceived to have a beginning and an end. But this is impossible.

He, then, who conceives of this being conceives of a being which cannot even be conceived not to exist; but he who conceives of this being does not conceive that it does not exist; else he conceives what is inconceivable. The nonexistence, then, of that than which a greater cannot be conceived is inconceivable.

IV. You say, moreover, that whereas I assert that this supreme being cannot be *conceived* not to exist, it might better be said that its nonexistence, or even the possibility of its nonexistence, cannot be *understood*.

But, it was more proper to say, it cannot be conceived. For if I had said that the object itself cannot be understood not to exist, possibly you yourself, who say that in accordance with the true meaning of the term what is unreal cannot be understood, would offer the objection that nothing which is can be understood not to be, for the nonexistence of what exists is unreal: hence God would not be the only being of which it could be said, it is impossible to understand its nonexistence. For thus one of those things which most certainly exist can be understood not to exist in the same way in which certain other real objects can be understood not to exist.

But this objection, assuredly, cannot be urged against the term *conception*, if one considers the matter well. For although no objects which exist can be understood not to exist, yet all objects, except that which exists in the highest degree, can be conceived not to exist. For all those objects, and those alone, can be conceived not to exist, which have a beginning or end or composition of parts; also, as I have already said, whatever at any place or at any time does not exist as a whole.

That being alone, on the other hand, cannot be conceived not to exist in which any conception discovers neither beginning nor end nor composition of parts, and which any conception finds always and everywhere as a whole.

Be assured, then, that you can conceive of your own nonexistence, although you are most certain that you exist. I am surprised that you should have admitted that you are ignorant of this. For we conceive of the nonexistence of many objects which we know to exist, and of the existence of many which we know not to exist; not by forming the opinion that they so exist, but by imagining that they exist as we conceived of them.

And indeed, we can conceive of the nonexistence of an object, although we know it to exist, because at the same time we can conceive of the former and know the latter. And we cannot conceive of the nonexistence of an object, so long as we know it to exist, because we cannot conceive at the same time of existence and nonexistence.

If, then, one will thus distinguish these two senses of this statement, he will understand that nothing, so long as it is known to exist, can be conceived not to exist; and that whatever exists, except that being than which a greater cannot be conceived, can be conceived not to exist, even when it is known to exist.

So, then, of God alone it can be said that it is impossible to conceive of his nonexistence; and yet many objects, so long as they exist, in one sense cannot be conceived not to exist. But in what sense God is to be conceived not to exist, I think has been shown clearly enough in my book.

V. The nature of the other objections which you, in behalf of the fool, urge against me it is easy, even for a man of small wisdom, to detect; and I had therefore thought it unnecessary to show this. But since I hear that some readers of these objections think they have some weight against me, I will discuss them briefly.

In the first place, you often repeat that I assert that what is greater than all other things is in the understanding; and if it is in the understanding, it exists also in reality, for otherwise the being which is greater than all would not be greater than all.

Nowhere in all my writings is such a demonstration found. For the real existence of a being which is said to be *greater than all other beings* cannot be demonstrated in the same way with the real existence of one that is said to be *a being than which a greater cannot be conceived.*

If it should be said that a being than which a greater cannot be conceived has no real existence, or that it is possible that it does not exist, or even that it can be conceived not to exist, such an assertion can be easily refuted. For the nonexistence of what does not exist is possible, and that whose nonexistence is possible can be conceived not to exist. But whatever can be conceived not to exist, if it exists, is not a being than which a greater cannot be conceived; but if it does not exist, it would not, even if it existed, be a being than which a greater cannot be conceived. But it cannot be said that a being than which a greater is inconceivable, if it exists is not a being than which a greater is inconceivable; or that if it existed, it would not be a being than which a greater is inconceivable.

It is evident, then, that neither is it nonexistent, nor is it possible that it does not exist, nor can it be conceived not to exist. For otherwise, if it exists, it is not that which it is said to be in the hypothesis; and if it existed, it would not be what it is said to be in the hypothesis.

But this, it appears, cannot be easily proved of a being which is said to be *greater than all other beings.* For it is not so evident that what can be conceived not to exist is not greater than all existing beings, as it is evident that it is not a being than which a greater cannot be conceived. Nor is it indubitable that if a being greater than all other beings exists, it is no other than the being than which a greater cannot be conceived; or that if it were such a being, some other might not be this being in like manner; as it is certain with regard to a being which is hypothetically posited as one than which a greater cannot be conceived.

For consider: If one should say that there is a being greater than all other beings, and that this being can nevertheless be conceived not to exist; and that a being greater than this, although it does not exist, can be conceived to exist; can it be so clearly inferred in this case that this being is therefore not a being greater than all other existing beings, as it would be most positively affirmed in the other case, that the being under discussion is not, therefore, a being than which a greater cannot be conceived?

For the former conclusion requires another premise than the predication, *greater than all other beings.* In my argument, on the other hand, there is no need of any other than this very predication, *a being than which a greater cannot be conceived.*

If the same proof cannot be applied when the being in question is predicated to be greater than all others, which can be applied when it is predicated to be a being than which a greater cannot be conceived, you have unjustly censured me for saying what I did not say; since such a predication differs so greatly from that which I actually made. If, on the other hand, the other argument is valid, you ought not to blame me for having said what can be proved.

Whether this can be proved, however, he will easily decide who recognizes that this being than which a greater cannot be conceived is demonstrable. For by no means can this being than which a greater cannot be conceived be understood as any other than that which alone is greater than all. Here, just as that which is greater cannot be conceived is understood, and is in the understanding, and not for that reason is asserted to exist in the reality of fact: so what is said to be greater than all other beings is understood and is in the understanding, and therefore it is necessarily inferred that it exists in reality.

You see, then, with how much justice you have compared me with your fool, who, on the sole ground that he understands what is described to him, would affirm that a Lost Island exists.

VI. Another of your objections is that any unreal beings, or beings whose existence is uncertain, can be understood and be in the understanding in the same way with that being which I discussed. I am surprised that you should have conceived this objection, for I was attempting to prove what was still uncertain, and contented myself at first with showing that this being is understood in any way, and is in the understanding. It was my intention to consider on these grounds, whether this being is in the understanding alone, like an unreal object, or whether it also exists in fact, as a real being. For if unreal objects, or objects whose existence is uncertain, in this way are understood and are in the understanding, because, when they are spoken of, the hearer understands what the speaker means, there is no reason why that being of which I spoke should not be understood and be in the understanding.

How, moreover, can these two statements of yours be reconciled: 1) the assertion that if a man should speak of any unreal objects, whatever they might be, you would understand, and 2) the assertion that on hearing of that being which does exist, and not in that way in which even unreal objects are held in concept, you would not say that you conceive of it or have it in your concept; since, as you say, you cannot conceive of it in any other way than by understanding it, that is, by comprehending in your knowledge its real existence?

How, I ask, can these two things be reconciled: that unreal objects are understood and that understanding an object is comprehending in knowledge its real existence? The contradiction does not concern me; do you see to it. But if unreal objects are also in some sort understood, and your definition is applicable, not to every understanding, but to a certain sort of understanding, I ought not to be blamed for saying that a being than which a greater cannot be conceived is understood and is in the understanding, even before I reached the certain conclusion that this being exists in reality.

VII. Again, you say that it can probably never be believed that this being, when it is spoken of, and heard of, cannot be conceived not to exist in the same way in which even God may be conceived not to exist.

Such an objection could be answered by those who have attained but little skill in disputation and argument. For is it compatible with reason for a man to deny the existence of what he understands, because it is said to be that being whose existence he denies because he does not understand it? Or, if at some time its existence is denied, because only to a certain extent is it understood, and that which is not at all understood is the same to him; is not what is still undetermined more easily proved of a being which exists in some understanding than of one which exists in no understanding?

Hence it cannot be credible that any man denies the existence of a being than which a greater cannot be conceived, which, when he hears of it, he understands in a certain degree; it is incredible, I say, that any man denies the existence of this being because he denies the existence of God, the sensory perceptions of whom he in no wise conceives of.

Or if the existence of another object, because it is not at all understood, is denied, is not the existence of what is understood in some degree more easily proved than the existence of an object which is in no wise understood?

Not irrationally, then, has the hypothesis of a being a greater than which cannot be conceived been employed in controverting the fool, for the proof of the existence of God; since in some degree he would understand such a being, but in no wise could understand God.

VIII. Moreover, your so careful demonstration that the being than which a greater cannot be conceived is not analogous to the not executed picture in the understanding of the painter, is quite unnecessary. It was not for this purpose that I suggested the preconceived picture. I had no thought of asserting that the being which I was discussing is of such a nature; but I wished to show that what is not understood to exist can be in the understanding.

Again, you say that when you hear of a being than which a greater is inconceivable, you cannot conceive of it in terms of any real object known to you either specifically or generally, nor have it in your understanding. For, you say, you neither know such a being in itself, nor can you form an idea of it from anything like it.

But obviously this is not true. For everything that is less good, in so far as it is good, is like the greater good. It is therefore evident to any rational mind that by ascending from the lesser good to the greater, we can form a considerable notion of a being than which a greater is inconceivable.

For instance, who (even if he does not believe that what he conceives of exists in reality) supposing that there is some good which has a beginning and an end does not conceive that a good is much better, which, if it begins, does not cease to be? And that as the second good is better than the first, so that good which has neither beginning nor end, though it is ever passing from the past through the present to the future, is better than the second? And that far better than this is a being—whether any being of such nature exists or not—which in no wise requires change or motion, nor is compelled to undergo change or motion?

Is this inconceivable, or is some being greater than this conceivable? Or is not this to form a notion from objects than which a greater is conceivable, of the being than which a greater cannot be conceived? There is, then, a means of forming a notion of a being than which a greater is inconceivable.

So easily, then, can the fool who does accept sacred authority be refuted, if he denies that a notion may be formed from other objects of a being than which a greater is inconceivable. But if any Catholic would deny this, let him remember that the invisible things of God, from the creation of the world, are clearly seen, being understood by the things that are made, even his eternal power and Godhead (Rom. 1:20).

IX. But even if it were true that a being than which a greater is inconceivable cannot be conceived or understood; yet it would not be untrue that a being than which a greater cannot be conceived is conceivable and intelligible. There is nothing to prevent one's saying *ineffable,* although what is said to be ineffable cannot be spoken of. *Inconceivable* is conceivable although that to which the word *inconceivable* can be applied is inconceivable. So, when one says, *that than which nothing greater is conceivable,* undoubtedly what is heard is conceivable and intelligible, although that being itself, than which a greater is inconceivable, cannot be conceived or understood.

Or, though there is a man so foolish as to say there is no being than which a greater is inconceivable, he will not be so shameless as to say that he cannot understand or conceive of what he says. Or, if such a man is found, not only ought his words to be rejected, but he himself should be condemned.

Whoever, then, denies the existence of a being than which a greater cannot be conceived, at least understands and conceives of the denial which he makes. But this denial he cannot understand or conceive of without its component terms; and a term of this statement is a *being than which a greater cannot be conceived.* Whoever, then, makes this denial, understands and conceives of that than which a greater is inconceivable.

Moreover, it is evident that in the same way it is possible to conceive of and understand a being whose nonexistence is impossible; but he who conceives of this conceives of a greater being than one whose nonexistence is possible. Hence, when a being—than which a greater is inconceivable—is conceived, if it is a being whose nonexistence is possible that is conceived, it is not a being than which a greater cannot be conceived. But an object cannot be at once conceived and not conceived. Hence he who conceives of a being than which a greater is inconceivable, does not conceive of that whose nonexistence is possible, but of that whose nonexistence is impossible. Therefore, what he conceives of must exist; for anything whose nonexistence is possible, is not that of which he conceives.

X. I believe that I have shown by an argument which is not weak, but sufficiently cogent, that in my former book I proved the existence of a being than which a greater cannot be conceived; and I believe that this argument cannot be invalidated by the validity of any objection. For so great a force does the signification of this reasoning contain in itself, that this being which is the subject of discussion, is of necessity from the very fact that it is understood or conceived, proved also to exist in reality, and to be whatever we should believe of the divine substance.

For we attribute to the divine substance anything of which it can be conceived that it is better to be than not to be that thing. For example: it is better to be eternal than not eternal; good, than not good; nay, goodness itself, than not goodness itself. But it cannot be that anything of this nature is not a property of the being than which a greater is inconceivable. Hence, the being than which a greater is inconceivable must be whatever should be attributed to the divine essence.

I thank you for your kindness both in your blame and in your praise for my book. For since you have commended so generously those parts of it which seem to you worthy of acceptance, it is quite evident that you have criticised in no unkind spirit those parts of it which seemed to you weak.

19

THE "QUINQUE VIAE" OF ST. THOMAS AQUINAS

Aquinas: Selected Passages *

THE existence of God can be proved in five ways. The first and more manifest way is the argument from motion. It is certain and evident to our senses that some things are in motion. Whatever is in motion is moved by another, for nothing can be in motion except it have a potentiality for that towards which it is being moved; whereas a thing moves inasmuch as it is in act. By "motion" we mean nothing else than the reduction of something from a state of potentiality to a state of actuality. Nothing, however, can be reduced from a state of potentiality into a state of actuality, unless by something already in state of actuality. Thus that which is actually hot as fire, makes wood, which is potentially hot, to be actually hot, and thereby moves and changes it. It is not possible that the same thing should be at once in a state of potentiality and actuality from the same point of view, but only from different points of view. What is actually hot cannot simultaneously be only potentially hot; still, it is simultaneously potentially cold. It is therefore impossible that from the same point of view and in the same way anything should be both moved and mover, or that it should move itself. Therefore whatever is in motion must be put in motion by another. If that by which it is put in motion be itself put in motion, then this also must needs be put in motion by another, and that by another again. This cannot go on to infinity, because then there would be no first mover, and, consequently, no other mover—seeing that subsequent movers only move inasmuch as they are put in motion by the first mover; as the staff only moves because it is put in motion by the hand. Therefore it is necessary to arrive at a First Mover, put in motion by no other; and this everyone understands to be God.

The second way is from the formality of efficient causation. In the world of sense we find there is an order of efficient causation. There is no case known (neither is it, indeed, possible), in which a thing is found to be the efficient cause of itself; for so it would be prior to itself, which is impossible. In efficient causes it is not possible to go on to infinity, because in all efficient causes following in order, the first is the cause of

---

* St. Thomas Aquinas (1225-1274), *Summa Theologica*, I, q. 1, art. 3, "Whether God Exists?" The translation is that of the Fathers of the English Dominican Province (London: Washbourne, 1911).

the intermediate cause, whether the intermediate cause be several, or one only. To take away the cause is to take away the effect. Therefore, if there be no first cause among efficient causes, there will be no ultimate cause, nor any intermediate. If in efficient causes it is possible to go on to infinity, there will be no first efficient cause, neither will there be an ultimate effect, nor any intermediate efficient causes; all of which is plainly false. Therefore, it is necessary to put forward a First Efficient Cause, to which everyone gives the name of God.

The third way is taken from possibility and necessity and runs thus. We find in nature things that could either exist or not exist, since they are found to be generated, and then to corrupt; and consequently, they can exist and then not exist. It is impossible for these always to exist, for that which can one day cease to exist, must at some time have not existed. Therefore, if everything could cease to exist, then at one time there could have been nothing in existence. If this were true, even now there would be nothing in existence, because that which does not exist only begins to exist by something already existing. Therefore, if at one time nothing was in existence, it would have been impossible for anything to have begun to exist; and thus even now nothing would be in existence—which is absurd. Therefore, not all beings are merely possible, but there must exist something the existence of which is necessary. Every necessary thing either has its necessity caused by another, or not. It is impossible to go on to infinity in necessary things which have their necessity caused by another; as has been already proved in regard to efficient causes. Therefore we cannot but postulate the existence of some being having of itself its own necessity, and not receiving it from another, but rather causing in others their necessity. This all men speak of as God.

The fourth way is taken from the gradation to be found in things. Among beings there are some more and some less good, true, noble and the like. But "more" or "less" are predicated of different things, according as they resemble in their different ways something which is in the degree of "most," as a thing is said to be hotter as it more nearly resembles that which is hottest; so that there is something which is truest, something best, something noblest, and consequently, something which is uttermost being; for the truer things are, the more truly they exist. What is most complete in any genus is the cause of all in that genus; as fire, which is the most complete form of heat, is the cause whereby all things are made hot. Therefore there must also be something which is to all beings the cause of their being, goodness, and every other perfection; and this we call God.

The fifth way is taken from the governance of the world; for we see that things which lack intelligence, such as natural bodies, act for some purpose, which fact is evident from their acting always, or nearly always, in the same way, so as to obtain the best result. Hence it is plain that not fortuitously, but designedly, do they achieve their purpose. Whatever lacks intelligence cannot fulfil some purpose, unless it be directed by some being endowed with intelligence and knowledge; as the arrow is shot to its mark by the archer. Therefore some intelligent being exists by whom all natural things are ordained towards a definite purpose; and this being we call God.

Synthesis of St. Thomas' Demonstration *

Before examining each of these (Thomistic) typical proofs in detail, we shall give a general proof which includes all the others, and which, we believe, most aptly illustrates what is commonly accepted as the essential point in establishing the existence of God. The principle of this general proof, i.e.: "The greater cannot proceed from the less," condenses into one formula the principles upon which our five typical proofs are based. These principles may be stated as follows: "*Becoming* depends upon *being* which is determined: *conditioned* being depends upon *unconditioned* being; *contingent* being depends upon *necessary* being; *imperfect, composite, multiple* being depends upon what is *perfect, simple* and *one; order* in the universe depends upon an *intelligent designer.*" The principles of the first three proofs especially emphasize the fact that the world depends for its existence upon a *cause,* while the last two principles stress the *superiority* and *perfection* of this cause. These may then be summed up in the formula: "The *greater* cannot proceed from the *less;* only the *higher* grade of being can explain the lower."

The general proof will have to be scientifically established by the five other proofs. Though it is in itself somewhat vague, it becomes strong and convincing when united with the others. We have here a concrete case of what the theologians teach about the natural knowledge of God. "Although the existence of God needs to be demonstrated," writes Scheeben (*Dogmatik,* II, n. 29), "it does not follow that its certainty is merely the result of a scientific proof, one of conscious reflection, based on our own research or on the teaching of others; nor does it follow that this certainty is due to the scientific accuracy of the proof. On the contrary, the proof required so that anyone may arrive at complete certainty is so easy and so clear that one scarcely perceives the logical process which it involves, and the scientifically developed proofs, far from being the means by which man first acquires certainty of the existence of God, merely clarify and confirm the knowledge which he already has. Moreover, since the proof, in its original form, presents itself more or less as an ocular demonstration, and finds an echo in the most hidden recesses of the rational nature of man, it establishes a conviction on this basis which is firmer and less open to attack than any other, no matter how ingeniously contrived, and which cannot be assailed by any scientific objection." Thus are verified the words of Scripture when it chides the

* Reginald Garrigou-Lagrange, *God: His Existence and His Nature,* Part I, Chap. III, n. 35. (St. Louis: Herder, 1934-1936).

pagans, not for having neglected the studies necessary for acquiring a knowledge of God, but for having violently suppressed the divine truth clearly made known to the mind of man (Rom. 1:18; 2:14). To deny the existence of God is an insult to nature (*mataioi phuseos;* Wisd. 13:1) as well as to reason (*Dixit insipiens in corde suo: non est Deus;* Ps. 13:1).

The general proof may be stated as follows, by ascending from the lower beings to man: We know from experience that there are beings and events belonging to different orders. Certain things in nature are inanimate (minerals); and there is the vegetative life (in plants), the sensitive life (in animals), and the intellectual and moral life (in man). All these things come into existence and disappear again, they are born and they die, which shows that their activity has a beginning and an end. Evidently they do not exist of and by themselves. What, then, causes them to come into being?

If there are things in existence at present, there must have been something in existence always. If at any particular moment of time nothing exists, then nothing will ever come into existence. "*Ex nihilo nihil fit.*" The principle of causality tells us that nothing can be the reason or cause of actual being. To say that the series of perishable things had or did not have a beginning does not solve the problem. If the series is eternal, it is eternally insufficient; for the perishable things of the past were just as indigent as those now existing, and not in any way self-sufficient. How would any one of them, not being able to account for its own existence, account for those that follow? This would be the same as admitting that the greater proceeds from the less. We must admit, therefore, that above perishable beings there is a *First Being,* who owes existence only to himself and can give it to others.

If living beings exist today, and if life is superior to brute matter, it could not have evolved from the latter, for to assert this would mean that the greater comes from the less, or, what amounts to the same, that *being* comes from nothing. Just as *being* as such, cannot come from nothing, living being cannot proceed from that which is not living and of a lower order than life. The First Being, must therefore have life. This necessary conclusion becomes practically evident to the senses if we suppose that it is an established fact of positive science that the series of living beings had a beginning.

If there is such a thing in the world today as intelligence and knowledge; if intelligence is superior to brute matter, to the vegetative and sensitive life; if the most domesticated of animals can never be trained so as to grasp the principle of sufficient reason or the first principle of the moral law; intelligence could never have evolved from these lower grades of being, but it is necessary to admit an intelligent being existing from all eternity. The intellectuality of that being cannot be, like ours, contingent; for, not being responsible for its existence, how could it account for that of others? This means that the First Being is of necessity *intelligent.* If everything originated from matter, from a lump of clay, how could human reason, or the mind of man, have evolved? "There is no greater absurdity than to admit that intelligent beings are the result of a blind and material fatalism," says Montesquieu. And how could there be order in the world without an intelligent designer?

If the series of rational principles, which dominate our reason and all reality, actual as well as possible, are necessary, and consequently *superior* and anterior to all contingent intellects and realities which they regulate, then they are independent of the latter, and there must always have been some intelligent being reigning supreme in the realm of the possible, the real, and the intellectual. This supreme intellect must have been in possession of a *first and unchangeable truth*. In other words, if the intelligible and its necessary laws are superior to the unintelligible and the contingent, they must have existed from all eternity, for they could not possibly have originated from that which in no wise contained them.

If, finally, there are in the world today morality, justice, charity, if we can attribute sanctity to Christ and Christianity, if this morality and this sanctity are of a higher order than what is neither holy nor moral, there must have been from all eternity a moral, just, good, and holy Being. The soul of a St. Augustine or a St. Vincent de Paul, the humblest of Christians for whom the words of the *Pater Noster* have a message to convey—is there anything more absurd than to say that these are the result of a material and blind fatality? Can the desire for God and for perfect holiness be explained apart from God? Can the relative be explained apart from the absolute? If the first principle of the moral law, namely, that we must do good and avoid evil ("Do your duty, let happen what may"), forces itself upon us with no less objectivity and necessity than the principles of speculative reason; if the really good, which is the object of our will (good in itself, superior to useful and delectable good), has a *right* to be loved and willed apart from the satisfaction and advantages to be derived from it; if the being capable of such an act of the will *must* so will, in order to retain its *raison d'être;* if the voice of conscience proclaims this right of the good to be loved, and afterwards approves or condemns without our being able to stifle the feelings of remorse; if, in a word, the right of good to be loved and practiced *dominates* our moral activity and that of societies, actual and possible, just as the principle of identity dominates the real, both actual and possible, then there must have been from all eternity a foundation for these absolute rights. These necessary and dominant rights cannot be explained and regulated by any contingent reality. Since they are above everything except the *Absolute Good,* it is only the latter that can explain their existence. If we are conscious of a moral law within us which is superior to all human legislation, there must be a *supreme legislator.*

Therefore, there must be a First Being, who is at the same time Life, Intelligence, supreme Truth, absolute Justice, perfect Holiness, and sovereign Goodness. This conclusion is based on the principle that "the greater cannot proceed from the less," which in turn is merely a formulation of the principle of causality. *"Quod non est a se est ab alio quod est a se."* That which has not its reason for existing in itself, must derive that reason from another being, which exists by and for itself. The lower grades of being, far from being able to explain the higher, can be explained only by the latter. The simplest of material elements, such as the atom and the crystal, far from being the principle of things, can be explained only by an idea of type or final end. The display in them of intelligent design can have been caused only by an intelligent designer.

The Import of St. Thomas' Demonstration *

Nowhere is the absence of an exposition of his own philosophy by Thomas Aquinas himself more seriously felt than on the question of the existence of God. Here especially do we have to show that St. Thomas is transforming all he borrows. This would be a great deal easier were it not that he constantly gives expression to his own meaning in a form already used by others before him. He nowhere offers an explanation of why he does this, and the historian is left to his own surmises. There may be several concurring reasons. The modesty of the man and the saint must have contributed something and also his sincere desire to make others as sure as he himself was of the very real agreement there is between faith and reason. Thus it was more important to show that the ways pursued in different philosophies lead to the same truth than to propose further demonstrations of a totally new kind. St. Thomas did not consider himself to be the first to prove effectively the existence of God. He did not think this as philosopher, and as theologian he would have shuddered at the very suggestion. Whatever his reasons, he borrowed the language of others. Thus the need here to scrutinize his texts in order to extract his personal thought from words and expressions which were not his own.

We can speak about his terminology and formulae this way when we become aware of the extreme diversity of their sources. St. Thomas borrows now from Aristotle, now from Avicenna, and now from St. John Damascene or St. Augustine. No matter how eclectic we suppose him to be, he cannot have collected thoughts so infinitely varied without modifying them considerably. We shall see that he did modify them, and his personal contribution to the problem was precisely the modification he imposed upon them. It mattered little to him that his proofs were of different origin; his hope was above all to show that they were all good, provided they could be made to come to the right conclusion.

Thus envisaged, the number of the Thomistic proofs for the existence of God loses considerable of its importance. Our attention has rightly

* Etienne Gilson, *The Christian Philosophy of St. Thomas Aquinas*, trans. by L. K. Shook, C.S.B. (New York: Random House). Copyright, 1956 by Etienne Gilson.

been called to "the empirical character of the five ways . . . a sort of stock-taking which makes no claim to be exhaustive, much less to present the constituent parts of a necessary division." Not only their number, but their original meaning in the doctrine from which they are borrowed loses much of its interest. The point in trying to get back to their original sense is less to determine what St. Thomas is preserving than to see what he is adding. Indeed it is perhaps rather to see, where he appears to be adding nothing, how he is transforming it into something else entirely by merely transposing it to another plane.

The proof by the first mover is characteristic in this regard and is more or less typical of the others. As we observed when analyzing it, it argues to the existence of a first desirable and immovable source of all the movement of the universe. We have also observed that such was Aristotle's position. It appears, however, at first glance, that St. Thomas could not hold this. The God of whom he is thinking, both as Christian doctor and philosopher, does not cause motion simply as a final cause but as an efficient cause, without, however, being moved himself, and remaining always separate. We have only two choices here. Either St. Thomas did not understand that Aristotle's proof could not be taken over as it stood, in which case he was guilty of misinterpretation; or he did understand this, and therefore could only press the proof by the first mover into service by giving it a new meaning.

Now there are many signs that St. Thomas's first mover is not a simple final cause. In the first place, it is remarkable that in the *Summa Theologiae* the immovable First Mover is not at all presented as being only a supreme desirable. Reading this text just as it is, everyone will understand it. Everyone understands it in fact to prove the existence of a first efficient cause of motion. One has only to read it again to be assured of this. But this is not all. The distinction between the Aristotelian level of substance and the Thomistic level of existence ought to intervene here, at least if we are to attribute to the texts of St. Thomas their Thomistic meaning. We all know that in Aristotle the motion of the heavenly bodies is the cause of all motion, the term "motion" being understood here as everywhere in the sense of "passing from potency to act." The generation of beings which we are constantly witnessing in experience are motions of this kind. They are, therefore, caused by the motion of the heavenly bodies. As the first cause of this motion is the immovable First Mover, then, even under the simple title of First Mover, it can be called the cause of all the beings succeeding one another in the world. Moreover, St. Thomas has strongly emphasized this in order to defend Aristotle against the charge of having made of God a mere moving cause. These common causes of beings, eternal and separated substances, are also supreme beings, and, consequently, causes of other beings. "Whence it is evident," concludes St. Thomas, "how false is the opinion of those who maintain that Aristotle did not think that God was the cause of the substance of the heavens but only of its motion." Indeed, "On this first principle, which is the first mover as end, depends the heavens, both as to the perpetuity of its substance and as to the perpetuity of its motion. Consequently, all nature depends on such a principle, since all natural beings depend upon the heavens and their motions." Let us go farther. Aristotle shows that the immovable First Mover is not only intelligible and desirable, but intelligent and living. In short, the First Mover is truly God. It is, therefore, God as immovable First Mover that Aristotle affirms to be the cause of motion and of substances.

Can we go beyond this point, without going beyond Aristotle? St. Thomas, who always brings Aristotle as close to the truth as he can, has at least tried to do so. He strives to make him say that all motion and all nature depend upon the First Mover, not only as upon a final cause, but upon a will. He makes the attempt in this additional remark: "We must pay attention to this, that Aristotle is here saying that the necessity of the first movement is not an absolute necessity, but a necessity depending upon an end. Now the end is that principle which he afterwards names God, to whom the end of motion is to assimilate beings (*inquantum attenditur per motum assimilatio ad ipsum*). On the other hand, the assimilation to a willing and intelligent being, as he shows God to be, is understood in terms of will and intelligence. Thus the products of art are assimilated to the artisan in so far as in them the will of the artist is fulfilled. It follows from this, therefore, that all the necessity of the first movement is subject to the will of God."

Strictly speaking, St. Thomas is not here going beyond the letter of Aristotle, save perhaps in speaking of Aristotle's God as having a will, when, in the passage from the *Metaphysics* upon which he is commenting, Aristotle does not say this. However, as Aristotle is there showing the immovable First Mover as supreme delectable and as living, he could strictly speaking be said to have a will. We say, strictly speaking, because Aristotle is only speaking in this Book XII, chap. VII of the *Metaphysics* of the life and pleasure of a Supreme Intelligence, which is also the Supreme Intelligible. But if we admit that this is so, all that St. Thomas can rightly draw from this text of Aristotle is that the first motion, cause of all others, is that of a will being assimilated to what the First Mover wills in willing itself, not a motion willed by a supreme will. In fact, St. Thomas says no more about it; so that even in his commentary upon it, the hiatus separating the "final cause" God of Aristotle from the "efficient moving cause" God of Thomism is still not removed.

But even if it were removed, we should have a second gap to cross, and this time a veritable abyss, because it separates the entitative being of nature or substance from existential being properly so called. St. Thomas always maintains, as we shall see better when we deal with creation, that Aristotle affirmed his immovable First Mover as the cause of the whole substance, and, consequently, of all substances. This is clearly what we have just found St. Thomas saying *a propos* of the text of the *Metaphysics*. There is nothing more interesting than to compare with his commentary the terms he uses when speaking freely and for himself about the moving causality of the Christian God. Since he has begun with Aristotle's proofs, it is still the God of these proofs with whom he sets out. But now it becomes evident that the entire substantialist metaphysic of Aristotle is transferred to a much more profound plane. "It has been shown above, by a demonstration from Aristotle, that a first efficient cause exists, which we call God. Now the efficient cause brings its effects to actual existence (*suos effectos ad esse conducit*). God is, therefore, the cause by which other things exist. It has also been shown by an argument of the same Aristotle that there exists an immovable First Mover whom we call God. Now in any order of motions whatsoever, the First Mover is the cause of all the motions in the series. Since therefore the motions of the heavens bring many things to exist, motions of which God has been shown to be the First Mover, it must be that God is the cause of the existence of many things."

The interpreter of St. Thomas has to make his choice. The first efficient cause cannot cause the existence of the effects which other causes produce if it does not first cause the existence of these causes. The immovable First Mover cannot cause the existence of the effects of the motions of the heavens if it does not first cause the existence of this motion. It would not cause it, if its action simply consisted in motivating by its presence the motion of a first movable. This would be to give to this first movable a motive for moving itself; it would not be to confer existence to its motion. It seems true to say that the Thomistic proofs for the existence of God are developed immediately upon the existential level as demonstrations that there exists a first moving cause of the heavenly motions and, through them, of the very beings that come to be owing to their influence; a first efficient cause of all the causes and of their efficacy; a necessary existant, cause of the actualization of all possibles; a first term in the orders of Being, Good, True, cause of everything contained in these orders; a Last End, whose existence is the why of every "why—something —exists."

Thus interpreted in the fullness of their meaning, the Thomistic proofs of the existence of God rejoin another order of considerations which we have already met several times. To say that an existing thing requires an extrinsic cause of its existence is to say that it does not contain it in itself. From this point of view, the proofs of the existence of God consist in constructing a chain of causes which binds all beings which are by another to the one being who is by itself. Beings by another, which have not in themselves the wherewithal to exist, are those same beings whose essence, we were saying, is distinct from their existence, as opposed to being by itself whose very essence is to exist. We can say, therefore, that all the Thomistic proofs for the existence of God amount, in the last analysis, to a search, beyond existences which are not self-sufficient, for an existence which is self-sufficient and which, because it is so, can be the first cause of all others.

The reason why St. Thomas did not directly approach the problem from this angle in the *Summa Theologiae* and in the *Summa Contra Gentiles* is no doubt the same as that for placing the proof by motion before the others. "The first and most manifest way," he says of this proof. It is the most manifest because there is no sensible experience more common and more striking than that of motion. If it is motion that is most apparent in the sensible world, it is the distinction between essence and act-of-being that is most secret. What indeed is this distinction if not the translation, in abstract terms, of the ontological deficiency revealed in a being by the fact that it changes, that it is only a cause in so far as caused, only a being in so far as it is a possible realized, and that it is neither first in its own order nor last in the order of ends? On the other hand, precisely because the distinction between essence and existence translates the state of second cause, whatever its order of causality, into one and the same formula, it qualifies all the proofs. It is not a sixth way. It is rather the ultimate metaphysical implication of the other five, in the light of the Thomistic interpretation of the notion of being.

It is therefore natural to find this interpretation in one of Thomas's more deeply metaphysical writings, his short treatise *On Being and Essence*. In this work dating from the beginning of his career, he inaugurated his method of entrusting his most personal contributions to the patronage of others. When, in this treatise, he has made his distinction between essence and existence, which we have dealt with above, St. Thomas continues as follows: "Whatever is proper to anything is either caused by the principles of its nature, as, for example, the aptitude for laughing in man, or comes to it by some extrinsic principle, as the light that is in the air under the influence of the sun. Now it cannot be that the act-of-being (*ipsum esse*) is caused by the very form or quiddity of the thing, caused, I say, as by an efficient cause, for then a thing would itself be the cause of itself, a thing would itself bring itself into existence, which is impossible. It is necessary, therefore, that everything whose act-of-being is other than its nature should have its act-of-being from another. And as whatever exists by another can be reduced to what is by itself as to its first cause, there must be one thing that is the cause by which all things exist, because it alone is the act-of-being. Otherwise we should have to go to infinity in causes, for anything that is not act-of-being only has a cause which makes it exist, as has been said."

Contrary to what we ourselves have once believed, this development is not intended by Thomas Aquinas to be a proof of the existence of God. It is not presented as such in *On Being and Essence*. Nor is it mentioned, in either one of the two *Summae,* as a supplementary way to the conclusion that there is a God. If one considers the problem closely enough, the reason why it should be so becomes apparent. An essential feature of a Thomistic way to the knowledge of the existence of God is that it should start from sense experience. Now, to the best of our knowledge, Thomas

Aquinas has never attempted such a demonstration. Nor does one see how the thing could be done. The distinction of essence and existence presupposes the very notion of the pure act of being which its alleged demonstrations are supposed to justify. What here is at stake is the metaphysical intuition of the first principle, which is the notion of being. At this highest metaphysical level, it is not a question of proof, but of sight.

The large number of Christian philosophers and theologians, even among the so-called Thomists, who have rejected the distinction of essence and existence understood in its Thomistic meaning, clearly shows that no demonstration is here at stake. Above all, the careful procedure of Thomas Aquinas himself in handling the notion invites us to consider it less as the conclusion of some dialectical argument than as a prime source of intelligibility whose existence is known by the very light it sheds upon all the problems of metaphysics. So Thomas Aquinas will not attempt to prove it, but we shall see him progressively leading us to it, starting from the very demonstrations of the existence of God, as if it were for him a question of purifying our sight until it becomes able to stand the light of the first principle.

In the present problem, the distinction of essence and existence throws into relief the existential nature both of the effect whose cause is being sought and of the very cause which explains it. This cause is a God whose essence is the very act-of-being *Deus cujus essentia est ipsummet esse suum*. A God of whom some go so far as to say that He has no essence or quiddity since He is all act-of-being: *non habet quidditatem vel essentiam, quia essentia sua non est aliud quam esse suum*. Otherwise put, God is actual being pure and simple, without any addition, distinct from any other existing thing because of His very purity, as a color existing in its pure state would differ from broken colors because of its purity and separation. Such is the God whom the proofs of St. Thomas strive for, but whom we only approach by meditation on that same Being whose existence they conclusively demonstrate.

This last aspect of the God of St. Thomas remains perhaps the least known by his interpreters. One hesitates between saying that it escapes them so often although it marks the point at which St. Thomas and Aristotle are farthest apart or that it escapes them for this very reason. In positing his immovable First Mover as a thinking thought, Aristotle had guaranteed the purity of the highest act by enclosing it in the splendor of divine isolation. Aristotle's God is not merely "separated" as ontologically distinct from everything else, but as ontologically absent from anything else. The only kind of presence He can fittingly have for things is the desire which they experience for Him and which moves them towards Him. Now this desire for God is their desire. It is of the being experiencing it, not of the being who is its term. It is quite otherwise in St. Thomas's world. The relation of things to God is defined there in the order of existence. This is why the dependence of things upon their principle attains there a depth that cannot be expressed either in Aristotle's language or Plato's. It is in its very existence that the universe of St. Thomas is a religious universe.

To formulate the relation of the world to God in the language of Plato, we must have recourse to the relations between image and model. St. Augustine normally used the same terminology and so too did St. Bonaventure and the thirteenth-century Augustinians. For all of these, the sensible world is a mirror in which reflections of God are to be found —a collection of images for an illustrated theology. The universe itself is indeed that. Christian spirituality could not consent to part with its divine "speculations" in the mirror of nature, so splendidly rationalized by St. Bonaventure, so divinely lived by St. Francis of Assisi. The question, then, is to know whether this kind of meditation gives an insight into the deepest metaphysical resemblance of things to God. The reply to this has to be affirmative, at least if the contemplation of God in the *being* of things penetrates to their *act-of-being*. It is true that things are good in so far as they are. It is true that they are beautiful. It is true that they are causes and that they have marvellous energy and fecundity in whatever they do. In all this they imitate God and represent Him. But the most marvellous of all the things a being can do is *to be*. Things exist, and this is what is most profound in them because in this they best imitate their cause. Herein lies the true meaning of the proofs for the existence of God—we come to *Him Who Is* by starting with those objects of which it can be said that they *are*. "Things which exist by God resemble Him, in so far as they are beings, as the first and universal principle of all that is."

20

THE EXISTENCE OF GOD IN ST. BONAVENTURE *

PHILOSOPHICAL reason has neither its origin nor its end in the natural universe: yet it must, as reason, conquer certain truths which, as systematized, form the very content of philosophy. The first, the most urgent is the existence of God; and it is also perhaps the easiest to seize, for it is in itself very evident—but this only if it presents itself in such a guise that nothing hinders us from perceiving it.

There are three errors which can hinder the effectiveness of the evidence of this truth: errors respectively of conception, of reasoning, of conclusion.

* We borrow the analysis of the arguments of St. Bonaventure (1221-1274) from Etienne Gilson's *Philosophy of St. Bonaventure*, trans. by Dom Illtyd Trethowan and F. J. Sheed (New York: Sheed & Ward, 1938), ch. III.

By the error of *conception* is meant a failure to understand fully and correctly the meaning of the word God. Such was the error, for instance, of the pagans, who saw in the term one particular attribute of God rather than God himself, and therefore applied it to any being superior to man and capable of foreseeing the future. Thus, owing to the incompleteness of their definition, they were able to adore idols and take them for gods, on the ground that they sometimes got—or thought they got—exact prophecies of things to come.

But further than that, errors of *reasoning* lie in wait for man—such as the folly of those who, from the fact that the wicked are not immediately punished for their crimes, argue to the absence of a universal order and therefore to the nonexistence of its author.

And finally doubt may arise from sheer incapacity to carry on a train of reasoning to its *conclusion:* for there are minds so immersed in matter that they cannot go beyond the data of sense but rest in the material world and think, as so many pagans thought, that as the world of bodies is the only reality, the lord of this visible world is the highest being conceivable; which is why the sun has found so many worshippers. So that —given the inability to *resolve*—that is, to pass beyond the appearances of things and discover their first principles—error and doubt are possible as to God's existence; but not for an intellect which defines, reasons and concludes correctly.

Yet there still remains the question of God's *cognoscibility*—to wit whether, even with all care for the proper functioning of our intellect, God does not by nature transcend us radically and so remains essentially unknowable to man. The answer is clear. Even before we come to the question of His existence, God appears to us as in Himself eminently knowable, as an object which by its own evidence offers itself to the grasp of our intellect. The word "to know" can mean two things: "to comprehend" and "to apprehend." To comprehend an object, one must be equal to it, in order to embrace it in its totality, and in this sense it is obvious that we cannot know God. But to apprehend a thing even though it may in itself exceed the limits of our understanding, it is sufficient that its truth should become manifest to us, that its presence should be attested to us by evidence. Now no reason can be shown why we should be incapable of apprehending God. In itself, such a being is at once the supreme intelligible, and the first principle of all our knowing. While if we consider ourselves, though our faculty of knowing is deficient and must so remain till we attain the Light of Glory, yet we are remarkably adapted to the knowledge—that is the apprehension—of such an object.

It might be urged in objection that there is a greater distance between our created intellect and the Uncreated Truth than between our senses and the intelligible element in things; and since our senses, which perceive the sensible, never rise to the intelligible, *a fortiori* our intellect cannot possibly rise to God. Such an objection confuses the categories of being and knowing; there is indeed a greater difference of *being* between the infinite God and a finite intellect than between finite senses and a finite intelligible. But from the viewpoint of *knowing*, the distance is less between the intellect and God than between the senses and the intelligible; for God and the soul belong to the same order of the intelligible, whereas sense and intellect do not.

Again it might be said that the finite cannot apprehend the infinite. But we must distinguish the infinity of mass—which involves extension in space and multiplicity—from absolute infinity, which implies perfect simplicity. God is an absolute infinite, perfectly simple: and while a finite body cannot apprehend an infinite mass (whose *infinity* is not at one instant present at any one of its points) yet a finite mind can apprehend an infinite that is perfectly simple: for if it apprehends it in one point, it apprehends it in its entirety; but one cannot *comprehend* it, for, though it is present in its entirety in every point inasmuch as it is simple, it is not comprehended in any, inasmuch as it is infinite. St. Augustine before St. Bonaventure and Descartes after him, have shown very forcibly the difference between comprehending an object by thought and making contact with it by thought; but neither of them seems to have shown with the same metaphysical profundity that the infinite can be apprehended only as infinite, by reason of its simplicity, despite the fact that it exceeds the compass of thought by reason of its infinity.

There remains a third objection—that for such an object no mode of knowing is conceivable. God must inform our intellect in order to be known by it; but He cannot become its form in any sense of the word; nor can He inform it by means of an image which our intellect would draw from Him by abstraction, for, to the sound Aristotelian, the image abstracted is more spiritual than the object it is abstracted from; and nothing can be more spiritual than God. But we shall have to see later whether there is not another mode of knowing God—whether it may not be that God—who is present to our soul and to every intellect by truth—informs it by means of a knowledge which He imprints upon it and which it does not abstract, a knowledge inferior to God since it is in man, but superior to the soul since it enriches it. A priori then, there is no sort of impossibility standing between the soul and the knowledge of God.

We can even go further. Not only God is not unknowable by man; the knowledge we have of Him is evident and easily acquired. We may take any one of three different ways of arriving at the fact of His existence; and each of these three brings us to a certitude as complete as it is humanly possible to desire.

The first way is based on the fact that the existence of God is a truth naturally innate in every rational soul. This "innateness" does imply that man sees God by His essence; it does necessarily imply even that he possesses by nature and with no sort of effort an exact knowledge of what the divine nature is; when we speak of an innate knowledge of God's existence, it is of His *existence* alone that we make the affirmation. Hugh of St. Victor gives the definite formula of this *innatism* when he says that God has measured out the knowledge man has of Him in such a way that we can never either totally comprehend His essence or be in total ignorance of His existence. It is essential to understand exactly what St. Bonaventure held on this delicate point.

To grasp his thought in all its complexity, we must first pose the problem in the precise terms that St. Bonaventure had inherited and adopted from St. Augustine. The question with which the philosophers of the school were above all preoccupied was whether the human soul can or cannot be ignorant of God. The affirmation of the innateness of the idea of God does, at first sight, come into collision with the plain fact that idolaters adore statues of wood and stone: how could this be, if the idea of God were inseparable from man's mind and born with it?

The reason, replies St. Bonaventure, is that between absolute knowledge of God and absolute ignorance, there are many possible degrees: above all there is a great difference between error as to His nature and ignorance of His existence. One knows God, in a sense at least, even when one holds mistaken views about Him. One man—the pagan, for instance, asserts that God is what in reality He is not: another asserts that God is not what He is—accuses Him, for instance, of not being just because He does not at once punish the impious: but each of them, though wrong about God's nature, affirms his existence. We may agree that *indirectly* they deny the existence of God, in this sense that what they affirm or deny is incompatible with the divine essence; but it cannot be said that the idolator is totally devoid of any idea of God, nor that he thinks that God does not exist. On the contrary, it is indeed God whose existence he affirms while in error as to His nature: and this can be proved.

In this sense St. Bonaventure interprets the famous phrase of St. John Damascene: *Nemo mortalium est, cui non hoc ab eo naturaliter insitum est, ut deum esse cognoscat.* Whereas St. Thomas reduces this to a mere affirmation of the innateness of that whereby we may acquire the knowledge of God, St. Bonaventure finds in it the formal assertion of the innateness of this knowledge itself—incomplete knowledge, assuredly, but one which excludes doubt and which all we see within us helps to make manifest. The thought of man aspires to wisdom, but the most desirable wisdom is that which is eternal; therefore it is above all the love of this wisdom that is innate in the human mind. But it is impossible to love that of which one is absolutely ignorant: therefore some kind of knowledge of this supreme wisdom must be innate in the human soul, and this is primarily to know that God Himself or Wisdom exists. The same line of thought may be applied to our desire of happiness; since such a desire cannot be conceived without a certain knowledge of its object, it follows that we must have an innate knowledge of the existence of God who is our Sovereign Good. The same again applies to our thirst for peace, for the peace of a rational being can reside only in a Being immutable and eternal; but this thirst supposes a notion or a knowledge of its object; the knowledge of a being immutable and eternal is then naturally innate in every rational mind.

How could it be otherwise? The soul is present to itself and knows itself directly, but God is eminently present to the soul, and just as the soul is intelligible to itself, so also is God. We have then an intelligible present to an intelligible. And though this supreme intelligible be superior—even so infinitely superior that there is no proportion at all between it and the being in which it resides—this fact proves nothing against the possibility of such a knowledge. In fact if, for knowledge, it were necessary that there should be proportion between the knowing subject and its object, the human mind would never arrive at any knowledge of God at all, for it cannot be proportioned to God by nature, by grace or by glory. But the proportion that would be required for a knowledge adequate to its object—and especially for a definition of essence—is not required for a mere awareness of its existence. A mere relation of aptitude, a certain compatibility suffice for an infinite God to be naturally knowable to us. And such a relation exists. The soul, as has been said, is naturally apt to know all because it can be likened to all; add further that it is specially apt to know God by this way of assimilation, because it is made in His image and likeness. Our innate knowledge of the existence of God is thus rooted in a profound harmony between the two intelligibles, of which the one is the cause and the archetype of the other.

The second line of proof of the existence of God is by way of creatures, the reason making a simple application of the principle of causality. By this principle we may rightly argue not only from cause to effect, but as legitimately from effect to cause; if God is truly the cause of things, it must be possible to discover Him in His effects. And this should be all the easier because the sensible is a way naturally leading to the intelligible and for an intellect wedded with matter as ours is, it would be actually impossible to seize God in His pure spirituality. So that we may rightly begin with his creatures in our approach to Him.

Given this, it matters little what starting point the reason chooses. Things are deficient in being not accidentally, nor according to one or other of their properties; they are essentially inadequate and incapable of self-sufficiency. So that if reason, armed with the principle of causality, sets out to develop the manifold relations binding cause and effect, any reflection or any property of the thing caused leads at once to the cause. Now things are quite obviously imperfect and finite, hence caused; but if there is anything that is brought into being, there must be a first being, for effect implies cause; if there is anything that is dependent upon another for its origin, its operation and its purpose, there must be a being that exists by itself, of itself and for itself; if there is a being that is composit, there must be, as the source of its existence, a being that is simple—for composition is an absence of simplicity; if there is a being compounded of potentiality and actuality, there must be one that is pure actuality, for nothing created is pure actuality; if there is a being in motion, there must be one unmoved, for motion is based on that which moves not—as the motion of the hand upon the relative immobility of the elbow, the motion of the elbow on the fixity of the shoulder, and so on; if there is a relative being, there must be an absolute—for every creature is in some genus or other: but what represents only one of the genera of being can account neither for itself nor for being: so that there must be an absolute being whence all others derive such being as they have.

From this it is immediately evident that the proofs St. Bonaventure bases upon the things of sense are offered to us with a certain unconcern. In any one of these lines of proof, he treats the starting-point as a matter of comparative indifference: and so no one of them is worked out with anything remotely resembling the carefully dovetailed argumentation of St. Thomas. This fact has been seized upon often enough as showing how unelaborated his thought was, and how he may have regretted, on this as on other points, that he did not make better use of the text of Aristotle, which shows how fundamentally critics have mistaken the significance and true direction of his thought.

The choice of a starting-point for these proofs appears to be a matter of indifference to him, and it so appears because he really held it so. What is more, he held it better not to choose, but rather to mass together as many proofs as possible, founded on the most diverse imaginable phenomena or natural properties. What, after all, was his purpose? Not to elaborate four or five proofs convincing by their own solidity, but rather to show that God is so universally attested by nature that His existence is almost self-evident, and scarcely needs demonstration.

St. Thomas is insistent that God's existence is not self-evident: obviously then he must give his whole mind to the choice of one of many starting-points specially apt for his purpose, and to the logical development of his proof. St. Bonaventure, on the other hand, insists that the whole of nature proclaims God's existence as a truth beyond the reach of doubt, if only we will take the trouble to look; in fact he is simply following out the Franciscan feeling of God's presence in nature, when he passes before us in review the long series of creatures each in its own way proclaiming the existence of God.

Just as he does not mind which of created things he takes as his starting-point, so he is not concerned to construct logical proofs to any great degree of elaboration. For to him proofs from things of sense are proofs not because they bring into play notions belonging to the intelligible order which imply God's existence. Any chain of reasoning must lose much of its significance, if it uses some prior experience sufficient of itself to prove the same conclusion. But, held St. Bonaventure, this is so here: our experience of God's existence is the very condition of the inference by which we claim to establish that God exists.

We think we are starting from strictly sensible data when we state as the first step in our demonstration that there are in existence beings mutable, composite, relative, imperfect, contingent: but in actual fact we are aware of these insufficiencies in things only because we already possess the idea of the perfections by whose standard we see them to be insufficient. So that it is only in appearance and not in reality that our demonstration begins with sense data. Our awareness, apparently immediate and primary, of the contingent implies an already existent knowledge of the necessary.

But the necessary is God: so that the human mind discovers that it already possesses a knowledge of the First Being when it sets out to prove that He exists.

Thus viewed, the proofs from the sense world in the systems of St. Bonaventure and St. Thomas are not really comparable. If the idea of God is innate, the world of sense cannot enable us to construct it, but only to discover it within ourselves: and the idea itself must of necessity be our real, if unrecognized, starting-point. Looked at more closely, the starting-point turns out to be the goal. If we have in us the idea of God, we are sure that He exists, for we cannot think of Him as nonexistent.

The second way then brings us back to the first; and the first opens up the third—that the existence of God is a fact immediately evident.

From the *Commentary* to the end of his career St. Bonaventure remained on this point the faithful disciple of St. Anselm. The existence of God, considered in itself, is absolutely evident.

A first principle is such that, once we understand the terms in which it is stated, we accept its truth: it does not require proof, because, in such a proposition, the predicate is implied in the subject. The proposition *God is* is of such a sort; for God, the supreme truth, is being itself, and such that nothing more perfect can be conceived; therefore He cannot not be, and the intrinsic necessity of His being is such that in some way it is reflected in our thought.

It is possible not to know what is meant by the word God: and one who is wrong about His essence will certainly not discover the necessity of His existence. But, if one knows, whether by reasoning or experience, or the teaching of faith, what the word means: or if one does but consider the innate idea of God that all men possess by nature; then the necessary existence of the divine being in itself will become a necessity also for our thought, and we shall be unable to think of Him as other than existence. It matters little, then, how the arguments are constructed: whatever the way, direct or round-about, they all bring us finally to one same identity.

Clearly, St. Bonaventure was very strongly drawn towards a still fuller simplification of the argument of St. Anselm, direct as it already was: by a rapid, though closely articulated, dialectical process the *Proslogion* constrains the mind to posit God as the being than which no greater can be conceived: but the dialectical process is now simplified by St. Bonaventure to the point of vanishing altogether.

For St. Anselm, the definition of God implied a content which our thought had to unfold in order to get at the conclusion involved in it. For St. Bonaventure, the same definition becomes an immediate evidence, because it participates in the necessity of its content. The metaphysical substratum of the proof, which St. Anselm was certainly feeling for, here attains full self-consciousness: it is because the necessity of the divine being is communicated to the mind thinking of Him that a mere definition can turn out to be a proof. Thus one might say: *tanta est veritas divini esse quod non potest cogitari non esse;* or rather, since that which cannot not be is greater than that which can not be, the being than which none greater can be conceived necessarily exists. But the formula can be simplified still further, and since the assertion of God's existence is founded upon the intrinsic evidence of the idea of God, it should suffice to place this idea before our eyes to ensure our perceiving its necessity; and since the antecedent is evident, the conclusion is evident likewise.

If we reflect upon the conditions on which rests the possibility of a knowledge of so exceptional an order, they will appear to be twofold. First, the necessity of the object. An argument of this sort is valid for God and for no other being; to urge as an objection, as was urged against St. Anselm, the case of an island such that none more beautiful can be conceived, is to show a lack of understanding of the problem involved. When we say "a being such that no greater can be conceived," no contradiction appears between the subject and the predicate: therefore, it is a perfectly conceivable idea. But when we say an island such that none more perfect can be conceived we are stating a contradiction, for an island is by definition an imperfect being: an imperfect being than which none more beautiful can be conceived is a contradiction in terms; and obviously one cannot prove the *existence* of anything by means of a definition which is contradictory and therefore impossible.

But it is not enough that the object of our knowledge should be necessary in itself. The necessity of its being is grounded upon identity in it of essence and existence; now this identity must be manifested to us in the identity of subject and predicate if this is to be a basis upon which the necessity of our judgment may rest. But such a transfer of necessity from the being to the judgment of the being is not mere hypothesis: it takes place really each time we think of Being, and it is in the profound metaphysical relation, in the relationship which binds the soul to God, that we must seek the ultimate justification for St. Anselm's argument and for all other proofs for the existence of God.

It is not that St. Bonaventure fails to realize the infinite distance separating human thought from such an object, but we have already noted that a being infinitely remote from another in the order of being can be immediately present to it in the order of knowledge; for this it is enough that these two beings should be analogous in nature even though they do not realize their nature in the same degree. The soul and God are two intelligibles. If our intellect were a pure intelligence like that of the angels, it would be able, without ever arriving at a total comprehension of God, to see Him perfectly, to seize the identity of His essence and existence; but even short of that, it can in virtue of such intelligibility as it has, seize the identity of the idea of His essence with the idea of His existence. And if it is sufficient that the idea of God should be in us, to enable us to posit the existence of its object, it is because there is no ontological argument in the sense in which Kant understood it. St. Bonaventure does not pass (illicitly) from the idea of the being; the idea is for him simply the mode whereby the being is present in his thought; there is therefore no real gap to be bridged between the idea of a God whose existence is necessary, and this same God necessarily existing.

Further, it would be a serious error to see in this attitude of the Seraphic Doctor nothing more than an unconscious dogmatism; never was dogmatism more aware of itself, nor more firmly based upon its metaphysical foundations. With St. Bonaventure the truths presupposed in St. Anselm's argument come into the foreground and, shown in their full evidence, in some sense absorb the proof. If, in fact, the line of argument of the *Proslogion* draws its value from the profound contact that our idea of God maintains with its object, it is rather the realization of this action of God in our thought that constitutes the proof of His existence, and not the analytical working out of the consequences involved in the notion we have of Him.

The problem then is reducible to the question whether God is or is not an object proportionate to our thought. We can be certain that He is; and we should have no hesitation on the point if we did not fall into the error of conceiving intellectual knowledge as analogous to sense knowledge. Every sensation implies an organ, that is a certain grouping of elements, organized and ordered in a definite proportion: a sensible object which lacks power to impress itself upon this organ remains unperceived, but a sensible object which exceeds its capacity introduces a disturbance into the organ and threatens its destruction—too bright a light dazzles, too loud a noise deafens. Further, the action which affects the sense organ is a kind of intrusion from without, since the object that excites it is normally an exterior object; so that it can be the cause of trouble. Finally, the sense does not turn inwards to perceive its object; on the contrary, it tends outwards, emerges from itself, is in a sense dispersed, so that it must inevitably be weakened. Intellectual knowledge is totally different; it depends upon no bodily organ and therefore no object can be disproportioned to it, either by excess or defect; on the contrary, it may be said that the more excellent an object is, the more easily will the mind comprehend it, for such an object of knowledge acts from within—that is, it penetrates our faculty of knowing and instead of being a cause of trouble to it, aids it, strengthens it, facilitates the exercise of its operation. St. Bonaventure illustrates this by a striking comparison: if mountains gave us the strength to carry them, we should carry a large mountain more easily than a small since the larger mountain would give us more strength than the small; just so, the divine intelligible aids our intellect to know in proportion to its immensity; and aids it all the more, in that it is for our knowledge not an exterior object only to be attained by our mind ranging outside itself, but an interior object about which it may recollect itself and so gain strength. It is therefore the irradiation of the divine object itself in the interior of our souls which is the metaphysical foundation of the knowledge we have of it, and it is in the order of being that St. Anselm's argument here finds its final justification.

We may now see how St. Anselm's argument from the idea of God is practically identical in St. Bonaventure's eyes with St. Augustine's argument from the existence of truth. This is so not only because truth is in fact God Himself, but also because each particular truth implies the existence of an absolute truth whereof it is the effect. Therefore to affirm any individual truth at all is to affirm the existence of God. This is even more perfectly evident if instead of affirming the truth of a particular proposition one affirms the existence of truth in general; for if one denies the existence of truth, the very declaration that truth does not exist implies that it is true that truth does not exist: if this is true, then something is true; and if something is true, then the first Truth exists. Therefore one cannot deny the existence of truth or the existence of God without in that very act affirming the thing denied.

Clearly these arguments of St. Augustine re-stated by St. Bonaventure imply the same metaphysic of being that is the basis of St. Anselm's argument. It is not in virtue of a purely dialectical analysis of abstract concepts that we can, starting from no judgment at all, proceed immediately to infer the existence of God; it is not simply a logical repugnance that makes it impossible for us to deny the existence of God without contradicting ourselves; this repugnance is but a sign of a metaphysical impossibility with which we are in conflict. If God is present in our soul by the truth which we discover therein, how can we deny Him in His own name? Since we know nothing save by His light, how can we affirm in the name of that light that the first light does not exist? This radical impossibility of denying God is therefore the effect left upon the face of our soul by the divine light.

Thus, the proofs of God's existence as St. Bonaventure states them support each other. What is more, they seem so closely related to one another that neither we, nor even he, can easily make any rigorous separation between them. We cannot return to the origin of any of them without returning to the same starting-point—a relationship between the soul and God such that God manifests Himself in the soul, is present there in the truth that it apprehends and is more interior to it than it is to itself—in a word, a natural aptitude of the soul to perceive God.

The definite orientation of St. Bonaventure's thought dooms to futility every effort to bring it within the same historic framework as that of St. Thomas. Such attempts may be more or less ingenious, and some of them indeed are of a very high philosophical quality; but if it is the task of philosophy to harmonize, it is the task of history to distinguish. St. Bonaventure's proofs and St. Thomas' cannot be placed in the same category save by each one leaving the category proper to it for an imaginary category invented by the historian. Such it would seem is the case with the celebrated *implicit* knowledge of God attributed by Lepidi and his disciples both to St. Bonaventure and to St. Thomas.

As far as St. Bonaventure is concerned we may unhesitatingly agree that his doctrine does in fact concede to man an implicit knowledge of God. The actual expression is used by him, and in the most definite way: *Omnia cognoscentia cognoscunt implicite Deum in quolibet cognito. Sicut enim nihil habet rationem appetibilis nisi per similitudinem primae bonitatis, ita nihil est cognoscibile nisi per similitudinem primae veritatis.* He even teaches more than once that we have a confused innate knowledge of God's existence, in so far as we naturally desire beatitude and we must of necessity have a certain knowledge of what we desire. But we must be clear as to the *Thomist* sense of the word "implicit"; it can be interpreted either as applying to something already virtually existent which has only to be developed like a seed, or as applying to something underdetermined to which some further addition will give determination. Now it seems clear that in such a system as that of St. Thomas no knowledge of God can be implicit in the first sense. It is impossible to suppose that any knowledge whatsoever should be originally given to us in the intellect itself. Since our intellect is, to begin with, a *tabula rasa* on which nothing is yet written, the idea of God is no more inscribed thereon than any other idea, and there is not a single text of St. Thomas that authorizes us to suppose that it is in any manner pre-formed in the intellect. If his philosophy allows the mind any innate content, we shall owe a great debt of gratitude to the historian who can show that it does. Meanwhile the interpretation which seems to me inescapable is the only one that the fundamental principles of his system allow: our intellect, a *tabula rasa*, contains originally no idea of God.

If the idea of God does not exist implicitly in the intellect itself, does it at least exist in the first of the ideas formed by the intellect, the idea of being? Notice first that as a consequence of the principle already studied, this first idea itself is not developed by the intellect as a virtuality drawn from its own substance: it is acquired and formed by contact with the sensible as all our ideas are to be. Its mode of birth already settles what its mode of development will be: just as the idea of being was not virtually pre-formed in the human intellect before any sensible experience, so equally it does not contain, virtually pre-formed, any distinct idea of God. It is neither in itself, nor in the idea it forms, that the soul possesses implicit knowledge of God; it is in its object, and it is there that it must necessarily seek it. The true signification of the term implicit is therefore not "virtual," but confused and indeterminate. And it is not from the content of the idea of being that thought, drawing upon its own substance, will bring forth the clear idea of God; it is a series of determinations, added to the idea of being by the intellect, in the course of its exploration of the world of sense, which is to determine and build up the idea of God.

If we examine every text of St. Thomas where there is any question of this confused natural knowledge, it will be seen that he nowhere presents the human soul as in possession of a notion whereof the content is to develop of itself, but only as in the presence of an object of which it has not yet explored all the riches or defined the nature.

Assuredly the object is present to the intellect, and, since the intellect apprehends it, it knows it in a certain manner; but the human soul can never draw from its natural desire of beatitude or its natural idea of being more than they actually contain, if it confines itself to this knowledge and love alone. The implicit virtualities that it hopes to find there are not contained in them, but only in the object—or in itself in so far as it is capable of becoming its own object. To render its implicit knowledge of God determined, our intellect then must have recourse to the sense experience by which in the first place it acquired this implicit knowledge. From the beginning of his career to the end St. Thomas never taught otherwise; intellectual light is a means of knowing, it is never an object known. A man may maintain the contrary and call himself a Thomist, but he is thinking as an Augustinian.

Very different is the position adopted by St. Bonaventure in face of this capital problem. He begins by distinguishing between two questions —the question of God's nature and the question of God's existence. It is possible to be in ignorance as to His nature, but not to be in ignorance concerning His existence; Christians, Jews, Saracens, even idolaters, all agree in admitting that a God exists, though they do not agree as to the nature of this God. If then we ask what can be implicit in the knowledge of God, attributed to us by St. Bonaventure, we arrive at the conclusion that it is solely the knowledge of the divine essence. Not only may the idolater fall into error as to the nature of God; we know that every reason not illuminated by the light of faith must of necessity fall into error. There is no natural reason, no matter how high, that can by its own strength rise to the idea of one God in three divine persons, and the experience of natural philosophy before the coming of Christ is a standing proof of this. Prior to revelation men were limited to an implicit knowledge of the Trinity. And this was attained by the best of them when they discerned, by the unaided effort of their reason, the attributes proper to persons whom they knew not.

But the thesis leaves the question of God's *existence* intact. Since in effect St. Bonaventure, differing from St. Thomas, holds that man has an innate idea of God and His existence, the knowledge we have of Him is necessarily inseparable from our thought; this it is which finds exterior manifestation in the gestures of the idolater and the beliefs of the heretic; it sets in motion our desire for God, directing it towards happiness, peace and goodness.

Thus upon this point we are obviously brought face to face with two profoundly different theories of knowledge: for St. Bonaventure the "implicit" really is the virtual—which can be developed from within, because, as we shall see, it does not distinguish intellect from the soul as an accident is distinguished from its substance; therefore it makes possible a direct presence of the soul to itself; and thereby allows it to decipher in its own substance the image which the Creator impressed upon it in the beginning. If this is really so, the human intellect is not a nucleus of white light which casts out its rays over objects to outline their contours: it is rather the direct movement of an intelligible substance (which is the soul), this substance being rendered intelligible by the presence of the divine action; that is why the implicit, which attains determination in St. Thomas by the intellectual exploration of the sensible, attains determination in St. Bonaventure by a deeper exploration of itself, by a progressive and increasingly powerful recognition of the intimate relationship which binds the human soul to God.

The same difference of point of view emerges again if St. Bonaventure is asked the question posed by St. Thomas: is the existence of God a *res per se nota?* There is a difficulty here in that the answer St. Bonaventure would give implies a question formulated somewhat differently. What the Seraphic Doctor asks is whether God's existence is a *verum indubitabile,* that is a truth that no right thought can possibly cast in doubt. To a question thus worded, St. Bonaventure replies in the affirmative and without the smallest reservation: God's existence is a truth which in no way lacks evidence, whether in itself or from the point of view of the proofs which establish it, or in regard to the knowledge we have of it. But it would be a mistake to identify the *verum indubitabile* of St. Bonaventure with the *per se notum* of St. Thomas. In Thomist doctrine the *per se notum* is a proposition such that its truth appears the moment the terms are understood in which it is constituted; but the *verum indubitabile* of St. Bonaventure is something simpler still, since the presence of the innate idea of God in our thought suffices of itself to prove His existence; on the other hand it may be more complex, since we sometimes reason from contingent things or particular truths to the existence of God.

In one case, that of St. Anselm's argument, both philosophers treat of a proposition whose predicate is necessarily included in its subject. But here the conflict between St. Thomas and St. Bonaventure is purely exterior and verbal, because the notions upon which the proof draws are not of the same order for both of them. When St. Thomas denies that the existence of God may become a thing self-evident, he is speaking of a concept constructed by our intellect by an innate faculty from materials drawn from the world of sense; but God is not included in the field of sense experience; a concept, therefore, drawn from that field cannot give us the intuition of His existence, but can only teach us as much as may be inferred by means of a causal and analogical line of reasoning. Our concept of the Divine essence grows progressively as we demonstrate God's existence; being the result of the proof, it cannot be its basis.

St. Bonaventure would undoubtedly agree that given such a theory of knowledge, God's existence can never be self-evident; but the idea of God that he attributes to us is of a very different nature. It is not an analogical construction of our intellect, it is innate; and it is not *our* activity that is its origin; we must know whence it comes, we must explain it by a cause. Thus St. Bonaventure dares to maintain that the simplest explanation of our idea of God is God. An idea which comes neither from things nor from ourselves can come from none other than God; it is in us as the mark left by God upon His work; it is therefore eminently qualified to attest irrefutably the existence of its object. The presence of the idea of God in the human soul would be unintelligible if it did not manifest the presence there, by way of truth, of a God truly existent.

Finally the very idea of a proof of God's existence does not refer to the same intellectual operation in the two systems. For St. Thomas, a proof remains what it is, no matter at what moment the intellect considers it: anyone who can understand the terms and the chain of propositions of which the proof from the First Mover is composed can understand and prove in his turn that God exists. For St. Bonaventure, by reason of the mystical turn of his mind, each kind of proof corresponds to a definite stage of the soul's return to God by ecstasy, and their order of succession depends upon the degree to which the human soul is penetrated by grace. The proofs of God's existence based upon the world of sense form in reality the first part of the soul's journey to God; already, therefore, they presuppose a supernatural aid, if not for their constitution as a logical series, at least that the mind may gain from them the uttermost evidence that is in them. The proofs of God's existence based upon the existence of truth, and St. Anselm's proof based upon the idea of God, demand still more—a purification of the soul by the acquisition of the virtues, a drawing upwards of the intellect and the will for which St. Bonaventure's mysticism is an initiation. They reveal their true meaning only to the soul already at the summit of the interior life and about to make contact with God by love.

Thus by reason of a difference in initial attitude, which later I shall have to discuss more closely, the two great mediaeval philosophers do not study the fundamental problem of God's existence in the same terms. That is why the solutions they offer are not strictly comparable. The replies of one can only be adapted to the questions formulated by the other if we adopt a point of view which belongs to neither of them.

1

PROOFS OF THE EXISTENCE OF GOD BY JOHN DUNS SCOTUS *

I. DOES AN ACTUALLY INFINITE BEING EXIST?

The proof falls into two principal parts, one dealing with the relative properties of the infinite being, viz. efficiency, finality, and eminent perfection; the second with the absolute property of actual infinity. The unicity of God, the subject of the following question, might be called the third part. Each of these parts includes several stages. There are three for instance, in regard to the demonstration of the relative properties. The first stage consists in proving that each of the three ways (efficiency, finality, and relative perfection) terminates in an actually existing being that is first in that respective order. What is interesting to note is that Scotus, unlike Henry of Ghent, or for that matter, St. Thomas, does not pause here to tell us that this first cause, or this ultimate end, or this supreme nature is God. In fact, he almost seems loath to use this term until he believes he has established the existence of a being so different and unique among existing things that we can attribute this name to it in a meaningful fashion. Consequently, in the second stage he proceeds to show that we can put an "equal sign," as it were, between the heads of the three orders. A first efficient cause will also be an ultimate end and vice versa. The third step is to show that this prerogative of being a first efficient cause, an ultimate reason, a supreme being in some hierarchy of things is not a trait that is common to several different kinds of beings, but a relative property of but one kind of being. It never will be, nor can it ever be, characteristic of more than one kind of nature. It is not, in a word, a specific trait, or still less, a generic property. That it is in addition an individual property, Scotus puts off to the last question: Is there but one God or infinite being?

This being then can meaningfully be called the *Ens Primum*. The second part of the proof, then, attempts to go beyond these relative traits to reveal some of the absolute properties of this first nature. The goal of this portion of the proof is to demonstrate that "some existing being is actually infinite." As preliminary steps to establishing infinity, Scotus essays to show that nothing can possess the relative attribute of the triple primacy without possessing knowledge, and love or volition.

* The following pages are the main part of the analysis of the demonstration of Duns Scotus (1265-1308) read by Allan B. Wolter, O.F.M., at the twenty-eighth meeting of the American Catholic Philosophical Association. Cf. *Proceedings*, Catholic University of America, 1954, p. 99.

Furthermore, this knowledge and love are identical with its substance. Finally, the knowledge of such a being is actually infinite. With these conclusions as premises Scotus sets up his proof that this being itself is actually infinite. The question "Does an actually infinite being exist?" then can be answered in the affirmative. In the question that follows, he raises the problem: "Can more than one such being exist?" or "Is there more than one God?" Contrary to many of the other scholastics, including his own teacher, William of Ware, Scotus believed that the unicity of God can be demonstrated. It is not simply an article of faith. His proof is based on the contradictions that arise from the assumption of more than one infinite intellect, infinite will, infinite good, infinite power, infinitely perfect being, or one absolutely necessary being. . . .

Part One: Proof of the Triple Primacy

(p. 101) In practically all versions of the proof, Scotus concerns himself simply with setting up what he considers to be the demonstration proper. Only by accident, as it were, do we discover later why he began the way he did and what he considered the basis for the truth and evidence of his initial premise. I say initial premise, because the proof is in form of an enthymeme, or rather a series of enthymemes.

The first conclusion he seeks to demonstrate is the possibility of an efficient cause which is first in the sense that it is not produced by any other efficient cause, nor does it depend on any such cause for the exercise of its causality. His proof runs as follows: "Something can be effected; therefore it is either produced by itself or by nothing or by something other than itself; not by nothing, for nothing produces nothing; nor by itself for nothing makes or begets itself; therefore it is produced by another. Call this other *a*. Now if *a* is the first efficient cause in the sense defined, well and good, our thesis is admitted. If, then, it is dependent on another efficient cause for either its being or its effectiveness, call this other *b*, and proceed as before. Either it is first, or it depends on another. Thus we have an infinite regress where every cause is itself secondary or dependent on some prior cause, or we have a first. But since a circle in causes is excluded and an infinite regress in an ascending order is impossible, a primary is necessary."

In typical dialectic fashion, Scotus raises two objections to this argument. We shall consider only the second for the present since it throws light on why he began his proof the way he did. The proof, it would seem, proceeds from contingent propositions and consequently is not a demonstration, for the premises assume the existence of something caused, and every such thing exists contingently. In answer Scotus replies: "I could indeed argue that some nature is effected because some subject undergoes change and therefore the term of change comes into existence in the subject, and consequently this term or composite is produced or effected. Formulated in this fashion, the first argument would be based on contingent but manifest propositions. However, to prove our conclusion, the argument can be reworded in such a way that it proceeds from necessary premises. Thus it is true that some nature is able to be effected, therefore, something is able to produce an effect. The antecedent is proved from this that something can be changed, for something is possible (possible being defined as opposed to necessary being) and this proposition follows from its essential or its possible being, and hence proceeds from necessary propositions."

(p. 105) The second objection Scotus raises to his demonstration is that the pagan philosophers and their followers admit that an infinity in an ascending order exists. On the assumption that the world is eternal and the process of generation and corruption of forms has gone on from all eternity, as Aristotle claimed, the famous problem: Is the egg or the chicken first? is meaningless, for there was never a first egg nor a first chicken.

In answer to this objection, Scotus calls attention to the distinction between essentially and accidentally ordered causes. This is not the classical distinction between *per se* and *per accidens* for the parent is a *per se* cause of the child. The distinction regards not primarily the being but the act of causation itself. Any cause that needs the co-causality of a second cause in the act of exercising its causality, depends on that second cause essentially, not accidentally. Such a relationship would obtain between the four classical causes of Aristotle. A material cause cannot "matter" unless a formal cause "forms" and vice versa. These intrinsic causes in turn depend essentially on extrinsic causes and according to the Aristotelian and mediaeval conceptions a hierarchy of efficient causes essentially ordered also existed. In the Christian notion of the relationship of God to the world, all secondary causes are related to the First Cause by an essential order of efficiency, for God must cooperate with them or at least conserve them and their powers in being.

(p. 107) Next Scotus sets up three propositions. First, an infinity of essentially ordered causes is impossible. Secondly, an infinity of accidentally ordered causes is impossible unless based on an essential order. Thirdly, if an essential order is denied, infinity is still impossible. The objection from the possibility of an infinite regress in causes then is invalid.

(p. 109) Consequently, some possible efficient cause must be first in the sense that it was never produced by any other efficient cause, nor does it depend on any such for the exercise of its causality.

Then we see the necessity of the first conclusion:

1) *It is possible that something is first in the order of efficient causality.* From this the second conclusion follows:

2) *A cause that is first in this sense is wholly uncaused.* That it has no efficient cause is clear. But if that be so it can have no final, nor material, nor formal cause. The reason is based on the mutual implications of causes. . . . From these two conclusions, the actual existence of the first cause can be inferred.

3) *Something first in the order of efficient causality actually exists and*

some nature actually existing is first in this way. This conclusion need cause no wonder, for it is a perfectly valid inference from the other two conclusions. . . . What has no cause can be possible only by being actual. If a first efficient cause is possible, it must exist. *Ab oportere ad esse valet illatio.*

Three similar conclusions follow regarding the order of finality. First, an ultimate end is possible, secondly it is totally uncaused, thirdly it actually exists. We shall not go into his proofs but simply note that he. employs the Aristotelian axiom used generally by the scholastics: *Omne agens agit propter finem.* Since an effect is possible only if an efficient cause is possible, and efficiency implies finality, the initial premise of the first way also provides the starting point of the *via finalitatis.*

Since the end must exceed in perfection anything which was given existence only for the sake of the end, an order of relative perfection must also exist. In such a hierarchy a most perfect thing exists. Hence Scotus draws three more conclusions. In the order of relative perfection a supreme nature is possible, secondly, it is uncaused, thirdly, it actually exists.

With the establishment of this triple primacy, the *first step* in the proof of the relative attributes is achieved.

The second is to show that each of these primacies implies the others. Scotus does this by way of two conclusions, the first of which is this: *A first efficient cause is also an ultimate end.* Proof is found in the way in which agent and end are related. "Every *per se* efficient cause acts for the sake of an end, and a prior cause for a prior end; therefore, the first cause acts for the sake of the highest end. But the first efficient cause does not act primarily or ultimately for the sake of anything other than itself; hence it must act for its own sake as for an end, and therefore the first efficient cause is the highest end. For if it were to act *per se* for the sake of an end other than itself, then something would exceed it in nobility, for if the end were anything apart from the agent intending the end, it would be more noble than the agent."

(p. 111) *The first efficient cause is also the supreme nature.* The proof is very brief. "Since the first cause is not a univocal but an equivocal cause with regard to the other efficient causes, it is therefore more eminent and noble than they, therefore the cause which is first is the most eminent."

The *third and final step* in the first part of the proof is to show that the threefold primacy is characteristic of but one kind of nature. The reason Scotus seems to have introduced this as a special conclusion is because of the notions the pagan philosophers held regarding the Intelligences. Some might object that these inferior "gods" could conceivably differ from one another in essence and nature and yet in regard to their immediate effects enjoy this triple primacy.

Scotus draws a preliminary conclusion: 1) *The efficient cause which*

possesses the aforesaid triple primacy is of itself necessary existence.
2) From this first conclusion, the principal thesis of this part can be inferred: *The triple primacy is a property of but one kind of nature.*
Three proofs are given. The first exploits the property of necessary existence: "If two necessary natures existed, some real character proper to each would distinguish one from the other. Let us call these differences A and B. Now either A and B are formally necessary or they are not. If we assume them to be necessary, then each necessarily existing nature will possess two formal reasons for its necessary existence, since in addition to A or B, each is formally necessary by reason of that part of its nature in which it is like the other. Now this is impossible, for since neither of the two reasons of itself includes the other, if either be excluded the being would still exist necessarily in virtue of the other and thus the being would be necessarily existent by reason of something, which if eliminated would still leave the nature existing as necessarily as before. On the other hand, if neither nature is formally necessary in virtue of these distinguishing characteristics, then the latter are not of the essence of necessary existence and consequently neither is included in a necessary being. For any entity which is not of itself necessary being is only possible (i.e. contingent) being. Nothing merely possible, however, is included in that which exists necessarily."

The other two proofs are drawn from the fact that the first nature is the first efficient cause and that it is the ultimate end. The universe cannot be the result of several efficient causes and ends that are not coordinated but quite independent of one another. As the order of relative perfection requires a hierarchy so also an order of efficiency or finality.

Scotus adds a confirmation to these proofs: "One and the same thing cannot be totally dependent upon two things, for then it would be dependent upon something which could be removed and still leave the thing in question as dependent as before. Hence, the thing would really not be dependent on it at all. Now other things depend essentially upon an efficient cause which is also their end as well as pre-eminent in perfection. Now these other beings cannot be dependent upon two such natures in just this triple way; consequently, there is but one nature on which beings depend in this fashion, and which therefore enjoys this triple primacy."

Part Two: Proof of the Infinity of God (p. 113)

Though Scotus elaborated a number of proofs for God's infinity, not all of which he considered of demonstrative force, the one that held the greatest fascination for him was one based upon the intellect of God, or more precisely, on the knowledge required in a being that is both the efficient cause and the last end. The argument obviously grew out of a constructive criticism of the Aristotelian argument for what we might call the "infinity" of the first mover elaborated in the *Physics*, VIII, c. 10, and *Metaphysics*, XII, c. 7. The argument from the "efficiency of the first mover," as Scotus calls it, maintains that the latter cannot be finite, "for it produces movement through infinite time, but nothing finite has infinite power." The first and most obvious weakness of this argument, of course, lay in the Aristotelian assumption that motion and time have had no beginning, which conflicted with the Christian belief of a creation in time. This difficulty, however, could be overcome if one could show that the first cause could have produced movement through an infinite time even though *de facto* it did not do so. But then another difficulty appears. Since at any given moment, only a finite expenditure of energy is required, the prolongation of such a finite effect over an infinite period of time would only prove an "intensive infinity." If some agent has the power to lift a finite weight of say 10 grams, we cannot conclude from the fact that this agent can continue to lift ten gram weights successively throughout an infinite period of time that it has the power to lift an infinite weight. We must first show that the power in question is intensively perfect or infinite, that is, at one at the same moment, it possesses sufficient power to produce the equivalent of the sum total of an infinite series of such effects. While Scotus tried to strengthen this argument from efficiency, it seems he was never fully satisfied with it and in the *De primo principio* it was finally relegated to the last place, among the arguments of doubtful efficacy. But if we assume that there is no limit to the possible creatures that God could create, even though at any given time only a finite number of such possibilities could be actualized, why not apply the previous type of argumentation to God's intellect instead of God's power? So Scotus reasoned. For while we need not say that whatever God can create over a period of time, he can create at one and the same moment, we must say that he has to know all the possible creatures simultaneously. Only prove that the number of possible entities is infinite and that God knows distinctly each of these infinite possibilities simultaneously, and you have a God of infinite knowledge. Show further that this infinite act of knowledge is really identified with the essence or substance of the First Being, and you have established the existence of an infinite being, for an infinite power cannot reside in a finite substance, according to Aristotle.

With this thought in mind, Scotus introduces four preliminary theses or conclusions to pave the way for his proof for God's infinity. They are 1) That the first being, whose existence he has established, has knowledge and volition; 2) that its self-knowledge and love, at least, are identical with its essence; 3) that no knowledge it possesses, even that of things other than itself, can be something accidental to its nature; and 4) that this knowledge is necessary, eternal and prior ontologically to the existence of the creatures themselves.

(p. 115) The proofs for these four introductory theses are derived in one way or other from the self-sufficiency of the first nature and the fact that it exceeds all others in perfection.

Once these preliminary conclusions are granted, the principal thesis is taken up: "From the fact that the first being knows distinctly everything that can be made, we argue as follows: The things that can be known are infinite, and they are actually known by an intellect that knows all things. But the intellect of the first being is of such a kind. I prove the antecedent and the consequent of this enthymeme. Things potentially infinite or endless in number if taken one at a time, are actually infinite if they are actualized at one time. Now what can be known is of such a nature so far as a created intellect is concerned, as is sufficiently clear. But all that the created intellect knows successively, the divine intellect knows actually at one and the same time. Therefore, the divine intellect knows the actually infinite. I prove the major of the syllogism, although it seems evident enough. Consider these potentially infinite things as a whole. If they exist all at once they are actually infinite or actually finite. If finite, then if we take one after the other eventually we shall know all of them. But if we cannot actually know them all in this way, they will be actually infinite if known simultaneously. The consequence of this enthymeme, I prove as follows. Whenever a greater number implies or requires greater perfection than does a smaller number, numerical infinity implies infinite perfection. An example: a greater motive power is required to carry ten things than to carry five. Therefore, an infinite motive power is needed to carry an infinitude of such things. Now in the issue at hand, since to know A is a perfection and to know B also, both A and B will never be known by one and the same act of knowledge unless the latter includes in a more eminent way the perfection of the other two. The same holds for three objects and so on *ad infinitum*."

A confirmatory proof of the same Scotus draws from the fact that the first being cannot depend upon creatures for its knowledge of them, yet knowledge of creatures it must have if it is truly the first cause in the sense established in the first part of the proof. The divine essence is so perfect an object of knowledge that it causes not only an intuitive vision of itself but of everything else as well, so that the presence of these secondary or lesser objects would contribute nothing to the perfection of the knowledge which the first being has of them by reason of the presence of its primary object. From this it follows that this primary object is infinitely knowable, for only if the superior object is infinite in cognoscibility, will it be impossible for the inferior object to add to it. But if it is infinitely knowable, then it is infinite in being, for according to Aristotle *unumquodque sicut se habet ad esse sic ad cognosibilitatem*.

In addition to this argument for infinity from the divine intellect, Scotus also examines other ways, e.g., from efficient causality, from finality and from eminence. From the use of such words as *suadetur, colora-*

tur, roboratur ultima probabilitas and the like, all of which qualifying expressions are absent in the proof from the intellect, it would seem he regarded only the latter as strictly demonstrative. . . .

II. IS THERE BUT ONE GOD?

The establishment of the existence of an infinite being represents as it were the peak of achievement of the human intellect in its upward striving from creatures to God. The fact that it comes at the very end of an *a posteriori* demonstration that began with creatures would already seem to indicate, says Scotus, that in this notion God is set apart, or distinguished most of all from creatures and to that extent, so far as our way of conceiving God is concerned, it comes closest to describing the unique essence of the Supreme Being, who described himself in a language that the mind of mortals could understand as simply I AM WHO AM.

. . . .

(p. 118) Of all the attributes that he could prove, Scotus at this point selects the one most pertinent to the subject at hand, God's unicity. And with this he concludes his proof for the existence of God.

His method is to exploit the various contradictions that would follow by reason of the absolute attributes of the several infinite beings. The first of his six demonstrations is based on the fact that an infinite being has an infinitely perfect intellect. This means, first of all, that its knowledge extends to everything knowable; secondly, whatever such a being knows it knows most perfectly; thirdly, this knowledge is independent of the causality of anything outside itself. Now if two gods existed, each infinitely perfect, one or the other of these three characteristics would have to be denied. Suppose, he says, there were two gods, A and B, each with infinitely perfect knowledge. If A's knowledge extends to all that is intelligible, it cannot assuredly exclude the infinitely intelligible B. Yet it cannot in any way depend upon B for this knowledge, for that would imperil its perfect independence. If it knows B at all, then, it must be by knowing its own self or substance, which is impossible, of course, for B must be wholly independent of A, and A can only know itself and what is contained therein either formally or virtually. Even if we assume, for the sake of argument, that A and B are similar and therefore A by knowing itself has some kind of knowledge of B, A's knowledge would still be imperfect, for it would not be intuitive, but by way of abstraction. In addition, it would be a knowledge through universal or common notions, so that the unique features which distinguish B from A would remain unknown. Furthermore, an additional difficulty arises, for we should have to assume that one and the same act of knowledge has two adequate objects, which are not only distinct but unrelated to each other by dependence, since by definition each good must be completely independent of the other.

Similar contradictions are developed in regard to the postulate of more than one infinitely perfect will, or infinite good, or infinite power, or infinitely perfect being, or more than one necessarily existing being. However, as the argumentation runs along the lines of the above we shall omit it in this summary account.

IV. The Existence of God in Modern Philosophy

22

THE EXISTENCE OF GOD BASED UPON THE IDEA OF GOD *

I. OUR IDEA OF GOD MUST BE TRACED TO GOD HIMSELF

THERE remains only the idea of God, concerning which we must consider whether it is something which cannot have proceeded from myself. By the name of God I understand a substance that is infinite (eternal, immutable), independent, all-knowing, all-powerful, and by which I myself and everything else, if anything else does exist, have been created. Now all these characteristics are such that the more diligently I attend to them, the less do they appear capable of proceeding from me alone; hence, from what has been already said, we must conclude that God necessarily exists.

For although the idea of substance is within me owing to the fact that I am substance, nevertheless I should not have the idea of an infinite substance—since I am finite—if it had not proceeded from some substance which was veritably infinite.

Nor should I imagine that I do not perceive the infinite by a true idea, but only by the negation of the finite, just as I perceive repose and darkness by the negation of movement and of light; for, on the contrary, I see that there is manifestly more reality in infinite substance than in finite, and therefore that in some way I have in me the notion of infinite earlier than the finite—to wit, the notion of God before that of myself. For how would it be possible that I should know that I doubt

* René Descartes (1596-1650). In his "Third Meditation," Descartes argues from the origin of that idea which must be traced to no other source than God Himself. In the "Fifth Meditation" he argues that we can think of the Most Perfect Being only as existent. Our extracts are taken from The Philosophical Works of Descartes, trans. by Elizabeth S. Haldane and G. R. T. Ross (New York: Cambridge University Press, 1931), Vol. I, pp. 165-171, 180-183.

and desire, that is to say, that something is lacking to me, and that I am not quite perfect, unless I had within me some idea of a Being more perfect than myself, in comparison with which I should recognize the deficiencies of my nature?

And we cannot say that this idea of God is perhaps materially false and that consequently I can derive it from nought (i.e. that possibly it exists in me because I am imperfect), as I have just said is the case with the ideas of heat, cold, and other such things; for, on the contrary, as this idea is very clear and distinct and contains within it more objective reality than any other, there can be none which is of itself more true, nor any in which there is less suspicion of falsehood. The idea, I say, of this Being who is absolutely perfect and infinite, is entirely true; for although, perhaps, we can imagine that such a Being does not exist, we cannot nevertheless imagine that His idea represents nothing real to me, as I have said of the idea of cold. This idea is also very clear and distinct; since all that I conceive clearly and distinctly of the real and the true, and of what conveys some perfection, is in its entirety contained in this idea. And this does not cease to be true although I do not comprehend the infinite, or though in God there is an infinitude of things which I cannot comprehend, nor possibly even reach in any way by thought; for it is of the nature of the infinite that my nature, which is finite and limited, should not comprehend it; and it is sufficient that I should understand this, and that I should judge that all things which I clearly perceive and in which I know that there is some perfection, and possibly likewise an infinitude of properties of which I am ignorant, are in God formally and eminently, so that the ideas which I have of Him may become the most true, most clear, and most distinct of all the ideas that are in my mind.

But possibly I am something more than I suppose myself to be, and perhaps all those perfections which I attribute to God are in some way potentially in me, although they do not yet disclose themselves, or issue in action. As a matter of fact I am already sensible that my knowledge increases (and perfects itself) little by little, and I see nothing which can prevent it from increasing more and more into infinitude; nor do I see, after it has thus been increased (or perfected), anything to prevent my being able to acquire by its means all the other perfections of the Divine nature; nor finally why the power I have of acquiring these perfections, if it really exists in me, shall not suffice to produce the ideas of them.

At the same time I recognize that this cannot be. For, in the first place, although it were true that every day my knowledge acquired new degrees of perfection, and that there were in my nature many things potentially which are not yet there actually, nevertheless these excellences do not pertain to (or make the smallest approach to) the idea which I have of God in whom there is nothing merely potential (but in whom all is present really and actually); for it is an infallible token of perfection in my knowledge that it increases little by little. And further, although my knowledge grows more and more, nevertheless I do not for that reason believe that it can ever be infinite since it can never reach a point so high that it will be unable to attain to any greater increase. But I understand God to be actually infinite, so that He can add nothing to His supreme perfection. And finally I perceive that the objective being of an idea cannot be produced by a being that exists potentially only, which properly speaking is nothing, but only by a being which is formal and actual.

To speak the truth, I see nothing in all that I have just said which by the light of nature is not manifest to any one who desires to think attentively on the subject; but when I slightly relax my attention, my mind, finding its vision somewhat obscured and so to speak blinded by the images of sensible objects, I do not easily recollect the reason why the idea that I possess of a being more perfect than I, must necessarily have been placed in me by a being which is really more perfect; and this is why I wish here to go on to inquire whether I, who have this idea, can exist if no such being exists.

And I ask, from whom do I then derive my existence? Perhaps from myself or from my parents, or from some other source less perfect than God; for we can imagine nothing more perfect than God; or even as perfect as He is.

But [were I independent of every other and] were I myself the author of my being I should doubt nothing and I should desire nothing, and finally no perfection would be lacking to me; for I should have bestowed on myself every perfection of which I possessed any idea and should thus be God. And it must not be imagined that those things that are lacking to me are perhaps more difficult of attainment than those which I already possess; for, on the contrary, it is quite evident that it was a matter of much greater difficulty to bring to pass that I, that is to say, a thing or a substance that thinks, should emerge out of nothing, than it would be to attain to the knowledge of many things of which I am ignorant, and which are only the accidents of this thinking substance. But it was clear that if I had of myself possessed this greater perfection of which I have just spoken [that is to say, if I had been the author of my own existence], I should not at least have denied myself the things which are the more easy to acquire, [to wit, many branches of knowledge of which my nature is destitute]; nor should I have deprived myself of any of the things contained in the idea which I form of God, because there are none of them which seem to me specially difficult to acquire; and if there were any that were more difficult to acquire, they would certainly appear to me to be such (supposing I myself were the origin of the other things which I possess) since I should discover in them that my powers are limited.

But though I assume that perhaps I have always existed just as I am at present, neither can I escape the force of this reasoning and imagine that the conclusion to be drawn from this is, that I need not seek for any author of my existence. For all the course of my life may be divided into an infinite number of parts, none of which is in any way dependent on the other; and thus from the fact that I was in existence a short time ago it does not follow that I must be in existence now, unless some cause at this instant, so to speak, produces me anew, that is to say, conserves me. It is as a matter of fact perfectly clear and evident to all who consider with attention the nature of time that, in order to be conserved in each moment in which it endures, a substance has need of the same power and action as would be necessary to produce and create it anew, supposing it did not yet exist, so that the light of nature shows us clearly that the distinction between creation and conservation is solely a distinction of the reason.

All that I thus require here is that I should interrogate myself, if I wish to know whether I possess a power which is capable of bringing it to pass that I who now am shall still be in the future; for since I am nothing but a thinking thing, or at least, since thus far it is only that portion of myself which is precisely in question at present, if such a power did reside in me, I should certainly be conscious of it. But I am conscious of nothing of the kind, and by this I know clearly that I depend on some being different from myself.

Possibly, however, this being on which I depend is not that which I call God, and I am created either by my parents or by some other cause less perfect than God. This cannot be, because, as I have just said, it is perfectly evident that there must be at least as much reality in the cause as in the effect; and thus since I am a thinking thing, and possess an idea of God within me, whatever in the end is the cause assigned to my existence, it must be allowed that it is likewise a thinking thing and that it possesses in itself the idea of all the perfections which I attribute to God. We may again inquire whether this cause derives its origin from itself or from some other thing. For if from itself, it follows by the reasons before brought forward, that this cause must itself be God; for since it possesses the virtue of self-existence, it must also without doubt have the power of actually possessing all the perfections of which it has the idea, that is, all those which I conceive as existing in God. But if it derives its existence from some other cause than itself, we shall again ask, for the same reason, whether this second cause exists by itself or through another, until from one step to another, we finally arrive at an ultimate cause, which will be God.

And it is perfectly manifest that in this there can be no regression into infinity, since what is in question is not so much the cause which formerly created me, as that which conserves me at the present time.

Nor can we suppose that several causes may have concurred in my production, and that from one I have received the idea of one of the perfections which I attribute to God, and from another the idea of some other, so that all these perfections indeed exist somewhere in the universe, but not as complete in one unity which is God. On the contrary, the unity, the simplicity or the inseparability of all things which are in God is one of the principal perfections which I conceive to be in Him. And certainly the idea of this unity of all Divine perfections cannot have been placed in me by any cause from which I have not received likewise the ideas of all the other perfections; for this cause could not make me able to comprehend them as joined together in an inseparable unity without having at the same time caused me in some measure to know what they are (and in some way to recognize each one of them).

Finally, so far as my parents (from whom I have sprung) are concerned, although all that I have ever been able to believe of them were true, that does not make it follow that it is they who conserve me, nor are they even the authors of my being in any sense, in so far as I am a thinking being; since what they did was merely to implant certain dispositions in that matter in which the self—i.e. the mind, which alone I at present identify with myself—is by me deemed to exist. And thus there can be no difficulty in their regard, but we must of necessity conclude from the fact alone that I exist, or that the idea of a Being supremely perfect—that is God—is in me, that the proof of God's existence is grounded on the highest evidence.

It only remains to me to examine into the manner in which I have acquired this idea from God; for I have not received it through the senses, and it is never presented to me unexpectedly, as is usual with the ideas of sensible things when these things present themselves, or seem to present themselves, to the external organs of my senses; nor is it likewise a fiction of my mind, for it is not in my power to take from or to add anything to it; and consequently the only alternative is that it is innate in me, just as the idea of myself is innate in me.

And one certainly ought not to find it strange that God, in creating me, placed this idea within me to be like the mark of the workman imprinted on his work; and it is likewise not essential that the mark shall be something different from the work itself. For from the sole fact that God created me it is most probable that in some way He has placed His image and similitude (in which the idea of God is contained) by means of the same faculty by which I perceive myself—that is to say, when I reflect on myself I not only know that I am something (imperfect), incomplete and dependent on another, which incessantly aspires after something which is better and greater than myself, but I also know that He on whom I depend possesses in Himself all the great things towards which I aspire (and the ideas of which I find within myself), and that not indefinitely or potentially alone, but really, actually and infinitely; and that thus He is God. And the whole strength of the argument which I have here made use of to prove the existence of God consists in this, that I recognize that it is not possible that my nature should be what it is, and indeed that I should have in myself the idea of a God, if God did not veritably exist—a God, I say, whose idea is in me, i.e. who possesses all those supreme perfections of which our mind may indeed have some idea but without understanding them all, who is liable to no errors or defect (and who has none of all those marks which denote imperfection). From this it is manifest that He cannot be a deceiver, since the light of nature teaches us that fraud and deception necessarily proceed from some defect.

But before I examine this matter with more care, and pass on to the consideration of other truths which may be derived from it, it seems to me right to pause for a while to contemplate God Himself, to ponder at leisure His marvelous attributes, to consider and admire, and adore the beauty of this light so resplendent, at least as far as the strength of my mind, which is in some measure dazzled by the sight, will allow me to do so. For just as faith teaches us that the supreme felicity of the other life consists only in this contemplation of the Divine Majesty, so we continue to learn from experience that a similar meditation, though incomparably less perfect, causes us to enjoy the greatest satisfaction of which we are capable in this life.

II. THE IDEA OF GOD IMPLIES EXISTENCE

. . . It is perfectly clear that all that is true is something, and I have already fully demonstrated that all that I know clearly is true. And even although I had demonstrated this, the nature of my mind is such that I could not prevent myself from holding them to be true so long as I conceive them clearly; and I recollect that when I was still strongly attached to the objects of sense, I counted as the most certain those truths which I conceived clearly as regards figures, numbers, and the other matters which pertain to arithmetic and geometry, and, in general, to pure and abstract mathematics.

But now, if just because I can draw the idea of something from my thought, it follows that all which I know clearly and distinctly as pertaining to this object does really belong to it, may I not derive from this an argument demonstrating the existence of God? It is certain that I no less find the idea of God, that is to say the idea of a supremely perfect Being, in me, than that of any figure or number whatever it is; and I do not know any less clearly and distinctly that an [actual and] eternal existence pertains to this nature than I know that all that which I am able to demonstrate of some figure or number truly pertains to the nature of this figure or number, and therefore, although all that I concluded in the preceding Meditations were found to be false, the existence of God would pass with me as at least as certain as I have ever held the truths of mathematics (which concern only numbers and figures) to be.

This indeed is not at first manifest, since it would seem to present the appearance of being a sophism. For being accustomed in all other things to make a distinction between existence and essence, I easily persuade myself that the existence can be separated from the essence of God, and that we can thus conceive God as not actually existing. But, nevertheless, when I think of it with more attention, I clearly see that existence can no more be separated from the essence of God than can its having three angles equal to two right angles be separated from the essence of a (rectilinear) triangle, or the idea of a mountain from the idea of a valley; and so there is no less repugnance to our conceiving of a God (that is, a Being supremely perfect) to whom existence is lacking (that is to say, to whom a certain perfection is lacking), than to our conceiving of a mountain which has no valley.

But although I cannot really conceive of a God without existence any more than a mountain without a valley, still from the fact that I conceive of a mountain with a valley, it does not follow that there is such a mountain in the world; similarly, although I conceive of God as possessing existence, it would seem that it does not follow that there is a God which exists; for my thought does not impose any necessity upon things, and just as I may imagine a winged horse, although no horse with wings exists, so I could perhaps attribute existence to God, although no God existed.

But a sophism is concealed in this objection, for from the fact that I cannot conceive a mountain without a valley it does not follow that there is any mountain or any valley in existence, but only that the mountain and the valley, whether they exist or do not exist, cannot in any way be separated one from the other. While from the fact that I cannot conceive God without existence, it follows that existence is inseparable from Him, and hence that He really exists; not that my thought can bring this to pass, or impose any necessity on things, but, on the contrary, because the necessity which lies in the thing itself, i.e. the necessity of the existence of God determines me to think in this way. For it is not within my power to think of God without existence (that is [to think] of a supremely perfect Being devoid of a supreme perfection) though it is in my power to imagine a horse either with wings or without wings.

And we must not here object that it is in truth necessary for me to assert that God exists after having presupposed that He possesses every sort of perfection, since existence is one of these, but that as a matter of fact my original supposition was not necessary, just as it is not necessary to consider that all quadrilateral figures can be inscribed in the circle; for supposing I thought this, I should be constrained to admit that the rhombus might be inscribed in the circle since it is a quadrilateral figure which, however, is manifestly false. [We must not, I say, make any such allegations because] although it is not necessary that I should at any time entertain the notion of God, nevertheless whenever it happens that I think of a first and a sovereign Being, and, so to speak, derive the idea of Him from the storehouse of my mind, it is necessary that I should attribute to Him every sort of perfection, although I do not get so far as to enumerate them all, or to apply my mind to each one in particular. And this necessity suffices to make me conclude (after having recognized that existence is a perfection) that this first and sovereign Being really exists; just as though it is not necessary for me ever to imagine any triangle, yet, whenever I wish to consider a rectilinear figure composed only of three angles, it is absolutely essential that I should attribute to it all those properties which serve to bring about the conclusion that its three angles are not greater than two right angles, even although I may not then be considering this point in particular. But when I consider which figures are capable of being inscribed in the circle, it is in no wise necessary that I should think that all quadrilateral figures are of this number; on the contrary, I cannot even pretend that this is the case, so long as I do not desire to accept anything which I cannot conceive clearly and distinctly. And in consequence there is a great difference between the false suppositions such as this, and the true ideas born within me, the first and principal of which is that of God. For really I discern in many ways that this idea is not something factitious, and depending solely on my thought, but that it is the image of a true and immutable nature; first of all, because I cannot conceive anything but God Himself to whose essence existence [necessarily] pertains; in the second place, because it is not possible for me to conceive two or more Gods in this same position; and, granted that there is one such God who now exists, I see clearly that it is necessary that He should have existed from all eternity, and that He must exist eternally; and finally, because I know an infinitude of other properties in God, none of which I can either diminish or change.

23

OUR KNOWLEDGE OF THE EXISTENCE OF GOD *

Ph. God having given to our souls the faculties with which it is adorned has not left himself without a witness; for the senses, perception, and the reason furnish us manifest proofs of his existence.

Th. God has not only given the soul faculties suitable for knowing him but he has also impressed upon it characters which indicate him, although the soul needs faculties to perceive these characters. But I do not wish to repeat the discussions we already had upon ideas and innate truths, among which I reckon the idea of God and the truth of his existence. Let us come rather to the fact.

Ph. Now, although the existence of God is the truth most easily proved

---

* Gottfried Wilhelm Leibniz (1646-1716), *New Essays Concerning Human Understanding,* trans. by Alfred Gideon Langley (New York: Macmillan, 1896), Bk. IV, ch. x. The book takes the form of a dialogue in which *Philalethes* represents Locke and *Theophilus* represents Leibniz. A brief statement of the argument is found in the *Monadology,* Nos. 31-45.

by the reason, and its evidence equals, if I am not mistaken, that of mathematical demonstrations, it yet demands attention. It needs at once only reflection upon ourselves and our own indubitable existence. Thus I suppose that *everyone knows that something actually exists*, and that thus there is a real being. If there is anyone who can doubt his own existence, I declare that I do not speak to him. We know also by an intuitive knowledge that *bare nothing cannot produce a real being*. Whence it follows, with mathematical evidences, that *something has existed from all eternity*, since everything which has a beginning must have been produced by something else. Now every being which draws its existence from another, draws also from it all it has, and all its faculties. The eternal source of all beings is then also the principle of all their powers, so that *this eternal being must be also all-powerful*. Further, man finds in himself knowledge. *There is*, then, *an intelligent being*. Now it is impossible for a thing absolutely destitute of knowledge and perception to produce an intelligent being, and it is contrary to the idea of matter, deprived of thought, to produce it of itself. The source of things is then intelligent, and *there has been an intelligent being from all eternity*. An eternal, very powerful, and very intelligent being is what we call *God*. If, however, anyone were found so unreasonable as to suppose that man is the only being having knowledge and wisdom, but that nevertheless, he has been formed by pure chance, and that it is the same principle, blind and without knowledge, which carries on all the rest of the universe I should advise him to examine at his leisure the wholly solid and emphatic censure of Cicero (*De legibus*, lib. 2). Certainly, he says, no one could be so foolishly arrogant as to think that he has within himself an understanding and reason, and yet that there is no intelligence governing the heavens and all this vast universe. From what I have just said it clearly follows that we have a more certain knowledge of God than of anything else outside of us.

Th. I assure you, sir, with perfect sincerity, that I am extremely sorry to be obliged to say something against this demonstration; but I do it solely in order to give you an opportunity to fill up the void. It is principally in the part where you conclude that something has existed from all eternity. I find therein some ambiguity, if that means *that there never has been any time in which nothing existed*. I admit it, and it follows truly from the preceding propositions by an inference wholly mathematical. For if there had always been nothing, there would always have been nothing, nothing being unable to produce a being; then we ourselves should not be, which is contrary to the first truth of experience. But the consequence appears at once, that by the statement that something has existed from all eternity, you mean an eternal thing. But it does not at all follow in virtue of what you have hitherto advanced, that if there has always been something, there has always been a certain thing, i.e. an eternal being. For certain opponents will say that I have been produced by other things, and these things by others. Further, if some admit eternal beings (as the Epicureans their atoms) they will not think themselves compelled for that reason to admit an eternal being who is the only source of all the others. For if they should admit that this which gives existence, gives also the other qualities and powers of the thing, they will deny that a single thing gives existence to the others, and they will say also that in each thing many others must concur. Thus we shall not reach by this alone a source of all the powers. Yet it is very reasonable to judge that there is one, and also that the universe is governed with wisdom. But when we believe matter susceptible of thought, we may be disposed to believe that it is not impossible that it may produce something. At least it will be difficult to bring forward a proof which does not show at the same time that it is wholly incapable of it; and, assuming that our thought comes from a thinking being, may we take it as admitted, without prejudice to the demonstration, that this must be God?

Ph. I do not doubt that the excellent man from whom I have borrowed this demonstration is capable of perfecting it; and I shall try to influence him to do so, since he could scarcely render a greater service to the public. You also desire it. This makes me think that you do not consider it necessary, in order to shut the mouths of atheists, to make everything revolve upon the existence of the idea of God in us, as some do, who attach themselves too strongly to this favorite discovery, even to rejecting all other demonstrations of the existence of God, or at least attempting to weaken them and forbidding to employ them as if they were weak or false; although at bottom they are proofs which show us so clearly and in a manner so convincing the existence of the sovereign being by the consideration of our own existence and of the sensible parts of the universe, that I think no wise man ought to resist them.

Th. Although I am for innate ideas, and in particular for that of God, I do not think that the demonstrations of the Cartesians drawn from the idea of God are perfect. I have shown fully elsewhere (in the "Actes de Leipsic" and in the "Mémoires de Trèvoux") that what Descartes had borrowed from Anselm, Archbishop of Canterbury, is very beautiful and really very ingenious, but that there is still a gap therein to be filled. The celebrated archbishop, who was without doubt one of the most able men of his time, congratulates himself, not without reason, for having discovered a means of proving the existence of God *a priori,* by means of its own notion, without recurring to its effects. And this is very nearly the force of his argument: God is the greatest, or (as Descartes says) the most perfect of beings, or rather a being of supreme grandeur and perfection, including all degrees thereof. That is the notion of God. See now how existence follows from this notion. To exist is something more than not to exist, or rather, existence adds a degree to grandeur and perfection, and as Descartes states it, existence is itself a perfection. Therefore this degree of grandeur and perfection, or rather this perfection which consists in existence, is in this supreme, all-great, all-perfect being; for otherwise some degree would be wanting to it, contrary to its definition. Consequently this supreme being exists. The Scholastics, not excepting even their Doctor Angelicus, have misunderstood this argument, and have taken it as a paralogism; in which respect they were altogether wrong, and Descartes, who studied scholastic philosophy quite a long time at the Jesuit College of La Flèche, had great reason for re-establishing it. It is not a paralogism, but it is an imperfect demonstration, which assumes something that must still be proved in order to render it mathematically evident; that is, it is tacitly assumed that this idea of the all-great or all-perfect being is possible, and implies no contradiction. And it is already something that by this remark it is proved that *assuming that God is possible, he exists,* which is the privilege of divinity alone. We have the right to presume the possibility of every being, and especially that of God, until someone proves the contrary. So that this metaphysical argument already gives a morally demonstrative conclusion, which declares that according to the present state of our knowledge we must judge that God exists, and act in conformity thereto. But it is to be desired, nevertheless, that clever men achieve the demonstration with the strictness of mathematical proof, and I think I have elsewhere said something that may serve this end. The other argument of Descartes, which undertakes to prove the existence of God because the idea of Him is in our soul, and [which] must have come from the original, is still less conclusive. For in the first place this argument has this defect, in common with the preceding, that it assumes that there is in us such an idea, i.e. that God is possible. For what Descartes alleges, that in speaking of God we know what we are saying, and that consequently we have an idea, is a deceptive indication, since in speaking of perpetual mechanical movement, for example, we know what we are saying, and yet this movement is an impossible thing, of which, consequently, we can have only an apparent idea. Secondly, this same argument does not sufficiently prove that the idea of God, if we have it, must come from the original. But I do not wish to delay here at present. You will say, sir, to me, that recognizing in us the innate idea of God, I ought not to say that we may question whether there is one. But I permit this doubt only in relation to a strict demonstration based upon the idea alone. For we are otherwise sufficiently assured of the idea and of the existence of God. And you will remember that I have shown how ideas are in us, not always in such wise that we are conscious of them, but always in such wise that we may draw them from our own depths and make them perceivable. And this is also my belief concerning the idea of God, the possibility and existence of which I hold to be demonstrated in more than one way. And the *pre-established harmony* itself furnishes a new and incontestable means of so doing. I believe also that nearly all the means which have been employed to prove the existence of God are good and might be of service, if we would perfect them, and I am not at all of the opinion that we should neglect that drawn from the order of things.

Ph. It will perhaps be proper to insist a little upon this question, whether a thinking being can come from a non-thinking being deprived of all sensation and knowledge such as matter may be. It is indeed quite evident that a part of matter is incapable of producing anything of itself, and of giving itself motion; its motion must then either be eternal or be impressed upon it by a more powerful being. If this motion were eternal, it would always be incapable of producing knowledge. Divide matter into as many little parts as you please, in order, as it were, to spiritualize it, give it all figures and motions you wish, make it a globe, a cube, a prism, a cylinder, etc., whose diameters are only the one-millionth part of a gry, which is one-tenth of a line, which is one-tenth of an inch, which is one-tenth of a philosophical foot, which is one-third of a pendulum, each vibration of which in the latitude of forty-five degrees is equal to one second of time. This particle of matter, small as it is, will act upon other bodies of a size proportional to itself no differently than bodies of an inch or a foot in diameter act among themselves. And we may hope as rationally to produce feeling, thought, and knowledge, by putting together gross parts of matter in a certain figure and motion, as by means of the smallest parts of matter in the world. These last knock, push, and resist each other just as the great ones do, and this is all they can do. But if matter could draw from its bosom feeling, perception, and knowledge, immediately and without machinery, or without the aid of figures and motions, then their possession must be an inseparable property of matter and of all its parts. To which one could add that, though the general and specific idea we have of matter leads us to speak of it as if it were a thing single in number, yet all matter is not properly one individual thing, which exists in a material being or a single body that we know or can conceive. So that if matter were the first eternal thinking being, there would not be one eternal infinite and thinking being but an infinite number of eternal infinite thinking beings, independent of one another, whose forces would be limited and thoughts distinct, and who consequently could never produce this order, harmony, and beauty which are seen in nature. Whence it necessarily follows that the eternal first being cannot be matter. I hope that you, sir, will be more content with this reasoning taken from the celebrated author of the preceding demonstration than you have appeared to be with his demonstration.

Th. I find the present reasoning the most solid in the world, and not only exact, but further profound and worthy of its author. I am perfectly of his opinion that no combination and modification of the parts of matter, however small they may be, can produce perception; forasmuch as the gross particles could not give it (as is manifestly admitted) and as all is proportional in the small parts to what may take place in the great. It is furthermore an important remark regarding matter which the author makes here, that it must not be taken as a thing single in number, or (as I have been wont to state it) as a true and perfect *monad* or *unity*, since it is only a *mass* of an infinite number of beings. Here this excellent author needed but a step to arrive at my system. For in fact I give perception to all these infinite beings, each one of which is like an animal endowed with a soul (or some active analogous principle which makes its true unity), together with what is necessary to this being in order to be passive and endowed with an organic body. Now these beings have received their nature, active as well as passive (i.e. what they have of immaterial and material), from a general and supreme cause, because otherwise, as the author very well says, being independent of one another, they could never produce this *order, harmony,* and *beauty* which are seen in nature. But this argument, which appears to possess only a moral certainty, is pushed to a necessity wholly metaphysical by the *new kind of harmony* I have introduced, which is the *pre-established harmony*. For each one of these souls expressing in its way what takes place outside of it and being unable to have any influence on other particular beings, or rather, being obliged to draw this expression from the depths of its own nature, each one must necessarily have received this nature (or this internal reason of the expression of that which is outside) from a universal cause upon which all these beings depend and which makes one perfectly in accord and correspondent with another; a thing impossible without an infinite knowledge and power and with an artifice great as regards especially the spontaneous agreement of the mechanism with the acts of the rational soul. The illustrious author (Pierre Bayle) who made objections against it in his wonderful Dictionary doubted, as it were, whether this condition of things did not surpass all possible wisdom, saying that the wisdom of God did not appear to him too great for such an effect, and recognized at least that never had the feeble conceptions we may have of the divine perfection been so set in relief.

Ph. How delighted I am at this agreement of your thoughts with those of my author. I hope you will not be displeased, sir, if I give you an account also of the rest of his reasoning upon this article. First he examines whether the thinking being, upon whom all the other intelligent beings depend (and with much stronger reason all other beings) is material or not. It is objected that a thinking being might be material. But he replies that if that were so, it is enough that this be an eternal being which has an infinite knowledge and power. Further, if thought and matter can be separated, the eternal existence of matter will not follow from the eternal existence of a thinking being. It will further be asked of those who make God material whether they imagine that every part of matter thinks. In that case it will follow that there would be as many Gods as particles of matter. But if each part of matter does not think, then there is a thinking being composed of non-thinking parts, which has already been disproved. To say that any single atom of matter thinks, and that the other parts, though equally eternal, do not think, is to make the *gratuitous* statement that one part of matter is infinitely above another and produces thinking beings not eternal. If we will have it that the thinking eternal and material being is a certain particular mass of matter whose parts are non-thinking, we fall back upon the view which has been disproved; for the parts of matter are united in vain, they can acquire only a new local relation, which cannot give them knowledge. It matters not whether this mass is at rest or in motion. If at rest, it is only an inactive mass which has no privilege above an atom; if in motion, since this motion, which distinguishes it from other parts, is destined to produce thought, all these thoughts will be accidental and limited, each part by itself being without thought, and having nothing which regulates its movements. Thus there will be neither freedom, nor choice, nor wisdom, any more than in simple brute matter. Some believe that matter is at least coeternal with God. But they do not say why; the production of a thinking being, which they admit, is much more difficult than that of matter which is less perfect. And perhaps (says the author) if we would withdraw ourselves a little from common ideas, give wings to our mind, and engage in the profoundest examination we could make of the nature of things, *we might be able to attain a conception, though in an imperfect manner, how matter may at first have been made, and how it commenced to exist by the power of this eternal first being.* But we should see at the same time that to give being to a spirit is an effect of this eternal and infinite power more difficult to comprehend. But because this would perhaps lead me too far (he adds) *from the notion upon which the philosophy now in the world is based,* it would not be excusable in me to deviate so far from them or to inquire, so far as grammar would permit, whether at bottom the commonly established opinion is contrary to this particular view; it would be wrong, I say, for me to engage in this discussion, especially *in this corner of the world,* where the received doctrine is good enough for my purpose, since it posits as an indubitable thing that if the creation or beginning of any *substance* whatever is once admitted, the creation of every other substance, except the Creator Himself, may with the same facility be assumed.

Th. You have given me genuine pleasure, sir, by giving me some account of a profound thought of your clever author, which his too scrupulous prudence has prevented him from producing in its entirety. It would be a great wrong, if he should suppress it and leave us there, after having made our mouths water. I assure you, sir, that I believe there is something beautiful and important concealed behind this enigmatical manner. The *substance* in large letters might make one suspicious that he conceives the production of matter in the same way as that of the accidents, which we find no difficulty in drawing from nothing; and in distinguishing his particular thought *from the philosophy now prevalent in the world or in that corner of the earth.* I do not know but that he had in mind the Platonists, who take matter as something fleeting and transitory, after the manner of the accidents, and had an altogether different idea of spirits and souls.

Ph. Finally, if some deny *creation,* by which things are made from nothing, because they cannot conceive it, our author, writing before he knew your discovery of the reason of the union of the soul and the body, holds against them, that they do not understand how voluntary movements are produced in bodies by the will of the soul, and they cease not to believe the fact, being convinced by experience; and he replies with reason to those who answer that the soul, being unable to produce a new motion, produces only a new determination of the animal spirits; he replies to them, I say, that the one is as inconceivable as the other. And nothing can be better said than what he adds on this occasion, that to wish to limit what God can do to what we can comprehend, is to give an infinite extent to our comprehension, or to make God himself finite.

Th. Although now the difficulty regarding the union of the soul and the body has in my view been removed, there remain difficulties elsewhere. I have shown *a posteriori* by the pre-established harmony, that all the monads have received their origin from God and depend upon Him. But we cannot comprehend the how in detail; and at bottom their conservation is nothing else than a continued creation, as the Scholastics have clearly recognized.

24

WHY THERE ARE ATHEISTS *

W E SAID in the beginning of this Theodicy that if there be a genuine proof of the existence of God, that proof must correspond to some common, daily, essential, and fundamental process of human reason; we have shown in the soul and human mind a universal tendency, which, ever desirous to enlarge, embellish, and raise to the infinite every trace of being, beauty, and goodness presented by the world, rises to God by this poetic process, which is but the impulse of reason. Most minds, even the simplest, reach God by this way. We have recognized that the proofs of God's existence given by true philosophers, from Plato to Descartes, are nothing but this common method translated into philosophic language. We have explained the essence of this process; we have asserted and shown, with Descartes and Leibnitz, that this proof is as rigorous as any mathematical proof; and lastly, we have shown that

* Alphonse Gratry (1805-1872), *Guide to the Knowledge of God: A Study of the Chief Theodicies,* trans. by Abby Langdon Alger (Boston: Roberts Bros., 1892), Part I, ch. IX.

this vital and fundamental process of the human mind is a universal process, of which the infinitesimal mathematical process is merely a special application.

It now remains for us to understand how, if it be true that the demonstration of the existence of God be the simplest and most spontaneous as well as the grandest and most essential of the acts of reason; if it be true that philosophy has described, analysed, and argued it with full details and precision, and that this demonstration has now clearly acquired mathematical certainty—it remains, we say, for us to understand how there can still be atheists, how there always will be, and how there is, at the present day, a school of atheism which is far more scientific than the old-fashioned atheism.

In the first place, there are atheists because man is a free agent, and because there are wicked men.

In fact, the proof of God's existence is not only the act and fundamental process of the rational life, it is also the act and fundamental process of the moral and practical life. That is to say, the operation of the mind which proves God answers to a moral act of the free will which loves and adores God. These two acts answer to each other in such a fashion that the moral act is the source, the point of support, the cause, of the rational act. For if the will refuse its action, reason cannot complete its own. The mind, when the heart does not adore God, cannot alone effect the true proof of the existence of God. It sees the reasons for it if they be pointed out, but does not believe them. It can repeat the lesson, if it choose to be a hypocrite, but it has no faith in God; and we find that the demonstration is only an argument without a basis, which, to a dry, abstract spirit, far removed from love and spontaneous worship, does not imply the reality of God's existence, but only the abstract idea of God.

So that, among men, those who reach God through love may reach him through reason; those who do not reach him through love can only reach him through reason in seeming, or actually turn their reason against him: I do not say that they do not at the same time turn reason against itself, but they turn their reason against God, and deny him in their intelligence because they have denied him in their affection.

Let us study more in detail the origin of atheism.

To do this, we must first recall the proof of the existence of God.

We consider the beings who surround us, we contemplate the world and our soul. We see therein being and life, although limited; traces of beauty and goodness, mingled with contrasts and changes. But the imperfect goodness of this world leads us to comprehend infinite goodness; its borrowed beauty, absolute beauty. For this world speaks and proclaims God. This is what the soul of every man should comprehend in the presence of this world, and such is the duty of his reason.

The duty of reason is to conceive the infinite through every trace of being, beauty, and goodness shown to us by creatures; and because they also everywhere show us limitations, void, evil, and imperfection, it is the duty of reason, as well as of will, to prevent us from pausing at knowledge or love in limited beings. To go beyond them, to seek the infinitely perfect being, manifestly different from all creatures, although evidently proclaimed by each—such is our duty.

But it is here that men part, and either advance towards God or hold aloof from him.

Who has not often hesitated before the complex vision of things? Now, the order and beauty of the world compel the soul to admiration, praise, hope, and faith in that invisible being whom all things proclaim and reveal. Again, the disorder and evil, the misery and brevity, of the present, above all, death, trouble us, sadden us, drive us to distrust, complaint and despair. In this hesitation, in this trial of reason and will, some upheld by the legitimate instinct of human nature—or, to speak better, by the contact of God with the root of the soul—maintain within them their ideal faith in the infinite perfection, substantial, actual and living. Others, despite the horror felt by their soul and the remorse of their reason, allow their ideal to be smothered by the sight of chance, their faith by the sight of obstacle, and, in answer to doubt, choose negation. These are the two moral and intellectual races which divide the world. There are minds and hearts which affirm, there are others which deny. Herein lies the whole question: God or not; yes or no.

Consider well that the choice is free. We are, by choice and freely, for God or against God.

The choice between these two paths is offered to every man, not only in his youth, but at every point of life. Every movement of our consciousness, every impression received from our fellow-creatures, may and should re-echo from ourselves and our fellow-creatures back to God, if, repelling and scorning the vanity, imperfection, and present misery of things, and of ourselves, a vigorous love of good—that is, virtue—lifts our soul towards the sovereign Good, the supreme perfection, transporting us from the finite to the infinite, from the transitory to the eternal. This is what Socrates meant by philosophizing, when he said: "To philosophize is to learn to die"; it is to learn to sacrifice accidental and transitory impressions, limited sensations, finite and transitory joys, to attain the substance itself of which they are the shadows. This progress towards the infinite by the sacrifice of the finite is the right path—the path of goodness and truth.

But if all the moments of consciousness, if all the impressions received from our fellow-creatures, far from re-echoing to God in our intelligence and affection, wrap us in selfishness and sensuality; if every pleasure and every pain nail us—to use Plato's vigorous expression—to the present and accidental point of life; if, far from raising us to the infinite and the immense, the present instant fixes us upon a point of the finite; if it not only detach us from the consciousness of God, but also from full consciousness of ourselves, from entire possession of our soul which is greater than the world, and reduce us to the proportions of a creature which is but a mere detail in the world—this degradation, which can only occur because we freely prefer the possession of self to that of God, and the external possession of the senses to the full and entire possession of self, sensuality to reason, pleasure to virtue and freedom—this continuous descent towards the lower, is clearly the false path, the path of evil and of error.

We are not sufficiently alive to the fact that man ascends or descends the ladder of life, as he may prefer, at every point in life. He tends, by such of his unbiassed actions, towards fulness of life or vacuity of life —that is towards an actual being more complete or more empty. We approach God, and *we are more;* we depart from him, and *we are less.* And this is the whole mystery of life—to advance towards God, or to depart from him. We know not the perpetual and universal history of the world and of every soul. Meantime, the tremendous drama does not pause. We steadily advance either towards God or towards nonentity. "The wicked man sinks towards nothingness," says the holy Scripture. This is why there are atheists.

Assuredly there are fearful moments for the soul, when, having sunk in some sort to a lower state of being—that is, to an enfeebled vitality —it is tempted to absolute incredulity; conscious of its degradation and decay, it is tempted to say, There is nothing but an empty void; there is nothing, there is no God. Because it is moving towards lesser being, it begins to believe in nonentity; just as, in the luminous moments of increasing life, the soul, conscious of growth and progress, conceives of being more and more, trembles with joy, and leaps by a mighty act of faith to the immediate certainty and absolute assertion of Being, that is, infinite Being.

So that, in reality, the mystery of good and evil, of truth and error, consists in attaining by free choice, to one of these extremes, to one of the two prime decisions, implicit universals, which are the foundation of every mind: *Being is,* or *Being is not*—a living, intimate, and incarnate double proposition, which every soul asserts at will and bears in its inmost core; of which the one, produced by free love of the supreme Good, is the very formula of evidence, *Being is;* the other, produced by that distaste for the supreme Good and that habitual choice of the lesser, which results from egoism, is the general formula of the absurd— that is, the most concise and most absolute of all contradictory propositions, *Being is not.*

Once more we have the two human tendencies, good and evil, truth and error; there are minds which affirm, because they love; there are minds which deny, because they do not love; absolute negation or absolute affirmation, Being or non-Being, God or no God, all or nothing.

Hence the noble words of Plato, which Leibnitz holds to be so true: "The philosopher and the sophist move in opposite directions; one advances towards being, the other towards nothing; and while the philosopher is dazzled by the too great clarity of his object, the sophist, on the contrary, is blinded by the darkness of his."

On this subject Leibnitz reports that the sophist Foe at the close of his life said to his disciples: "This is the basis of all things—there is nothing; nonentity is the principle of all things." We know that India is full of this insensate nihilism. Greek sophists, Gorgias among others, taught it; Plotinus renewed it; and in our day a whole school of philosophers teaches it.

Thus there are atheists; there have been such in all ages; there will always be such, because evil plants radical incredulity and absolute negation in perverse hearts. Atheism, says Plato, is a disease of the soul before it is an error of the mind.

This is why there is a modern school of atheism more scientific than the ancient one.

It is because, as practical atheism is and can be nothing but the will itself directed in a sense contrary to the moral laws, so speculative atheism is only the reason directed in a sense contrary to the laws of logic, whence results this strange consequence, that in philosophy the theory of atheism is nothing but the demonstration of the existence of God taken inversely. The actual demonstration of the existence of God being mathematically exact, and having clearly become so by the labors of the seventeenth century, it follows that the actual theory of atheism, which is the same demonstration reversed, is in a certain sense exact, and, I ought even say, true—true, in that it entails at the close of the argument a manifest absurdity; which must be so, since a correct train of reasoning must reduce to an absurdity the hypothesis that there is no God.

Contemporary atheism proceeds as follows. To the sight of finite beings, who only exist up to a certain point, and not beyond it, to the sight of created perfections and their limitations, it applies in an inverse sense the process which rises to God. Instead of destroying the limitation and raising the perfections to the infinite, it destroys the perfections and raises the limitation to the infinite; and it thus succeeds in asserting that *absolute nonentity exists,* and that there is no other absolute being than this nothingness.

Whence it follows that "Being and Nothing are identical" or that "Being is Nothing." These two propositions exist textually in Hegel's works, and he constantly repeats them. They are, as we see, the statement of absolute absurdity. This is inevitable. The process which, applied correctly, gives us truth itself, must produce pure absurdity when applied in a contrary sense.

Thus we have in contemporary atheism a demonstration by means of the *reductio ad absurdum,* of the existence of God.

But what is truly monstrous, and what is peculiar to the present school of atheists, is that it clings with desperate determination to this radical absurdity, and intrenches itself in it. It asserts that the formula,

"Being is nothing," is the principle of philosophy, and that starting from this principle, logic must be transformed. "The time has come," says Hegel, "to transform logic"; and this transformation consists chiefly in denying the *principle of contradiction*—that is, in maintaining that in all things we can and ought to assert at the same time for and against, in the same sense and in the same connection.

So that a new system of logic, absolutely contradicting the old one, has been taught in Europe for the last forty years, successfully, brilliantly—nay, more, with such raciness of reasoning that logic, reversed as it is by this school, will come forth more fully developed than it was, because several points hitherto unknown, or undemonstrated, will thus be demonstrated to absurdity. This is an important fact, a solemn and critical moment in the history of the human mind. This fact, rich as it is in consequences and instruction, will be the object of minute study in our Treatise on Logic. We shall then see how modern sophistry, which has built up in the nineteenth century a powerful school of atheism, is simply and precisely Descartes turned wrong side out, Leibnitz reversed.

25

WHY SHOULD GOD NOT EXIST? *

WE HAVE devoted long chapters to justify and illustrate by means of images taken from nature, and from human and social life, the striking words of Jules Simon we chose as epigraph: "The idea of God is the cross-road at which all the lines of human thought meet."

From nature we inquired why it exists and what is the explanation of its wonderful order; from human life we asked an account of its origins, of its laws and of its destiny; from society we inquired how it came to be, what is the source of the authority which binds its members, and how it hopes to reach the goal of its efforts.

To all these questions we found only one acceptable answer.

We concluded that nature, human life and social life rest upon God and on the idea of God; upon God, for without God nothing is possible; on the idea of God, for outside of Him nothing is intelligible. The whole course of the world is but a varied expression of His power; all spiritual life is but a varied expression of our idea of God; all that exists is but a varied reflection of His being.

To affirm His existence is the first condition of all thinking, of all awakening of conscience, of all being, because He is Truth, and Good,

* Antonin Gilbert Sertillanges, O.P. (1863-1948), *Les Sources de la croyance en Dieu* (Paris: Perrin, 1913), ch. XVIII.

and Being, and thereby the source of all that is true, and good and real outside of Him.

The denial of Him would mean throwing everything into nothingness; denying that He exists and is the true Light would mean casting all into darkness. Now we cannot believe that nothing exists, and that all is darkness, for how could we think of nothingness without making it a being, or imagine that we see darkness without endowing it with colors?

Few minds would dare to assume that nature is but an illusion, that the ideas which are the life of the soul are nothing, that there is no truth, no error, no good, no evil, no obligation, no sanction, no legitimate authority, no social progress. And yet, as I have tried to show, all this we should hold, if there were no God.

Having done this, and not to omit anything that might make our positions clear, I may say a word regarding the positive arguments against the existence of God.

"Why should God not exist?" is a strange question; and yet we must face it, so deeply perturbed are many minds in this age of confused discussions.

Recent works have raised dust around our concept of God which we must brush away. Moreover, this will give a chance to clarify certain points we had to overlook in the preceding chapters.

I shall be brief; a whole treatise as large as this one would be needed to solve all the problems which would arise; I shall limit my study to what is indispensable to repel the attacks and to strengthen our convictions.

After I have blown away the dust to which I have just referred, if there remains any, it will, I hope, be like that evening dust which is not dense enough to hide the sun, but which, on the contrary, adds to its brilliancy by surrounding it with mystery, by forming around it a golden aura that seems to be an emanation from its substance. We may then see that the sun is the centre of our small universe, since it is source of light, and draws that universe through space as the mantle in which we are clothed, as some protective wings, as the source from which our life has drawn its flame, and without which we fall into slumber, the image of the total death to which, but for God, man and all that is in man would be lost.

I

When we speak of God we naturally picture Him as a real being, transcendent, distinct from His creatures, living His own life, as well as being the life principle of other living beings. We refrain from the verbal subtleties which, while retaining the word God, use their ingenuity to deny His reality. We have long been on our guard against the mystical terminology which empties the divine of its substance at the very moment when it makes a show of reverence to it and covers it with the flowers of pious rhetoric.

To the idea of the true God, of the living and personal God—which we shall define below—it is customary to oppose three main objections: a so-called *scientific* one; a *popular* one, and a *philosophical* one, the only one that has the right to be considered.

The first objection reads: there is no God, because there is no need of God. It is not enough to look upon Him as on the fifth wheel of a car; since there is no need of God, His existence must be denied; for it is only to explain some effect that we could bring in some invisible cause, and no effect that we know requires a transcendent explanation. Physical events have a physical explanation, and voluntary acts proceed from the will. Thus the whole course of the world is well explained in this way, and there is no need to bring in God.

It is easy to see why such an objection should not detain us one moment. It would mean challenging our whole demonstration, and wasting our time in proving in detail that all physical and human activity must ultimately be traced to divine casuality, if we allowed ourselves to be upset by such peremptory assertions.

Nature explains everything, and it explains nothing; the human will gives only a partial explanation of certain facts, which needs to be supplemented.

In the words of Leibnitz, physical and free agencies account for particular facts, not for all facts, which means that through them we know the proximate cause of each individual phenomenon; but there are other causes, and the proximate cause itself needs to be put into action.

A proximate cause is itself an effect; how then could it claim to be an adequate cause, when it is an effect? If you have a son, evidently, you are his cause; but your father too is the cause of your son, even before you, though in an indirect manner. We can view nature as a mother; but she is also a daughter, for she can by herself explain neither her own existence, nor her activity, nor the ends she pursues.

We grant that *this* explains *that;* but how is it that we have *this* and *that?* This order involves *that* order; but whence is the former order of which the latter is merely a manifestation? Is the seed less in need of explaining than the tree? It needs an explanation for two reasons: first to explain its existence as an *object,* then also to account for its power to act.

Now if the universe is a tree, nature itself, in which we recognize the principle of that tree—that prodigious chaos in which throb all things before they come to be, in which once, before the dawn of the worlds, in that remote time which Scripture calls "the beginning," everything was involved in mystery—was but a seed, and I ask where is the tremendous Sower who has cast into space the germs of such colossal creatures, destined to such a grand future, to such limitless expansions.

As for the human will, we know that it too is the germ of a world. For is not life a world, which had an origin like the universe; does it not also evolve through phases and crises, through complex phenomena, in light and in darkness, in weakness and in power, but always diverse like the events of nature among which it stirs?

We cannot explain life, whether it be individual or social, without a first datum which we might call a synthesis, without the human soul endowed with its faculties, which, with the aid of the resources of its environment will give rise to the whole history, the history of the world, and the history of each one of us.

Now has the human soul, which is the seed of history as the original chaos was the seed of the worlds, its explanation in itself? It has not, since it comes to be; since it is subject to change, since it gives evidence of failure. There must then exist a sower of souls as well as a sower of worlds. They fall from heaven into the bosoms of mothers, if I may use such an image, as the pollen carried by the wind falls into corollas.

No one can father spirits but the first Spirit. Not that the like only can beget the like; but everything requires a proportionate cause, and the flesh, which alone takes part in the generation of a man, is not a cause capable of producing a spirit.

We shall not repeat all these arguments; it is enough to bind them into a sheaf; they are like a bunch of flowers laid before the feet of the First Cause, from which we can make a whip to stir the atheist's slumber, or chastise his mental perversion.

The second objection from the existence of evil is of the same order. We gave two answers: one regarding evil in nature and evil as it affects man; the other regarding individual and collective evil. In both cases, whether it affects nature or mankind, not only did we see no reason to deny God's existence, but rather an argument, though an indirect one, in support of it.

Evil is only an accident to the good; disorder a derogation to order; a blemish is an evidence of the merit of the work; an abortion, a deviation of the orientation of the genitive power. The mere fact of failures is evidence of purpose, order, good, value and finality.

We sought also some way of effecting, by means of good and evil, a sort of synthesis which would be a real good, analogous to a musical accord of dissonant notes. Such attempts, we said, are to be made with hesitation; for we know too little, and our life is too short to permit us to embrace at one glance, as we should to form a correct judgment, the immensity of Creation; but if we are utterly ignorant, we have no right to sit as judges, we should keep silent. God reveals Himself in good, and hides in evil; but a hidden being is not nothing, and can manifest its power without unveiling its mystery.

In the case of man, evil, which is then called suffering, or inner contradiction, or mediocrity, did not appear to us as a scandal but rather as a starting point for rising to the First Cause. The feeling we have of all that, we said, is the exact measure of the range of our aspirations. Could we suffer, if we did not pursue happiness: Could we experience inner contradiction, if we did not love the good? Could we have that sense of mediocrity, whatever may be the level of our life, if we had not immense aspirations? Is not that flight, never satisfied but indefatigable, the proof that our nature bears the stamp of the infinite, and that the goal it pursues without attaining it in this life, does connote the presence of a creative action issuing from an agent infinitely rich?

All that we admit, it is useless to insist. Let us be content to remove the scandal of evil, to replace our illusion with a sense of reality, to rise from the entrancing spectacle of little details to the summits from which we shall grasp even a small portion of the universal plan.

We make our own life the measure of everything, and therefore we hunger for immediate solutions of the problems which the universe poses before us. We forget that, according to Alphonse Karr's witty saying, "God is solvent, but does not pay every Saturday." All things work towards their end; but that end is not at our feet tomorrow. When the knights of Peter the Hermit were on their way, and, already tired, reached the frontiers of Hungary, we are told that as soon as they sighted some village steeple, they asked: Is not this Jerusalem? We too wish that the lasting City in which the Divine plan will be unfolded, should appear at every turn of the road. No, the eternal City is built stone by stone; it is with short and vacillating steps that we advance towards it. We must wait and refrain from summary judgments.

To tell God that His world is full of evil, and therefore He does not exist is a mark of signal childishness. We ought to ponder, and to let our dwarf pride look with contempt upon the gigantic works which surround us; we should try, in the depth of our souls, to reach that eternal self which cannot be deceived by the illusions of life, because it transcends matter, lives outside of the limits of time, and must be found, at the moment when it will be given the solution of the problem of evil, living, but speechless, and plunged into the humility of its nothingness, but also lifted up by love and its enlightened free will, to the sight of what it could only surmise so long as it had only confidence in the veiled bounty which it apprehends in the present life.

But the third objection which I called philosophical demands greater attention. Examining it more closely will put us on the way to find a truth of sovereign importance with which I would like to close these studies on God and belief in God.

II

Some philosophers say: God does not exist because His existence is impossible.

What we call God is an infinite being. Now, an infinite being cannot exist apart from the world. If such a being exists it must be all; if it is not all, you must admit that it does not exist. An infinite God should absorb all that exists, and those who affirm His existence would not themselves exist.

What we call God is conceived as endowed with personality; but a person is the very opposite to an infinite; for it can be conceived only in opposition to what is not it, while an infinite excludes nothing except the exclusion that would be imposed upon it.

What we call God is the Absolute, viz. a being which is independent, whose whole life is contained in it, and admits of no necessary relationship with what it is not. But such could not be a personal God who must needs have many relations to what are called his works.

What we call God, in fine, is the Perfect, and from a perfect being an imperfect work could not emanate, even for a moment, even in the smallest detail.

The last objection brings us back to the problem of evil, though from a different point of view. When we dealt with it, it was, so to speak, God's morality that was challenged; here it is God's very nature. Instead of saying God *must not,* now they say God *cannot.* The moral argument has been turned into a metaphysical argument. Has it thus gained strength? We shall see. But we must begin by noting the conclusion that would be drawn, if we admitted the cogency of the foregoing objections.

Some would purely and simply deny God's existence. Others, and their number increases daily, under the pretext of clearing it from the difficulties, transform the concept of God, and rob it of any value for men who want to live by it.

The living God, we are told, does not exist; what exists is the *divine.* Make God an ideal, we shall agree. Call this ideal God, if you are so minded; that is the name men use to designate it; we shall adopt that name; but we shall know that this name, *person,* really connotes only a *thing,* and that this thing is an idea. The idea of the good, of the perfect, of the infinite, such for us is God. This idea, because it is forced upon us, and because we have a tendency to reify all ideas, takes in our eyes the figure of a person; but we must rid ourselves of this age-long illusion. God is but the category of the ideal, the extreme limit our mind guesses or dreams of, of the true, the beautiful, the good, being itself, unless you say that God is the universe itself which is conceived under all these transcendent forms, because it realizes them in part and strives incessantly towards their perfect realization.

Here we are confronted by Idealistic Pantheism. We have met it more than once, and we pointed out in passing its dissolving nature and the frail character of its principles. That doctrine is a wonderful illustration of the saying of Montaigne: "The most subtle wisdom is the source of the most sublime folly." It has proved useful in disengaging many souls from heavy materialism; but, by going far beyond truth, it has fallen into the opposite excess which is almost as noxious an error.

Materialism and Pantheism seem to bear some relation to the two worst vices which afflict our moral nature. Materialism favors sensuality, and Pantheism the pride of science. The former is plunged entirely into matter; the latter seeks to rise above, and overlord its principle. But as observation finds excessive pride often leading to vice, Pantheism is all rigged up to lead us to the extreme of sensuality.

In every age Pantheism has been the religious and moral plague of the human race. It makes religious feeling subtle to the point of making it out and out inconsistent and consequently of robbing it of all moralizing power; it absorbs all personal feeling, rolls man up in his dreams, and, for the benefit of these dreams, breaks the very springs of an active will.

In the social domain, as a consequence, Pantheism leans fatally to absolutism, as statesmen have observed and as is proved by history. Liberal institutions are found in nations that honour personality. If personality is drowned into the great cosmic All, the chance is that it will also be absorbed into the great political All, viz. into the State. Then the way is opened to despotism, or to socialism and communism in which there is no room for individuality.

Whatever consequences may thus already be drawn against Idealistic Pantheism from its moral and social effects, we must meet the arguments it opposes to us. They are specious, but only specious. We know how they run; let us seek the answer to them.

Pantheists claim that the Infinite cannot exist apart by itself in an existence that would allow other existences, which, against all logic, would make only an addition to the infinite.

Are men who reason thus sure that they are not the prey to an enormous illusion? Why could not an infinite exist apart, and the only one of its nature? Is not its very infinity the ground of its distinction from other beings? What is self-existent and therefore independent of any cause, since it is the cause of all that exists; what possesses existence to the point that existence is its essential attribute, or rather what does not *possess*, but *is* its existence, since for it, to exist is to be itself, as to be itself is to exist; what lives in this way, and bears no other definition, must by that alone be essentially distinct from what exists only because it made it. What we call beings, have only a borrowed name, a name they borrow from God, since God alone, the source of existence, explains how they come to exist. Now, can we identify a spring and a stream, in their respective natures? No, streams are streams and can run side by side, forming a network and bearing similar names; but the spring is unique, and is isolated by virtue of its function.

If it exists, the Divine Being must be essentially distinct from every other being. Let no one object that it does not exist for the very reason that ascribing existence to it would mean to separate and isolate it from all the other beings. Let no one argue either, that it is all, lest there be something outside of it, which would destroy its infinity.

I see the difficulty. If the infinite is isolated in itself, instead of including every being in itself, what lies outside of it must be added to what it includes, and therefore that pretended infinite would no longer be an infinite by the very fact that we would have our own existence.

This illusion is based upon a defective way of looking upon God and the world, and the poverty of our language is partly responsible for that illusion. Human language is not appropriate to such a lofty use; it fails as soon as it is applied to something above the common usage. Reflection must step in to correct it, and drive away, by means of certain distinctions, the equivocations it would allow.

When then we speak of God and of the world, and say: They are, we seem to treat them *ex aequo* as regards the value we ascribe to the word *to be* in each case, and that is the reason why our opponents can say: first, if God is and is infinite; and then if the world is and is not God, then we have God and the world, the infinite plus something, which is absurd.

But that reasoning is illusory. It is as bad reasoning as if one would say: here is a tube fifty centimeters long, and another thirty centimeters long; therefore their united dimension is eighty cubic centimeters. How would he answer if he were shown that the two tubes belong to a telescope and are inserted one in the other?

Apart from the crudeness of the illustration we have here the same false reasoning. The divine being on the one hand, and the created being on the other, do not add up as two values of the same kind. When we say: God is, and when we say: Man is, we use the same words for lack of others, but one must realize that they are not used in the same sense. Applied to God the term *to be* sounds with fulness of meaning, since God who is by Himself, and exists by virtue of His nature, can be truly defined: "HE WHO IS." Man, or any creature also *is* but its existence is a borrowed existence always dependent on its source.

That truth Plato had perfectly understood, and, quite contrary to our opponents, instead of changing the roles and conceding a full being to the world, leaving only the shadow to God, he said that it is God who truly exists, and that our own being is but the shadow and the reflection of God's being.

Now, if Plato was right, our opponents' objection falls. They may no longer say: The Infinite cannot exist apart without being shadowed by the finite. Would indeed the eternal Sun lose anything of its brightness, if the creature, that reflection and shadow of it, were projected on the wall of time and space?

God without the world is no less infinite. God and the world are no more than God; for what God confers He does not lose, as creatures participate in His being without taking that being from Him.

God *has* all being, even though He *is* not all being. He carries all in Himself and possesses all, even what is not He.

Now, if this answer is understood, all the others can be easily solved. They all rest upon the same confusions. Either they disregard the total dependence of the creature on the First Cause; or they disregard the special transcendent character of their mutual relations.

For instance, how do Pantheists regard *personality?* God, they claim, cannot be personal, because by its personality a being is opposed to every other being, and, if so, a personal Infinite would be limited.

But, in the first place, it is not true that personality essentially *involves* opposition; it is something positive, it means an independent self-conscious being. It is only by accident that, with us, personality means negation of something. In God, it does not necessarily imply opposition. Moreover, there is in God enough opposition to something else, for Him to be called a person. God is not the world; and the world is not God. God is the source from which the world originates. That should be enough to mark the distinction, and even opposition, between the personal God and the world which depnds upon His will.

It is enough to remember that the opposition we have in mind is that of the spring to the streams which emanate from it, and that it does not alter the character of absolute dependence, and, if I may say, envelopment of creatures by God.

Again, we are told: If God exists, his name is the Absolute, and this means that in virtue of His infinity, His life must be self-centered and in no way related to anything outside of Him, and that all the functions ascribed to Him regarding creatures would ultimately imply that He is not Absolute.

That argument involves the same confusion of ideas. God, no doubt, has His own life. He could receive nothing that does not already belong to His essence, nor lose anything of Himself by imparting it to others. Being is His own essence; He alone can make others participate in it; His ownership of being is not affected by the fact that others may borrow it. Even what He imparts remains God's possession; how then could He be imagined to lose what He gives. The relation arising from His creative actions does not link Him with something alien to Him; it is the creature which is dependent on the spring from which incessantly flows its being. Our conception of the Absolute therefore involves no limitation of it. The relations we posit between it and the world, always as a result of the poverty of our language, mean relations, not from it to us, but from us to it, and they leave it with its fulness of being, its independence, and its ideal perfection. The ocean of being does not suffer any ripple from the least touch; no wave breaks its surface or upsets its calm.

In fine, we are absolutely certain that God is the Perfect, and that nothing but something perfect can emanate from Him. But this must be rightly understood. God can produce no evil; but some evil can arise from the good that He produces. It is enough that His wisdom be capable of directing it to some ultimate good and of bringing into it the temporary or relative that may result from His action.

This can be explained by an easy example. The creation of a lamb was not an evil, neither the creation of a lion. But when lion and lamb meet evil occurs, the lamb dies. The problem is whether from this death, viewed in the general plan of the world, some good greater than that sad death cannot result; and it is the task of the Divine wisdom to provide for that.

Whatever may be the success of that intervention, it is easy to answer the present objection which must be kept upon the metaphysical level. Not only is it possible that imperfection may mar the work of the Perfect; but it cannot be otherwise; for to exclude imperfection and therefore evil from His works, the Perfect would have to impart His own nature, and that is impossible. God is Perfect because He is infinite; and the infinite cannot create another infinite.

All that He can produce must needs belong to some genus and species, and, while possessing some degree of goodness, have more or less of that generic and specific goodness. Now, as soon as they enter relations, the difference of nature and the various degrees of perfection among things are bound to bring about some evil. The sun cannot rise over the ocean without causing the evaporation of water and giving rise to clouds; an ox cannot tread a meadow peacefully but heavily without crushing the grass, and causing the death of thousands of plants. Except by creating a world perfectly still like dead crystals, the Creator could not avoid evil. He has preferred to make use of evil, and if that does not make Him unwise, still less is it out of harmony with His essence. The very perfection of that essence is one more reason why the universe cannot be like unto Him.

There remains the matter of degrees of perfection. Some may find too weak the amount of good the world exhibits, and too high the amount of evil. But what a rash judgment! Those who pass it are totally ignorant of its grounds; they do not know the facts, since, lost as they are in a little corner of space and time, they are incapable of embracing their whole course; and the laws are beyond their grasp, since their overweening but feeble reason should not dare to draw rules for the actions of the Creator.

The Infinite has reasons of His own; no one is admitted into His counsels, and all that we can allow human reason without insulting it by ascribing to it a pride of madness, is that for it the problem of evil is a mystery. I am willing to grant the existence of that mystery, and I do not pretend to have offered a solution of it in this brief discussion, no more than I claim to be able to solve all the difficulties which rise in my mind from considering the existence of the Infinite, the existence of the finite, and the transcendental relations which link together two orders of reality which are so radically distinct from each other.

From every direction, when we deal with those problems, clouds pile up and night grows darker. To speak of God is to grind a mystery. But would not the world itself be a mystery without God? Would not human life too be a heap of mysteries? We have taken our flight to God that we may come out of night and nothingness; shall we now turn away from God because of the overflowing light and the rich existence we find in Him?

If anything comes clear from these thorny discussions, it is the extreme partiality of those who oppose God; it is, on the one hand, their tender exigencies, and, on the other, their unconquerable fear of mystery, when applied to God in whom it should be expected, and the amount of mystery they tolerate in their denials. I have noticed that tendency, and I dare to think the reader will appreciate it.

Let us resign ourselves to our powerlessness to understand the Ineffable; nevertheless, let us affirm His existence, because without Him nothing can exist, and nothing is intelligible. The Infinite, on the one hand, and, on the other, the synthesis of the Infinite with the finite, are mysteries we should not dream of fathoming; but the existence of the finite about us without that of the Infinite, its cause, is not a mystery, but an absurdity, and between the two common sense is quick in choosing.

Common sense says: God exists, I have real evidence for this assertion; I cannot reject it without giving the lie to my reason and its highest principles; nor to my life and to all that lives, nor to their most profound needs. It will add: God is mystery; but how could it be otherwise? Is it in our power to conceive the conditions of Infinite existence, its way of subsisting, the manner in which it can create, carry on, and bring back to itself all reality. All that is hidden for me; all that I can know about it is the necessity of these transcendental affirmations. The attributes I ascribe to God are but the expressions of His necessary existence. If I see from afar something that moves like arms, and cry: That is a man, I should not later say: he has but one arm. In the same way, after I have acknowledged the existence of God, because there must exist a First Being, an unmoved Mover, a Cause of causes, and Intelligence, source of all truth, a Will, source of all good, an intelligent and holy Power capable of giving a sanction to duty, a living Ideal which is the basis of human ideals, how can I, in the light of all that, deny that God is powerful, intelligent, good, just, self-conscious and living?

However, I realize that those terms applied to the Infinite must take another connotation and be transfigured to the point of having no limit. True, Spinoza has written: "All determination is a limitation." These words are true, but on the condition that the *negation* spoken of be the negation of all limitation, and that the *determination* make God a self-subsistent, and therefore a limitless Being. And I insist that, applied to god, the words: *good, just, intelligent, powerful, living* or *being*, may, while retaining their import, lose their restrictive character, and clothed with infinity, rise to the height which they connote.

It is not only in our days that spiritualist philosophers have written that, strictly speaking, no word of the human language applies to God. We stammer and we own that we can do nothing else. But our opponents too stammer, and their stammering is wrong, since they dare to deny in matters that call for the sovereign affirmation of silence.

When we deal with God, let us hold our tongue, but let our silence be an act of adoration, a falling of our mind prostrate in presence of perfections which are too lofty for even the words of genius to reach them; too dazzling not to make faint the human mind's ray of light; too inaccessible to permit the scaffolds of our systems to attain up to the fronton of the temple, on which the mystical triangle shows forth its undecipherable symbol; where the giant's hand cannot reach, where the birds stop, but only to find their aliment in the cracks of the eternal stones, not to judge of the structure, not to analyse its forms, nor to measure its dimensions.

26

A SKETCH OF AN ADEQUATE DEMONSTRATION OF
THE EXISTENCE OF GOD *

IN THE passage of *The Two Sources* in which he examines the problem of the existence of God, Bergson offers the view that the problem can and must be approached *experimentally*. "Indeed we fail to see how philosophy could approach the problem in any other way. Generally speaking, we look at an object as existing if it is perceived, or might be perceived. Such an object is therefore presented in actual or possible experience. No doubt you may construct the idea of an object or of a being, as the geometrician does for a geometrical figure; but experience alone will decide whether it actually exists outside the idea thus constructed. Now, you may assert that this is just the question, and that the problem precisely is to know whether a certain Being is not distinctive from all other beings in that He stands beyond the reach of our experiences, and yet is as real as they are. Granted, for this once, although an assertion of this kind, with its attendant arguments, appears to me to imply a fundamental illusion. But then you must prove that the Being thus defined, thus demonstrated, is indeed God." Then Bergson goes on to a criticism of the God of Aristotle, "adopted with a few modifications by most of his successors," and he re-

* Fernand van Steenberghen, "Le problème philosophique de Dieu," *Revue Philosophique de Louvain*, Vol. 45 (1947), pp. 301-313. This is the conclusion of the article.

marks that there is an abyss between the God "most men have in mind" and the God of Philosophy "whom mankind has never dreamed of invoking."

We may grant at once that the Prime Mover or Pure Act of Aristotle is not the true God that we seek; when, at the beginning of our study, we must clear the notion or the "nominal definition" of God which was to help us to state the problem, we took care to meet the current notion men have of God as the center of religion; we asked whether Philosophy could establish the existence of a "Creator who governs the universe." Here, therefore, as indeed in the philosophy of St. Thomas and of all the great scholastic masters, we deal with the same God of whom Bergson speaks; it is quite incorrect to say that the God of Aristotle has been adopted "with but slight modifications" by the Christian disciples of the Philosopher, for there is a far greater abyss between Aristotle's "Prime Mover," and the "infinite Creator and Ruler" of Thomistic metaphysics, than between this Creator and the God of Christian revelation.

Our true disagreement with Bergson, therefore, does not regard the notion of the true God, which is the very *subject* of the problem, but the *method* of solving it; Bergson appeals to the experience and the testimony of the mystics because he questions the possibility of a rational demonstration, which amounts to a denial of the possibility of metaphysics.

Those who think they should adopt the French philosopher's empiricist and agnostic attitude would have no other resource than to follow likewise his manner of seeking God and we have not thought of condemning that method, in spite of the reservations it calls for from the strictly scientific point of view. It is reasonable and prudent to rely upon the convergent testimonies of witnesses like John of the Cross, Teresa of Jesus, Francis de Sales and so many other great Christian mystics; it is reasonable and prudent to accept the testimony of the Apostles and, above all, of Christ Himself, and admit the existence of God as a *fact;* certain minds which lean toward positivism will always find this empirical method, this manner of finding God as a duly attested fact, more satisfactory and more convincing than all metaphysical arguments. Nothing forbids us to respect that preference.

But there are other minds which are more exacting. They want to attain a *personal evidence,* where such evidence is within the reach of man, and they ask whether the existence of God cannot become the object of a rational assent based upon a critical investigation. We think that metaphysics can give a positive answer to that question, and the last part of our study is devoted to the task of making it evident.

It is easy to understand why the discussion of the problem of the existence of God belongs to metaphysics. As the science which deals with "what is, in so far as it is," Ontology alone has the task of discovering the general laws of reality and of bringing as far as possible into light the mystery of existence. Owing to the transcendental import of the concept of being, which is its formal object, Metaphysics, alone among all sciences, knows no limit to its range, which embraces all that exists; it is therefore the only science that can raise the problem of "the ultimate reasons," or of the "first causes." It is therefore its business to tell us whether the transcendent Being whom we have defined "Creator and Ruler of the universe" finds a place in the metaphysical synthesis, and must be accepted as the ultimate explanation of what exists. We shall see that an affirmative answer must be given to that question.

The metaphysical reflection which ends in the affirmation of God involves two steps. In the first, the existence of an *absolute, or unconditioned reality* is established. In the second, proof is given that that absolute reality must be looked for *beyond the realm of finite beings,* in other words that the Absolute transcends the finite, or is infinite.

The first step is easy to cover, and it is significant that it has been covered by all great thinkers, with the exception of those who have allowed themselves to tumble into absolute phenomenism or radical empiricism. This part of the demonstration can be summed up in a brief, clear formula, which appeals to most minds: "Since something exists, something must be self-existent." The evidence of the compound proposition is based on the fact that its contradictory immediately appears to be untenable; for the assertion: "Nothing exists" is evidently false, and even involves an evident contradiction, since to assert that nothing exists, one must exist; as to the proposition "all that exists owes its existence to another," it also involves an evident contradiction, since what is affirmed as "totality" in the subject is denied as "totality" in the predicate, since "something other" than the "totality" is posited.

Of course philosophical critics do not see the issue in this simple way. If one wants to carry methodical doubt to the end and meet all the possible demands of criticism, one will have to proceed more slowly and more prudently.

First, one will establish against Scepticism the *validity of the assertion* and, against radical Phenomenism the validity and the import of *the affirmation that something exists.*

Then one will show *the analogical and transcendental character of the idea of being,* which allows us to synthetize, not only all the data of our experience, but all that could exist beyond the range of our experience: in one word, to grasp really, though confusedly, through our thought all that exists.

Lastly, one will show that the integral object of intelligence, thus grasped confusedly by an act of thinking possessed of transcendental import, has the nature of an *absolute value.* For what is opposed to nothing can be related to nothing, can depend on nothing; now the whole of reality is opposed to nothing; therefore it cannot be relative, it is absolute or unconditioned. This means that at least *something* in the whole sphere of existence must be self-existent and be the source of the existence of all the rest. In one word, there exists an absolute, unconditioned or uncaused reality.

This first stage of the proof of God's existence is found in various forms in most of the classical arguments for the existence of God. Aristotle rejects the explanation of motion by an infinite series of "movers" because it is absurd to assume that all that exists is dependent or conditioned; without "*first* mover" or "*unmoved* mover," motion is inexplicable. St. Augustine invokes the necessity of admitting the existence of an *eternal* reality *necessary by nature*. St. Anselm's being "quo majus cogitari non potest" has *necessary existence* as an essential attribute. Avicenna rises from composite contingent beings to the Being whose definition is that it is, or *whose essence is its existence. The* first three *viae* in St. Thomas' *Summa theologica* reject the *"regressus in infinitum"* because an *absolute principle* is required as the source of that which exists; the *"maxime ens"* of the *"quarta via"* is the *uncaused or unconditioned cause* of all that participates in the plenitude of being. In one word, aseity is an essential attribute of God in the eyes of all thinkers who affirm the existence of a personal God, and likewise in the eyes of the pantheists the real principle to which they seek to link the universe is primarily conceived as, and often expressly called "the Absolute."

The second *stage* of the metaphysical demonstration of the existence of God is more difficult and proves to be a stumbling block for many metaphysicians. It can be set forth in this way.

The metaphysical analysis of finite being as such reveals that every finite being is essentially related to something else, and that the whole order of finite beings is related to some transcendent reality. This is evident from the consideration either of the *existence*, or of the *action* of the finite.

What, in the very *existence* of the finite, is the sign of an essential relativity? It is not its *composite nature* as such, for, even after it has been duly established, it remains mysterious, and nothing can be directly inferred from it. Neither is it *finitude* as such, for nothing permits us to affirm *a priori* that the Absolute cannot be finite; a finite being is a being distinct from other beings, whose own reality is distinct from that of other beings, which, in regard to it, are also finite; this "relation of opposition" when it is considered exclusively in itself, does not *of itself* involve a real interdependence of those beings. What makes manifest the fundamental relativity of finite beings is their mutual *analogy* which evidences their *basic similitude in spite of their diversity;* this similitude is utterly inexplicable so long as we consider only finite beings. For, as we have just said, finite beings are different from one another, alien to one another, limited by one another; hence none of them can be the adequate cause of another, by imparting existence to it or creating it, for we can conceive of no opposition between a being and the cause that created it, as it is wholly precontained in that cause; and yet, as beings, they are wholly similar to one another, they have a real basic "kinship," a "family look" which must have a *raison d'être,* not to be unintelligible; this deep ontological kinship has no other explanation than their *common dependence* upon one single Cause which transcends all finite beings, and therefore is infinite.

As regards *activity,* the argument is still more striking, but it assumes the truth that every finite being is by nature an active principle. I believe that this truth can be established by beginning with a metaphysical analysis of our personal activity (of which we are all conscious), and by showing that the *necessary and sufficient* condition of our own activity is found also in every finite being. The finite being therefore is *active by nature,* which means that it strives to perfect itself by entering into relation with other finite beings. Now such a condition betrays an all-around and essential indigence and dependence.

In the first place, the active being is dependent because it is *perfectible:* an absolute being cannot grow in perfection, because perfectibility implies the possibility of coming under the influence of an agent. As it is by nature perfectible, the finite being must be dependent.

Moreover, the active being is dependent because of its *positive seeking* of other beings to help it in becoming perfect. As this active tendency is essential to it, it involves an essential relativity.

The dependence of the active being is also evidenced from other aspects of activity, but an analysis of the whole doctrine of activity would be required for an exact apprehension of its nature.

Therefore, whether we consider the finite being in its existence or in its activity, it appears to be wholly relative, conditioned or dependent. An "absolute finite being" involves a logical contradiction.

However, could we not conceive the finite being as related *to the other finite beings,* and conditioned by *the whole order of finite beings,* which would be the absolute reality and the key to the solution of the whole problem?

This last attempt to explain the finite by the finite is quite illusory, and only fancy can give it the appearance of consistency. The order of finite beings has no reality beyond the finite beings themselves; a group of beings, every one of which is dependent on others for its very existence, and none of which can account for the existence of the others, is totally dependent as a group. A new global effect can be obtained by the synthesis of several elements, provided each of these elements is endowed with a degree of efficiency: thus a vault can be built of many stones, because each stone brings in its cohesion, its shape and its weight; several horses can set in motion a car which only one horse could not pull, because each one contributes to the global effect with its own muscular power. But an absolute being cannot result from the multiplication of wholly relative beings, no more than a car could be moved by a team of wooden horses. In other words, the ontological similitude and the activity of finite beings remain unexplained, even if we bring in the whole order of them. Their essential similitude is not based upon their order as such, it is rather the similitude that is the basis of the order. As to their activity, it confers a new perfection to the whole order, because it is by its activity that each finite being actually expands and enriches itself; but if the order of finite beings is perfectible, it is evident that it cannot constitute an absolute reality, since every change implies dependence.

Thus we reach the end of the second stage of our demonstration, and we can conclude as follows: every finite being considered apart from the others and from the whole order of finite beings discloses a complete indigency, dependence, or relativity, in regard to a reality which transcends the finite, that is to say, a reality which is not finite, but infinite. In this, as in the first stage, supplementary explanations would be required to give full satisfaction to the demands of philosophical criticism. We should have to expound and examine deeply the whole metaphysics of the finite to grasp the full force of the demonstration I have just sketched briefly. We should have above all to bring into light the doctrine of *analogy*, the doctrine of *activity* and the metaphysical *principle of causality* which is the true spring of the argument.

Such is, in its broad lines, the effort of reflection which, starting from the most elementary assertion, "Something exists," leads us to the summit of human thought and the culminating point of metaphysics, with the affirmation of the existence of the Infinite Being, creator of all finite beings and of their whole order. We must add a few complementary remarks to give its full force to this reflection or demonstration.

It is not difficult to grasp the *sinew of the proof.* It is the radical antinomy between the *absolute* and the *finite* which drives us logically to affirm the existence of a Being which transcends the finite. We may then sum up as follows the proof of the existence of the Infinite Being: there exists an absolute reality (such is the conclusion of the first stage of the demonstration); now this absolute reality is not to be found in the order of finite beings; therefore it transcends the finite, or is infinite. On the other hand, since the whole order of finite beings is relative, it can be related only to the infinite reality which transcends it, which means that it is entirely the effect of the Infinite Being.

Does this Infinite Being whose existence is thus revealed to us *answer the description of God* we gave at the start of our inquiry, when we set forth this nominal definition of God: "A Creator and ruler of the universe"? To give an adequate answer to this important question, we should here undertake to deduce the attributes of the Infinite Being. I limit myself to saying that, once we have vindicated the affirmation of the Infinite Being, total cause and creator of the order of finite beings, it is easy enough to show that this Infinite Being is *only one,* that He is eminently *personal*, that His creative power is *intelligent* and *benevolent*, and that His *providence* embraces the universal order with all its elements. At the end of this deduction we meet again fully the nominal definition we set forth at our starting point.

Is a *popular* statement of the proof of the existence of God possible? It is in the "psychological preparation"; it is very useful provided it is offered for what it is worth, and not as an apodictic and complete demonstration; to undergraduate students, for example, after unfolding this psychological preparation, it will be shown that the problem of the existence of God is essentially a *philosophical* problem which, as it presupposes training in philosophy, can be examined scientifically only in the graduate course. The real proof, viz. the metaphysical proof, can be stated in a popular way in the same measure as Metaphysics itself; now here two extremes are to be guarded against, namely the exaggeration and the underestimation of the difficulty of that kind of reflection; presented in its broad outline and in "human" terms, the proof we have outlined seems to be accessible to every intelligence that has been trained to reflect on abstract subjects; those who would want to go further may be required to make a greater effort and to get more deeply initiated into metaphysical investigation.

Let us return briefly to the *method* we have used in our argument and try to see why any truly satisfactory proof must be reduced to the following. The problem is to reach the "Creator of the Universe," the only adequate Cause of all that is not Himself. This is possible only if, after having shown that we must admit an Absolute, we thus *go beyond the finite as such*. For, if we were content with going beyond *certain categories* of finite beings (material beings, for example), we would have to establish the relativity of the *other* finite beings that may exist beyond the categories we have considered, and thus we would lose the right to posit the Absolute as *infinite*. Now, to prove that there is only one First Cause, we must know that it is infinite; therefore, if we should reason from only one category of finite beings, we could not arrive at one only Absolute, nor at one only Creator of all.

Two elements therefore are indispensable in every rigorous proof of the existence of God: the realization of the necessity of an Absolute and that of the relativity of the finite being as such. These two mental acts essentially belong to the metaphysical order of thought, and that is sufficient ground for rejecting as insufficient any proof that does not reach the metaphysical level. On the other hand, the realization of the relativity of the finite as such can be got only from a metaphysical analysis of its *existence* or of its *activity*, for those are the only two aspects under which we can reach any finite being.

In the light of these remarks it would be easy to show in detail the weak points of the many arguments we have rejected as unacceptable. Some neglect showing that we must admit an Absolute. Others are content with showing the contingency of certain categories of beings. Others use defective ways of proving the relativity of finite beings, whether they argue from the real distinction between essence and existence, or the fact that existence does not enter into the definition of finite being (which, besides, is inaccurate), or the very notion of finite being which would directly imply the existence of the Infinite; or at last, the hierarchy of finite beings which would imply an absolute maximum at its summit. Others pretend to reach the Infinite Being without recourse to the relativity of the finite as such, and by a mere appeal to the dynamism of the intellect. We have shown the defects of these various methods.

By way of illustration and to make more evident the insufficiency of the *quinque viae* taken literally, let us for a moment resume our examination of the *prima via*. As we said above, we find in it, at least implicitly, the first stage of the metaphysical argument in the words by which St. Thomas rejects the explanation of change by recourse to an infinite series of "moved movers"; "*hic autem non est* (this hellenism means "it is not possible," "it is not licit") *procedere in infinitum, quia sic non esset aliquod primum movens, et per consequens nec aliquod aliud movens, quia moventia secunda non movent nisi per hoc quod sunt mota a primo movente.*"

Let us first remark that this text makes no explicit reference to an absolute *being*, but to an absolute *mover*, that is to a moving cause which does not receive the motion which it imparts; now, as we have seen, there is a way to show directly, and rather easily, the existence of an absolute reality, from the mere fact that all cannot be relative or dependent on a cause.

Now, what is the immediate conclusion of the *prima via?* As we saw before, its premises permit the conclusion that we must go beyond the range of experience, where everything is subject to becoming, to find *one or many immutable sources* of the many changes we observe here below. That is all, and when St. Thomas adds immediately: "et hoc omnes intelligunt Deum," he knows very well that such an affirmation is elliptic and requires to be explained.

How can we pass from this rather vague conclusion to the affirmation of the true God, that is of the "Creator and ruler of the universe"? To show that there is *only one* absolute and immutable Principle of motion, one must prove that it is *infinite;* and to prove that it is infinite and transcendent over all finite reality (not only over the world of our experience), we should prove that *all* finite reality is by its very nature contingent or relative; we have then to proceed to the second stage of the metaphysical argument.

And it is this method that St. Thomas himself uses in his *Summa theologica.* He seeks to prove that an immutable Being (conclusion of the *prima via*) could not be composed of essence and existence (Qu. III, a. 4), nor could it admit of any composition (Qu. III, ar. 7), for any kind of composition would imply the presence in it of a *potential* element which would be incompatible with immutability. As it is an

Esse subsistens, this immutable Being must be *infinite* (Qu. VII, ar. 1), and therefore *one only* (Qu. XI, ar. 3). We shall not dwell on the difficulties of the rather complex deduction (this complexity is inevitable in the *prima via* which, instead of going straight to the goal and showing the relativity of the finite, takes the roundabout way of the changes which are observed in the material world). What we want to stress is that *this deduction clearly implies a metaphysical analysis of the finite being as such,* in other words, the second stage of the metaphysical argument we have set forth. A being "made up of essence and existence" is nothing but a "finite" being, since in the eyes of St. Thomas, the union of essence and existence is what constitutes the finite being, and explains how it can *exist* and *be finite;* hence to say that every being made up of essence and existence is a being in potency to change, means that every finite being is subject to change, is a "moved mover" and therefore is a relative and conditioned being, and it is on that ground that St. Thomas posits the existence of the Infinite Being. Actually the *prima via* has been merely the first step in an argument the essence of which is to be found in later questions of the *Summa.*

Existentialism is now the fashion. As a philosophy of living experience or concrete "subjectivity," and as a philosophy of the human condition or of an existence full of tragedy and mystery, existentialism fosters a deep distrust, and often open hostility to concepts, reason, and argument; it is anti-rationalist and, no doubt, in a large measure, anti-intellectualist. We may pass over atheistic existentialism, which is a philosophy of the absurd and of despair, to which the contemporary intellectual and moral dismay, too often united with a snobbism of bad taste, insures momentary success. But there is a "right wing" existentialism, even a Christian existentialism, which appeals to good minds by its concrete method and its acute sense of reality. What aid could we expect from this method in our quest for God?

The reader who has followed our study with some degree of attention will have no difficulty in anticipating the direction of our answer. The existentialist method has already yielded remarkable fruits with its penetrating, often ingenious, and at times genial exploration of the inexhaustible world of human experience; in this domain existentialism brings a contribution of high value to what we have called "the psychological preparation" for the proof of the existence of God: the radical indigence and precariousness of the human condition, the sense of sin and the sense of death, the dramatic aspiration of man to happiness, justice and immortality, the perfect communion of souls, etc.; all that is excellent and only reminds us of the famous sayings of an Augustine, a Pascal, an Ollé-Laprune, a Blondel, and many others. In as far as existentialism would refrain from using other methods than those of empiricism and phenomenology, one can rest assured that it will not go beyond that "psychological preparation," for God is not an object of human experience, the Infinite is not the *immanent* goal of our aspirations, but the *transcendent* Principle and End of the universal order, the Creator. If by chance existentialism consents to break the barriers of empiricism and to enter the field of metaphysics, in its search of the metempirical conditions or implications of the facts of experience, it will be able to do so only with the aid of conceptual and discursive thought; for that is the only means at our disposal to carry us beyond the range of experience and to formulate laws regarding the finite being as such. Now to be able to affirm the existence of the Infinite Being we have to rise up to the conditions of existence which are common to all finite beings and make evident their fundamental relativity.

To have the right to challenge this conclusion, existentialism would have to prove that we possess, beyond the range of conceptual knowledge, I know not what intellectual intuition which would enable us to reach the personal Infinite in a more direct and more concrete manner. But, barring the appeal to mystical experience (and in this case we leave the ground of philosophy), nothing leads us to anticipate the discovery of such an intuition; the repeated failures of all the attempts made in this sense in the course of history, from Plato to Bergson, leaves very little hope to the incorrigible Utopians who dream for us of an angelic way of knowing; the essays accomplished heretofore by the best representatives of the new school in their search for God are not such as could weaken our scepticism; the more so as as the analysis of man's consciousness makes extremely improbable the existence in us of the mysterious power they dream of; for conceptual and discursive thought seems to be the mode of intellection befitting a consciousness endowed with the power of assimilation and stimulated by an experience made up of sensorial perceptions, and of a certain consciousness of subjective activity. When based upon such an experience, conceptual and discursive activity is quite capable of leading us to the knowledge of the Infinite, and we do not see why a specific intuition should be needed to attain it.

Hence, whatever may be the resources and the interest of the existentialist methods in their proper fields of application, metaphysical reflection elaborated as a result of our conceptual and discursive activity remains indispensable for the solution of the most fundamental problems, not to mention the fact that it is the summit of our spiritual life.

We must make a last remark. We have just seen that the scientific, rigorous and complete proof of the existence of God is of necessity metaphysical. Nay more, it is identical with the essential processes of metaphysical thinking, and the affirmation of the Infinite Being is in truth the natural crowning of the science of being as being. It is from its metaphysical character that this proof derives its absolute rigor, and its unequaled scientific value, and, consequently, its certainty in a supreme degree, the metaphysical certainty. But it is also the metaphysical character of that proof that baffles many minds. Once he has reached that summit in his intellectual life, man is caught in a kind of vertigo and anxiety, because his need of intuition and his sensibility no longer find satisfaction in this line of thinking. This is the source of the psychological uneasiness that some are prone to experience before the most rigorous metaphysical demonstrations. But we should not forget that we must adore God "in spirit and in truth," nor that true wisdom urges us to react against such unjustified impressions and such demands of the carnal man. Every man is a metaphysician unconscious of his power, for every being endowed with intelligence is haunted by the need of understanding reality. This sleeping metaphysician must be awakened and his benumbed curiosity must be stimulated. God has endowed us with intelligence primarily that we may seek Him, and our effort to find Him will not be disappointed.

27

THE EXISTENCE OF GOD AND MODERN NATURAL SCIENCE *

ACCORDING to the measure of its progress, and contrary to the affirmations advanced in the past, true science discovers God in an ever-increasing degree—as though God were waiting behind every door opened by science. We would even say that from this progressive discovery of God, which is realized in the increase of knowledge, there flow benefits not only for the scientist himself when he reflects as a philosopher—and how can he escape such reflection? but also for those who share in these new discoveries or make them the object of their own considerations. Genuine philosophers profit from these discoveries in a very special way, because when they take these scientific conquests as the basis for their rational speculations, their conclusions thereby acquire greater certainty, while they are provided with clearer illustrations in the midst of possible shadows and more convincing assistance in establishing an ever more satisfying response to difficulties and objections.

Thus stimulated and guided, the human intellect approaches that demonstration of the existence of God which Christian wisdom recognizes in those philosophial arguments which have been carefully examined throughout the centuries by giants in the world of knowledge, and which are already well known to you in the presentation of the five ways which the Angelic Doctor, St. Thomas, offers as a speedy and safe road to lead the mind to God. We have called these arguments "philosophical." This does not mean that they are aprioristic, as they are

* His Holiness, Pope Pius XII (1876-1958). From an address to the Pontifical Academy of Science, November 22, 1951, trans. and published by the National Catholic Welfare Conference, Washington. Introduction, pp. 3-5.

accused of being by a narrow-minded and incoherent positivism. Even though they draw their demonstrative force from the power of human reason, they are nevertheless based on concrete realities established by the senses and by science.

In this way both philosophy and the sciences, by means of activities and methods which are analogous and mutually compatible, carry on their work. Though in different measures, they all make use of both empirical and rational elements and cooperate in harmonious unity for the discovery of truth.

But if the primitive experience of the ancients could provide human reason with sufficient arguments for the existence of God, then with the expanding and deepening of the field of human experiments, the vestiges of the Eternal One are discernible in the visible world in ever more striking and clearer light. Hence it seems helpful to re-examine on the basis of new scientific discoveries the classical proofs of the Angelic Doctor, especially those based on motion and the order of the universe (*Sum. theol.* 1, 2, 3); that is to say, to inquire if, and in what degree, a very profound knowledge of the structure of the macrocosm and the microcosm contributes toward strengthening these philosophical arguments.

It is also helpful to consider, on the other hand, if and to what degree these proofs have been weakened, as is not infrequently affirmed, by the fact that modern physics has formulated new basic principles, ruled out or modified certain ancient ideas, whose content was perhaps judged in the past to be fixed and definitive, such as time, space, motion, causality, substance—all of which concepts are supremely important for the question which now occupies us. The question, then, is not of inquiring into the physical foundations from which they flow, although limitations of time will oblige Us to restrict Our attention to only some few of these foundations. There is no reason to be fearful of surprises. Not even science itself aims to go outside the world which today, as yesterday, presents itself through these "five modes of being" whence the philosophical demonstration of the existence of God proceeds and draws its force.

PART TWO

The Nature of God and Divine Life

Section One

The Analogical Character of Our Knowledge of God

28

HOW GOD IS KNOWN BY US *

a. God can be known in this life by natural reason. XII, 2.

OUR natural knowledge begins from sense. Hence our natural knowledge can go as far as it can be led by sensible things. Our mind cannot be led by sense so far as to see the Essence of God; because the sensible effects of God do not equal the power of God as their cause. Hence from the knowledge of sensible things the power of God cannot be known; nor therefore can His Essence be seen. But because they are His effects and depend on their cause, we can be led from them so far as to know that God exists, and to know of Him what must necessarily belong to Him, as the First Cause of all things, exceeding all things caused by Him.

Hence we know that He has to do with creatures so far as to be the cause of them all; also that creatures differ from Him inasmuch as He is not in any way part of what is caused by Him; and that creatures are not removed from Him by reason of any defect on His part, but because He superexceeds them all.

b. A name can be given to God. XIII, 1.

According to the Philosopher, words are signs of ideas, and ideas are the similitude of things; it is thus evident that words relate to the meaning of things through the medium of the intellectual conception. It follows that we can give a name to anything in as far as we understand it. It was shown (Qu. XII, ar. 11-12) that in this life we cannot see the essence of God; but we know God from creatures as their principle, and

* St. Thomas Aquinas, *Summa Theologica*, Ia, q. 12, art. 2, q. 13, art. 1, 2, 5.

also by way of excellence and remotion (of defect). In that way therefore he can be named by us from creatures, nevertheless not so as to express by the name what belongs to the Divine Essence in itself; as the name *man* expresses the essence of man as he really is, since it signifies the definition of man in his essence; for the idea expressed by the name is the definition.

c. Some names can be applied to God substantially. XIII, 2.

Negative names applied to God or signifying His relation to creatures manifestly do not at all signify His substance, but rather express the distance of the creature from Him, or His relation to something else, or rather, the relation of creatures to Himself.

As regards absolute and affirmative names of God, as: *good, wise,* and the like, various and many opinions have been given. For some have said that all such names although they are applied to God affirmatively, nevertheless have been brought into use more to express some remotion from God, rather than to express anything that exists positively in Him. Hence they assert that, when we say that God lives, we mean that God is not like an inanimate thing; and so in like manner the same applies to other names; this was taught by Rabbi Moses. Others that these names applied to God signify His attitude towards creatures: as in the words, *God is good,* we mean, God is the cause of goodness in things; and the same rule applies to other names.

Both of these opinions, however, seem to be untrue for three reasons: for in neither of them can any reason be assigned why some names more than others are applied to God. For He is assuredly the cause of bodies in the same way as he is the cause of good things, therefore if the words, *God is good,* signified no more than, *God is the cause of good things,* it might in like manner be said that God is a body, inasmuch as He is the cause of bodies. So also to say that He is a body implies that He is not a mere potentiality, as is primary matter. Second, because it would follow that all names applied to God would be said of Him by way of being taken in a secondary sense, as healthy is secondarily said of medicine, forasmuch as it signifies only the cause of health, in the animal which primarily is called healthy. Third, because this is against the intention of those who speak of God. For in saying that God lives, they assuredly mean more than to say that He is the cause of our life, or that he differs from inanimate bodies.

Therefore it must otherwise be said that these names signify the divine substance, and are predicated substantially of God, although they fall short of expressing the full representation of Him. Which is proven thus. For these names express what God is, so far as we can understand Him. Our intellect knows God from creatures; therefore it knows Him as far as creatures are capable of giving a true and adequate representation of Him. It was shown above that God presupposes in Himself the possession of all perfections belonging to all creatures, so that He is considered as simply and universally perfect. Hence every creature represents Him as far, and is like Him as far as it possesses some perfection, but not as representing Him as if He belonged to the same species, or genus, but as the excelling principle in regard to whom the effects are defective; still, however, possessing some kind of likeness in themselves as effects; as the forms of the inferior bodies represent the power of the sun. This was explained above in treating of the divine perfection. Therefore the aforesaid names signify the divine substance, but in an imperfect manner, as creatures also represent it imperfectly. So when we say, God is good, the meaning is not, God is the cause of goodness, or, God is not bad; but the meaning is, Whatever good we attribute to creatures pre-exists in God, and in a more excellent and higher way. Hence it does not follow that God is good because He causes goodness; but rather, on the contrary, He causes goodness in things because He is Himself good; according to what Augustine says, *Because He is good, we are.*

d. What is said of God and of creatures is not univocally predicated of
    them. XIII, 5.

Univocal predication is impossible between God and creatures. The reason of this is that every effect which is not an adequate result of the power of the agent cause, receives the similitude of the agent, not in its full degree, but in a measure that falls short of the agent, so that what is divided and multiplied in the effects resides in the agent simply, and in the same manner; as for example the sun by the exercise of its own power produces manifold and various forms in all inferior things. In the same way, as said above, all perfections existing in creatures divided and multiplied, pre-exist in God simply and united. Thus, when any name expressing perfection is applied to a creature, it signifies that perfection distinct in idea from other perfections, as, for instance, by this name *wise* applied to a man, we signify some perfection distinct from a man's essence, and distinct from his power and existence, and from all similar things; whereas when we apply it to God, we do not mean to signify anything distinct from His essence, or Power, or Existence. Thus also this name *wise* applied to a man in some degree describes and comprehends the things signified; whereas this is not the case when it is applied to God; but it leaves the thing signified as uncomprehended, and as exceeding the signification of the name. Hence it is evident that this name *wise* is not applied in the same way to God and to man. The same rule applies to other names. Hence no name is predicated univocally of God and of creatures.

Neither, on the other hand, are names applied to God and creatures in a purely equivocal sense, as some have said. If that were so, it follows that from creatures nothing could be known or proved about God at all; but everything would be exposed to the fallacy of equivocation. Such a view is against the philosophers, who proved many things about God, and also against what the Apostle says: *The invisible things of God are clearly seen from the things made* (Rom. I:20). Therefore it must be said that these names are said of God and creatures in an *analogous* sense, that is, according to the sense of proportion.

This occurs in two ways as regards the use of names: either according to the proportion of many things to one, as for example when we speak of urine and medicine, in relation to health of body, of which the former is the sign and the latter the cause, or because one thing has proportion to another, as health is said of medicine and animal, since medicine is the cause of health in the animal body. In this way some things are said of God and creatures analogically, and neither in a purely equivocal nor purely univocal sense. For we can name God only from creatures. Thus, whatever is said of God and creatures, is said in the order that exists of a creature to God as its principle and cause; wherein pre-exist excellently all perfections of things. This mode of community of idea is a mean between pure equivocation and simple univocation. For in analogies the idea is not, as it is in univocals, one and the same, yet also it is not totally diverse as in equivocals, but it must be said that a name used in a multiple sense signifies various proportions as regards some one thing; as health applied to blood signifies the sign of animal health, and applied to medicine signifies the cause of health.

9

ST. THOMAS AND ANALOGY *

T HE basic proposition in the doctrine of Thomistic analogy, in its strict and proper meaning, is that whatever perfection is analogically common to two or more beings is intrinsically (formally) possessed by each, not, however, by any two in the same way or mode, but by each in proportion to its being. Knowledge, for example, is possessed by men, by angels and by God, but not in the same way; the way in which men know is proportionate to the being which men have and likewise for angels and for God. There is thus a strict proportion of proportions in which the terms of one proportion are not proportionate to the terms of the other proportion, but the whole proportion between the terms on one side of the relation is proportionate to the whole proportion between the terms on the other side of the relation. Thus, in the analogous statement, "Knowledge is to the angel as knowledge is to

* Gerald B. Phelan (1892-   ), *Saint Thomas and Analogy,* "The Aquinas Lectures, 1941" (Milwaukee: The Marquette University Press, 1941), pp. 23-30, 38-43.

man," knowledge in the first case (angelic knowledge) is not directly compared to knowledge (human knowledge) in the second case (in other words, the term knowledge does not mean the same thing when predicated of angel as it does when predicated of man); nor is "angel" directly compared with "man"; or, in other words, man is not said to be an angel nor an angel to be a man.

What is stated is that the proportion between knowledge and angel *holds*, i.e. angels know *as* angels are; and the proportion between knowledge and man *holds*, i.e. men know *as* men are; and further (and finally) that there is proportion between the way the first proportion *holds* and the way the second proportion *holds*. Of course, the ultimate basis upon which such analogies rest is the proportion existing between the essence (*quod est*) and existence (*esse*) of every being that is; from it follows that every metaphysical perfection, every metaphysical concept and every metaphysical term is of its very nature analogical. This is indeed a very far-reaching statement for it implies that whenever one uses such a common word as "is" or "true" or "good," or any other term expressing a metaphysical or transcendental object of thought, the meaning of that word never remains exactly the same but is always proportionate to the nature of the being of which it is said.

This type of analogy, the analogy of proportionality, is the only true metaphysical analogy. All the other analogies fail to fulfil the requirements of metaphysical analysis for two reasons:

1. Because the perfection or character which is predicated of two or more beings is possessed intrinsically by only one of the beings in question and is merely transferred by the mind to the others.

2. Because the perfection or character which is predicated of two or more beings, although possessed intrinsically by each of the beings in question, is possessed by all in the same manner or mode, albeit in unequal degrees.

Since Cajetan's *De Nominum Analogia* it is customary to deal with the doctrines of analogy in the philosophy of St. Thomas under the general headings of analogy of inequality, analogy of attribution and analogy of proportionality—"which corresponds exactly with the three types of analogy which St. Thomas himself distinguished in his *Commentary on the Sentences of Peter Lombard (In Sent.*, d. 19, q. 5, a. 2 ad 1). Cajetan's terminology is, indeed, found elsewhere throughout the writings of St. Thomas, but in this particular passage he definitely describes each type. Given that in any analogical predication, as distinguished from univocal and equivocal predications, one term is predicated of another in a meaning which is neither entirely the same nor entirely different, the terms in which St. Thomas describes the three types of analogy just alluded to are more revealing than Cajetan's terminology.

Cajetan's analogy of inequality is described by St. Thomas as that in which there is proportion in the *being* of the analogated perfection but not in the *concept* of it. That is to say: 1. that the concept of the analogated perfection is univocal and, since a concept is the intellectual representation of the quiddity of its object, the analogated perfection is itself univocal in its very quiddity; 2. that this univocal quiddity exists intrinsically in two or more beings in a more or less perfect manner according to (proportionate to) the nature of each. It is obvious that in this type of analogy we are dealing with a generic perfection unequally shared by the species within the genus. Not only is this a rather thin sort of analogy but may be regarded, as Cajetan regards it, as "utterly alien to analogy." Nevertheless it is to this type of analogy that many philosophers have had recourse in a vain endeavour to escape the inexorable logic driving them on to monism.

The second type of analogy, which Cajetan calls the analogy of attribution, is described by St. Thomas as that in which the analogated perfection exists intrinsically in only one of the analogates (and is, therefore, univocal), and is applied by the mind proportionately to others on the basis of some relation to causality existing between the prime analogate and the minor analogates. Here we have to deal once more with a case of ontological univocity coupled with a logical use of the univocal term after the manner of a true analogy. The procedure is, of course, logically valid and, no doubt, of considerable importance in dialectics; but, once more we have on our hands a type of analogy which is far too weak to bear the weight of metaphysical or transcendental predication.

It will not be surprising to find a number of idealists using arguments based upon this type of analogy to maintain the necessary distinction between the Absolute and the Relative (by whatever names they may be called in different systems of idealism), for idealism always explicitly or implicitly reduces metaphysics to logic and erroneously applies procedures valid in dealing with the *entia rationis* of logic to the *entia realia* of ontology.

St. Thomas' description of the third type of analogy—Cajetan's analogy of proportionality—demands that the analogated perfection be not univocal either in its *being*, or in the *concept* of it, but, on the contrary, that it both exists intrinsically in all of the analogies and in each according to a different mode. This is, indeed, a difference in the very likeness and a likeness in the very difference; not merely a mingling of likeness and difference wherein likeness is based upon a formal identity and difference is based upon a formal diversity. This true analogy; for it is *in being* (*essendo*) that all beings are one yet the very *being* (*esse*) by which they are one is diverse in each, though proportionate to the essence of each.

The peculiar type of proportionality which is at the root of the metaphor and of symbolism cannot be regarded as a proper proportionality upon which metaphysical reasoning can be based because the perfection symbolically or metaphorically analogated is univocal and it is only *used* analogically to designate a certain likeness in relations. The analogated perfection is not of itself and intrinsically analogous and this is the essential requirement of a truly metaphysical analogy.

. . . .

In discussing the analogy of proportionality St. Thomas distinguishes between proportionality properly so-called and improper proportionality or symbolic analogy (*De Veritate*, II, 2 c.). The latter is of no importance for the solution of metaphysical problems since it is based upon a relation of *effects* rather than upon a relation of *causes*. Because an eagle is what it is, its flight is more sweeping and exalted than the flight of other birds; because a great orator is what he is, his eloquence is likewise more sweeping and exalted than that of other speakers. So we call Bossuet the Eagle of Meaux. But nothing in such a metaphor indicates either what an eagle *is* or what Bossuet *is*. There is, indeed, a certain proportion of proportions involved, namely the relation of an eagle to its flight and the relation of the orator to his eloquence; but to call Bossuet an eagle gives no indication with regard to the nature of Bossuet or to the being which he exercises.

Should one attempt to use this sort of analogy as the basis of a philosophy—as Vaihninger has done in *The Philosophy of "As If"*—the result will be just nothing. In other words, philosophy will disappear, to be replaced by rhetoric, poetry or pure imagination. We shall be dealing with a universe of "as if," but not with a universe of being.

The only analogy which is adequate as a metaphysical principle is the analogy of proportionality properly so-called.

An analogy of proper proportionality is founded upon the ontological (transcendental) relation in which each being stands to every other being in virtue of the very act of existence whereby all that is exists. Beings are analogical in *be-ing*. That is to say, every being exercises the act of existence (*is*) in proportion to its essence.

The analogy of proper proportionality alone accounts for the diversity of beings and their unity in being. The Heraclitean-Parmenidean dilemma can be overcome only by the recognition of the intrinsic, formal, necessary, entitative unity of that which is actually diverse. The basis of diversity in beings is the division of being by potency and act—existence (*esse*) is diversified by essence (or form) and in beings in which there is diversity within the essence, that diversity is caused by the composition of matter and form and numerical diversity results from the quantitative determination of the material thing through the division by its matter. In each of these (and all other) cases of diversity, one of the constituent elements of the beings in question is actual with respect to the other which is potential. Essence is potency in respect to existence; matter is potential with respect to form; quantity is potential with respect to informed matter. Diversity results from the manifold limitations of act by potency.

Yet within that very diversity, unity is present by reason of the intrinsic order of all that is in any way whatsoever, to the act of existence, really and formally, though proportionately, possessed by each. The unity of beings in being is necessarily an analogical unity. Were it univocal, diversity would be unintelligible; were it equivocal, nothing would be intelligible. And it is for this reason that St. Thomas says: "In analogicals it is not *diverse realities* which fall under consideration but *diverse modes* of existence of the selfsame reality" (Penido, *Le Rôle de l'analogie en Théologie dogmatique*).

By reason of the analogy of being in *be-ing* it is possible to demonstrate the existence of God, not, indeed, merely as the prime analogue in analogy of attribution, but as the Cause (analogically understood according to an analogy of proper proportionality) of the being of all that exists. For the very notion of cause is itself an analogical notion and any demonstration of the existence of the Cause of *being*, although it may virtually contain an analogy of attribution, derives its probative force from the likeness of proportions which must exist between beings which *are* only by participation and Being which *is* in its own right. It is this analogy which gives validity to all positive predication with respect to God in whom all positive perfections subsist intrinsically and formally, not merely attributively (as Meister Eckhart would have it), nor symbolically (as Maimonides contends), but according to an analogy of proper proportionality.

While univocity—the realm of clear and distinct ideas—is the arch-enemy of metaphysics, and equivocity leads but to agnosticism and the intellectually void and barren sterility of pragmatic agitation, analogy is the salvation of philosophy. It does not give the mind the complete and full satisfaction which only the intuitive grasp of Being can afford. Yet, on the other hand, neither does it sound the knell of intellectual despair (as do all empiricisms based on univocity). Experience is respected and intelligence is honoured. But the mystery of Being remains a mystery, a challenge to the thought of men, a stimulus to reflection and a lure to the inquiring mind, urging it ever inward with a divine curiosity and a humble confidence towards an ever-increasing understanding of the world of beings which Being has created.

Section Two
The Nature of God

I. The Metaphysical Attributes of God

30

AQUINAS: SELECTED PASSAGES *

Note: The term "metaphysical" is used to designate such attributes of God as relate to His nature rather than to His actions. Because they aim principally at differentiating God from creatures, these attributes are sometimes called "negative" although they express real perfections of God. St. Thomas deals with such attributes in Questions three to eleven of the First Part of his Summa Theologica. *We shall quote only the most pertinent articles dealing with Simplicity, Infinity, Existence in all things, Immutability, Eternity, and Unity.*

I. Simplicity (q. 3, art. 7):

THE absolute simplicity of God may be shown in many ways. First, from the previous articles on this question. There is neither composition of quantitative parts in God (for He is not a body), nor composition of form and matter; nor does His Nature differ from His Personality, nor His Essence from His Existence; neither is there in Him composition of genus and difference, nor of subject and accident. Therefore, it is clear that God is nowise composite but is altogether simple. Second because every composite being is posterior to its component parts, and is dependent on them; whereas God is the first Being. Third, because every composite thing must have a cause, for things in themselves different cannot amalgamate unless something causes them to unite. But God is uncaused, since His is the First efficient cause. Fourth, because in everything composite there must be potentiality and actuality (which is not so in God); but either it is one of the parts that

---

* St. Thomas Aquinas, *Summa Theologica*, I.

actuates another, or at least all the parts are potential to the whole.
Fifth, because nothing composite can be predicated of any single one of
its parts. And this is evident in a whole made up of dissimilar parts; for
no part of a man can be called a man, nor any of the parts of the foot,
a foot. In wholes made up of similar parts, although something which is
predicated of the whole may be predicated of a part (as even a part of
the air is air, and a part of water, water), nevertheless something is predicated of the whole which cannot be predicated of any of the parts; for,
not because the whole volume of water is two cubits, can any part of it
be two cubits. Thus in everything composite there is something which is
not the whole. But, even if this could be said of whatever has form, viz.,
that it has something which is not the whole, as in everything white
there is something which has not the formality of whiteness; nevertheless in the form itself, there is nothing besides itself. Since God is absolute form, or rather absolute being, He can be in no way composite.
Hilary implies this argument, saying: *God is strength, is not made up of
things that are weak; nor is He who is light, composed of things that
are dim.*

II. Infinity (q. 7, art. 1):

All the ancient philosophers attribute infinity to the first principle,
and truly so; considering that things flow forth infinitely from the first
principle. Because some erred concerning the nature of the first principle, as a consequence they erred also concerning its infinity; forasmuch
as they asserted that matter was the first principle; consequently attribut-
ing to the first principle a material infinity, to the effect that some infinite body was the first principle of things.

We must consider that a thing is called infinite because it is not finite;
whereas matter is in a way made finite by the form, and the form by
matter. Matter is made finite by the form, inasmuch as matter, before it
receives its form, is in a state of potentiality as regards many forms; but
on receiving a form, it is terminated by that one. Again form is made
finite by matter, inasmuch as form, considered in itself, is common to
many; but when received in matter, the form is determined to that one
particular thing. Matter is perfected by the form by which it is made
finite; therefore the infinite as attributed to matter, by itself contains
the idea of something imperfect, for it is as it were formless matter.
Form is not made perfect by matter, but rather is contracted by matter;
and hence the infinite, regarded on the part of the form not determined
by matter, contains the idea of something perfect. Being in itself is the
most formal of all things, as appears from what is shown above (qu. 4,
On the Perfection of God). Since the Divine Being is not a being received in anything; but is His own subsistent Being as was shown above
(qu. 3, On the Simplicity of God), it is clear that God Himself is Infinite and Perfect.

III. Existence in All Things (q. 8, art. 1):

God is in all things; not, indeed, as part of their essence, nor as an accident; but as an agent is present to anything upon which it works. As an agent must be joined to anything wherein it acts immediately, and touch it by its own power; hence it is proved that the thing moved and the mover must be joined together. Since God is Existence itself by His own Essence, so created existence must be His proper effect; as to ignite is the proper effect of fire. God causes this effect in things not only when they first begin to exist, but as long as they are preserved in existence; as light is caused in the air by the sun as long as the air remains illuminated. Therefore as long as a thing exists, God must be present to it, according to its mode of existence. The existence (*esse*) of anything is all the closer to it and all the more profoundly belongs to it as the formal idea of all that is in it. . . . Hence it must be that God exists intimately in all things.

IV. Immutability (q. 9, art. 1):

From what precedes (the demonstration of God from the fact of motion, qu. 2) it is shown that God is altogether immutable. First because it was shown that there is some first Being, whom we call God; and that this first Being must be Pure Act (*Actus Purus*), without any potentiality; for the reason that potentiality is absolutely posterior to act. Everything which is in any way changed, is in some way a potentiality. Hence it is evident that it is impossible for God to be in any way changeable. Second, because everything which is moved, remains as it was as regards some term, and passes away as regards some other term; as what is moved from whiteness to blackness, remains the same in substance; thus in everything which is moved, there is some kind of composition to be found. It has been shown above (qu. 3, On the Simplicity of God), that in God there is no composition; for He is altogether simple. Hence it is manifest that God cannot be moved. Third, because everything which is moved acquires something by its motion, and attains to what it had not attained previously. As God is Infinite, comprehending in Himself all the plenitude of perfection of all Being, He cannot acquire anything new, nor extend Himself to anything whereto He was not extended previously. Hence motion in no way belongs to Him. So, some of the ancients, constrained as it were, by the truth, decided that the First Principle was immovable.

V. Eternity (q. 10, art. 2):

Note: *Having defined eternity as "the whole, simultaneous and perfect possession of interminable life" (art. 1), St. Thomas proceeds to the demonstration of God's eternity (art. 2):*

As we attain to the knowledge of simple things by way of compound things, so we must reach to the knowledge of Eternity by means of Time. which is nothing but motion numbered by *before and after*. Since succession occurs in every motion, and one part comes after another, the fact that we reckon before and after in motion, makes us apprehend Time, which is nothing else but the measure of before and after in motion. In a thing bereft of movement, which is always the same, there is no before and after. As the idea of Time consists in the numbering of before and after in motion; so likewise in the apprehension of the uniformity outside of motion, consists the idea of Eternity.

Likewise things are said to be measured by Time which have a beginning and an end in Time, because in everything which is moved there is a beginning, and there is an end. Whatever is wholly immutable, as it can have no succession, so it has no beginning, and it has no end.

Thus Eternity is known from two sources: first, because what is eternal is interminable that is, has no beginning nor end (that is, no term in either way); second because Eternity has no succession, existing whole all at once.

The idea of Eternity follows Immutability, as the idea of Time follows motion, as appears from the preceding article. Hence, as God is supremely immutable, it supremely belongs to Him to be Eternal. Nor is He Eternal only; but He is His own Eternity; whereas no other being is its own duration, as no other is its own existence. God is His own uniform Being; and, hence as He is His own Essence, so He is His own Eternity.

VI. Unity (q. 11, art. 3):

That God is one can be shown from three sources. First from His Simplicity. For it is manifest that the reason why anything is this particular thing cannot be communicated to many. Whatever makes Socrates a man can be communicated to many; whereas, what makes him this particular man, is only communicable to one. Therefore, if Socrates were a man by what makes him this particular man, as there cannot be many Socrates, so there could not in that way be many men. This belongs to God alone; for God Himself is His own Nature, as was shown above (qu. 3). Therefore, in the very same way God is God, and He is this God. Impossible it is therefore that many gods should exist.

Second, this is proved from the Infinity of His Perfection. It was shown above (qu. 4), that God comprehends in Himself the whole perfection of being. If then many gods existed, they would necessarily differ from each other. Something would belong to one, but not to another. If this were a privation, one of them would not be absolutely perfect; if a perfection, one of them would be without it. So it is impossible for many gods to exist. Hence also the ancient philosophers, constrained, as it were by

truth, when they asserted an infinite principle, asserted likewise that
there was only one such principle.

Third, this is shown from the unity of the world. All things that exist
are seen to be ordered to each other; and some serve others. Things that
are diverse have not the same order, unless they are ordered thereto by
one. Many are reduced into order by one better than by many because
what is one by itself is the cause of one, and many are only accidentally
the cause of one, inasmuch as they may be in some way one. Since what
is first is most perfect, and absolutely so of itself, and not accidentally, it
must be that the first which reduces all into one order should be only
one. And this one is God.

31

THE ATTRIBUTES OF GOD ACCORDING TO ST. AUGUSTINE *

F OR St. Augustine, God is Truth. In Him there is no distinction between idea and actuality; He is the living unity of eternal ideas.
He is, not merely to a certain point; He is, in the fulness of the
sense. He is His very essence.

This notion of God cannot be enlarged, but it can be made more explicit and thus yield what we call the divine attributes.

I. Immutability

First of all, Truth is immutable, and from this attribute which is constantly recalled by St. Augustine, all the other attributes are derived.

In the works of St. Augustine the word "immutable" is so often attached to the word "truth," that it appears to be its natural epithet.
Particularly in the first *Dialogues*, St. Augustine unites the two terms
without explaining their logical connection; he is content with apprehending it, and giving it a forceful expression.† But he also frequently
points out the impossibility of separating the notions of God and of
immutability.

God, he says, is immutable, because He is at the summit of Being:

* Charles Boyer, S.J., *L'idée de vérité dans la philosophie de saint Augustin* (Paris:
Beauchesne, 1941), pp. 114-128. Printed by permission of the publisher. Translation
prepared by the editor.

† *De ordine* ii. 19. 50: "Nec si omnis iste mundus concidat, poterit ista ratio non
esse." *Soliloquium* i. 15. 28-29: "Nonne tibi videtur intereuntibus rebus veris veritatem
non interire?" And *ibid.* ii. 2. 2: "Nullo modo igitur occidet veritas." *De immortalitate
animae* 2: "Et semper eodem modo est, *Duo* et quattuor sex." And others.

"God is the supreme essence, that is to say, He is supremely, and is therefore unchangeable." *

"God is the sovereign good, above all good, and, for that reason, is the unchangeable good." † Now, the supreme Being, the sovereign Good, is the true Being and Good, the Being and Good which are not participations of the idea of Being or of the idea of Good, but the very idea of Being and the very idea of Good, and consequently the Truth, which is the adequation of the idea of reality.

"Would Thy proper name be Being if everything that exists outside of Thee were not, compared to Thee, as though it had no true existence?" ‡ But how does immutability follow from the truth or fulness of being? To change means to acquire or to lose some form of being. To receive a new form implies that one is lacking that form.§ Now in Truth, which is the supreme form, no form can be lacking. It is not enough to say that it possesses all perfections; it is those perfections, and that is why it is Truth. But nothing can be added unto itself. Therefore Truth can acquire no new perfection. "There is nothing in that simplicity that could have acquired or regained its own form, but the form itself is there; therefore the eternal immutable substance is not lacking any form; it is itself its form." || Could it suffer any loss? First by itself? But what is the true Being does not destroy itself, for, if it should tend to nonbeing, it would make clear that it has received being and is not being itself.¶ By the action of some nature opposed to its own? But there is no such nature; for to the true Being there is no contrary but nothingness.

St. Augustine loves to reverse that deduction, and he often says: "God is the supreme being, because He does not change" [*Ideo illum summum esse, quia nulla mutabilitate proficit seu deficit.—Epist.* 118, c. 3, n. 15]. The reason for this is that immutability is the sign by which we recognize the true being, or rather, the changes we observe in the objects of our experience are the proofs that they are not Truth itself. The whole philosophical section of the *De vera religione* [chapters 30-40] is

* "*Quum* enim Deus summa essentia sit, hoc est *summe* sit, et ideo immutabilis sit . . ." (*De civitate Dei* xii. 2).

† "Summum bonum quo superius non est Deus est: ac re hoc incommutabile bonum est," the opening phrase of *De natura boni contra Manichaeos*. Again, "Quare mutabilia? Quia non summe sunt" (*De vera religione* xviii. 35). ". . . Quod enim vere est incommutabiliter manet" (*De fide et symbolo* iv. 7).

‡ *Enarrationes in Psalmos* cx. 10. St. Augustine himself, in chapter 10 of the eleventh book of *The City of God*, unites the idea of immutability with that of supreme Being, and this again with that of Truth, "Est itaque bonum solum simplex, et *ob hoc* solum incommutabile, quod est Deus." But what is it to be simple? ". . . Natura dicitur simplex, cui non sit aliquid habere quod vel possit amittere; vel *aliud sit habens, aliud quod habet*" (*ibid.*). But, the identity of that which possesses and that which is possessed is, for St. Augustine, truth.

§ "Quaelibet res, si quam habet formam non ei opus est accipere quod habet" (*De libero arbitrio* ii. 17. 45).

|| *De Trinitate* xv. 16. 26.

¶ See *De civitate Dei* xii. 3.

based upon that principle: nothing that undergoes changes is the actualization of its idea. However, immutability, in spite of its close connection with Truth, is not the note by which we could define the nature of Truth. We conceive it only as a resultant, an attribute of it. Truth is not Truth as such because it is immutable. It is Truth because it is the adequation of the idea with being. From that adequation immutability follows.

II. Eternity

On the contrary, immutability implies eternity, or rather, it is eternity itself, the definition of which involves immutability. "The character by which we distinguish eternity from time is that there is no time without movement or change, while in eternity there is no change." As early as the time when he wrote the *De musica*, Augustine had expressed the same idea when he said: "in the things above there is no time, because there is no change whatever." Eternity is the immutability of God considered in relation to time, as time is the mobility of things considered in relation to eternity. At times St. Augustine opposes, not time, but the mobility of creatures to the eternity of God. In eternity he sees the mode in which God is immutable [*Aeternitas qua est immutabilis Deus*].

That reduction of eternity to immutability is very important. It permits us to conceive eternity otherwise than as an endless time; and it justifies the formula which St. Augustine used quite early, and which is an epitome of his teaching on this matter: "In what is really eternal nothing lapses into the past, nothing is yet to come, but everything is." In his *Confessions* he develops the same idea: "Nor dost Thou by time precede time; else wouldst not Thou precede all times. But in the excellency of an ever-present eternity, Thou precedest all time past, and survivest all future times, because they are future, and when they have come they will be past; but Thou art the same, and Thy years shall have no end. Thy years neither go nor come; but ours both go and come, that all may come. All Thy years stand at once since they do stand; nor were they, when departing, excluded by coming years, because they pass not away; but all these of ours shall be when all shall cease to be." How could one express more clearly the truth that in God life is wholly actual in one instant.

It is the nature of truth which demands and makes clear the eternity of the Being in which it stands in its fulness. We already have the proof of it, since, at bottom, immutable and eternal are synonymous. But at times St. Augustine applies the word to eternity. "God is," he says, "He truly is, and by the very fact that He is, He has neither beginning nor end"; and even more explicitly: "In everything that moves I find a past and a future; but in the Truth that lasts I find neither past nor future, but only the present, and that without any change, which is not found in creatures. Look at things subject to change. You will have to say:

'That has been.' 'This will be.' Think of God, and you will have to say: 'He is, because in Him, nothing has been, and nothing is to be.' It you seek to be, you must rise above time." The meaning of the whole passage is determined by the exclamation: "O Truth which truly is."

Plotinus too holds eternity to be an intrinsic attribute of the intelligible being; and for him it derives from the fulness of that being which needs no future to be completely actualized. "Truth does not consist in the agreement of one thing with another, but in the agreement of each thing, of which it is the truth, with itself. To be a real whole, this true whole must be all, not only in the sense that it is all things, but also in the sense that it lacks nothing. If so, for it nothing is *to be*; for to say that some thing is *to be* for it would imply that, before, it was lacking that thing." St. Augustine had early made this doctrine his own. Already when he lived in Cassiciacum, the words: truth, true being, immutability and eternity, were associated under his pen and explained one another, with the difference that, more positively than Plotinus, he identified eternity with the divine essence. "In the nature of God," he says, ". . . there is only what *is*, and it is eternity itself" [*In Dei autem natura . . . est tantum id quod est, et ipsa est aeternitas*].

III. Immensity

Above time because He is Truth, God is also, and much more, above space; we say, "much more," because our soul is already outside of space by its higher activities, while it remains "extended" in time. "If the soul," he says, "which goes through so many changes, . . . is not diffused or extended in space, but, by the impetus of its energy, overcomes all spaces; what thoughts and feelings must we have about God Himself, who stands firm and immutable above all rational beings, and imparts to every one what it needs?" And yet our soul can only approximate Truth, while God is Truth itself, the site of unextended Ideas. The Teacher of Hippo explained it in this way: "God inhabits light inaccessible, but that light is not a disc like the sun, and our eyes of flesh cannot apprehend it. To know it, one has to see what truth is, and what are wisdom and righteousness." Therefore God is nowhere as in a place; though we may not say absolutely that He is nowhere. Since Truth exists, we have the right to ask where it is. Provided we understand it in the right way, we must say that God is everywhere: "Make an effort, my brethren, to conceive how the light of truth and wisdom is everywhere within reach of all; think of the light of righteousness which dawns upon your minds as soon as you think of it." In the east as well as in the west, righteousness reveals itself to anyone who seeks it. What does that mean if not that "God is bound to no place, but is everywhere in Himself"?

As he tells us in the *Confessions,* it was by pondering the nature of truth that St. Augustine gradually broke with the Manichaean materialism and began to conceive God as a Spirit. "Is Truth, therefore, nothing because it is neither diffused through space, neither finite, nor infinite? And Thou didst cry to me from afar, 'Yea, verily, I am who I AM.'" He had apprehended that light while meditating on the works of the Neo-Platonists; and that explains why the words he uses when he speaks of God's nonspatial immensity, and of God's nonlocal presence in creatures always remind us of the words of Plotinus. A letter written in 413 in which he explains to a holy woman how God knows no space, gives us a clear idea of the process by which we can reach the concept of the immateriality of the Truth which, in us, is immaterial, and, *a fortiori*, of the Truth which enlightens us.

IV. Simplicity

Immutable, eternal, unextended in space, such are the characteristics we perceive in Truth; and the ground of these attributes is always the same: that which really *is* admits of no division and multiplicity of parts. Therefore St. Augustine was bound to stress the attribute which is based upon a principle so fruitful: the divine simplicity. He did so more and more as he went on, but even before he was raised to the episcopate, he had asserted with great clearness: "In the divine substance, we cannot imagine that the substance is one thing, and that its attributes are another thing distinct from the substance." Taking this premise as a basis he was, all through his works, to identify life, intelligence, beatitude, power, greatness, and the three divine Persons with the essence of God. In the last book of the *De Trinitate* he enumerates twelve attributes of God and goes on to show that all those attributes and all others that could, not unbecomingly, be ascribed to God, are all found involved in any one of them.

Now we believe we can show that it was by a deeper analysis of the idea of truth that St. Augustine built his doctrine on this point as all the others. Here is the principle which he sets forth to establish the simplicity of God: "God is what He has" [*Ideo simplex dicitur, quoniam quod habet, hoc est*]. Man may possess wisdom, he is not wisdom. When one possesses a perfection and is not that perfection, he only participates in that perfection, he does not exhaust it. There is but one way to have full possession of it: it is to be identical with it. Up to that point, one may reflect it, and be an incomplete imitation of it; but there is disparity between the image and the pattern, the real and the ideal, being and the idea of it. Truth, on the contrary, is the adequation of being to its idea, and this adequation is none other than God. Hence God, or Wisdom, or Life, or Intelligence, or Power, or all these together are one. He writes in the *De Trinitate*: "In things which are great by partaking of greatness, to which it is one thing to *be,* and another to *be great* as a great house, and a great mountain, and a great mind; in these things, I say, greatness is one thing, and that which is great because of

greatness, is another, and a great house, certainly, is not absolute greatness itself. But that is absolute greatness by which not only a great house
is great, and any great mountain is great, but also by which every other
thing whatsoever, which is called great, is great; so that greatness itself
is one thing, and those things are another which are called great because
of it. And this greatness certainly is primarily great, and in a much more
excellent way than those things which are great by partaking of it. But
since God is not great with that greatness which is not Himself, so that
God, in being great, is, as it were, partaker of that greatness; otherwise
that will be a greatness greater than God, whereas there is nothing
greater than God; therefore, he is great with that greatness by which He
Himself *is* that same greatness." Every one of the divine attributes is thus
identical with the divine nature, and, consequently, identical with each
of the others. The reason is that Truth is simple [*Simplex est natura
veritatis*]. Shall we then say that, by virtue of His simplicity, God is
beauty or power as well as truth? It is true that St. Augustine states it
explicitly [*Eadem veritas quae illa omnia*]. The fact remains that to
reach that conception he used the idea of truth.

V. Ineffability

When he reached the summit of his doctrine regarding God, St. Augustine met a difficulty which was so serious that it might have proved
fatal to the whole structure. If to be true, Wisdom must be identified
with Being, Beauty, Greatness, Power and all the others, does it still remain true wisdom, and can we still attach a fitting meaning to the term?
Has not our concern with forming a correct concept of Truth paved the
way to agnosticism? Or at least are we not returning to Plotinus and setting God above the intelligible?

As early as his first *Dialogues*, St. Augustine asks himself by what name
he should call God, and he answers: "Everyday expressions present themselves, but they have been rendered sordid by things of lesser worth."
These words are found in the passage which is perhaps the most dependent on Plotinus that the author ever wrote: purification, and vision of
God, the Father of Truth, are there rendered in terms which seem rather
transcribed from the *Enneads* than interpreted by the enthusiastic reader
of the "books of the Platonists." And yet, in those passages, contemplation remains an intellectual act. The eyes *see;* it is the *sight* of Beauty
that is promised. After he returned to Africa, Augustine gave expression
of the same thought in a truly personal form which, afterward, he would
only elaborate. "Nothing is said about God that is entirely fitting. To
feed our mind and to reach what no human word can express, we use
the terms we have at hand." It was the Manichaeans' railleries about
Biblical anthropomorphisms that afterwards led St. Augustine to a critical examination of even the highest terms which we apply to God. He
gives his thought on this point in four main passages, in every one of

which he sets it in the same order and in very similar terms; from this we are led to believe that they contain the same doctrine, and that these texts throw light on one another.

None of the names given to God are fitting unless they undergo a deep transformation. This is readily granted regarding certain coarse expressions. What is God's anger, when we say that He is angry, but His power to punish? What is His jealousy but unruffled justice? What is His repentance but immutable foreknowledge? But we have to go further: the words "justice" and "foreknowledge," noble as they are, are no fitting description of the nature of God. God is beyond justice, if we mean only human justice, which is only too human. By way of example, let us examine more closely how unfitting is the term: "foreknowledge." Can we say that God foresees, when everything is present to Him? Is His knowledge altered by the temporal apparition of things? Hence, when we speak of God we should use the term, "knowledge," and not, "foreknowledge." And even then we should remember that His knowledge is not like ours, based upon learning and memory. Is not one then deluding himself who applies to God terms which we use also about men? Far from it. "The application of the same terms to God and to men is not useless. We learn them from our daily life and find their illustration in manifold experience, and they help us in some degree to understand the sublime divine truths. If, for instance, we take away from human knowledge its changes and its progress from one thought to another; when we draw from memory and bring under the eye of our mind what was not there before, and thus jump from one to another portion of our recollections, in which consists our knowledge in parts, to use the words of the Apostle; if I take away all that and leave only the splendor of a truth which is lasting and makes all things clear by one act of eternal contemplation—though I should not speak of leaving it, since it is not found in human knowledge—if I concentrate my thought upon it, then, I have some idea of God's knowledge, and I have the right to apply that term to God and to man, for, when he knows, man knows something." But these removals or negations of created imperfections, this effort to reach the absolute, requires trained minds [Vi a paucis et spiritualibus intelleguntur]. To reach the absolute does not mean simply accumulating attributes, it means searching into their deep meaning and refining it; it requires, not words only, but silent reflection; and that of which thought catches a glimpse by rising above words cannot properly be expressed in words [Cui honorificum potius silentium quam ulla vox humana competeret]. Indeed there is a great analogy between the terms St. Augustine uses to express his teaching and the vocabulary of Plotinus. But we have no right to infer from that any identity of thought between the Teacher of Hippo and the founder of Neo-Platonism, at least as the latter is generally interpreted. St. Augustine does not set God above the intelligible, above Justice as such for example. It is in the passage in which he deals most profoundly with this problem, and in which he states that, absolutely speaking, no name can be applied to God, that he points out how it is possible for us to form some idea of the divine knowledge (*Insinuatur mihi utcumque scientia Dei* [*De diversis quaestionibus*, II, qu 2, n. 3]), and even, in some degree, to understand in some manner God's jealousy. He rejects the idea of a God without attributes.

If there is in the whole Augustinian theology a divine attribute that is set forth in special relief, it is the one which is in greatest opposition to the transcendental indeterminateness of the One, namely the personality of God. For St. Augustine God is a Being who has consciousness of itself and of its works; had he doubted it, he would not have written the *Confessions*, that intimate dialogue of Augustine's heart with the heart of his God. How could Truth exist, if there were no thought? If the human artist is intent on his work and obeys the peremptory rules he has learned from God, could we imagine the supreme Artist not having a perfect knowledge of what He creates? "Can you imagine Him who made your eyes not looking at you?" All creatures are, in various degrees, imperfect truths; and some of them, participated ideas; the highest degree revealed in experience is the genius of the artist, or the thought of the contemplative; but the supreme degree is Truth completely actualized, it is Thought itself. Such is the conception of God that we find in the *De ordine*, in the *De musica*, in the *De libero arbitrio*, as well as in the *De civitate Dei*. It is fundamental in St. Augustine's philosophy; or rather, it is the epitome of his philosophy. If we try to form an idea of immutable knowledge, we shall get a glimpse of "the splendor of an unchanging truth which enlightens everything through a unique and eternal contemplation," and that Truth is God. No doubt the perfect apprehension of such a splendor is above our intelligence, nay, above every finite intelligence; but it is not above the divine intelligence. As for us, our power to know God is both affirmed and limited in one sentence of the *De Trinitate*, "God is more truly thought than He is uttered, and exists more truly than He is thought."

II. The Essence of God Is His Existence

32

AQUINAS: SELECTED PASSAGES *

Ar. 3: God is the same as His Essence or Nature.

To UNDERSTAND this, it must be noted that in things composed of matter and form, the nature or essence must differ from the individual, because the nature or essence connotes only what is included in the definition of the species; as human nature connotes all that is included in the definition of man, for it is precisely by this connotation that a man is a man. Particular matter, with all the accidental individualizing qualities, is not included in the definition of the species. This particular flesh, these bones, that blackness, this whiteness, etc., are included in the definition of a man, therefore this flesh, these bones, and the accidental qualities distinguishing that particular matter, are included in human nature; and yet are included in this man. So a man has something more in himself than his human nature. Consequently human nature and a man are not identical; but human nature is taken to mean the formal part of a man, because connotating principles are regarded as the constituent formality in regard to the individualizing matter. In anything not composed of matter and form, individualization cannot be due to individual matter—that is to say, to *this matter*—but the very forms themselves are individualized of themselves. Hence the forms themselves must be self-dependent individuals. Therefore individual and nature in them are identified. Since God is not composed of matter and form, He must be His own Divinity, His own Life; and whatever else is thus predicated of Him.

Ar. 4: God is not only His own Essence, but also His own Existence.

This may be shown in many ways. First, whatever a thing has besides its essence must be caused either by the constituent principles of that essence; like a property that follows from the species—as the faculty of laughing is proper to a man—and is caused by the essential constituent principles of the species; or by some exterior agent; as heat is caused in

* St. Thomas Aquinas, *Summa Theol.*, I, q. 3, art. 3-4.

water by fire. Therefore, if the existence of a thing differs from its essence, then this existence must be caused either by some exterior agent or by its essential constituent principles. It is impossible for a thing's existence to be caused solely by its essential constituent principles, for nothing can be the sufficient cause of its own existence; so long as existence is caused at all. Therefore, that thing the existence of which differs from its essence, must have its existence caused by another. This cannot be true of God; because we call God the first efficient Cause. Therefore it is impossible that in God His Existence should differ from His Essence. Second, existence is that which makes every form or nature actual; for goodness or humanity are only spoken of as in act, because they are spoken of as existing. Therefore, existence must be compared to essence if they differ, as actuality to potentiality. Therefore, since in God there is no potentiality (ar. 1), it follows that in Him existence does not differ from essence. Therefore His Essence is His Existence. Third, because, just as that which has caught fire, but is not itself fire, is on fire by participation; so that which has existence, but is not its own existence, exists by participation. God is His own Essence; if, therefore, He is not His own Existence, He will not be the First Being—which is absurd. Therefore God is His own Existence; and not merely His own Essence.

33

HAEC SUBLIMIS VERITAS *

I T IS hardly credible that the existential nature of the problem of the existence of God ever had to be discovered. It is even less credible that Christian theologians had to discover the existential nature of the Christian God. Was it not enough to open the Scriptures in order to discover it there? When Moses wished to know the name of God in order to reveal it to the Jewish people, he directly addressed God Himself and said to Him: "Lo! I go to the children of Israel, and I shall say to them: the God of your fathers sends me to you. If they ask me His name, what shall I say to them?" And God said to Moses: "I Am Who Am." And He added: "Thus will you reply to the children of Israel: He Who Is sends me to you." (Exod., III, 13-14) Since God Himself called Himself I am, or Who is, as the name properly belonging to Him, how could Christians have ever been ignorant that their God was the supremely existing being?

We do not say that they did not know this. Indeed, everyone believed it, many struggled to understand it, and a certain number before St. Thomas carried the interpretation even to the level of metaphysics. Cer-

---

* Etienne Gilson, *The Christian Philosophy of St. Thomas Aquinas*, trans. by L. K. Shook, C.S.B. (New York: Random House). Copyright, 1956 by Etienne Gilson.

tainly the identification of God and Being is the common possession of Christian philosophers as Christian. But the agreement of Christians upon this point did not prevent philosophers from being divided on the interpretation of the notion of being. Holy Scripture provides no treatise on metaphysics. The first Christians who wanted to think philosophically about the content of their faith had at their disposal only the philosophical techniques elaborated by the Greeks for altogether different ends. The history of Christian philosophy is in large measure that of a religion becoming progressively conscious of philosophical notions which as a religion it could, strictly speaking, do without. But she recognized more and more clearly that these notions were capable of defining the philosophy of those faithful who wished to have one. It is easy to understand how Christian thinkers had to struggle a long time in order to clarify the meaning of this basic text of Exodus. It was only gradually that a metaphysical interpretation was found. The mere inspection of the two distinct notions of being which turn up in the study of the problem of the existence of God is enough to show us this. History permits us to make a living analysis by comparing the essentialist interpretation of the text of Exodus, at which St. Augustine finally stopped, with the existential interpretation of the same text developed by St. Thomas Aquinas.

St. Augustine was so sure that the God of Exodus was Plato's being that he wondered how to explain the coincidence without admitting that Plato had somehow or other known Exodus: "But what makes me almost subscribe to the idea that Plato was not completely ignorant of the Old Testament is that when an Angel conveys the words of God to the holy man Moses, who asks the name of the one who is ordering him to proceed to the deliverance of the Hebrew people, the reply is this: 'I am Who am; and you are to say to the children of Israel: it is He Who is who has sent me to you.' As if, in comparison with him who truly is because he is immovable, he who has been made movable did not exist. Now Plato was intensely convinced of this and he took great care to say so." Clearly, the Being of Exodus is here conceived as the immovable entity of Plato. Reading these lines, we are bound to suspect that the accord at which Augustine marvels conceals a little confusion.

Such, indeed, was St. Augustine's notion of God and being. "The first and highest being is that which is entirely immovable, and which can say by full right: 'I am Who Am; and you will tell them, He Who is has sent me to you.'" But Augustine had a very deep sense of the difficulty of the problem, and he never, perhaps, expressed his final thought on this question better than in a homily on the Gospel of St. John. It is better to cite the entire text because we can sense in it both the depth of Augustine's Christian feeling and the Platonic limits of his notion of being.

Nevertheless, pay good attention to the words spoken here by Our Lord, Jesus Christ: if you do not believe that I am, you will die in your sins (John, VIII, 24). What is this: si non credideritis quia ego sum? I am, what? There is nothing added; and because there is nothing added, his word embarrasses us. We were waiting for him to say what he was, yet he did not say it. What did we think he was going to say? Perhaps, *if you do not believe that I am the* Christ; *if you do not believe that I am,* the Son of God; *if you do not believe that I am* the Word of the Father; *if you do not believe that I am* the author of the world; *if you do not believe that I am* the former and reformer of man, his creator and recreator, he who made him and remade him; *if you do not believe that I am* that, *you will die in your sins.* This *I am,* he says he is, is embarrasing. For God also had said to Moses: *I am Who Am.* Who can say rightly what is this *I am?* By his angel, God sent his servant Moses to deliver his people from Egypt (you have read what I am saying here, and you knew it, but I am recalling it to you); God was sending him trembling, reluctant but obedient. In order to find some excuse Moses said to God who, he knew, was speaking to him through the angel: if the people ask me, who then is the God who sent thee? What shall I reply? And the Lord said to him: *I am who am;* then he repeated: *it is He Who Is who has sent me to you.* Here, again, he did not say: *I am* God; or *I am* the maker of the world; or *I am* the creator of all things; or again, *I am* the propagator of this very people who must be liberated; but he only said this: *I am Who Am;* then, *you will say to the children of Israel, He Who Is.* He did not add: *He Who Is* your God; *He Who Is* the God of your fathers; but he only said this: *He Who Is sent me to you.* Perhaps it was difficult for Moses, even as it is difficult for us too—and even more difficult for us—to understand these words: *I am Who Am;* and, *He Who Is, has sent me to you.* Moreover, even if Moses understood them, how could they to whom God was sending him have understood them? God has then postponed what man could not understand and added what he could understand. This he added, indeed, when he said: *I am the God of Abraham, and the God of Isaac, and the God of Jacob* (Exod., III, 13-15). This, you can understand; but what thought can comprehend *I am?*

Let us pause here briefly to greet in passing this first meeting, in God's own words, between the God of Abraham, of Isaac and of Jacob and the God of the philosophers and scholars. Augustine knows very well that it is the same God. No more than the people of Israel can he hesitate over the identity of the living God of Scripture. But it is the *Qui est* that intrigues him, for God no more explained it to Moses than to Augustine or to us, as if, having revealed to men the truth that saves, He had reserved the understanding of it to the patient efforts of the metaphysicians. However, faithful to the teaching of the "interior master," Augustine is going to pray here to God Himself to enlighten him on the meaning of His words.

I am going to speak, now, to Our Lord Jesus Christ. I am going to speak to him and he will hear me. For I believe that he is present; I do not doubt it in the least, since He said: *Behold I am with you even to the consummation of the world* (Matt., XXVIII, 20). O Lord, our God, what have you said: *If you do not believe that I am?* Indeed, of all you have made, what is there that is not? The heavens, are they not? The earth, is it not? And the things that are on the earth and in the heavens, are they not? And the very man to whom you are speaking, is he not? If they are, if all these things you have made are, what then is being itself—*ipsum esse*—which you reserved for yourself as something proper to you, and which you have not given to others, in order to be the only one to exist? Must we then understand: *I am Who Am,* as if the rest were not? And how are we to understand the *If you do not believe that I am?* Those who understood it, then, were they not? Even if they were sinners they were men. What are we to do? Let being itself—*ipsum esse*—say what it is; let it speak it to the heart; let it say it within; let it speak it within; let the interior man understand it; let thought understand that to be truly is, to be always in the same way.

Nothing could be clearer than this statement: *vere esse est enim semper eodem modo esse . . .* To identify thus the true being (*vere esse*) which God is with "immovable being" is to assimilate the *Sum* of *Exodus* to the οὐσία of Platonism. Here we are again face to face with the same difficulty we had when it was a question of translating this term in the dialogues of Plato. The Latin equivalent of οὐσία is *essentia* and it seems, certainly, that Augustine identified in his mind the God of Abraham, of Isaac and of Jacob with that alone which, being immovable, can be called *essentia* in all the fullness of the term. How would it be otherwise since to be is "to be immovable"? Hence this formal statement of the *De Trinitate:* "Perhaps it ought to be said that God alone is *essentia.* For he alone truly is, because he is immovable, and it is this he declared for Moses his servant when he said *I am Who Am* and *you will tell them that it is He Who Is who has sent me to you (Exod., III, 14)."* Hence the divine name of names, *Sum,* is best translated into philosophical language by the abstract term *essence* which itself denotes the immutability of "*that which is.*"

We see here the source of that doctrine of divine *essentialitas* which was later through St. Anselm to influence so profoundly the theology of Richard of Saint-Victor, Alexander of Hales and St. Bonaventure. To pass from this philosophical interpretation of the Text of *Exodus* to the one St. Thomas was going to propose, it was necessary to bridge the gap between being of essence and being of existence. We have seen how St. Thomas's proofs for the existence of God have prepared that bridge. It only remains to recognize the proper nature of the God whose existence they have demonstrated, that is, to recognize Him as the supreme act of being.

There is nothing more convincing in this regard than the order followed by the *Summa Theologiae.* Knowing that a thing is, one has only to ask in what way it is, in order to know what it is. Indeed, and we shall have to say why, we do not know what God is, but only what He is not. The only conceivable manner of circumscribing His nature is therefore to remove successively from our notion of Him all the modes of existing which cannot be His. Now it is remarkable that the first of the ways of being which St. Thomas eliminates as incompatible with the notion of God is composition. He does this by establishing at the outset that God is simple, not in the hope of giving us a positive concept of a simplicity like God's but to make us conceive of Him, at least negatively, as the being free from all composition whatsoever. What can we hope to find at the end of the analysis announced if not *being*, free from all that is not being? To progress towards this conclusion will be to do no more than to make evident a notion virtually included in the proofs for the existence of God.

In following St. Thomas's analysis it is well to fix the attention at least as much on the reasons for which all compositions are eliminated one after the other as on the nature itself of the compositions thus eliminated. Let us begin with the grossest among them, that of conceiving of God as a body. To eliminate body from the notion of God, it is enough to look again at the principal proofs of His existence. God is the first immovable mover; now no body moves unless it is moved; God is therefore not a body. God is the first being, and is therefore being in act, *par excellence;* now all body is continuous and, as such, divisible to infinity; all body is therefore divisible in potency; it is not being, in pure act; hence, it is not God. The existence of God has already been shown to be the most noble of *beings;* now the soul is more noble than the body; it is impossible therefore that God is a body. Clearly, the principle dominating these various arguments is one and the same. In each case, it is a question of establishing that whatever is incompatible with the pure actuality of being is incompatible with the notion of God.

According to this principle, we must deny that God is composed of matter and form, for matter is what is in potency, and since God is pure act, without any mixture of potency, it is impossible that He is composed of matter and form. This second conclusion immediately entails a third. According to our definition, essence is only substance as intelligible through the concept of its quiddity and susceptible of definition. Thus understood, essence expresses, before anything else, the form or nature of substance. It includes whatever falls under the definition of species, and only this. For example, the essence of man is *humanitas,* which notion covers everything by which man is man—a reasoning animal composed of soul and body. It is to be noted, however, that essence embraces only that part of the substance which all substances of the same species have in common and not what each substance possesses as an individual. It is of the essence of humanity that every man should have a body. But the notion of humanity does not include the very body, the members, the flesh, the particular bones belonging to the substance of a given man. All these individual determinations belong to the notion of man since no man can exist without them. Thus, man (*homo*) is said to designate the complete substance taken with all the specific and individual determinations which render it capable of existing, whereas humanity designates the essence or formal part of the substance, man. It is the element which defines man in general. From this analysis, it follows that in all substances composed of matter and form, substance and essence do not exactly coincide. Since there is more in the substance man than in the essence humanity, man and humanity are not wholly identical. Now we have said that

God is not composed of matter and form. There cannot, then, be in Him any distinction between essence on the one hand and substance or nature on the other. We can say that man is man in virtue of his humanity but not that God is God in virtue of His deity. God (*Deus*) and deity (*deitas*) and anything else that can be attributed to God by way of predication are all one and the same thing.

This last formula enables us to recognize at once the opponents whom St. Thomas had in mind in this discussion and at the same time to understand the exact meaning of his position. At the point of his analysis just reached, St. Thomas has not yet arrived at the order of existence, the ultimate term towards which he is tending. Thus far it is only a question of a notion of God which does not go beyond substantial being. What he is asking himself is simply whether on this level which is not yet that of the act of being, it is possible to distinguish God's substance (what God is) from His essence (that by which He is). In this case, that by which God is God, is called His deity and the problem is reduced to asking whether God (*Deus*) is distinct from His *deitas* or identical with it.

This thesis came from a Platonism different from St. Augustine's, that of Boethius. It is a rather curious fact that Plato's thought should have exercised so profound an influence on the thought of the Middle Ages which knew almost nothing of his works. But his thought reached the Middle Ages through several schools which he had directly or indirectly influenced. We have already met the Platonism of St. Augustine and its derivatives, and we shall be meeting the Platonism of Dionysius the Areopagite and its derivatives. But we must also take into account that of Alfarabi, Avicenna and their disciples, as well as that which falls under examination here, the Platonism of Boethius, by no means the least important.

There have then been several forms of Platonism, not just one, behind medieval philosophies, and it is important to know how to distinguish them. But it is important also to remember that by their relationship to a common origin, these various Platonisms have constantly tended to reinforce one another, to unite, and sometimes even to become confused. The Platonic current is like a river issuing from St. Augustine, being enlarged by the tributary from Boethius in the sixth century, from Dionysius, Scotus Erigena in the ninth century, from Avicenna and the *Book of Causes* in the twelfth century. Other less important tributaries like Hermes Tresmegistus, Macrobius and Apuleius, for example, can be cited, as well as the translation of the *Timaeus* by Chalcidius, with its commentary, the only fragment of Plato himself which was, if not known, at least used during the high Middle Ages. Thus St. Thomas found himself face to face with many allied forms of Platonism to which he had sometimes to adjust himself, which he had sometimes openly to combat, and against which he had always to be on guard.

In the case in question, the root common to the Platonism of Boethius and Augustine is the ontology which reduces existence to being and con-

ceives of being as *essentia*. But this principle is developed differently by
Boethius than by St. Augustine. Boethius seems to have begun with the
celebrated remark made by Aristotle, as it were in passing, which was to
give rise to such numerous commentaries: "what man is is different from
that fact that he is" (II *Anal.*, II, 7, 92 b 10-11). This remark could have
introduced, *a propos* of a question of logic, the frequently discussed
problem of the relation between essence and existence. Aristotle himself
never raised the problem, for the simple reason that, as his faithful com-
mentator Averroes very well saw, he never made the distinction between
what substances are and the fact that they are. Aristotle is not saying in
this passage that the essence of a substance is distinct from its existence,
but simply that one cannot conclude from the mere definition of substance that it exists.

When in his turn Boethius took up the problem, he raised it to the
plane of metaphysics. The very obscurity of his terse definitions tended
to focus the attention of his commentators upon them. Boethius distinguished between being and what is: *diversum est esse et id quod est*.
But his distinction between *esse* and *id quod est* does not mark a distinction between essence and actual existence. It designates, rather, the
distinction between the thing itself that is (*id quod est*) and the form
(*esse*) whereby it is that which it is. For this reason, the form (*esse*) of
a substance is also called its *quo est:* that by which the substance is. Such
a form is simple by definition; *ipsum esse nihil aliud praeter se habet
admixtum;* on the contrary, the *quod est* only exists in so far as it is
informed by the form that gives it being: *quod est, accepta essendi forma
est atque consistit.*

To comment on Boethius through Gilbert de la Porrée is certainly to
explain *obscurum per obscurius*. However his modern commentators interpret Gilbert himself, they agree that, in his texts, "one must not
translate *essentia* by essence. This term evokes, in its true meaning, a
distinction, within being itself (essence and existence), which did not as
yet exist in Latin thought. *Esse*, too, is taken as a form. *Esse* and *essentia*
are in this sense equivalents. God's *essentia* is the *esse* of all being and, at
the same time, form *par excellence.*" Since it is here a question of a basic
metaphysical position it was to dominate even the problem raised by the
notion of God. Indeed, Gilbert conceived God, the form of all being,
as Himself defined by a form determining our notion of Him as God.
Thought, therefore, would conceive of this *quod est,* which God is, as
determined to being by the form *divinitas*. It is impossible to think that
Gilbert conceived of God as composed of two really distinct elements,
God (*Deus*) and divinity (*divinitas*), but he seems at least to have admitted that as far as we are concerned, God can only be conceived as a
quod est informed by a *quo est,* which is His divinity. The influence of
this doctrine has been considerable. Accepted or amended by some, condemned by others, it has left its traces even upon those who rejected it

most energetically. This is hardly surprising, because philosophers frequently reject consequences whose principles they still accept. In order to set aside Gilbert's doctrine, it was necessary to pass beyond the realism of *essentia* to that of existence. In brief, it was necessary to bring about that philosophical reform which we associate with the name of St. Thomas Aquinas.

Put in terms of Thomistic philosophy, the distinction between *Deus* and *divinitas* was equivalent to conceiving of the divine being as a kind of substance determined to be such by an essence which would be the essence of divinity. It may be that this conclusion is practically inevitable so long as one seeks to circumscribe the divine being by the conceptual definition of an essence. Even if he affirms, as does Gilbert, that God is His divinity, whoever seeks to define such an essence can only do so by conceiving of God as being God by the very *divinitas* that He is. This is to reintroduce into Him, at least in what concerns thought, a distinction between potency and act, incompatible with the pure actuality of the divine being. In order to overcome this difficulty we must, with St. Thomas, pass beyond the identification of God's substance with his essence and posit the identity of his essence with His very act-of-being. What distinguishes his position from that of the followers of Gilbert is not that it gives testimony of a more lively sense of the divine simplicity. All Christian theologians know that God is absolutely simple; and they say so, but not in the same way. The lesson St. Thomas gives us here is that we cannot say this properly if we remain on the plane of substance and essence, which are objects of quidditative concepts. The divine simplicity is perfect because it is the simplicity of pure act. We cannot define it; we can only only affirm it by an act of the judging faculty.

In order to understand the position of St. Thomas on this decisive point, we must first remember the privileged role he attributes to *esse* in the structure of the real. For him each thing has its own act-of-being. Let us say, rather, there is no real apart from distinct acts of existing, by virtue of each of which a distinct thing exists. We must, then, posit as a fundamental principle that everything is, in virtue of the act of existing proper to it: *unumquodque est per suum esse*. Since it is here a question of a principle, we can be certain that its scope extends even to God. It would perhaps be better to say that it is the very being of God which is at the basis of the principle. For God is, as the third proof for His existence shows, the necessary being. He is therefore an act of existing of such a kind that His existence is necessary. This is what is meant by being necessary *per se*. To posit God in this way is to affirm an act of existing which needs no cause of its own existence. Such would not be the case were His essence distinguished, in so far as it is, from His existence. If, indeed, the essence of God determined in any degree this act of existing, the latter would no longer be necessary. God is, therefore, the act-of-being that He is. Such is the meaning of the expression: *Deus est suum esse*. Like whatever exists, God is by His own act-of-being; but, in His case alone, we have to say that *what* His being is is nothing else than that by which He exists, namely, the pure act of existing.

Any one of the proofs for the existence of God would lead to the same conclusion precisely because they all set out from contingent existences in order to reach the first *esse* which causes them. As St. Thomas himself says of this thesis: it can be shown in many ways. God is the first cause; He has therefore no cause; now God would have a cause if His essence were distinct from His existence, because then it would not be enough, in order to exist, to be what He is. It is therefore impossible that God's essence be anything other than His act-of-being.

We can begin too, if it seems preferable, from the fact that God is act, free from any potency. Then the question is: What is most actual in all given reality? According to our analysis of the metaphysical structure of the concrete the answer must be: The act-of-being, because to be is the actuality of all form, or nature. Actually to be good is to be a good being which exists. Humanity only has actual reality in an actually existing man. Let us suppose, therefore, that the essence of God were distinct from His existence. The divine act of existing would then be the act of the divine essence. This latter would therefore be, with regard to God's *esse,* as potency to act. Now God is pure act; therefore, His essence must be his very act-of-being.

It is possible also to proceed even more directly, starting from God posited as being. To say that God's essence is not His *esse* would be to say that *what* God is has *esse* but is not itself *esse.* Now what has the act-of-being but is not the act-of-being is only by participation. Since, as we have just seen, God is His essence or His very nature, He is not by participation. This is, moreover, what we mean when we call Him the first being. Thus God is His essence, and His essence is the act itself of being; He is, therefore, not only His essence but His act-of-being.

Such is the God whom the five proofs of St. Thomas seek and finally attain by five different ways. The question here was incontestably a philosophical one. Historically located, this conclusion appears to be the result of an effort extending over several centuries to attain the very root of being, which was then to become identified with the act-of-being. Going beyond the Platonic ontology of essence and the Aristotelian ontology of substance, St. Thomas in one long stride also went beyond both the first substance of Aristotle and the God *essentia* of St. Augustine and his disciples. St. Thomas never says that God has no essence. If we think of his many opportunities to say this, we must presume that he had good reasons for avoiding the expression. The simplest reason is probably that, since we only know beings whose essence is not their act-of-being, it is impossible for us to conceive of a being without essence. Also, in the case of God, we conceive less of an act-of-being without essence than of an essence which, by passing as it were to its limit, comes at length to be one with its own act-of-being. Moreover, the case is similar with all the attributes of God in the doctrine of St. Thomas. Just as we do not say that God has no wisdom, but that His wisdom is His own being, so we do not say that He has no essence but that His essence is His act-of-being. To grasp in one glance the extent of St. Thomas's reform on the plane of natural theology, we have only to measure the distance separating the God *essentia* of St. Augustine from the God of St. Thomas whose *essentia* is, as it were, absorbed by its *esse*.

However, this pure act of being which St. Thomas the philosopher met at the end of metaphysics, St. Thomas the theologian had met too in Holy Scripture. It was no longer the conclusion of rational dialectic but a revelation from God Himself to all men that they might accept it by faith. There is no doubt that St. Thomas thought that God had revealed to men that His essence was to exist. St. Thomas is not lavish with epithets. Never did a philosopher yield less frequently to the temptation to wax eloquent. Here, however, seeing these two beams of light so converging that they fused into each other, he was unable to withhold a word of admiration for the overwhelming truth blazing forth from their point of fusion. He saluted this truth with a title exalting it above all others: "God's essence is therefore His act-of-being. Now this sublime truth (*hanc autem sublimem veritatem*), God taught to Moses when Moses asked what to reply if the children of Israel should ask His name. (*Exod.* III, 13). And the Lord replied: I am Who Am. You may say this to the children of Israel: *He Who Is* has sent me to you. Thus He showed that His proper name is *Who Is*. Now every name is intended to signify the nature or essence of something. It remains then that the divine act-of-being itself (*ipsum divinum esse*) is the essence or nature of God."

Let us note well that for St. Thomas this revelation of the identity of essence and existence in God was the equivalent of a revelation of the distinction between essence and existence in creatures. *Who Is* signifies: He Whose essence is to exist; *Who Is* is the proper name of God; consequently, the essence of anything that is not God is not to exist. We could, if we had to, make this simple inference by our reason. But we do not have to, the text is explicit: "It is impossible that the substance of any being other than the First Agent be its very act-of-being. Hence the name which *Exodus* (3:14) gives as the proper name of God, *Who Is*. It belongs properly to Him alone that His substance be nothing other than His act-of-being."

These positions have two principal consequences. First, Thomistic existentialism concerned not merely natural theology, but theology in the strict sense. It is here indeed a question of a literal interpretation of the word of God. To appreciate the importance of what is at stake we have only to compare St. Thomas's interpretation of the text with St. Augustine's. When St. Augustine read the name of God, he understood "I am he who never changes." St. Thomas reading the same words understood them to mean "I am the pure act-of-being."

Whence, this second consequence, that no historian can consider St.

Thomas's thinking to be a combination of distinct schools of thought. Neither the identity of essence and existence in God nor the distinction between essence and existence in creatures belongs to the *revelatum*, properly so-called, since neither of these truths is beyond the range of natural reason considered as a judging faculty. Both are, nevertheless, for St. Thomas part of the revealable, and even of the revealable which has been revealed. Nowhere, perhaps, can we see more clearly how complex is the economy of revelation, the act by which God makes Himself known to man, in the teaching of St. Thomas. St. Thomas was far from believing or having others believe that God had at one time revealed to Moses the twenty-second chapter of Book II of the *Summa Contra Gentiles*. If anyone should think this, it is not St. Thomas who is naïve. God has given us His name; it suffices that man believe it lest any false god afterwards seduce him. But the theology of the Christian Doctors is only revelation investigated by reason working in the light of faith. Time was necessary for reason to do its work. St. Augustine was on the right path; St. Thomas but followed the same road to its end. Everyone is free to imagine St. Thomas's genius as a living classification of the sciences. But those of us who do this will soon be at grips with this thorny problem: Is it St. Thomas the theologian who, reading in *Exodus* the identity of essence and existence in God, taught St. Thomas the philosopher the distinction between essence and existence in creatures? Or is it St. Thomas the philosopher who, pushing his analysis of the metaphysicial structure of the concrete even as far as the distinction between essence and existence, taught St. Thomas the theologian that *He Who Is* in *Exodus* means the *Act-of-being?* St. Thomas himself as a philosopher thought of these two propositions as the two sides of one and the same metaphysical thesis. And from the day he understood them, he always thought of them as being in Holy Scripture. The word of God is too profound for human reason to exhaust its meaning. But it is always the same meaning of the same word which the reason of the Doctors of the Church ever pursues to depths more and more profound. The genius of St. Thomas is one and his work is one. One cannot separate, without destroying its perfect balance what God has revealed to men from the meaning of what He has revealed.

This sublime truth is, for the historian at least, the key to the understanding of Thomism. His best interpreters have all seen this, and we need only repeat it after them. But each age repeats it in its own way, because new obstacles arise to obscure the meaning of the fundamental notion of existing. Today two distinct causes are moving concurrently in this direction. On the other hand, the permanent tendency of the human understanding to feed on quiddities inclines us to break up the unity of Thomism into a mosaic of essences. These, like the pieces in a jig-saw puzzle, are arranged side by side, powerless to communicate with one another. On the other hand, the progress of historical studies reveals for us in ever-increasing number the doctrinal sources on which St. Thomas drew in order to construct his work. So much is this so, that his work is apt to appear more and more as a mosaic of borrowed fragments of whose heteroclite nature he seems to have been unaware.

Thomism, indeed, can appear as the emptiest or fullest of philosophies, as the most inconsistent of eclecticisms or the luckiest stroke of drilling ever attempted through the thickness of concrete reality, according as it is interpreted as a logic of abstract being or a metaphysic of the act-of-being. We must, then, be neither scandalized nor disturbed when some find fulness and light where others find but obscurity and emptiness. St. Thomas's philosophical work is above all else the first discovery, through human reason, of the *Ultima Thule* of metaphysics. It is difficult to reach it and almost as difficult to stay there. This, however, is what we must try to do in following, even to its final consequences, this sublime truth— *hanc sublimem veritatem*—whose light illumines the whole of Thomism.

At the beginning of this quest, let us provide ourselves with this formula, the fullest and clearest of all those which Thomas himself has provided: "Being (*esse*) is used in two senses. In the first it denotes the act-of-being (*actum essendi*). In the second it denotes the composition of the proposition made by the mind in joining a predicate to a subject. If we take being in the first sense, we cannot know what God's being is (*non possumus scire esse Dei*), any more than we can know His essence. But we can know that the proposition we form about God in saying 'God is' is true; and we know this from His effects."

III. The Transcendence of God

34

IS GOD ORGANIC WITH THE WORLD? *

A. EXPOSITION

ONE argument which maintains that God is organic with the world is based on the notion of creation. . . . The traditional notion of creation meets with general ridicule. Professor Pringle-Pattison classes it "in the same circle of ideas as the waving of a magician's wand," and by the use of the same magic wand discards the doctrine as worthy of "no place in serious thinking or in genuine religion." James classes it as "the produce of childish fancy," and as lacking "sweep and infinity enough to meet the requirements of even the illiterate natives of India. . . . The vaster vistas which scientific evolutionism has opened,"

* Fulton J. Sheen, *God and Intelligence in Modern Philosophy* (London: Longmans, Green, 1935), Part II, ch. VI, III.

he says, "and the rising tide of social democratic ideals, have changed the type of our imagination, and the older monarchical theism is obsolete or obsolescent. The place of the Divine in the world must be organic and intimate. An external creator and his institutions may still be verbally confessed at church in formulas that linger by their mere inertia, but the life is out of them; we avoid dwelling on them, the sincere heart of us is elsewhere." Like other terms in philosophy, creation has changed its meaning. With M. Bergson it means "novelty," with Howison it simply means "the eternal fact that God is a complete, moral agent, that His essence is just a perfect conscience," or else the moral recognition of God by the republic of spirits. For Professor Ward it means "internal limitation"; while it assumes almost the meaning of "created" with Professor Alexander. God in the sense of the universe tending toward deity is "creative only of deity. God, then, like all other beings in the universe —for Space-Time itself is not in the universe, whereas God, since His deity is part of the universe, is in it—is in the strictest sense *not a creator, but a creature*. I need hardly say I do not mean that He is a creature of our imagination or of our thought. He is the infinite creature of the universe of Space-Time." Although the term *creation* has, for these philosophers, lost its meaning, it has not lost it use. The most generally accepted interpretation in these days, and certainly the sanest, is that of Professor Pringle-Pattison. There are moments when it approaches the traditional notion, and we would often interpret him in that sense were it not for the ridicule he directs against it, thus forbidding such an interpretation. In an effort to escape a false statement of the problem by Janet, namely, that there is a moment when God alone was, and then a next moment when God and the world were, he makes God and the world eternal. We create a difficulty for ourselves, he says, "by substantiating God as a solitary unit apart from the universe in which He expresses Himself." "This solitary, ante-mundane Figure is a residual of a primitive and pictorial fashion of thinking. Creation must be regarded as an eternal act, an act grounded in the Divine nature, and therefore, if we are to use the language of time, coeval with the Divine existence." There is no priority of the infinite over the finite. "Creation is an eternal act or process which must be ultimately understood not as the making of something out of nothing, but as a self-revelation of the Divine in and to finite spirits."

B. CRITICISM

Apart from individual differences among philosophers, creation *ex nihilo* is rejected because of a confusion, into which they have fallen, and the clarifying of this confusion is the answer to their positive doctrines.

The confusion results from *spatially imagining* creation instead of *intelligibly understanding* it. Two quite distinct and separate problems are rolled up into one. The comprehension of the notion of creation depends on their distinctness. One is a *chronological* problem, the other is *ontological*.

The chronological problem is concerned with the time element. The Pluralists along with Professor Pringle-Pattison insist on the eternity of the universe, there being "no priority of the infinite over the finite." As far as reason is concerned, this notion is in perfect accord with St. Thomas.

There is no metaphysical necessity for the *commencement of the world*. *Reason* alone cannot prove that the world had to have a beginning, nor can it prove that it could not have had a beginning. "It cannot be demonstrated that man, or heaven, or a stone did not always exist. Likewise, neither can it be demonstrated on the part of the efficient cause which acts by will. For the will of God cannot be investigated by reason. . . . But the Divine will can be manifested by *revelation,* on which faith rests. Hence, that the world began to exist is an *object of faith,* but *not of demonstration or science*. And it is useful to consider this, lest any one presuming to demonstrate what is of faith should bring forward reasons which are not cogent, so as to give occasion to unbelievers to laugh, thinking that on such grounds we believe things that are of faith" (*S.T*. Ia, p. 46, art. 2 c.).

So far as reason is concerned, the world need not necessarily have a beginning; time might go on forever as far as human science is concerned; there might be a kind of eternal flux and flow of universal nature. In this sense, and from the point of view of reason, a philosopher may see no reason for denying the eternity of the universe, and thus consider God and the world existing co-eternally.

But for Christians, this conception is untenable. We know by revelation that the world is finite in duration in the past. This is a fact, but an indemonstrable fact; it is a knowledge, but an incommunicable knowledge—as certain as it is incommunicable.

It is at this point that the position of Professor Pringle-Pattison appears illogical. Throughout his work there is a splendid attempt to reveal the love of God as communicating Himself to us, and a recognition of the Incarnation as the sublime reconciliation of the transcendence and immanence of God. Scripture is quoted, and Christian thought prevails throughout. But if revelation is worthy of credence in the case of the Incarnation, it is worthy of credence in the case of creation. There seems to be no valid reason for accepting it in one case and denying it in the other.

So much for the chronological problem, which is purely accessory. The ontological problem is much more important. Here we prescind from the time-element. The problem is now transcendental and not one of duration. Whether the world existed eternally or not does not affect this problem. If it existed eternally, it is eternally insufficient. Neither does the hypothesis of evolution affect the problem in any way, as James and his disciples would have us believe. The idea of evolution answers the question of the temporal relations of beings one to the other. What temporal bonds are between them? How do they succeed? Are they causes, effects, conditions, of such and such a kind? The idea of creation refers to something entirely different, as it is a question of the transcendent relation between being as such as its First Cause. Evolution is a problem of the before and after; creation is a problem of the above. "Evolution is concerned with a relation in a circle; creation is a tangential problem" (Sertillanges).

Whether being is evolving or not, whether it is perpetual or not, it must have a source. As it is the most universal effect, it must have the most universal cause. If being is not evolving, but is perpetual, then there must be a source for being. If there is evolution, there is a double cause for the existence of God, because God must be postulated, first as the source of being as such (God Creator); secondly as a source of being inasmuch as it is in evolution (God First Mover); and thirdly, as cause of the order according to which the world evolves—that is, the intelligibility which it expresses and the ends which it realizes (God, Word; God, Alpha and Omega; God, Beginning and End). The vaster vistas which scientific evolution has opened in no way affect creation, any more than the invention of machinery affected the necessity of manufacture. The *how* of a process never dispenses with the explanation of the *why*. It does little credit to a philosopher to say that contentment with the regress to a God-Creator, or some similar notion, is the true mark of speculative indolence (Von Hartmann).

Apart from this, creation has been brought into disrepute among philosophers by their spatially imagining a sort of nothing from which the world was made, and conceiving the creative act as a becoming, or a movement, or a change. It is quite true that we often imagine creation as two moments—one in which there was God, and the second in which there was the world. Explaining what he believes to be the traditional notion, a contemporary (Pringle-Pattison) writes: "God is conceived as a pre-existent, self-centered Person to whom, in His untroubled eternity, the idea of such a creation occurs, one might almost say, as an afterthought. The inspiration is forthwith put into execution; the world is created by the word of His power. A universe is summoned into existence and stands somehow there, as shapes and figures might appear at a sorcerer's word of command, or as temples and towers rise like an exhalation before the eyes of a dreamer." This is a fine example of creation spatially imagined, in which there are two moments, a before and an after; and two terms, a *terminus a quo* and a *terminus ad quem*.

Creation is not made up of two moments, one of labour and the next of rest. *Creation is not change; it is a relation.* St. Thomas, speaking on this point, says: "Creation is not change, except as to a mode of understanding. For change means that something should be different now from what it was previously. But in creation, *by which the whole sub-*

stance of the thing is produced, the same thing can be taken as different now and before only according to our way of understanding, so that a thing is understood first as not existing at all, and afterwards as existing. But as action and passion coincide as to the substance of motion, and differ only according to diverse relations (*Phys.* III, text 20, 21), it must follow that, when motion is withdrawn, only diverse relations remain in the Creator and in the creature."

In things which are made without movement, as in creation, to become, and to be already made, are simultaneous. In these things, that which is being made is; but when we speak of its being made we mean that it is produced by another. Hence, since creation is without a movement, a thing is being created and is already created at the same time. There is then no passage from nothing to being, as if nothing were a "stuff," or an abyss, first, because nothing cannot be the subject of a phenomenon, and, secondly, because being nothing it cannot be first nothing and then something. Creation is intelligible only as a relation—real in us, and logical in God. Creation of the world by God means that the world has its reason of being in God, it depends on God, in its entirety, which includes the duration which is its measure. Or, more briefly, creation is the dependence of finite being on its First Cause.

Thus absolute dependence of created being on God is the evidence of the omnipotent power of God. Power, says St. Thomas, is not to be judged uniquely by *what* is made, but also by *how* a thing is made. The greater the heat, the more it heats and the more quickly it heats. The creation of some finite effect would not show forth the omnipotent power of God, but the creation *ex nihilo* does. However small a being is, and however finite it is, to create it from nothing requires an infinite power, which can belong only to an infinitely perfect Being. In creating there is no addition made to the infinity of God's Being, because it is not in the same order as the Being of God. Being in an inferior order is possible, because of the analogy of *being.* Nor is there more being in the world after creation than before. Suppose that there was only one man in the world who had knowledge. Knowledge would be quantitatively and qualitatively one in such a case. Now suppose that learned men should teach a populated world. What would be the result? Knowledge would increase quantitatively; instead of there being one man who knows, there would be millions. But qualitatively the knowledge would remain the same. There would be no more knowledge qualitatively in the world than before.

The comparison is feeble, but it helps to illustrate the point in question. Creation is an increase of being *extensively* but not *intensively.* There are more beings in the world after creation than before, but there is no more *being;* there are more good things, but the good is not multiplied. Creation introduced the word "have" into the world to denote participation. Before creation there was no such thing as "having"; there was only *being.*

The misunderstanding on this point usually arises from a spatial conception, according to which God is understood mathematically. The being of God is not *quantitative;* it is Divine. Being Divine, it possesses the fulness of perfection, and nothing can be added to it. What is created is related to the uncreated as a point to a line, there being no proportion between the one and the other. A line added to a point does not make it greater, nor does a created good increase the goodness of God. The finite, therefore, being placed outside of the infinite as an *extensive* increase of being, offers no contradiction, and in fact is in perfect accord with the perfection of God; for it allows Him causality, without which He would not be perfect.

But to place the finite in the infinite, then God is both finite and infinite, and "this is not a mystery as is creation, but the absurd" (Garrigou-Lagrange). Neither can it be said that the creative act implies a change in the Divine Will, simply because at a given moment God became a creator in time. By His *power* God was never a creator in time, because the power is identical with Him from all eternity. The Divine Will is not like our will, which needs external help and other faculties to make it efficacious. There is a change, but the change is in *creatures,* not in God. Creation is an eternal act which terminates at its objects when God wills it. If there is anything new in God, it is only a logical relation, and even that is from our point of view.

St. Thomas, on this point, touches the root of the problem in saying that "the will does not act according to the *mode of its being,* but according to the *mode of its resolution.*" The Divine Will embraces not only what the effect will be, but when it will be. A king, for example, decides to make war within a year. When a year comes, the war is carried on without the least change in the will of the king, his resolution remaining the same as during the preceding year. There is a change, but the change is wholly on the part of the soldiers. St. Augustine has used another figure to show that the newness of Divine effect does not imply newness of action in God. Without any change the sun illumines the earth, heats it, nourishes, hardens some things, softens others, dries up others, raises vapour and vegetation, and strengthens the feeble. All the change is on the part of its *terminating object;* it is not on the nature of the sun. If there is no change in God, there is certainly no necessity that He should create one kind of world more than another. He is not bound to create the best possible world as Leibnitz contended; for otherwise He would lack a sufficient reason. The sufficient reason for an act of the will is to be found, not in the object absolutely considered, but in consideration of the end in view. The present world, then, is the best world possible for the end God had in view in creating it.

35

GOD AND THE MONISTIC IDEOLOGIES *

To DENY the existence of a supreme being, of an *ens realissimum*, is from every point of view impossible. Even the solipsist, by asserting that he can admit as real nothing except himself, affirms the existence of a supreme being. So also with the monist. The realest of beings, the only real being, says the complete materialist, is the universe of matter, and the idealist and the pantheist make analogous assertions. From this it follows that the true quarrel of the theist with his several opponents arises not because they deny the existence of a supreme being but because they mistake its nature. In the strict theist it is permissible, consistent, and inevitable to condemn all these opponents as atheists. For him they are atheists, as he must understand that term, in that either they make formal denial of the reality of a being infinitely perfect and distinct from the changing universe of experience; or, while admitting the actuality of an infinite mind, they deny that it is transcendent both as to nature and existence with regard to finite things. God is real to these last, claims the theist, only as identified with the reality we know and of which we are parts.

Hence the theistic objection to every monism, idealistic as well as materialistic, Heraclitean as well as Eleatic, is not that it is in error as to the existence of a supreme being, but that its error is more profound: it is totally in error as to the nature of this *ens realissimum*. Hence also the theist holds that the monist is totally in error as to the nature of the self and all the things of its knowledge and experience. It is impossible that a judgment of the character of particular things and a calculus of their value be made otherwise than in accordance with affirmations as to the nature of that whole of which they are held to be parts. It is upon the basis of this necessity, together with some of its logical and practical consequences and implications, that an argument for the existence of God, perfect and personal, may be constructed.

In every system of ideas there is a single idea upon which the entire system is raised. Better, in every system of ideas, by the very fact that it is a system, there is a single basic judgment, a fundamental principle, in which the basic idea is given expression and meaning. It is only in judgments, in affirmations and denials, that concepts are actual and become

* John K. Ryan (1897-   ), "God and the Monistic Ideologies," *The New Scholasticism*, Vol. IX (April, 1935), 134-146.

dynamic and effective.* Especially is this true with reference to an integrated view of reality, a complete and coherent system of thought. In such a system the basic idea must be given meaning and strength by its expression in a single judgment upon which all other judgments of existence, nature and value will depend. Thus in materialistic monism the basic principle is the assertion that all reality is body, and according to the demands of this dogma must answer to the particular problems that present themselves to be made. So also with idealistic and pantheistic monisms: their particular affirmations and denials, their appraisals and preferences are all given vitality, form, color and character by their basic idea and principle. So also with theism and atheism: in the one is found as its fundamental and dynamic principle the affirmation of the existence of God; in the other, the denial of real existence to God. In the theistic affirmation is found the reason for a complete and integrated view of all things, for a definite calculus of values, for a complexus of norms and sanctions that will determine conduct as well as thought. In the basic and initial denial pronounced by atheism is found the reason for a different interpretation of reality, for a different estimation of the character and worth of particular things and a different set of criteria for the governance of human life and human relations.

To any complete ideology, such as those that have been mentioned, there are certain tests that must be put. The first of these is the test of consistency. Since all particular judgments in a system of thought ultimately rest upon a single basic judgment, it is of logical necessity that all particular judgments be consistent with this basic judgment and with one another. Any system of thought that claims to be comprehensive must be able to harmonize, integrate and synthesize seeming contradictions. It must admit and face genuine difficulties and make genuine efforts to solve them in terms of its fundamental principle. If it is unable to meet and solve its difficulties, that is a defect that may amount to a self-refutation. The principle of contradiction still stands: when an ideology cannot rid itself of certain particular concepts and judgments that stand in irreconcilable opposition to its basic principle, then it is of logical necessity to condemn and reject the system itself.

That there are certain concepts and judgments that we cannot rid ourselves of is indicated by reflection and experience. With regard to ourselves we make certain pronouncements both as to existence and value that we cannot forsake. We recognize ourselves as individuals, real, distinct from all other things, possessed of a supreme value to ourselves. We may indulge, for the moment, in the make-believe of methodic or

* This is a logical and epistemological thesis that cannot be developed here. The position taken is substantially in agreement with what I take to be Ludwig Wittgenstein's doctrine in the same reference. Cf. his *Tractatus Logico-Philosophicus* (London: Kegan Paul, 1922), p. 50: *"Nur der Satz hat Sinn; nur in Zusammenhange des Satzes hat ein Name bedeutung. . . . Der Ausdruck hat nur im Satz Bedeutung. Jede Variable laesst sich als Satzvariable auffassen."*

universal doubt, but we know that it is only a game, that not even for the moment can we question these immediate certitudes. Nor can we cast them aside at the command of some assertion or supposition as to the ultimate nature of reality. The immediate makes itself felt as such and claims its priority of consideration and respect. Convictions that spring spontaneously from the deepest instincts and strongest impulses of our nature warn us, if they are in contradiction to some metaphysical principle, to test that principle and to reject it if it provides no basis for our most significant concerns and knowledge. Thus it is possible, expedient and necessary to make what may be called an *a posteriori* application of the test of consistency to any general theory of reality.

A second test to which any system of thought must submit is pragmatic. It is a necessity of our unique and unitary nature to give outward expression of our inward thought. Thought is made for action, not in any restricted Bergsonian sense, but in the familiar and genuine sense that, in more or less complete fashion, men inevitably translate their thoughts and theories into deeds and practices. No real system of thought ever remained solely in the ideal order, and this for two reasons. The men and women who produced that system of thought did so largely because of external forces and conditions. In turn, having given more than a merely notional assent to their principles, they show this by applying these principles to actual conduct. It is only by such practical application, and usually over a long period of time, that a complete system of thought can be developed. Such development is found only in a vast Platonic dialogue acted out in the course of generations by countless men and women of varying temperaments, interests and abilities.

The pragmatic test shows itself to be another test of consistency for a complete ideology. A complete system of thought must be "worked out," its implications made clear, its effects established, not only in the realm of mind but in the actual world of men as well. We are men, not angels, and our dual nature demands that this second consistency show itself as a harmony between inner thought and the outward social and moral order of things. We demand of an ideology that it prove itself by establishing an actual and advantageous order in our affairs. Especially do we demand of a new and revolutionary ideology that it show itself in its effects as an advance over what went before. A system of thought in opposition and contradiction to a previous system cannot be judged favorably if it fails to accord with our natural human demand for improvement and progress.

It is evident that these tests can be applied only to a genuine system of thought. They can be made only when a way of thinking has actually been developed in the minds and lives of many men, when it has ceased to be the private property of single individuals and has become a communal and social affair. As long as a doctrine remains merely individual and inchoate the tests that are made for its validity and consistency are merely tentative and speculative. Its real nature and worth can only be determined when it has attained the maturity of widespread and unambiguous action. These facts may be illustrated by past and present attempts to determine the truth or falsity of the atheistic ideology by a consideration of the nature and condition of a society of atheists.

In previous centuries it proved impossible to apply the tests of consistency and advantage to the atheistic ideology for the more than sufficient reason that such an ideology did not exist. It is true that in the last three centuries, for instance, there have been many individual men and women who have made formal denial of the existence of God or who gave formal assent to one or another of the several monistic doctrines. Yet the beliefs and assertions of such men and women did not constitute a complete and efficacious atheistic ideology. They were living not in a social order produced and maintained by atheism, but in a world that was essentially theistic in origin, development and structure. However unconsciously and inadequately, they were living lives based upon the theistic principle. The full meaning of the opposing doctrine to which they had given assent could not be discerned by them for the reason that they could not possibly see its full development in thought and practice, or experience the effects of its assumption of command in the order of action as well as in the order of thought.*

This inadequate and deceptive character of what may be called an abstract consideration of atheism is illustrated in a striking manner by Bayle's seventeenth century reflections upon the possibility of a society of atheists.† Even more strikingly is this illustrated by Voltaire's consideration of the matter and his criticism of Bayle.‡ Of Voltaire especially must it be said that he was naïve, ingenuous, in some of his observations on this subject, strange as this may sound of him. The reason is that in the seventeenth and eighteenth centuries, atheism had still to become more than a personal matter. As a result it could not be seen in its maturity and proper setting as a genuine system of thought and action. It had yet to be taken as a basic principle upon which a new interpretation of reality, a new estimation of the worth of things, a new set of criteria for the governance of human life would be founded.

In our own century another situation presents itself. Today it is necessary as well as possible to apply our tests of consistency and advantage to a mature and efficacious theory of reality based upon a denial of the existence of God. It is not meant that theism has been defeated and displaced, but that in our world the opposing doctrine has emerged as something more than a matter of isolated and private thought. It now appears as a widespread, dynamic and revolutionary doctrine, the deter-

---

* For a good statement of a somewhat similar aspect of this fact cf. George Hayward Joyce, *The Principles of Natural Theology* (New York: Longmans, Green, 1924), pp. 162-163.

† Pierre Bayle, *Pensées Diverses sur la Comète, édition critique . . . publiée par A. Prat* (Paris: Société des Textes Français Modernes: Édouard Cornély et Cie., 1911), Nn. 161-168.

‡ Voltaire, *Dictionnaire Philosophique* (Paris: 1816), article: *"Athéisme."*

mining force in the production of new social and political orders. Of this Russia is, of course, the prime example. So also may be instanced the shape that things more and more assume in Mexico. Nor are many other parts of the world so utterly different. More and more throughout the civilized world, totalitarian and absolutistic doctrines of one kind or another make themselves felt as dominant factors in the affairs of men and nations. In the case of certain of these ideologies their advocates make explicit protestations of their theistic good faith. Yet close scrutiny of the essentials of these doctrines and observation of their practices and results reveal them as the antithesis of any genuine theism. In the case of such totalitarian theories the old distinction between formal and practical atheism takes on a new significance. Their true meaning and character are most fully and convincingly revealed by their actual development and application.

Necessarily and obviously all these doctrines are theories of human conduct. Their concern, immediate, final, and exclusive, is with man's nature and existence. Hence it is necessary to determine the meaning and place of the concept of man in these systems of conduct and to show what changes they have made from the traditional idea of man as a moral agent. That idea, as has already been stated, showed man as an individual of a nature both unitary and unique. In it he was seen as a moral agent, a being equipped with intelligence and will, and therefore able to make moral decisions. Man was pronounced to be the possessor of certain natural rights, natural duties and natural dignities. Of his natural duties he could not divest himself, nor could his fellows divest him of his natural rights and dignities. Not merely an animal, and, a fortiori, not merely a machine, each individual man was conceived to be the equal of his fellows in essential character and value, so that no man, whether by his own decision or that of others, could be made a mere means to their advantage or pleasure. Natural dignity, natural worth, natural right, natural duty—these were essentials of that traditional concept of man.

Does this concept of man remain a part of any radical and effective atheistic ideology? Advocates of such an ideology may answer that if it does not, it is because its place has been taken by a larger and richer concept of man. Does it not follow that to remove from our speculations and activities the idea of a God by whom and for whom man is made is to raise his status, to make him a genuine and absolute end-in-himself? No longer is he a subject, either in concept or practice, to any higher being. More than that, man himself is seen as the supreme being, for only in him has reality reached its highest form and become self-conscious, intelligent and self-determining. Man is a moral agent, but in a higher way: he is now the source of all moral distinctions. No longer is he the mere subject of a rigid, objective, externally imposed moral law; he is now recognized as the adequate source of all moral distinctions. Counterpart to the denial that morality is an imposition from outside runs a loftier affirmation: "And you shall be as gods, knowing good and evil." An autonomous morality, humanly instituted and sanctioned, is therefore held to be a consequence of this enlarged and enriched concept of man. Viewed thus realistically and as he is in himself, man does not cease to be himself and become superman, but he does take his rightful place as the highest of beings. Such is the asserted concept of the nature and position of man in the developed doctrine of modern atheism.

Taking this concept of man as a point of departure, there is necessity as well as advantage in extending and making more definite this realistic view of man that the atheistic ideology demands. Such realism will depart from the abstract consideration of Man, it will leave behind, for a time, the universal idea of Man, and concern itself with the actual basis of the abstract and universal idea, that is, with individual men. Such realism will be answered and satisfied only by ascertaining the actual position and uses of individual men in a society produced, informed and governed by the atheistic ideology. Does such a society manifest, by its treatment of the individual man, the sure consequences of an enlarged and enriched concept of the individual man? Or does such a society, by its treatment of the individual, give evidence that its judgment of man's nature is false, and that this falsity springs directly and immediately from the falsity of that denial of God's existence which is basic to the entire system?

It is the second question that must be answered affirmatively. In the actual application of this ideology in its several forms, no individual man is conceived and treated as an end-in-himself. The individual is there looked upon as a mere means to the good of others or of the state and is held to be without absolute value or any essential dignity. Regarded as the subject of innumerable natural duties, he is yet denied the possession of the correlatives of such duties, that is, inalienable and necessary natural rights. Before the authority of the state's ends and the demands of the common good, the individual finds himself stripped of the rights which he thought had been made secure by centuries of labor, sacrifice and penalty. "Life, liberty and the pursuit of happiness" possess a social meaning but do not name natural and inalienable individual rights. Or they may be said to pertain, even in the case of the fundamental right to life itself, not to concrete, individual men but to Man in the abstract and the ideal.

The denial and practical destruction of the individual man's right to life is an essential and distinctive phenomenon of the atheistic ideology in action. A necessary consequence of the conception and treatment of men as means to be used by the state, this destruction of the right to life manifests itself in various ways. Forms of it are found in the secret hatred and fear of life that are birth prevention and abortion. Publicly and officially, it is expressed still more explicitly by the literal destruction of political opposition, by the violence and bloodshed of class-hatred and class-warfare, by the liquidation of entire castes and classes. Or it may take the form of the deliberate sacrifice of groups or blocks of the population, sometimes as an exemplary or punitive measure, sometimes as a means to furthering an economic plan. All these, it must be insisted, are necessary consequences and explicit manifestations of a fundamental judgment as to the character of the individual life and the uses to which it may be put.

The most striking instance of this judgment in action will be found in the total warfare that can be waged in its fulness only by the totalitarian state, that is, when the state is itself an expression of the monistic docrine. Such a state in its genuine form, as in Russia, is a determination of a philosophical absolutism that is formally and explicitly atheistic. Hence, when such a state wages war, when it attempts, in the words of Clausewitz's perfect definition, to impose its will by violence upon another nation,* it is to be predicted that the destruction of individual lives will take place upon an unprecedented scale. Since the individual is seen only as a means to ends that the state has in view, he will be put to more complete uses than in the past. Thus the mass slaughter of troops that took place in the last war, will be repeated in a larger way. Looked upon as mechanisms and instruments, equally with arms and explosives, individual men will be used precisely in the same way. Distinctions as to the value in use between the living machines and the non-living machines will inevitably be made upon the basis of expediency rather than upon any intrinsic superiority of right found in the one and not in the other. Again, in the total war waged by the totalitarian state, the asserted right to life of the non-combatant will be disregarded. There does not seem to be any ground for thinking that civil populations will be exempt from direct and devastating attacks with their attendant destruction of life in a manner and upon a scale that can only be known by experience. Finally, it is to be expected that in such warfare prisoners will be destroyed, especially if they have been taken in large numbers and if it would entail sacrifice and difficulty to respect and maintain them. In this logic there is no reason for according to the enemy-alien treatment that is impossible for the native.

Such things are the inevitable results of a principle in action. The complete monistic logic cannot be otherwise than in the direction of an effective destruction of the individual man's right to life and, a fortiori, of all other rights. In actual development and application the non- and anti-theistic ideology shows itself as a system of thought and conduct in which men cannot be conceived and treated as moral agents, possessed of certain fundamental natural rights and endowed with an essential value and dignity. Yet it is impossible for us to rest satisfied with such doctrines and with the situations that they produce. We deem it an enormity to hold that human beings, ourselves and others, must be thought of and may be used as things of no more or even less value than ma-

* Cf. Karl von Clausewitz, *Vom Kriege* (Berlin, 1832), Vol. 1, p. 4.

chines and chemicals. The deepest impulses of our nature unite with the clearest intuitions of our minds in pronouncing such judgments to be false and their consequences to be evil. A higher conception of human nature and human conduct forces itself so persistently and powerfully upon us that it necessitates attention and consent. For this higher conception any acceptable system of thought must have a place. Unable to provide a place for this conception, an ideology, no matter how grandiose and elaborate in its claims, stands self-condemned.

Which ideology, the theistic or the atheistic, fails before this test? Theism with its basic affirmation of the existence of a personal God and atheism with its negation of His existence stand in contradiction to one another. To prove that the one is true is to prove that the other is false; to prove that the one is false is to prove that the other is true. To show that the basic judgment of atheism provides no basis for certain necessary judgments as to the character and value of the individual is to indicate the falseness of that judgment. To show that it leads to enormities of thought and action is to indicate again the falseness of that basic judgment, and the truth of its contradictory. Or to put it in other terms, the disastrous consequences and inconsistencies of the atheistic ideology are in themselves compelling reasons for asserting the truth of the theistic affirmation. Indirectly and by negations we are led to recognize that it is only in the light of and in harmony with an idea of God, real, personal, and perfect, that we can know ourselves as we are. Directly and positively, from our sure recognition of our own nature, its rights, duties, and dignities, that is, from the truth of our judgments on man, we arise to the sure recognition that God exists. We proceed from the idea of man, based upon and reflective of the reality that is man, to the idea of God and affirmation of His reality.

This argument is not merely pragmatic in character. It is not argued on utilitarian principles that admission must be made of the existence of God, infinite, personal and provident, because only by such admission can actual human persons, their lives, rights and dignities, be safeguarded and respected. It is not argued here that recognition of God's existence is expedient as a mere regulative principle of human conduct. Fictionalism is as unwarranted and dangerous in theodicy as in other fields of philosophy. In theodicy even more than in other fields of philosophy a mere pragmatism is unwarranted and dangerous, since theodicy by its very nature deals not solely with consequences and effects but with their ultimate and adequate source and cause. Thus the present argument does not urge that men act "as if" God is real. Its force is that negatively, from the disastrous effects of an actual and dynamic atheism, and positively, from our ineluctable perception of what man is and how he ought to be treated, we arrive at the necessary conclusion that God does and must exist.

Nor is this argument ontological, that is Anselmian, in character. Its movement is not from the idea of God to the reality of God, but from the idea and reality of man to the idea and reality of God. That man knows by his very nature is a truth older than Aristotle. In the knowledge that man has acquired, the apprehension of his own essential nature holds a place that is high and sure. Most persistent of all man's judgments is his judgment of his own character and worth. Denied in theory and action, it persists in reasserting itself in the heart and mind of the race because it expresses a permanent and unchanging truth. To that truth with all it implies and demands the negation that is atheism is in contradiction. All tests of consistency, both of thought and action, show that a denial of God leads to a denial of man. Or, as it has recently been expressed, the testimony of modern history is that "man without God is no longer man." * Positively, such tests and testimony tell us that the reality of man as a moral person of inviolable dignity and worth must be affirmed, and that such an affirmation can be made only in company with another that is both higher and deeper—the affirmation of the reality of God, first and final cause of all things and of all values.

* Nicholas Berdyaev, *The End of Our Time* (New York: Sheed and Ward, 1933), p. 54.

Section Three
Divine Life

I. Life Is a Proper Attribute of God

36

AQUINAS: SELECTED PASSAGES *

LIFE is in the highest degree properly in God. In proof of which it must be considered that since a thing is said to live in so far as it operates of itself and not as moved by another, the more perfectly this power is found in anything, the more perfect is the life of that thing. In the first place the end moves the agent. The principal agent is that which acts through its form, but sometimes uses some instrument that acts not by virtue of its own form, but of the principal agent, and does no more than execute the action. There are things that move themselves, not in respect to any form or end naturally inherent in them, but only to the executing of the act of movement; the form by which they act, and the end of the action being alike determined for them, by their nature. Of this kind are plants, which move themselves according to their inherent nature, with regard only to executing the movements of growth and decay.

Other things have self-movement in a higher degree, that is, not only with regard to executing the movement, but even as regards the form, the principle of movement, which form they acquire of themselves. Of this kind are animals, in which the principle of movement is not a naturally implanted form; but one received through sense. Hence the more perfect is their sense, the more perfect is their power of self-movement. Such as have only the sense of touch, as shellfish, move only through the motion of expansion and contraction; and thus their movement hardly exceeds that of plants. Whereas such as have the sensitive power in perfection, not merely so as to recognize touch and connection, but objects apart from themselves, can move themselves to a distance by progressive motion.

* St. Thomas Aquinas. *Summa Theol..* I, q. 18, art. 3.

Although animals of the latter kind receive through sense the form that is the principle of their movement, nevertheless they cannot of themselves propose to themselves the end of their operation, or motion; for this has been implanted in them by nature; and by natural instinct they are moved to any action through the form apprehended by sense. Hence such animals as moved themselves in respect to an end they themselves propose are superior to these. This can only be done by reason and intellect; whose province it is to know the proportion between the end and the means to that end, and duly co-ordinate them. Hence a more perfect degree of life is that of intelligent beings; for their power of self-movement is more perfect. This is shown by the fact that in one and the same man the intellectual faculty moves the sensitive powers; and these by their command move the organs of motion. Thus we see that the art of navigation rules the art of ship-designing; and this in its turn rules the art that is only concerned with preparing the material for the ship.

Although our intellect moves itself to some things, yet others are supplied by nature, as are first principles, which it cannot doubt; and the last end, which it must always will. Hence, although with respect to some things it moves itself, yet with regard to other things, it must be moved by another. That being whose nature is its intellect itself, and which, in what it naturally possesses, is not determined by another, must have life in the most perfect degree. Such is God; and hence in Him principally is life. From this the Philosopher concludes, after showing God to be intelligent, that God has life most perfect and eternal, since His intellect is most perfect and always in act.

37

THE INNER LIFE OF GOD *

GOD exists, but what does He? What is His action? This question at once rises in our thoughts. As soon as the mind has recognized the existence of a being, it asks how this being lives; and still more so in regard to God, who, as the principle of beings, excites within us a thirst for knowledge of Him, so much the more ardent and just as His action is the model of all action, and His life the pattern of all life. What then is the life of God? How does He employ His eternity? This is doubtless a bold question. Nevertheless, it is a question

* Henri Lacordaire, O.P. (1802-1861), *Jesus Christ, God and Man*, Conferences delivered at Notre Dame de Paris, trans. by a Dominican Tertiary (Manchester: Robinson, 1902). We insert this Conference, realizing that it is a piece of sacred eloquence rather than a strictly philosophical essay, because we have found nowhere else such a fine analysis of the inner life of God.

which men ask, and which they desire to solve. But how is it to be solved? How are we to penetrate the divine essence in order to catch a glimpse of the incomprehensible movement of an eternal, infinite absolute, and immutable spirit?

Three doctrines come before us. One of these, Aristotle, affirms that God is condemned by the sovereign majesty of His nature to an isolation dreadful to imagine; that, alone in Himself, He contemplates Himself seeing only Himself, and loves Himself with a love which has no other object than Himself; that in this contemplation and this love, eternally solitary, the nature and perfection of His life consist.

According to the second doctrine (Pantheism), the universe shows us the life of God, or, rather, is in itself the life of God. We behold in it His permanent action, the scene upon which His power is exercised, and in which all His attributes are reflected. God is not out of the universe any more than the universe is out of God. God is the principle, the universe is the consequence, but a necessary consequence, without which the principle would be inert, unfruitful, impossible to conceive.

Catholic doctrine condemns these two systems. It does not admit that God is a solitary being eternally employed in a sterile contemplation of Himself; nor does it admit that the universe, although it is the work of God, is His proper and personal life. It soars above these feeble ideas, and, bearing us with the word of God, beyond all the conceptions of the human mind, it teaches us that the divine life consists in the co-eternal union of three equal persons, in whom plurality destroys solitude, and unity division; whose thoughts correspond, whose love is mutual, and who in this marvelous communion, identical in substance, distinct in personality, form together an ineffable association of light and love. Such is the essence of God, and such is His life, both powerfully expressed in the words of the Apostle St. John: *There are three who give testimony in heaven, the Father, the Word, and the Holy Ghost* (1 John 5:7).

Here, and very soon after having promised you light, it would seem that I am leading you into a maze of darkness; for, can anything be conceived more formidable to the mind than the terms by which I have expressed, according to the Scriptures and the Church, the relations that constitute the inner life of God? Do not, however, yield to this first impression; trust rather to my promises, since they are those of the Gospel, wherein is written: *I am the Light of the world.* And again: *He that followeth me walketh not in darkness, but shall have the light of life* (John 8:12). Yes, be confident, count upon God, who has proposed nothing to you unnecessary to be believed, and who has hidden marvelous treasures in the most obscure mysteries, as He has hidden the fires of the diamond in the depths of the earth. Follow me, let us pass the pillars of Hercules, and, leaving truth to fill our sails, let us fearlessly advance even to the transatlantic regions of light.

We would understand something of the divine life: the first question, therefore, we have to ask is: What is life? For, as long as we do not know what life is in itself, it is clear that we shall not be able to form any idea of the life of God. What, then, is life? In order to understand this, we must learn what being is; for life is evidently a certain state of being. We thus arrive at that first and supreme question: What is being? And we shall solve it by seeking for what is permanent and common in the infinitely varied beings which surround us. Now, in all of these, whatever their name, their form, their degree of perfection or inferiority, we find a mysterious force which is the principle of their substance and organization, and which we call activity. Every being, even the most inert in appearance, is active; it condenses, it resists foreign efforts, it attracts and incorporates to itself elements which obey it. A grain of sand is in contest and in harmony with the whole universe, and maintains itself by that force which is the very seat of its being, and without which it would become lost in the absolute incapacity of nothingness. Activity, being the permanent and common characteristic of all that is, it follows that being and activity are one and the same thing, and that we are warranted in making this definition: Being is activity. St. Thomas Aquinas gave us an example when having defined God, who is being in its total reality, he said: *God is Pure Act.*

But activity implies action, and action is life. Life is to being what action is to activity. To live is to act. It is true that spontaneous, and, above all, free action, being perfect action, the birth or apparition of life is generally marked at the point where that kind of action is manifested. Thus we say that the stone is, that the plant grows, that the animal lives; but these different expressions mark only the gradations of activity, whose presence, how feeble soever it may be, everywhere constitutes the living being.

We know what life is. Let us advance another step; let us learn what are its general laws, and then apply them to God.

The first general law of life is: *The action of a being is equal to its activity.* In fact the action of a being can be limited only by a foreign force, or by its own will. Now a foreign force checks it only at the point where its own energy ceases, and as to its own will, should it possess any, that necessarily bears it as far as it can reach by its own nature. An action superior to its activity is impossible to it; an action inferior is insufficient; an action equal to its activity is the only action that places it in harmony with itself and with the rest of the universe. Therefore, whether you consider the general movement of the worlds or the tendency of each being in particular, you will find them all acting to the measure of their forces, and placing limits to their ambition only because they exist to their faculties. All, and man among the rest, advance as far as they can; all, having reached the point which exhausts and stops them, write like the poet, proudly accusing their own powerlessness: *Sistimus hic tandem nobis ubi deficit orbis.*

The first general law being recognized, I at once draw some conclusions from it touching the life of God; for, as the action of a being is equal to its activity, and as God is infinite activity, it follows that in God there is infinite action or, to speak more clearly, that infinite action constitutes in God the very life of God. But what is an action? Nature and mankind are composed only of a tissue of actions; we do nothing else from the moment of our birth to our death. Nevertheless, do you know clearly what an action is? Have you ever weighed the sense of that word which comprises all that passes in heaven and upon earth? An action is a movement; it is impossible for us to conceive its nature under a more clear and general form. The body moves when it acts, thought moves when it works, the heart moves when it conceives affections; from wheresoever the action comes, the tongue has but one term for expressing it. All is in movement in the universe, because all therein is action, and all therein is action, because, from the atom to the planet, from the dust even to intelligence, all is activity. But movement supposes an object, an end to which the being aspires. I move, I run, I risk my life. Why? What do I seek? Apparently I seek something wanting to me and which I desire; for if nothing were wanting to me, my movement would have no cause, repose would be my natural state, immobility my happiness. Since I move, it is to act; the act is at the same time the motive and the end of movement, and consequently action is a productive movement.

Do not grow weary of following me; it is true I am leading you by ways whose outlets perhaps you do not yet see; you are passengers in the ship of Columbus, you seek in vain the star that announces the port to you; but take courage, you will soon hail the shore, it is already near.

Action is a productive movement, as I have just shown, and, as action is the consequence of activity, it follows that production is the final end of activity, that is to say of being, since being and activity are one and the same thing. But in what proportion does being produce? Evidently in proportion to its activity, since, according to the first general law of life, the action of a being is equal to its activity. Therefore, to live is to act; to act is to produce; to produce is to draw forth from self something equal to itself. Doubtless we can conceive a production inferior to the being from which it emanates; but that production, were it to take place, would not be the principal act of such life, it would but be necessarily an accidental thereto. Every being tends to produce in the plenitude of its life, and it attains the natural term of its ambition only by drawing from itself something equal to itself. It is easy to prove this by observation, after having established it by reasoning. In what, for instance, consists the painful labor of the artist? The artist has had in his soul a vision of the Beautiful and the True; the horizon has opened before him, and in the luminous distance of the infinite he has seized an idea which has become his own, and which torments him day and night. What would he do, and what is it that troubles him? He would produce what he has seen or heard; he thirsts to make a piece of canvas, a stone, or words, express his thought as it is in himself, with the same clearness, the same force, the same poesy, the same tone. As long as he does not obtain that desired equality between his conception and his style, he is troubled and desponding, for he remains beneath himself and sheds burning tears over the inefficacy of his genius, which is as a reproach and as death to him. *From him to whom much is given,* says the Gospel, *will much be required.* Such is the law of production, in the order of nature and art, as in the order of virtue.

But in order for life to produce something equal to itself, it must produce life; in order for the living being to produce something equal to itself, it must produce a being like itself, or in other words, it must be fruitful. Fecundity is the extreme and complete term of production, which is itself the necessary term of activity. Thus we learn and lay down that second general law of life: *The activity of a being is resumed in its fecundity.*

Here the spectacle of the world around us is so striking, that it is almost needless to invoke it. Where in nature can we find any being so abject and disinherited as not to have received from God the grace to produce a being like itself, to see itself in another emanating from itself? The plant ceases not to sow in the earth the germ that multiplies it; the tree sheds around it and confides to the winds of heaven the mysterious seeds that assure to it a numerous offspring; the animal gathers its little ones to its unfailing breasts; and, last of all, man, spirit and matter, combines in his fragile life the double fecundity of the senses and thought. He bequeaths himself as a whole to a posterity which perpetuates him by the soul as much as by the body, a father twice blessed and doubly immortal. Shall I dare to advance further, and, passing from man to the opposite frontiers of life, show you the prodigy of fecundity even in those beings to whom science refuses organization, and which, notwithstanding their apparent insignificance, still find in themselves the power to seduce nature and be perpetuated in its bosom by alliances that manifest their vital energy? In vain, from one pole to the other, from man to the worm of the earth, I seek sterility. I find it only in one place and in one thing—in death. So that we may say with rigorous exactness, that life is fecundity, and that the fecundity is equal to the life.

Let us now lift up our eyes, for we can do so: let us turn them towards God. If what we have said be true, God, being infinite activity, is also, and even thereby, infinite fecundity. For, if He were active without being fruitful, one of two things would follow: either His action would be unproductive, or He would produce only outside of Himself, in the region of the temporary and the finite. To say that the action of God is unproductive, is to say that He acts without cause, and that His life is consumed in the powerlessness of eternal sterility; to say that His action is only productive outside of Himself, is to say that His life is not His own, which is absurd, or that the universe is His life, which brings us to pantheism. We must then conclude that the life of God is exercised within Himself by an infinite and a sovereign fecundity. Do not seek beforehand how this adorable mystery is accomplished; do not hurry your curiosity beyond the light and the abyss. Be masters of yourselves, examine the point you are investigating, hear the sounds that you hear, and no more. The Infinite, in heaven, is seen at a glance; here upon earth, it is difficult for us to lift even a little of the veil that hides it from us.

I ask you now but one thing, I ask you if you can form any idea of being without the idea of activity; any idea of activity without the idea of production; any idea of production without the idea of fecundity? I ask you if your mind consents to pronounce this judgment: God is infinite activity which ends in infinite sterility. You may say: He sees and loves Himself, is this nothing? Yes, but His regard and His love are sterile; does that satisfy you? What! Your regard and your love are fruitful; they produce a living being like yourself, equal to you, in whom you see and love yourself; and God, the principle and pattern of all things, does not possess, under an infinite and supernatural form, the mystery which you possess under a finite and natural form! His outer activity is great enough to give life to the universe, whilst His inner and personal activity is to produce nothing but the silence of unmeasured solitude! Is fecundity then a calamity, and sterility a state of perfection? If it be a state of perfection, do you not see that God contains them all in a supereminent degree? We must then conclude with St. Thomas Aquinas, in his marvelous treatise on the Divine Persons: "The consequence of all action being something which proceeds from that action, even as there is an outer procession that follows the outer action, there is also an inner procession that follows the inner action . . . and thus the Catholic faith establishes a procession in God" (Ia, qu. 27, 1).

Let us still advance and ask why fecundity is the sum term of the activity of beings? Why beings tend to produce other beings like themselves, and, in fact, do produce them? The reason of this is contained in the very idea of activity and action. For an action is a movement; a movement supposes a starting-point, which is the acting being and a relation between the principle and the end of movement, which is the desired being. Without that relation there would be no cause of movement, and, consequently, no more action, no more activity, no life, no being, nothing. Relation is the very essence of life, and we have but to examine our own life to find abundant proof of it. What do we do from the first of our days even to the last? We hold relations with God, with nature, with men, with books, with the dead, and with the living. The very time which measures our age is a relation, and our mind would lose itself in vainly endeavouring to imagine life otherwise than as an invisible tissue of numberless relations.

What then is a relation? It is more than needful for us to know, since it is the last link of our whole being. A relation consists in the bringing together of two distinct terms. The perfect conjunction of these terms is unity, their perfect distinction is plurality, and, consequently, their perfect relation is unity in plurality. Survey the whole web of our relations, you will find nothing else there. The life of your intelligence is unity of mind in plurality of thoughts; the life of your body is unity of action in plurality of members; your life as a family is unity of affection and interests in plurality of persons; your life as citizens is unity of origin, duties, and rights in plurality of families; your Catholic life is unity of faith and love in plurality of souls tending towards God; and so is it with all the rest. What am I now doing? Why are my words addressed to you? What is there between them and this audience? Nothing, if it be not that my soul seeks yours to lead it to the seat of a light which, without destroying the distinction between your personality and mine, would, nevertheless, bring us together in the present unity of the same hope and in the future unity of the same beatitude.

Now this marvel of unity in plurality could be produced only by the likeness of beings, and the likeness of beings supposes their equality by their community of origin. Fecundity, which produces beings like their authors and like each other, is then the natural principle of unity in plurality; that is to say, of the relations that form the life of beings by the continuous totality of their acts. It is true that we hold relations with beings to whom we are neither drawn by a similar origin nor by an exact likeness: but these relations are also feeble and distant, and the degree of likeness is always marked by the degree of kindred, which measures the strength and the intimacy of the relations. Thus members of the same family are nearer to each other than fellow-citizens; nations of the same race are more closely united than nations of different races; and all created beings derive from God, their common Father, the reason of likeness and relations, more or less direct, which bind them together in the vast unity of nature.

We are then entitled to lay down this third general law of life: *The end of fecundity is to produce relations between beings, that is to say, to give an object to, and a reason for, their activity.*

Already you cease to wonder at those prodigious words by which the Apostle St. John defined the divine life for us: *"There are three who give testimony in heaven, the Father, the Word, and the Holy Ghost, and these three are one"* (1 John 5:7). You see that the mystery of life is a mystery of relations, that is to say, a mystery that involves these two terms—unity in plurality, plurality in unity. But before we arrive at a still more formal conclusion, let us halt for a moment to consider the effects of relations in beings.

Life is not the only phenomenon they offer to us. Above the movement that mingles and bears them onward, we find a charm which we call beauty. Beauty is the result of order; wherever order ceases, beauty vanishes. But what is order if not the unity which shines in a multitude of beings, and which, notwithstanding their distinctions and their variety, brings them together again in the splendor of a single act?

Goodness is the sister of beauty. It is the gift which beings reciprocally make of their advantages, and consequently it is also the effect of relations. In order to give and to receive, it is necessary at least to be two.

Thus life, beauty and goodness, have one and the same principle, which is unity in plurality; and to refuse this double character to God is at once to refuse life, beauty, and goodness to Him. Would you do this? Even should you not understand how one and the same being could realize in Himself one and many, unity and plurality, would that feebleness of your intelligence destroy the chain of the reasonings and observations which have initiated us into the most profound secrets of the nature of things? But let us meet the difficulty face to face.

God is one; His substance is indivisible because it is infinite; this is beyond doubt for faith as for reason. God cannot, then, be many by the division of His substance. But if He is not many by the division of His substance, how can He be many? How can a being who is one and indivisible at the same time be many? Gentlemen, I require but one word, and I ask you in return: Why should God need to be many? Is it not in order to possess relations in Himself, those relations without which we can neither conceive activity, nor being? Let the substance of God, then remain what it is and what it should be—the seat of unity; and let it produce in itself, without being divided, terms of relation, that is to say, terms which are the seat of plurality in relation to unity. For those two things, one and many, are alike necessary in order to form relations; and if the substance of God were divisible, unity being wanted thereto, relations would be wanting too.

I divine your thoughts. You would tell me that you do not even understand the expressions which I employ, and that there is manifest contradiction between the idea of an unique substance and the idea of several terms of relation to be contained therein without dividing it. I will show you that it is not so, and, had you but the intelligence of a child, it would suffice to enable you to follow me and to render justice to truth.

I stretch forth my hand. Where is it? In space. What is space? Philosophers have disputed about its nature; some have thought that it is an exceedingly delicate and subtle substance; others that it is something void, a simple possibility of receiving bodies. Whatever it may be, whether substance or not, space manifestly is a capacity constituted by three terms of relation: length, breadth, and height; three terms perfectly distinct, equal, inseparable save by an abstraction of the mind, and yet in their evident distinction forming together but one single and indivisible extent, which is space. I say that length, breadth, and height, are terms of relation, that is to say, terms which relate to each other, since the sense of length is determined by the sense of breadth, and so on. I say that these terms of relation are distinct from each other; for it is manifest that length is not breadth, and that breadth is not height. I say, in fine, that these three terms, notwithstanding their real distinction, form but one and indivisible extent. This, moreover, is perfectly clear to the senses as to the mind. There is, then, neither obscurity, nor contradiction, in this proposition: God is a unique substance, containing in His indivisible essence terms of relation really distinct in themselves.

Shall I give a more positive example than that of space? For, notwithstanding the reality of space, you may perhaps accuse it of being a kind of abstraction. Take, then, the first body you meet with. Every body, whatever it may be, a stone or a diamond, is comprised under the three forms of length, breadth, and height. Prisoner of extent, it bears it in its simple and triple form, and becomes wholly incorporated in it by a reciprocal penetration which makes of both one single thing. Body is space, and space is body. Length, breadth, and height are body, inasmuch as it is long, inasmuch as it is wide, inasmuch as it is high. Divide the body as you will, change its innermost nature at pleasure, the same phenomenon of unity in plurality will always subsist; so that there is nothing in nature, space and body, that which contains and that which is contained, which does not fall under this definition as simple as it is marvelous—an unique substance in three terms of relation really distinct from each other.

The universe speaks then like St. John. Not only does it contain nothing contradictory to the logical rectitude of the expressions which represent the mystery of the divine life; not only do these expressions take in it the character of a general and algebraic formula of beings; but the force of analogy leads us also to apply this formula to the very principle of beings, to that Being Who should have placed in His works a copy only or a reflection of His own nature.

As soon, however, as we apply expressions or laws of the visible order to God, their proportions at once become changed, because they pass from the region of the finite to that of the infinite. You must not wonder, then, if Catholic doctrine teaches you that terms of relation take, in God, the form of personality. Let us clearly understand this word. Every being, by that alone that it is itself and not another, possesses what we call individuality. As long as it subsists, it belongs to itself; it may increase or decrease, lose or gain; it may communicate to others something of itself, but not itself. It is itself as long as it is; none other is or will ever be so, save itself. Such is the nature and force of individuality. Suppose now that the individual being possesses consciousness and knowledge of its individuality, that it sees itself living and distinct from all that is not itself, it would be a person. Personality is no other thing than individuality having consciousness and knowledge of itself. Individuality is the characteristic of bodies; personality is the characteristic of spirits. Now God is an infinite spirit; all that which constitutes Him, substance and terms of relation, is spirit. Consequently each term of the divine relations possesses consciousness and knowledge of itself, sees itself distinct from the others as terms of relation, one with them as substance; its distinction marks its relative individuality; consciousness and knowledge of its individuality make it a person. Imagine space becoming a spiritual being, you will have before you an analogous phenomenon. Length, breadth, and height would possess consciousness and knowledge of their relative individuality, consciousness of their absolute unity in space; they would be one by substance, many by distinction raised to the state of personality.

It remains for us to consider how many persons there are in God, how and in what order they are manifested in Him.

Up to this point we have only employed analogies drawn from external nature, but, now, having to consider the number and genesis of the divine persons, we must seek in more distant regions a light approaching nearer to the light of God.

Our horizon and light are not limited to external nature. We come in contact therewith in our own body; but it is out of us, even of our body, and in addition it is but dust and ashes; and if we possess something of God, it is but a vestige and not an image of Him. Let us leave the dust and limit, and enter into ourselves: Are we not spirits? Yes, I am a spirit. In this material sepulchre which I inhabit as a traveler, a light has been kindled, an immaterial and pure light enlightening my life, which is my true life which descends from eternity, and leads me thitherward as to my origin and nature. Why do I speak of time and space? Who shall stay me in these abject comparisons? Ah, I feel that you are ready to upbraid me. You wonder that I imprison my soul and your own in these inanities of the universe, where I see shadows only, and touch but the dead; from whence I have drawn only faint and defaced images of truth. You impatiently expect me to open to you the area of a higher vision; I feel that it is there before us. I see that which is unseen, I hear that which is not heard, I read that which has neither form nor color. Truth has still a veil, but it is its personality; it still has secrets, but they are the last. Nature, withdraw; and let us behold God in the spirit!

The mind lives, like God, of an immaterial life, and consequently it knows that life in which the senses have no part, and which is that of God. What, then, does the mind, when shut up within itself, imposing silence on all the rest, it lives of its own life? What does it, gentlemen? Two things only—two inexhaustible acts, which are constantly renewed, which never tire, and whose progress forms its own labor and delight— it thinks and it loves. First, it thinks, that is to say, it sees and combines objects divested of matter, form, extent, and horizon; a kind of universe before which the one that we inhabit by the senses is but a close and dreary dungeon. It dilates in the boundless sea of ideas. It calls into life, to form its own life, nameless and endless worlds which obey it with the quickness of lightning. It may be ignorant of their value and disdain them; pure contemplation will be the more burdensome to it that it exercises it the less and enchains its faculties to the abasements of the body. But I speak not of these treasons of the mind against itself; I speak of the mind as it is of its own nature, as it lives when it wills to live at the height where God has placed it. It thinks, then, this is its first act.

But thought; is it the mind itself, or something distinct from it? It is not the mind itself, for thought comes and goes, whilst the mind always remains. I forget on the morrow the ideas of the eve; I call them up and dismiss them; sometimes they beset me in spite of myself; my thought and my mind are two. I speak to myself in the solitude of my understanding; I interrogate myself. I answer to myself, my inner life is but a continual and mysterious colloquy. And yet I am one. My thought, although distinct from my mind, is not separated therefrom; when it is present, my mind sees it in itself. I am at the same time one and two. My intellectual life is a life of relation; I find again therein what I have seen in external nature, namely, unity and plurality—unity resulting from the very substance of the mind, plurality resulting from its action. What, indeed, would the action of the mind be, if it were unfruitful? What would be its reason, its end, its object? The mind, like the whole of nature, but in a much higher manner, is then prolific. Whilst bodies divide in order to multiply, the mind, created in the likeness of God, remains inaccessible to all division. It engenders its thought without emitting any of its incorruptible substance; multiplies it without losing anything of the perfection of unity.

You see that in rising from the outer to the inner life—from the life of the body to that of the mind—we find again the same law; but we find it, as was inevitable with an increase of light and precision. Bodies, notwithstanding their marvelous relations, kept us too far from God; the mind has borne us even to the sanctuary of His essence and His life. Let us enter, or at least, if we are forbidden to pass certain limits, let us approach as near as divine goodness will permit us.

God is a spirit; His first act is, then, to think. But His thought could not be like ours, multiple, unceasingly appearing but to vanish, and vanishing but to appear again. Ours is multiple, because since we are finite we can but represent to ourselves one by one the objects susceptible of being known to us; it is liable to perish, since in the crowding out of our ideas one upon another, the second dethrones the first, and the third overthrows the second. On the contrary, in God, whose activity is infinite, the mind at once engenders a thought equal to itself, which fully represents it, and which needs no second expression, because the first has exhausted the abyss of things to know, that is to say, the abyss of the infinite. That unique and absolute thought, the first-born and the last of the mind of God, remains eternally in His presence as an exact representation of Himself, or, to speak the language of the sacred books, as "His image, the brightness of His glory, and the figure of His substance" (2 Cor. 4:4; Heb. 1:3). It is His word, His utterance, His inner word, as our thought is also our utterance and our word; but differing from ours inasmuch as it is a perfect word which speaks all to God in a single expression, which speaks it always without repetition, and which

St. John heard in heaven when he thus opened his sublime Gospel: "In the beginning was the Word, and the Word was with God, and the Word was God" (John 1:1).

And even as in man the thought is distinct from the mind without being separated therefrom, so in God, the thought is distinct without being separated from the divine mind which produces it. *The Word is consubstantial with the Father,* according to the expression of the council of Nicaea, which is but the forcible expression of truth. But here, as in the rest, there exists a great difference between God and man. In man the thought is distinct from the mind by an imperfect distinction, because it is finite; in God, the thought is distinct from the mind by a perfect distinction, because it is infinite; that is to say that in man the thought does not attain to becoming a person, whilst in God it does attain thereto. The mystery of unity in plurality is not totally accomplished in our intelligence, and this is why we cannot live of ourselves alone. We seek from without the aliment of our life; we need a foreign support, a thought other than ours, and yet closely allied to it. In God plurality is absolute as well as unity, and therefore His life passes entirely within Himself, in the ineffable colloquy between a divine person and a divine person, between a Father without generation and a Son eternally engendered. God thinks, and He sees Himself in His thought and in another so akin to Him as to be but one with Him in substance; He is Father, since He has produced in His own likeness a term of relation really and personally distinct from Him; he is one and two in all the force which the infinite gives to unity and duality; in contemplating His thought, in beholding His image, in hearing His word, He is able to utter in the ecstasy of the highest, the most real paternity: "Thou art my Son, today I, have begotten Thee" (Ps. 2:7). Today! In this day which has no past, nor present, nor future; in this day which is eternity, that is to say, the indivisible duration of unchanging being. Today! For God thinks today; He engenders His Son today, He sees Him today, He hears Him today, He lives today in that ineffable act which has neither beginning nor end.

But is this all the life of God? Is the generation of His Son His sole act, and does it consummate with its fecundity all His beatitude? No, gentlemen; for, in ourselves, the generation of thought is not the term where our life ends. When we have thought, a second act appears; we love. Thought is movement which brings its object into ourselves; love is a movement which draws us out of ourselves towards that object in order to unite it to us and ourselves to it, and thus accomplish in its fulness the mystery of relations, that is to say, the mystery of unity in plurality. Love is at the same time distinct from the mind, and distinct from the thought; distinct from the mind in which it is engendered and in which it dies; distinct from the thought by its very definition, since it is a movement of drawing together, whilst the thought is a simple perception. And yet it proceeds from the one and from the other, and forms but one with both. It proceeds from the mind, whose act it is, and from the thought, without which the mind would not see the object which it should love; and it remains one with the thought and the mind in the same fount of life where we again find all the three, always inseparable, and always distinct.

In God it is the same. From the coeternal regard interchanged between the Father and the Son, springs a third term of relation, proceeding from the one and the other, really distinct from them, raised by the force of the infinite to personality, and which is the Holy Ghost, that is to say, the holy, the unfathomable and stainless movement of divine love. As the Son exhausts knowledge, the Holy Ghost exhausts love in God, and by Him the cycle of divine fecundity and life closes. What more could be possible to God? As a perfect Spirit He thinks and He loves; He produces a thought equal to Himself and with His thought a love equal to both. What more could He desire to produce? And what more could you desire if, like Him, you possessed unbounded thought and unbounded love in the unity of your substance? But, poor as we are, thought and love are in our soul only a perception and a possession of a foreign object; we are obliged to leave ourselves in order to seek our life, to appease our thirst for knowledge, our hunger for love. And instead of turning to the only source of truth and charity, which is God, we wed ourselves to nature, which is but a shadow; to the life of time, which is but death. Or, returning to ourselves in a hopeless effort, we ask from our powerlessness the accomplishment of the one and triple mystery which is divine felicity; we endeavour to satisfy ourselves in the pride of solitary thought, in the delight of personal love, and, like dust which consumes itself, we waste away in a withering grasp of egotism which would be infinite if nothingness could be infinite.

O, lift up your eyes to heaven! There is life because there is true fecundity. It is there that the spectacle of the laws of nature, and the study of the laws of your mind lead you. All teaches you that being and activity are one and the same thing, that activity is expressed by action, and that action is necessarily productive or fruitful; that the end of fecundity is to establish relations between similar beings; that relation is unity in plurality, from whence results life, beauty, and goodness. And that thus God, the infinite being, is infallibly the most magnificent totality of relations, perfect unity and perfect plurality, the unity of substance in the plurality of persons; a primordial mind, a thought equal to the mind that engenders it, a love equal to the mind and the thought whence it proceeds; all three, Father, Son, and Holy Ghost, ancient as eternity, great as infinity, one in beatitude as in the substance from whence they derive their identical divinity. Behold God! Behold God, the cause and pattern of all beings! Nothing exists below which is not a vestige or an image of Him, according to the degree of its perfection. Space reveals Him in its single and triple plenitude; bodies proclaim Him in the three dimensions which constitute their solidity; the mind shows us a nearer vision of Him in the production of the two highest things of this world, if indeed they are of this world, namely, thought and love; in fine, the very tissue of the universe which consists of relations, is before us, as it were, a picture which the divine passes over, penetrates, and so gives above the visible heaven a glimpse of the invisible heaven of the Trinity.

All laws take their source in this seat of primordial relations. If human society would aspire to perfection, it has no other model to study and to imitate. It will find there the first social constitution in the first community; equality of nature between the persons who compose it; order in their equality, since the Father is the principle of the Son and the Holy Ghost proceeds from the Father and the Son; unity, the cause of plurality; thought, receiving from above its being and its light; love, terminating and crowning all the relations. These laws are full of beauty, and if legislators could realize them upon earth, they would produce a work whose privilege and secret have until now belonged to the Catholic Church alone.

Let us halt here. I have not demonstrated the mystery of the Trinity to you, but I have placed it in perspective, where pride will not mistake it without insulting itself. Let us forgive that satisfaction to pride if it be jealous of claiming it. For yourselves, inspired by humbler and higher wisdom, give thanks to God, who, in revealing to us the mystery of His life, has not overwhelmed our intelligence by a sterile light, but has given to us the key of nature and our own mind.

II. Divine Knowledge

38

ITS EXISTENCE AND PERFECTION *

Art. 1: In God there exists the most perfect knowledge.

To prove this, we consider that intelligent beings are distinguished from non-intelligent beings because the latter possess only their own form; whereas the intelligent being naturally has also the form of some other thing; for the idea of the things known is in the knower. Hence it is manifest that the nature of a non-intelligent being is more contracted and limited; whereas the nature of intelligent beings has a greater amplitude and extension; therefore the Philosopher says that "the soul is in a sense everything." The contraction of the form comes

* St. Thomas Aquinas, *Summa Theol.*, I, q. 14, art. 1, 4.

from the matter. Hence, as we have said above, forms accordingly as they are the more immaterial, approach more nearly to a kind of infinity. Therefore it is clear that the immateriality of a thing is the reason and rule of its cognoscibility; and the mode of immateriality is the mode of knowledge. Hence, as the Philosopher says, plants do not know, because they are wholly material; sense knows in proportion as it receives images free from matter, and the intellect is still further cognoscitive, because it is more separated from matter, and unmixed. Since God is in the highest degree of immateriality, it follows that He occupies the highest place in knowledge.

Art. 4: God's intellect is His Substance.

If it were not His Substance, then something else, as the Philosopher says, would be the act and perfection of the Divine Substance; to which the Divine Substance would be related, as potency to act; which is altogether impossible. The act of understanding is the perfection and act of the intelligent agent. We must consider how this is. As laid down above, to understand is not a progressive act to anything extrinsic; but remains in the operator as his own act and perfection; as existence is the perfection of the one existing. As existence follows on the form, so in like manner to understand follows on the intelligible idea. In God there is no form apart from His Existence. Hence as His Essence itself is also His intelligible species, it necessarily follows that His act of understanding itself must be His Essence and His Existence.

39

THE OBJECT OF DIVINE KNOWLEDGE *

Art. 2: God understands Himself of Himself.

. . . Since God has nothing in Him of potentiality, but is Pure Act, the intellect and the object in Him are altogether the same; so that He neither is without the intelligible species, as is the case with our intellect regarded as potentiality; nor does the intelligible species differ from the substance of the divine intellect, as it differs in our intellect regarded as actually intelligent; but the intelligible idea itself is the divine intellect itself, and thus He understands Himself by Himself.

Art. 3: He also perfectly comprehends Himself.

. . . God knows Himself as perfectly as He can be known. For everything is knowable according to the mode of its own actuality. A thing is not known as a potentiality, but as an actuality. The power of God's

* Summa Theol., I, q. 14, art. 2, 5, 6, 11.

own knowledge is as great as His actual existence; because from the fact that He is Actuality separated from all matter and potentiality, He is knowable in a corresponding degree. It is manifest that He knows Himself as much as He is knowable; and for that reason perfectly comprehends Himself.

Art. 5: God necessarily knows things other than Himself.

It is manifest that He perfectly understands Himself; otherwise He would not be perfect, since His Existence is His Intelligence. If anything is perfectly known, its power is also perfectly known. The power of anything can be perfectly known only by knowing to what its power is extended. Since the divine power extends itself to other things by the very fact that it is the first effective cause of all things, God must necessarily know things other than Himself. This appears still more plainly if we add that the existence itself of the first efficient cause, that is God, is His own intelligence. Whatever effects pre-exist in God, as in the First Cause, must be in Him according to an intelligible mode. Everything which is in another, exists in it according to the mode of that other's existence. . . . So we say that God sees Himself in Himself, because He sees Himself by His Essence; and He sees other things not in themselves, but in Himself; inasmuch as His Essence contains the similitude of other things besides Himself.

Art. 6: He knows them by a proper, and not only by a general knowledge.

. . . To know a thing in general and not in particular, is to have imperfect knowledge of it. Hence our intellect, when it passes from potentiality to act, proceeds first to a universal and confused knowledge of things, before it knows them in particular; as coming from the imperfect to the perfect. If the knowledge of God regarding other things were only universal and not special, it would follow that His intelligence would not be absolutely perfect; therefore neither would His being be perfect. We must therefore hold that God knows other things than Himself with a proper knowledge; not only as beings, but as distinguished from each other.

Art. 11: He knows them also individually.

. . . Since God is the cause of things by His knowledge, His knowledge is extended as far as His causality extends. As the active power of God extends itself not only to forms, which are the source of universality, but also to matter, . . . the knowledge of God must extend itself to singular things, which are individualized by matter. Since God knows other things than Himself by His Essence, as being the Model of all things, as their active principle, His Essence must be the sufficing principle of knowledge as regards all things made by Him, not only in the universal, but also in the singular. . . .

40

KNOWLEDGE OF FUTURE CONTINGENTS *

God knows future contingent things.

In evidence of this, we must consider that a contingent thing can be considered in two ways: first, in itself, as actual, in which sense it is not considered as a future thing, but as a present thing; not as contingent, but as determined in one; and in that way it can infallibly be the object of certain knowledge, as for instance to the sense of sight; as when I see that Socrates its sitting down. In another way, a contingent thing can be considered as it is in its cause; and in that sense it is considered as a future thing, and as a contingent thing not yet determined to one; forasmuch as a contingent cause has relation to opposite things, and in that sense a contingent being is not subject to any certain knowledge. Hence, whoever knows a contingent effect in its cause, has merely a conjectural knowledge of it. God knows all contingent things not only as they are in their causes, but also as each one of them is actually (*actu*) in itself. Although contingent things become actual successively, nevertheless God knows contingent things not successively, as they are in themselves, as we do; but He knows them all at once; because His knowledge is measured by eternity as also His existence; for eternity existing all at once comprises all time. Hence all temporal things are present to God from eternity, not only in the manner that He has ideas of all things before Him, as some say; but because His glance is carried from eternity over all things, as they are in their presentiality. Hence it is manifest that contingent things are infallibly known by God, inasmuch as they are subject to the divine sight in their presentiality; still they are really future contingent things in relation to their own proximate causes.

An Interpretation †

What we have just said of God's knowledge of things may be applied to His foreknowledge of future contingent things and especially of future free actions. It is a defined dogma of the Catholic Church that God knows them from all eternity. St. Thomas (I, q. 14, ar. 13) views this problem as a particular case of the general doctrine established in the

* *Summa Theol.*, I, q. 14, a. 13.

† Reginald Garrigou-Lagrange, *God: His Existence and His Nature*, Part II, Art. II, Vol. II, 71-91. (St. Louis: Herder, 1934-1936).

eighth article of the same question, that the knowledge of God is the cause of things. The Molinists, on the contrary, seek to separate the thirteenth article of St. Thomas from the eighth, as if God's knowledge of future free actions were an exception to the general law that "God's knowledge is the cause of things." . . .

Does this mean, as the Molinists would have it, that God's knowledge which is the cause of all things is not the cause of future contingent things, or at least of the conditionally free acts of the future, and that here we have an exception to the principles regulating the divine knowledge in general?

In this case we should have to say that the principle of causality admits of an exception, and we should have to maintain that the conditionally free acts of the future do not come from God, the First Being. Moreover, we should have to maintain that God's knowledge is *passive* with regard to the conditionally free acts of the future, and that it is determined by them instead of determining them. Now, there is nothing more absurd than to admit a passivity in pure Act. Finally, we should have to admit, as we shall see, that these conditionally free acts of the future have been all along determined of themselves, and this is the denial of freedom to these acts.

Moreover, we shall show that St. Thomas in various passages teaches most emphatically that *God knows the free acts of the future in the divine decree by which they are made present to Him from all eternity* (*De Veritate*, qu. 2, ar. 12 ad 12um). In the article we have quoted, St. Thomas presupposes that the divine decree is the cause of all things, past, present, or future; but, as he is here concerned merely with God's knowledge of the free acts of the future, he defers, until treating the subject of the divine will (I, qu. 19, ar. 8; qu. 22, a. 4) the question how this divine will is infallibly efficacious without doing any violence to to our free will.

In the *Contra Gentiles* (I, ch. 68), St. Thomas reunites these two aspects of the question so as to prove that God knows the secret movements of our will. His answer is as follows: "God knows them in Himself in so far as He is the universal principle of all beings and of all modes of being. . . . Since the divine Being is the first of all beings and the cause of all beings, so the divine intellect is the first of intellects and the cause of all created intellectual operations. In knowing His being, God knows, therefore, whatever there may be in being, and in knowing His intellect and His will, He knows all thought and all volition. . . . The control which our will has over its acts, and in virtue of which it can, if it chooses, will or not will, presupposes that it is not by its nature determined to a certain act, and excludes the violent effort of an external agency, but not the influence exerted upon it by the supreme cause from which both being and action proceed. Moreover, the universal causality of the First Cause extends to our free acts, so that in knowing Himself God knows them.

We find St. Thomas teaching the same about the divine will (I, qu. 19, ar. 8), His providence (I, qu. 22, ar. 2 ad 4um), His governance of the world (I, qu. 103, ar. 5-8), His knowledge of our secret thoughts (I, qu. 57, ar. 4; *De Malo*, qu. 16, ar. 8).

How can God's eternal and infallibly efficacious decree leave the will free? St. Augustine (*Liber de corruptione et gratia*, c. 16), in the explanation he gives of St. Paul's words (Phil. 2:13), "For it is God who worketh in you, both to will and to accomplish," answers as follows: "Certainly we will, when we will; but He causes us to will what is good. . . . Certainly it is we who act when we act; but He causes us to act by enabling the will to act efficaciously. . . . When He says: I will cause you to act, what else does this mean than that He will take away the stony heart which was the cause of your inaction, and that He will give you a docile heart so that you will act?" In the fourteenth chapter of the same work, St. Augustine again writes: "God has power over the heart, moving it from within, and He draws human beings to Himself by their wills influencing them; if, therefore, when God willed to establish kings on earth, *The wills of human beings are more in His power than in their own*, who else causes it that chastisement is wholesome and that the heart being contrite there should be amendment of life?"

St. Thomas likewise reconciles the infallibility of divine foreknowledge and the freedom of our acts by appealing to the transcendent efficacy of the divine will. He writes: "When a cause is efficacious to act, the effect follows upon the cause, not only as to the thing done, but also as to its manner of being done or of being. Thus from defect of active power in the seed it may happen that a child is born unlike its father in accidental points that belong to its manner of being. Since, then, the *divine will is perfectly efficacious, it follows not only that things are done, but also that they are done in the way that He wills.* Now God wills some things to be done necessarily, some contingently, to the right ordering of things, for the building up of the universe. Therefore to some effects He has attached necessary causes that cannot fail; but to others defectible and contingent causes from which arise contingent effects" (I, qu. 19, ar. 8).

Under the leadership of a great general, the soldiers do not only *what must be done*, but as it must be done. "There is a way of doing things." And the way of a great general passes on to his soldiers. Far more so is this, too, the case with God as regards those beings created by Him.

There is certainly a *mystery* in this; it is that of the divine action between which and our own there is only a similarity by way of analogy, it not being possible for us to know for certain the mode of divine action. But who could demonstrate that there is any *contradiction* in maintaining that the *Creator of the free will who is more intimately associated* with *the will than freedom itself is,* can *infallibly move the will to determine itself freely to act?* Infallibility is not necessity.

We often say: I will see you without fail tomorrow. And, without failing to do so, we accomplish freely what we previously decided upon doing. Why could not God make us do freely what He Himself from all eternity had decided upon our doing? Since our will has the unlimited range of universal good by which it is specified, why, under the influence of the divine movement, can it not retain a dominating and active indifference concerning a particular good, this latter being deemed incapable of invincibly attracting it? The connection between our will and this finite good remains always something contingent. In willing this good, the will *has the power* not to will it. The will, by reason of its universality, goes beyond it. It is that which makes the act terminating our deliberation as a *free act.* "It would be absurd to say," as Bossuet remarks, "that our own decision takes away our liberty. It would be no less absurd to say that God has taken it away by His decree. And just as our will in determining itself to choose one thing rather than another, does not take from itself the power of choosing between two things, we must conclude likewise that this decree of God does not do so." (*Traité du libre arbitre,* ch. 8).

How could the divine motion destroy the contingency of the relationship existing between our will and a finite good, a contingency which arises from the will not being necessitated in making a decision? Not only does God safeguard the freedom of our act, but He brings it about with us when the deliberation has become a reality. *The divine motion cannot do violence to our freedom, for it exerts its influence in conformity with the natural inclination of the will. First of all it takes the will on to its adequate object, which is universal good; and only after that does it direct the will toward an inadequate object consisting of some particular good.* Viewed in the first way, the divine motion *effects the freedom* of the act. It exerts its influence interiorly in the very depths of the will taken in the fullest capacity of its willing. It carries it confusedly through all the degrees of good before inclining it to reach out for some particular good (John of St. Thomas, in I, qu. 19, d. 5, a. 6).

If there were any contradiction in maintaining that God can move our wills infallibly and freely, then the necessary application of the principle of causality is what would involve us hopelessly in absurdity. Let us not forget that what comes first in liberty is not human liberty. The idea of liberty is applied only *analogically* to God and human beings. There is merely a similarity of proportion between created liberty and the absolute liberty of God. It is a particular case of the mystery of the coexistence of finite beings with the infinite Being. How can the finite being exist apart from the infinite Being? It can exist only on condition that it is caused by Him and remains absolutely dependent upon Him. How can a secondary liberty exist apart from the primary liberty? It can exist only on condition that it is caused and moved by the latter, so that the faculty of willing passes from a state of *passive indifference* to one of *active indifference* contained in the very choice made by the faculty. Thus all the perfections of this secondary liberty pre-exist eminently from all eternity in the primary liberty.

Why would God not have the power to produce infallibly in us and with us the freedom of our acts? It is certain that God cannot produce a vital act in a stone, since such an act must proceed from a vital power; but He can produce such an act in a living being. It is certain that God cannot produce a free act unless it be determined freely on our part. But why could He not move the will *fortiter et suaviter,* "vigorously and gently," to determine itself to act? "If the will were so moved *by another,* as in no way to be moved *from within itself,* the act of the will would not be imputed for reward or blame. But since its being moved *by another* does not prevent its being moved from *within itself,* it does not thereby forfeit the motive for merit or demerit" (I, qu. 105, ar. 4, ad 2um et 3um).

To maintain that God, as first cause, cannot produce with us and in us the free mode of our acts, is to maintain that a *mode of being* cannot be produced by the prime Being, who is the Creator of all the being there is outside Himself. Contrary to this, we must say with St. Thomas (I, qu. 22, ar. 4, ad 3um) that *"necessary and contingent are consequent upon being as such.* Hence the mode both of necessity and of contingency falls under the foresight of God, who provides universally for all being." St. Thomas explains this point more clearly in his commentary on the *Perihermeneias* of Aristotle (B. I, lect. 14), saying: "We must conceive of the divine will as existing outside of the order of created beings, as a cause which produces the whole of being, and all the differences and modes of being. Now the necessary and contingent are precisely the primary modes into which being is divided." In his commentary on Aristotle's *Metaphysics* (B. VI, lect. 3), St. Thomas uses the same formal expressions.

We may sum up all this teaching in the famous passage of the *Summa* (I, qu. 83, ar. 1): "Free will is the *cause* of its own movement, because by his free will man moves himself to act. But it does not of necessity belong to liberty that what is free should be the first cause of itself, as neither for one thing to be the cause of another need it be the first cause. God, therefore, is the first cause who moves causes both natural and voluntary. And just as by moving natural causes He does not prevent their acts being natural, so by moving voluntary causes *He does not deprive their actions from being voluntary; but rather is He the cause of this very thing in them;* for He operates in each being according to its own nature." According to St. Thomas, intrinsically efficacious grace does not destroy the freedom of our acts, but is the cause of it.

When we come to speak of God's omnipotence, we shall have to define more clearly the nature of the divine motion. We will also solve the objection made against Thomism on this point, when we discuss the antinomies with reference to freedom.

This sublime teaching of St. Thomas finds its confirmation in the fact that according to the Thomists, every other explanation of God's fore-knowledge of the future inevitably ends in contradiction. We speak here of a contradiction and not of a mystery, because these theories, instead of descending from universal and necessary principles to explain a particular and obscure case, propose from the outset a gratuitous solution that involves the very denial of the absolute universality and necessity of the principles.

To explain God's foreknowledge of the free acts of the future, Molina proposed a theory that no one, so far as he knew, had ever taught. We would look in vain for such a theory in the writings of earlier theologians or the Church Fathers. Molina says: "God has a very profound and unfathomable comprehension of each free will. He sees clearly what each free cause would do of its own accord in such and such circumstances, and even in an infinite number of circumstances. This view which God has, we call "middle knowledge."

The knowledge is called middle by reason of its proper object, which is the conditional future or the conditionally free act of the future. It is intermediate between the purely possible which is the object of God's knowledge of simple intelligence, and the contingent future which is the object of God's knowledge of vision. By this middle knowledge, according to Molina, God knows, previous to any determining decree, how a free will would act if placed in certain circumstances, and how in certain other cases it would decide otherwise. After that God decides, according to His benevolent designs, to render this free will effective by placing it in those circumstances more or less favorable or unfavorable to it.

So then, according to Molina, God by His "supercomprehensive knowledge of secondary causes," *sees in the free cause itself,* that in certain circumstances this cause will act in such a manner, and that it will determine itself to act in this way. The divine foreknowledge is not the result of a more or less probable conjecture, but is an *infallible* knowledge of the conditional future.

To this the Thomists have always replied that the middle knowledge conceived to safeguard the freedom of the human will, virtually implies the denial of it. How can God see in a cause, which by its nature is undetermined as to whether it will act or not, that it will *de facto* act? The supercomprehensive knowledge of a cause cannot enable any one to see in it a determination which is not there. And if, in reply, we are told that this determination is known through the circumstances in which the free will would be placed, the theory ends fatally in determinism, which is the denial of free will. The foreseeing of the circumstances may enable one, indeed, to form conjectures, but not to have an infallible knowledge of the conditionally free acts of the future. Cardinal Mazzella, S.J. admitted this to be so, in agreement with the Thomists.

With Suarez and many Molinists, Cardinal Mazzella tries to defend the middle knowledge by saying that God sees the conditional futures neither in His will nor in ours nor in the motives or circumstances influencing the act, but that He sees them in their *objective or formal truth* (*De gratia*, disp. 3, ar. 7).

But the Thomists reply by asking how, previous to any decree from God, a conditionally free act of the future is objectively true rather than false. Suarez and Mazzella prove it in the following manner: "Of two conditional contradictory propositions, such as: If Peter were placed in these circumstances, he would sin or he would not sin; the one is definitely true and the other definitely false. It is impossible, indeed, for both to be true and both to be false. Therefore the infinite intelligence which penetrates all truth, sees certainly which of the two is true and which is false."

The Thomists reply that this is still the denial of free will. From it we should even be led to conclude that, previous to any divine decree, God can see which of the following contradictory propositions is true: The world will exist (come into existence), the world will not come into existence. From this it would follow that creation is no longer a free act, and the divine will would be subjected to the logical fatalism of the Stoics. As Cicero relates (*De divinatione*, I, 55), the Stoics really intended to prove determinism by the argument that, of two contradictory propositions, one is necessarily true. Therefore of the two propositions "A will be, A will not be," the necessity of one of them, at the very moment when I am uttering it, excludes the possibility of the other: "From all eternity is the flow of imperishable truths."

Suarez forgets that Aristotle, in his *Perihermeneias* (B. I, c. 9,), has shown that of two contradictory propositions which are particular ones and which concern a contingent future event, neither is *positively* true or false. If it were otherwise, as Aristotle remarks, the truth would be in determinism and our choice would not be a free one.

In vain some Molinists seek to avoid the difficulty by saying that God knows the truth of conditionally future things not in themselves but in His own essence, which contains eminently all truth.

It is clear that a contingent truth cannot be determined in the divine essence previous to any divine decree. It would be present there *on the same grounds* as absolutely necessary truths, and hence would be a necessary truth.

St. Thomas wrote concerning prophecy as follows: "The contingent free things of the future are not knowable in themselves, because their truth is not determined. Contingent things of the future, the truth of which is not determined, are not knowable in themselves" (II-II, qu. 171, ar. 3).

Concerning the Molinists and in general those who defend the theory of middle knowledge, Leibniz remarks: "It is amusing to see how they torment themselves to find a way out of a labyrinth when there is absolutely no way out. . . . Therefore they will never get out of the difficulty unless they admit that there is a predetermination in the preceding state of the creature which inclines it to act" (*Théodicée*, P. I, sec. 48). In these words just quoted, Leibniz gives us his own solution, which is psychological determinism, in which there is nothing left of liberty except the name.

"It is sufficient," he says, "for the creature to be predetermined by its previous state, by which it is swayed more one way than the other. And all those closely associated actions of the creature and of all creatures were represented in the divine intellect and known to God by His knowledge of simple intelligence, before He had decreed to give them existence. From this we see that, to account for God's foreknowledge of things, we can dispense with both the middle knowledge of the Molinists, and predetermination such as it was taught by Bannez or Alvarez" (*op. cit.*, sec. 47). Leibniz is consistent, but he ends in determinism. Does not the theory of middle knowledge also lead inevitably to this conclusion?

This is not the only inconvenience of this theory. It attacks God's universal causality and supreme dominion over all things, and consequently renders His knowledge passive with regard to our free determinations of which we alone are the cause. God ceases to be the universal cause of being, since the free determination on our part, which is some being, is not produced by Him in us and with us. He is no longer master of the will; His grace remains powerless, *it loses its suavity of appeal because it has lost its power.* There is also no more need of praying to the Savior, of placing all our hope and trust in Him instead of in ourselves. The soul, in the grip of temptation, cannot say to Him: "Convert me, and I shall be converted; for Thou art the Lord my God" (Jerem. 31: 18). God is no more the cause of our good than the cause of our bad deeds, since it depends solely upon our free will whether divine grace is effective or ineffective.

Man alone is the cause of his freely determining himself to act and of the good use he makes of grace. Contrary to the words of St. Paul, it is man himself who does the distinguishing. "For who distinguishes thee," says the Apostle, "what hast thou that thou hast not received" (Cor. 4:7).

Instead of viewing our will and the divine motion as *two total causes,* one of which is subordinate to the other in such a way that *our act,* so far as there is good in it, *comes entirely from God as the primary cause,* and *entirely from man as the secondary cause,* the Molinists view them as *two partial causes,* like two men hauling a boat. Hence God's external causality, as it affects us, proves to be rather mediocre and is like created causality. Our free will *participates* with God in the work of salvation and claims the better part of it. Since God's knowledge is no longer the cause of our free acts, the result is that it must be passive with regard to them. Instead of determining them, it is determined by them. And what is more inadmissible than to admit a state of passivity in the Being who is pure Act?

Certainly, Thomism has its obscurities. It does not take upon itself to show how the transcendent efficacy of the first cause, instead of clashing with our freedom, brings about in us and with us even that our acts are performed freely, in such a way that we still remain responsible. It is only by way of analogy that we can acquire a knowledge of the supreme efficacy of the first creative cause; what properly constitutes it as such remains essentially a mystery to us.

Father Lepidi very truly says: "So long as each of the two systems, the Thomistic and the Molinistic, confines itself to a consideration of the strength of its position and attacks the other in its weak points, there will be no end to this controversy. The two systems must be compared, as regards their development and their conclusions, elucidated by the general and evident rules which are admitted by both sides. If we proceed in this manner, undoubtedly there will still remain many profound obscurities in the two systems, which the intellect will never succeed in clearing up. But at least it will be seen that the obscurity in the Thomistic system is due to the weakness of our poor intellect which, though it knows that between the divine and human causality there is harmony prevailing, is unable to know how this is so. On the other hand, the obscurity in the opposing system results in veritable impossibilities" (*Opuscules philos.*, ch. 1).

The controversy between Thomism and Molinism may be reduced to this: Does Thomism end in obscurity through the legitimate and necessary application of the most universal of first principles (identity, causality, and the universal causality of the prime agent)? It is difficult to deny this. In virtue of the principle of identity, God alone is His own existence. It follows that He alone is His actuating principle, for operation follows being; and as God alone is His own being, so He alone is His principle of action. No created being exists of itself. Consequently no created being acts of itself; it receives its existence from God and can act only in so far as it is moved by the primary cause; a created intellect acts only as moved by the primary intellect; secondary freedom viewed precisely as freedom acts only so far as it is moved by the primary freedom. All movement implying the participation of a pure perfection (*simpliciter simplex*), of an absolutely simple one, evidently is dependent upon the corresponding divine perfection. It is absolutely impossible for anything which is contingent not to be caused by necessary being, the source of all being. What is not self-existent, exists by reason of another which is self-existent. The principles of Thomism are such that it fears neither logic nor mystery. It is even logic which causes Thomism to end in obscurity. How does the supreme efficacy of God's creative power produce in us and with us, *suaviter et fortiter*, the freedom of our acts? A method of reasoning that is most rigorous cannot lead us into an obscurity in which a contradiction would be lurking. It is only a mystery we have here, a result of the mystery of creation (the co-existence of the finite and the Infinite), which is analogous to the mystery of how we are to reconcile God's liberty with His immutability. There would be no contradiction unless, as Hegel would have it, reality were fundamentally a realized contradiction.

Molinism also has its obscurity, which is middle knowledge. But how does it arrive at this latter? Is it by the necessary application of the most universal of first principles which dominate the whole science of theology even to its last details? Is it not rather that by this system a solution may be found for a special difficulty concerning the freedom of the human will? This method of procedure may be adopted in polemical arguments, but it is not the method of science. The Thomist synthesis has given proofs of its capacity regarding all points of theological knowledge. Molinism is merely an opinion in a particular controversy. In the solution of particular and obscure cases, we must start from evident and universal principles. In these cases we cannot propose, regardless of the principles, an apparently convenient solution with uncertain advantages obtained by the denial of the very principles. It would be said that we are afraid to face both logic and the mysterious. In the obscurity to which this method would lead us, there would be hidden, not a mystery, but a veritable contradiction or antinomy. By this faulty method, Molinism is induced, first of all, to admit that there is an exception to the principle of causality; that the entity of future free acts does not come from God, the first Being (simultaneous concurrence). In the second place, Molinism is induced to maintain that God's knowledge is passive with regard to the conditionally free acts of the future, which determine this knowledge instead of being determined by it. Thus middle knowledge, by positing a passivity in pure Act, could not be a pure perfection, one which is *simpliciter simplex* (absolutely simple). It is an anthropomorphic idea which attributes to God a human perfection. Lastly, this theory, conceived to safeguard the freedom of the human will, must end logically in the determinism of the circumstances.

All these impossibilities are a confirmation of the teaching given us by St. Thomas, and before him by St. Augustine, a doctrine which faithfully reflects the Gospel narrative and the teaching of St. Paul, who says: "It is God who worketh in us both to will and to accomplish, according to His good will" (Phil. 2:13). "Who distinguisheth thee? Or what hast thou that thou hast not received?" (1 Cor. 4:7). "So then it is not of him that willeth, not of him that runneth, but of God that showeth mercy" (Rom. 9:16). To depreciate the meaning and import of these texts is to rob the word of God and theology of its treasures, of its simplicity, and of its depth of meaning.

Another Interpretation *

A problem of special difficulty is presented by the question of God's knowledge of our future free actions. Indeed, the idea of such knowledge is so perplexing to the human mind that many non-Catholic writers have declared the problem insoluble, and have maintained that we must needs either give up man's freedom or else admit that God does not possess a foreknowledge of the free choices of the human will. In previous centuries this generally led to a denial of human freedom. More recently thinkers have adopted the other alternative, and have maintained that in this regard, at least, the Divine knowledge is limited. Yet, as will appear, there is a profound divergence of opinion among them, when it comes to the question how that prescience is to be explained.

The fact that God possesses such a foreknowledge can be demonstrated in various ways. One argument may be drawn from the Divine Infinity. God, as we have seen, is the real End in the cognitive order. From this alone it follows as of necessity that He cannot become aware of anything not already known to Him. To admit that His mind could learn a truth of which He was previously ignorant, would be to allow that there is potentiality in the Divine Intellect; that it is not infinite, not *Actus Purus*. Hence whatever our explanation of that foreknowledge may be, or even if we should be unable to provide an explanation, the reality of God's prescience must be granted. . . .

Again God, it will be admitted, knows those truths, when they actually come to pass. Even those who deny that a free act is knowable before the elective choice is made do not dispute that God knows it as soon as it takes place. But God's knowledge, as we have seen, is eternal. For Him there is no flow of time. To us, who belong to that flow, whose existence is realized point by point, each event which has already happened stands in a different relation according to its place in the time-series; while future happenings, as yet, have no actuality and are only knowable insofar as they are determined in their causes. But to God, Who is outside the time-series, the relation borne by every such act is always the same. He sees the whole course of time as a present reality. Events, which to us are future, He beholds now. Thus the very condition of God's existence demands His foreknowledge of the whole future. Indeed, it is hardly accurate to speak of foreknowledge or of prescience in this connection; for those terms are not applicable from the point of view of eternity. God *knows* the future, He does not *foreknow* it. . . .

Another argument may be derived from God's government of the world. Although the proof may not possess the apodictic certainty of the two,

* George Hayward Joyce, S.J. (1864-1943), *Principles of Natural Theology* (London: Longmans, Green, 1934), ch. XI, pp. 3-4.

which we have just given, its grounds are so weighty that it can hardly fail to recommend itself to the rational judgment. God, as we have seen, is the Author of all nature. All the beings which constitute the great whole, and all the events which take place within it, are due to Him as their First Cause. But His government of the universe is directed to a definite end. . . .

But if this is so—if the world is a place where God realizes in all its details an immense scheme of providential wisdom, in which the principal part is the training of free agents—He must know how such agents will act when called on to choose between two courses. Were it otherwise— were He ignorant what the outcome would be—His providence would not be, as reason and experience seem to assure us, a process of supreme wisdom, carried on in view of a definite end. He who does not know how subordinate agencies will act cannot shape his means, save in a halting and imperfect way, to the attainment of his purpose. We must either admit that God knows the future free acts of His creatures, or admit that His providence is marred by frequent failures and often at fault; that He, Who is infinite alike in wisdom and power, often adopts the wrong means for the achievement of His purpose; and that in the attainment of His ends He is at the mercy of His creatures. Such a conclusion the intellect instinctively rejects. . . .

In the light thus thrown on the Divine foreknowledge it is of interest to consider the familiar objection that what God foresees must necessarily take place; and that, this being so, it is impossible that man's actions should be free, necessity and freedom being mutually exclusive. St. Thomas, dealing with this difficulty, points out that a free action, so soon as it is actually realized, becomes in virtue of the principle of contradiction, necessary. It cannot both be and not be. Since, then, it has actually occurred, it cannot be otherwise. Thus it is open to a man to walk or sit still. But granted that he has chosen to walk, it is impossible that he should be sitting still. Now, the Divine knowledge, as we have seen, regards things in their actual occurrence as present happenings, since there is for God no such thing as future time. But when we say that if God foresees a thing it must necessarily take place, we are considering the thing, not in relation to its physical causes, but as an object of Divine knowledge. The necessity, then, which we affirm of it belongs to it under that aspect—not in virtue of the manner of its causation, but in so far as it is viewed as an actual occurrence. This, as is manifest, is in no way incompatible with contingency in regard of its immediate physical cause. The objection as stated is fallacious because it fails to distinguish two totally different aspects; and thus confuses the necessity which belongs to an event considered as an actual occurrence, with the very different necessity proper to the effects of causes which are determined to a single mode of action.

Yet in affirming that a Divine knowledge of the future in its utmost detail is compatible with full elective freedom, we have not solved, nor even touched, the question *how* God knows what choice will be made. It is impossible that He should be dependent for His knowledge upon His creatures. Yet if it were granted that He knows the free choice before the creature makes it, we should be affirming such dependence. We should be allowing that the Divine mind acquires from the creature a knowledge which He does not otherwise possess. God's knowledge must be due to His own infinite perfection alone. The creature's choice may be a condition; but the source of the knowledge must be sought in God Himself. On this point all the Scholastic thinkers are at one. But as regards the manner in which the knowledge is to be explained they are sharply divided. The question is hotly debated between the advocates of two rival theories—the theory of physical premotion and the theory of the *scientia media*.

The theory of physical premotion teaches that the source of God's foreknowledge is to be sought in the decree by which He has determined what the future choice of the will shall be, and in accordance with which He *premoves* the will to its act.

God's premotion, as we are told by the defenders of this view, is always such as corresponds with the nature which receives it; and He premoves rational agents in such a way that they choose freely and not by constraint. In this manner, it is contended, the divine decree accounts for God's foreknowledge of the future volition without destroying the freedom of the act.

Those thinkers, on the other hand, who find themselves unable to reconcile the notion of predetermination with that of freedom, hold that God, in virtue of His essential perfection, knows what choice each human will would make in any given circumstances in which it might be placed. Knowing thus what the agent would do in a particular set of conditions, He knows what it actually will do in virtue of His decision to bring about those conditions and not others. This Divine decree is the medium in which God knows our future free actions only because He possesses antecedently a knowledge of the conditional future. However we are to explain this latter knowledge, we are compelled, they consider, to admit its existence. Apart from this the foreknowledge of free actions is a sheer impossibility.

This Divine knowledge of the conditionally future action is termed *scientia media* or "mediate knowledge," an expression employed by way of contrast with two other Scholastic terms. If we consider God's knowledge in regard of its different objects, we may usefully distinguish His knowledge of mere "possibles" from His knowledge of those things which at some time or other have been, or will be, realized. The former is called *scientia simplicis intelligentiae;* the latter *scientia visionis.* An event, however, which would take place in certain given circumstances is something more than a mere possible, but is less than an event actually to be realized. Hence God's knowledge of free actions, viewed as conditionally future, is conveniently designated by the term "mediate knowledge."

The respective merits of these two theories were earnestly contested at the beginning of the seventeenth century between theologians of the Dominican and Jesuit Orders, the former contending for physical pre-motion, the latter for *scientia media*. The debate was theological rather than philosophical, the actual point at issue being the mode in which Divine grace influences the will in the performance of the good act. Yet the Dominican teaching on efficacious grace necessarily involved the theory of physical premotion, as did the Jesuit teaching that of the *scientia media*. The theological aspect of the question lies, of course, altogether outside our scope in the present work. Our defence of *scientia media* must be based on grounds of reason alone. It is summed up in the contention that unless this knowledge be admitted, we are forced to deny either the divine foreknowledge or human freedom. Only on this supposition can both be true.

Yet when such knowledge is attributed to God, care must be taken to avoid anthropomorphism. We are not to be understood as signifying that the Divine knowledge passed through successive stages corresponding to the terms *scientia media* and *scientia visionis;* that God first saw which alternative a man would in fact adopt in each several situation in which he might be placed, and that subsequently, having decreed to place him in such and such circumstances rather than in others, He beheld in virtue of His knowledge the actual course of future events. This would be to suppose that God's knowledge can pass from indefiniteness, that it can be first incomplete and then complete. His knowledge of the future has been from all eternity the absolutely complete knowledge of the *scientia visionis*. The triple distinction which we have drawn expresses, not three stages in God's knowledge, but three modes in which by reason of our creaturely limitations we are compelled to think of His knowledge. They are based upon the stages of knowledge in which man envisages the objects he himself calls into being. We attribute them to God because His infinite knowledge must in some manner equivalently contain them. When, e.g., an artist paints a picture, it comes before his mind (1) as a mere possible which he might produce, if he so desired. This is followed by an act of will in virtue of which his idea passes into the stage of practical knowledge (*scientia practica*) and he contemplates the object (2) as about to exist in the future. Finally, after execution, he sees it (3) as a real thing. Here are three stages really distinct from each other. There is nothing like this in God's knowledge. From all eternity He contemplated by the *scientia visionis* the actual free choice which will in fact be made. Yet our supposition of a Divine knowledge antecedent to the decree to realize a particular course of events, though an unreal supposition, is representative of a veritable reality in the only way in which it lies in our power to represent it. The course of events proceeds precisely *as if* God at a given moment foresaw what decision my free will would adopt, were He to abstain from any act of free will on His part. Divine knowledge, while eternally contemplating the future as actualized, nevertheless contains within itself all that could be found in the successive stages which analogy with human knowledge leads us to distinguish.

It may be frankly admitted that it is beyond our power to give any explanation how God can know the choice which a free agent would make, were he placed in given circumstances. Yet this inability on our part constitutes no objection to the theory; for it arises from the very nature of the case. Our knowledge of God, as we have frequently had occasion to urge, is restricted within narrow limits. We know Him as the first principle of created being, and can affirm of Him the perfections which this involves; beyond this our knowledge is negative. The Divine attributes, which do not belong to this class, merely deny in His regard the imperfections which attach to finite things. But no analysis of what is involved in God's relation to the world as its efficient, exemplar and final cause, will show us the manner in which He knows the truths with which we are here concerned. We can deny of this knowledge all dependence on the creature; and we can reject any explanation which is inconsistent with the freedom of the secondary agent. But we can go no further. It is idle for us to seek to know the *how* of the Divine knowledge. The data for such an enquiry are absolutely lacking to us.

Note: The author in the rest of the chapter discusses the relative merits and defects of the Molinist and Thomist theories.

III. Divine Will

41

ITS EXISTENCE, OBJECT, AND FREEDOM*

Art. 1: There is will in God.

There exists Will in God; as there is Intellect; for will follows upon intellect. As natural things have actual existence by their form, so the intellect is actually intelligent by its intellectual form. Everything has this aptitude towards its natural form, that when it possesses it not it tends towards it; and when it possesses it is at rest therein. It is the same with every natural perfection, which is a natural good. This aptitude to

---

* St. Thomas Aquinas, *Summa Theol.*, I, q. 19, art. 1, 2, 3, 8.

good in things without knowledge is called natural appetite. Whence also intellectual natures have a like aptitude to good as apprehended through its intellectual form; so as to rest therein when possessed, and when not possessed to seek to possess it, both of which pertain to the will. Hence in every intellectual being will exists, just as in every sensible being there is animal appetite. And so there must be Will in God, since there is Intellect in Him. And as His Intellect is His own Existence, so is His Will.

Art. 2: God wills things apart from Himself.

God not only wills Himself, but other things apart from Himself. This is clear from the comparison which we made above [ar. 1]. Natural things not only have a natural inclination towards their own proper good, to acquire it if not possessed, and, if possessed, to rest therein; but also to spread abroad their own good amongst others, so far as possible. Hence we see that every agent, in so far as it is perfect and in act, produces its like. It pertains, therefore, to the nature of the will to communicate in so far as possible to others the good possessed; and especially does this pertain to the Divine Will, from which all perfection is derived in some kind of likeness. Hence, if natural things, in so far as they are perfect, communicate their good to others, much more does it appertain to the Divine Will to communicate by likeness its own good to others, as much as is possible. Thus, then, He wills both Himself to be, and other things to be; but Himself as the end; and other things as ordained to that end; inasmuch as it befits the Divine goodness that other things should be partakers therein.

Art. 3: The Divine Will is free.

There are two ways in which a thing is said to be necessary, namely absolutely, or by supposition. . . . As to things willed by God, we must observe that He wills something of absolute necessity; but this is not true of all that He wills. The Divine Will has a necessary relation to the Divine goodness, since that is its proper object. Hence God wills His own goodness necessarily, even as we will our own happiness necessarily; and as any other faculty has necessary relation to its proper and principal object, for instance the sight to colour, since it tends to it by its own nature. God wills things apart from Himself in so far as they are ordered to His own goodness as their end. In willing an end we do not necessarily will things that conduce to it, unless they are such that the end cannot be attained without them; as, we will to take food to preserve life, or to take ship in order to cross the sea. But we do not necessarily will things not indispensable for attaining the end, such as a horse for a journey which we can take on foot, for we can make the journey without one. The same applies to many other means. Hence, since the goodness of God is perfect, and can exist without other things inasmuch as no perfection will accrue to Him from them, it follows that His willing things apart from Himself is not absolutely necessary. Yet, it can be necessary by supposition, for supposing that He wills a thing, then He is unable not to will it, as His will is not mutable.

Art. 8: The Divine Will imposes necessity on some things willed, but not on all.

The reason of this some have chosen to assign to intermediate causes, holding that what God causes by necessary causes is necessary, and what He produces by contingent causes is contingent.

This does not seem to be a sufficient explanation, for two reasons. First, because the effect of a first cause is contingent on account of the secondary cause, from the fact that the effect of the first cause is hindered by deficiency in the second cause, as the sun's power is hindered by a defect in the plant. No defect of a secondary cause can hinder God's Will from producing its effect. Second, because if the distinction between the contingent and the necessary is to be referred only to secondary causes, this must mean that the distinction itself is independent of the Divine intention and Will; which is inadmissible. It is therefore better to say that this happens on account of the efficacy of the Divine Will. When a cause is efficacious to act, the effect follows upon the cause, not only as to the substance of the effect, but also as to its manner of being and of being made. From defect in the active power in the seminal element it may happen that a child is born unlike its father in accidental points, that belong to its manner of being. Since the Divine Will is perfectly efficacious, it not only follows that things are made that God wills to be made, but made also in the way that He wills. God wills some things to be made necessarily, some contingently, to the right ordering of things, for the building up of the universe. Therefore to some effects He has attached necessary causes; but to others defectible and contingent causes; from which arise contingent effects. Hence it is not because the proximate causes are contingent that the effects willed by God happen contingently, but because God has prepared contingent causes for them, it being His Will that they should happen contingently.

42

DIVINE LOVE *

Art. 1: Its existence.

. . . Love is naturally the first act of the will and appetite; for which reason all the other appetitive motions presuppose love, as their root and origin. Nobody desires anything nor rejoices in anything, except as a

* *Summa Theol.*, I, q. 20, art. 1, 2,

good that is loved; nor is anything an object of hate except as opposed to the object of love. Similarly, it is clear that sorrow and other things like it, must be referred to love as to their first principle. Hence, in whomsoever there is will and appetite, there must also be love. If the first source is wanting, all that would flow from it is also wanting. It has been shown that Will exists in God, and hence we must attribute love to Him.

Art. 2: God loves all existing things.

All existing things, in so far as they exist, are good, for the existence of a thing is itself a good; and, similarly, whatever perfection it possesses. It has been shown above (qu. 19), that God's Will is the cause of all things. It must needs be, therefore, that a thing has existence, or any kind of good, only inasmuch as it is willed by God. To every existing thing, then, God wills some good. Hence, since to love anything is nothing else than to will good to that thing, it is manifest that God loves everything that exists. Yet not as we love. Since our will is not the cause of the goodness of things, but is moved by it as by its object, our love, whereby we will good to anything, is not the cause of its goodness; but conversely its goodness, whether real or imaginary, calls forth our love, by which we will that it should preserve the good that it has, and receive besides the good it has not. To this end we direct our actions. The love of God, however, infuses and creates goodness.

PART THREE

God and His Creatures

Section One

God and the Existence of Creatures

I. Divine Omnipotence

43

AQUINAS: SELECTED PASSAGES *

All confess that God is omnipotent, but it seems difficult to explain in what His omnipotence precisely consists; for there may be a doubt as to the precise meaning of the word "all" when we say that God can do all things. If we consider the matter aright, since power is said in reference to possible things, this phrase, *God can do all things,* is rightly understood to mean that God can do all things that are possible; and in this respect He is omnipotent. According to the Philosopher, a thing is said to be possible in two ways: in regard to some power, as whatever is subject to human power is said to be possible to man. God cannot be said to be omnipotent merely because He can do all things that are possible to created nature; for the Divine Power extends much farther. If, however, we were to say that God is omnipotent because He can do all things that are possible to His power, there would be a vicious circle in explaining the nature of His Power. For this would be saying nothing else but that God is omnipotent, because He can do all that He is able to do.

It remains, therefore, that God is called omnipotent because He can do all things that are possible, absolutely; which is the second way of saying that a thing is possible. For a thing is said to be possible or impossible absolutely, when regard is had merely to the terms. It is absolutely possible, because the predicate is not repugnant to the subject, as that Socrates should sit; and absolutely impossible when the predicate is absolutely repugnant to the subject, as, for instance, that a man is a donkey. It must be remembered that since every agent produces an effect like itself, to each active power there corresponds a thing possible as its proper object according to the nature of that act on which its active power is

* St. Thomas Aquinas, *Summa Theol.,* I, q. 25, art. 3.

founded; for instance, the power of giving warmth is related as to its proper object to everything that is capable of being warmed. The Divine Existence, however, upon which the nature of power in God is founded, is infinite, and is not limited to any genus of being, but possesses within itself the perfection of all being. Whence, whatever has or can have the nature of an entity is numbered among the absolutely possible things; and it is in respect of these that God is called omnipotent. Nothing is opposed to the idea of entity except nonentity; that, therefore, is repugnant to the idea of an absolutely possible thing, coming within the scope of the Divine Omnipotence, which implies existence and non-existence at the same time. For such cannot come under the Divine Omnipotence, not because of any defect in the Power of God, but because it has not the nature of a feasible or possible thing. Therefore, everything that does not imply a contradiction in terms, is numbered among those possible things in respect of which God is called omnipotent. Whatever implies contradiction does not come within the scope of Divine Omnipotence, because it cannot have the nature of possibility. Hence it is better to say that such things cannot be done, than that God cannot do them. Nor is this contrary to the word of the Angel, saying: *No word shall be impossible with God*. For whatever implies a contradiction cannot be true; because no intellect can possibly conceive such a thing.

II. Creation

44

NOTION AND TIME OF CREATION *

Qu. 45, ar. 1: To create is to make something from nothing.

We must consider not only the emanation of a particular being from a particular agent, but also the emanation of all being from the universal cause, which is God; and this emanation we designate by the name of creation. Now what proceeds by particular emanation, is not presupposed to that emanation; as when a man is generated, he was not before, but man is made from *not-man*, and white from *not-white*. Hence if the emanation of the whole universal being from the first principle be considered it is impossible that any being should be presupposed before this emanation. For nothing is the same as not being. Therefore as the generation of a man is from the *not-being* which is *not-man*, so creation, which is the emanation of all being, is from the *not-being* which is *nothing*.

* *Summa Theol.*, I, q. 45, art. 1, 2, ad 2um; q. 46, art. 1, ad 6um, art. 2.

Q. 45, art. 2 ad 2um: Creation is not change.

Creation is not change except according to a mode of understanding. For change means that the same thing should be different now from what it was before, as in motion according to quantity, quality and place, but sometimes it is the same being but in potentiality, as in substantial change, the subject of which is matter. But in creation, by which the whole substance of a thing is produced, the same thing can be taken as different now and previously according to the intellect only, so that a thing is understood as first not existing to all, and afterwards as existing. But as action and passion coincide as to the substance of motion and differ only according to diverse relations (*Phys. III*), it must follow that when motion is withdrawn, only diverse relations remain in the Creator and in the creature. But because the mode of signification follows the mode of understanding as was said above (qu. 13, ar. 1), creation is signified by mode of change and on this account it is said that to create is to make something from nothing; though *to make* and *to be made* are more suitable expressions here than are *to change* and *to be changed*, because *to make* and *to be made* import a relation of cause to the effect, and of effect to the cause, and import change only as a consequence.

Q. 46, art. 1 ad 6um: Creation was not *ab aeterno*.

The first agent is a voluntary agent. And although He had the eternal will to produce some effect, yet He did not produce an eternal effect. Nor is it necessary for some change to be presupposed, not even on account of imaginary time. For we must take into consideration the difference between a particular agent, that presupposes something and produces something else, and the universal agent that produces the whole. The particular agent produces the form, and presupposes the matter; and hence it is necessary that it introduce the form in due proportion to a suitable matter. Hence it is correct to say that (such an agent) introduces the form into such matter, and not into another, on account of the different kinds of matter. But it is not correct to say so of God Who produces form and matter together; whereas it is correct to say of Him that He produces matter fitting to the form and to the end. But a particular agent presupposes time just as it presupposes matter. Hence it is correctly described as acting in time *after* and *not* in time *before*, according to an imaginary succession of time (coming) after time. But the universal agent who produces the thing and time also, is not correctly described as acting now, and not before, according to an imaginary succession of time succeeding time, as if time were presupposed to His action; but He must be considered as giving as much time to His effect as He willed, and according to what was fitting to demonstrate His power. For the world leads more evidently to the knowledge of the Divine creating power, if it was not always, than if it had always been; since everything which was not always manifestly has a cause; whereas this is not so manifest of what always was.

Q. 46, art. 2: Faith, not reason teaches the non-eternity of the world.

By faith alone do we hold, and by no demonstration can it be proved, that the world did not always exist. . . . The reason of this is that the newness of the world cannot be demonstrated on the part of the world itself. For the principle of demonstration is the essence of a thing. Now everything according to its species is abstracted from *here* and *now;* whence it is said that universals are everywhere and always. Hence it cannot be demonstrated that man, or heaven, or a stone were not always. Likewise neither can it be demonstrated on the part of the efficient cause, which acts by will. For the will of God cannot be investigated by reason, except as regards those things which God must will of necessity; and what He wills about creatures is not among these, as was said above (qu. 19, ar. 3). But the Divine will can be manifested by revelation on which faith rests. Hence that the world began to exist is an object of faith, but not of demonstration or science. And it is useful to consider this, lest anyone presuming to demonstrate what is of faith, should bring forward reasons that are not cogent, so as to give occasion to unbelievers to laugh, thinking that on such grounds we believe things that are of faith.

45

THE BEGINNINGS OF THE UNIVERSE ACCORDING TO SCIENCE *

LET us now turn our attention to the past. The farther back we go, the more matter presents itself as always more enriched with free energy, and as a theater of vast cosmic disturbances. Thus every-thing seems to indicate that the material universe had in finite times a mighty beginning, provided as it was with an indescribably vast abun-dance of energy reserves, in virtue of which, at first rapidly and then with increasing slowness, it evolved into its present state.

This naturally brings to mind two questions:

Is science in a position to state when this mighty beginning of the cosmos took place? And, secondly, what was the initial or primitive state of the universe?

The most competent experts in atomic physics, in collaboration with astronomers and astrophysicists, have attempted to shed light on these two difficult problems.

A. THE BEGINNING IN TIME

First of all—to quote some figures—which aim at nothing else than to give an order of magnitude fixing the dawn of our universe, that is to

* Pope Pius XII, *op. cit.*

say, its beginning in time—science has at its disposal various means, each of which is more or less independent from the other, although all converge. We point them out briefly:

1) Recession of the Present Nebulae or Galaxies:

The examination of various spiral nebulae, especially as carried out by Edwin W. Hubble at the Mount Wilson Observatory, has led to the significant conclusion, presented with all due reservations, that these distant systems of galaxies tend to move away from one another with such velocity that, in the space of 1,300 million years, the distance between such spiral nebulae is doubled. If we look back into the past at the time required for this process of the "expanding universe," it follows that, from one to ten billion years ago, the matter of the spiral nebulae was compressed into a relatively restricted space, at the time the cosmic processes had their beginning.

2) The Age of the Solid Crust of the Earth:

To calculate the age of the original radioactive substances, very approximate data are taken from the transformation of the isotope of uranium 238 into an isotope of lead (RaG), or of an isotope of uranium 235 into actinium D (AcD), and of the isotope of thorium 232 into thorium D (ThD). The mass of helium thereby formed can serve as a means of control. This leads to the conclusion that the average age of the oldest minerals is at the most five billion years.

3) The Age of Meteorites:

The preceding method adapted to determine the age of meteorites has led to practically the same figure of five billion years. This conclusion assumes special importance from the fact that today the interstellar origin of meteorites is generally admitted by all.

4) The Stability of the Systems of Double Stars and Starry Masses:

The oscillations of gravitation between these systems, as also the attrition resulting from tides, again limit their stability within a period of from five to ten billion years.

Although these figures may seem astounding, nevertheless, even to the simplest of the faithful, they bring no new or different concept from the one they learned in the opening words of Genesis: "In the beginning . . . ," that is to say, at the beginning of things in time. The figures We have quoted clothe these words in a concrete and almost mathematical expression, while from them there springs forth a new source of consolation for those who share the esteem of the Apostle for that divinely inspired Scripture, which is always useful "for teaching, for reproving, for correcting, for instructing" (2 Tim. 3:16).

B. INITIAL STATE OF THE UNIVERSE

In addition to the question of the age of the cosmos, scholars have with similar earnestness and liberty of research and verification, turned their daring genius to the other problem which has already been mentioned and which is certainly more difficult, concerning the state and quality of primitive matter.

According to the theories serving as their basis, the relative calculations differ in no small degree from one another. Nevertheless, scientists agree in holding that not only the mass but also the density, pressure, and temperature of matter must have reached absolutely enormous proportions, as can be seen from the recent work of A. Unsold, director of the Observatory of Kiel. (*Kernphysik und Kosmologie* in the *Zeitschrift für Astrophysik*, 24, B, 1948, pp. 278-305). Only under such conditions can we explain the formation of heavy nuclei and their relative frequency in the periodic system of the elements.

Rightly, on the other hand, does the mind in its eagerness for truth insist on asking how matter reached this state, which is so unlike anything found in our everyday experience, and it also wants to know what went before it. In vain would we seek an answer in natural science, which declares honestly that it finds itself face to face with an insoluble enigma. It is true that such a question would demand too much of natural science as such. But it is also certain that the human mind trained in philosophical meditation penetrates more deeply into this problem.

It is undeniable that, when a mind enlightened and enriched with modern scientific knowledge weighs this problem calmly, it feels drawn to break through the circle of completely independent or autochthonous matter, whether uncreated or self-created, and to ascend to a creating Spirit. With the same clear and critical look with which it examines and passes judgment on facts, it perceives and recognizes the work of creative omnipotence, whose power, set in motion by the mighty "Fiat" pronounced billions of years ago by the Creative Spirit, spread out over the universe, calling into existence, with a gesture of generous love, matter bustling with energy. In fact, it would seem that present-day science, with one sweeping step back across millions of centuries, has succeeded in bearing witness to that primordial "Fiat lux" uttered at the moment when, along with matter, there burst forth from nothing a sea of light and radiation, while the particles of chemical elements split and formed into millions of galaxies.

It is quite true that the facts established up to the present time are not an absolute proof of creation in time, as are the proofs drawn from metaphysics and Revelation in what concerns simple creation, or those founded on Revelation, if there be question of creation in time. The pertinent facts of the natural sciences to which We have referred, are awaiting still further research and confirmation, and the theories founded on them are in need of further development and proof before they can provide a sure foundation for arguments which, of themselves, are outside the proper sphere of the natural sciences.

This notwithstanding, it is worthy of note that modern scholars in these fields regard the idea of the creation of the universe as entirely compatible with their scientific conceptions and that they are even led spontaneously to the conclusion by their scientific research. Just a few decades ago, any such "hypothesis" was rejected as entirely irreconcilable with the present state of science.

As late as 1911, the celebrated physicist Svante Arhenius declared that "the opinion that something can come from nothing is at variance with the present-day state of science, according to which matter is immutable" (Die Weltgebaude im Wandel der Zeiten, 1911, p. 362). In this same vein we find the statement of Plato: "Matter exists. Nothing can come from nothing, hence matter is eternal. We cannot admit the creation of matter" (Ultramontane Weltanschauung und Moderne Lebenskunde, 1907, p. 55).

On the other hand, how different and much more faithful a reflection of limitless visions is the language of an outstanding modern scientist, Sir Edmund Whittaker, member of the Pontifical Academy of Science, when he speaks of the above-mentioned inquiries into the age of the world: "These different calculations point to the conclusion that there was a time, some nine or ten billion years ago, prior to which the cosmos, if it existed, existed in a form totally different from anything we know, and this form constitutes the very last limit of science. We refer to it perhaps not improperly as creation. It provides a unifying background, suggested by geological evidence, for that explanation of the world according to which every organism existing on the earth had a beginning in time. Were this conclusion to be confirmed by future research, it might well be considered as the most outstanding discovery of our times, since it represents a fundamental change in the scientific conception of the universe, similar to the one brought about four centuries ago by Copernicus" (Space and Spirit, 1946, pp. 118-119).

III. Preservation

46

AQUINAS: SELECTED PASSAGES *

BOTH reason and faith bind us to say that creatures are kept in being by God. To make this clear we must consider that a thing is preserved by another in two ways. First, indirectly, and through something else (*per accidens*); thus a person is said to preserve anything by removing the cause of its corruption, as a man may be said to preserve a child, whom he guards from falling into the fire. In this way God preserves some things, but not all, for there are some things of such a nature that nothing can corrupt them, so that it is not necessary to keep them from corruption. Secondly, a thing is said to preserve another directly and in itself, namely, when what is preserved depends on the preserver in such a way that it cannot exist without it. In this manner all creatures need to be preserved by God. For the being of every creature depends on God, so that not for a moment could it subsist, but would fall into nothingness, were it not kept in being by the operation of the Divine power, as Gregory says (*Moral.*, XVI).

This is made clear as follows: Every effect depends on its cause, so far as it is its cause. But we must observe that an agent may be the cause of the *becoming* of its effect, but not directly of it *being*. This may be seen both in artificial and in natural things; for the builder causes the house in its *becoming*, but he is not the direct cause of its *being*. For it is clear that the *being* of the house is the result of its form, which consists in the putting together and arrangement of the materials, and results from the natural qualities of certain things. Thus a cook dresses the food by applying the natural activity of fire; thus a builder constructs a house, by making use of cement, stones and wood which are able to be put together in a certain order and to preserve it. Therefore the *being* of a house depends on the nature of the materials, just as its *becoming* depends on the action of the builder. The same principle applies to natural things. For if an agent is not the cause of a form as such, neither will it be directly the cause of *being* which results from that form; but it will be the cause of the effect in its *becoming* only.

Now it is clear that of two things in the same species one cannot directly cause the other's form as such, since it would then be the cause

* *Summa Theol.*, I, q. 104, art. 1.

of its own form, which is essentially the same as the form of the other; but it is the cause of this form for as much as it is in matter—in other words, it may be the cause that *this matter* receives *this form*. And this is to be the cause of *becoming*, as when man begets man, and fire causes fire. Thus whenever a natural effect is such that it has an aptitude to receive from its active cause an impression specifically the same as in that active cause, then the *becoming* of the effect, but not its *being* depends on the agent.

Sometimes, however, the effect has not this aptitude to receive the impression of its cause, in the same way as it exists in the agent; as may be seen clearly in all agents which do not produce an effect of the same species as themselves; thus the heavenly bodies cause the generation of inferior bodies which differ from them in species. Such an agent can be the cause of a form as such, and not merely as existing in the matter, consequently it is not merely the cause of *becoming* but also the cause of *being*.

Therefore as the becoming of a thing cannot continue when that action of the agent ceases which causes the *becoming* of the effect; so neither can the *being* of a thing continue after that action of the agent has ceased, which is the cause of the effect not only in *becoming* but also in *being*. This is why hot water retains heat after the cessation of the fire's action; while, on the contrary, the air does not continue to be lit up, even for a moment, when the sun ceases to act upon it, because water is a matter susceptive of the fire's heat in the same way as it exists in the fire. Wherefore if it were to be reduced to the perfect form of fire, it would retain that form always; whereas if it has the form of fire imperfectly and inchoately, the heat will remain for a time only, by reason of the imperfect participation of the form of heat. On the other hand, air is not of such a nature as to receive light in the same way as it exists in the sun, which is the principle of light. Therefore, since it has no root in the air, the light ceases with the action of the sun.

Now every creature may be compared to God, as the air is to the sun which enlightens it. For as the sun possesses light by its nature, and as the air is enlightened by sharing the sun's nature; so God alone is Being by virtue of His own Essence, since His Essence is His existence; whereas every creature has being by participation, so that its essence is not its existence. Therefore, as Augustine says (*Gen. ad lit.* IV.): *If the ruling power of God were withdrawn from His creatures, their nature would at once cease, and all nature would collapse.* In the same book he says: *As the air becomes light by the presence of the sun, so is man enlightened by the presence of God, and in His absence returns at once to darkness.*

Section Two
God and His Co-operation with Creatures

I. Divine Concurrence with Creatures

47

AQUINAS: SELECTED PASSAGES *

SOME have understood God to work in every agent in such a way that no created power has any effect in things, but God alone is the immediate cause of everything wrought; for instance, that it is not fire that gives heat, but God in the fire, and so forth. But this is impossible. First, because the order of cause and effect would be taken away from created things; and this would imply lack of power in the Creator; for it is due to the power of the cause, that it bestows active power on its effect. Secondly, because the active powers which are seen to exist in things, would be bestowed on things, to no purpose, if these wrought nothing through them. Indeed, all things created would seem, in a way, to be purposeless, if they lacked an operation proper to them; since the purpose of everything is its operation. For the less perfect is always for the sake of the more perfect; and consequently as the matter is for the sake of the form, so the form which is the first act, is for the sake of its operation, which is the second act and thus operation is the end of the creature. We must therefore understand that God works in things in such a manner that things have their proper operation.

In order to make this clear, we must observe that as there are four kinds of causes; matter is not a principle of action but is the subject that receives the effect of action. On the other hand, the end, the agent, and the form are principles of action, but in a certain order. For the first principle of action is the end which moves the agent; the second is the agent; the third is the form of that which the agent applies to action (although the agent also acts through its own form); as may be clearly

* *Summa Theol.,* I, q. 105, art. 5.

seen in things made by art. For the craftsman is moved to action by the end, which is the thing wrought, for instance a chest or a bed; and applies to action the axe which cuts through its being sharp.

Thus then does God work in every worker, according to these three things. First as an end. For since every operation is for the sake of some good, real or apparent; and nothing is good either really or apparently, except as far as it participates in a likeness to the Supreme Good, which is God; it follows that God Himself is the cause of every operation as its end. Again it is to be observed that where there are several agents in order, the second always acts in virtue of the first; for the first agent moves the second to act. And thus all agents act in virtue of God Himself; and therefore He is the cause of every action in every agent. Thirdly, we must observe that God not only moves things to operate, as it were applying their forms and powers to operation, just as the workman applies the axe to cut, who nevertheless at times does not give the axe its form; but He also gives created agents their forms and preserves them in being. Therefore He is the cause of action not only by giving the form which is the principle of action, as the generator is said to be the cause of movement in things heavy and light; but also as preserving the forms and powers of things; just as the sun is said to be the cause of the manifestations of colours, inasmuch as it gives and preserves the light by which colours are made manifest. And since the form of a thing is within the thing, and all the more, as it approaches nearer to the First and Universal Cause; and because in all things God Himself is properly the cause of universal being which is innermost in all things; it follows that in all things God works intimately. For this reason in Holy Scripture the operations of nature are attributed to God as operating in nature, according to Job 10:11: *Thou hast clothed me with skin and flesh; Thou hast put me together with bones and sinews.*

48

INTERPRETATION *

1. DIVINE CONCURRENCE

WHEN we assert God's concurrence with created causes, we signify far more than is implied by merely terming Him the First Cause of their various activities. The latter expression does not explicitly convey a distinct relation to the effect produced, but might be almost equally well employed if the causality exercised by Him consisted simply in an initial impulse given to the secondary agent. By concur-

* George Hayward Joyce, S.J., *Principles of Natural Theology*, ch. XVI, pp. 3-6.

rence is signified that God cooperates directly in the production of every effect due to a created cause; that throughout the process He is exerting an efficient causality proper to Himself, so that the result in all its stages is partially attributed to His direct agency. On this point all adherents of the Scholastic system are at one, though, as will appear, when they come to explain how God's cooperation is exercised, they are divided into two opponent schools. Yet all acknowledge that the divine concurrence is a necessary deduction from first principles. A proof of this conclusion may be briefly given as follows. Finite being in all its forms is a direct effect of God's efficient causality. In this all finite things resemble one another, that they *are;* and this common feature must be attributed to one and the same cause, which can be none other than the Subsisting Being, God Himself. But the operations of finite causes are productive of being, substantial or accidental, hence it is manifest that in every operation of a finite cause there is a divine concurrence in virtue of which it is productive of its effect.

It is hardly necessary to point out that the conclusion here reached in no way involves us in the opinion that God is the sole cause, and that the causality of finite agents is only apparent. It is true that some have been found to maintain that created things cannot be more than "occasional causes"; that they are destitute of active powers capable of affecting what is external to themselves; and that the changes which they seem to produce are really wrought by God, who supplies for their incapacity by acting on their behalf. St. Thomas informs us on the authority of Maimonides that some of the mediaeval Arabian philosophers had adopted this view (*De Potentia,* q. 3, ar. 7). More recently a similar error was defended by some of the later Cartesians. Recognizing that the Cartesian system afforded no real explanation how material and immaterial substances could act upon each other—how material things could give rise to concepts in the mind, or volitions formed within the soul could result in external changes, they cut the knot by a theory of occasional causes. God, they said, produces in the intellect the concepts which represent external things, but which cannot arise from our perception of them; and when we form a volition, it is He who really effects these changes in the external order, which correspond to our purpose. The Scholastic doctrine of concurrence is far removed from any such paradoxes. It attributes to secondary causes the exercise of a veritable causality.

It has already been said that there is a difference of opinion among Scholastic philosophers regarding the mode of the Divine activity. Some hold with St. Thomas that the concurrence is required for the production of the actions; that its function is to confer upon the finite agent that premotion without which it cannot act at all; that it is prior, not in time, but in the order of causality to the activity of the creature. It is, they contend, a *concursus praevius.* Many, however, are found who adopt the opinion defended by Suarez and maintain that the influx of the

First Cause has regard, not to the agent as such, but to the effect, viz. the resulting action. Premotion, they hold, is unnecessary, since the powers of the created cause require no complement to enable them to exercise their efficiency. Divine concurrence is requisite, for upon it the new effect depends for its being. But neither in the order of time nor in the order of causality is this concurrence prior to the action of the creature; it is, on the contrary, a *concursus simultaneus*.

In view of much that has been said in previous chapters it must be evident to every reader that in our opinion the former of these positions alone is tenable. We have urged in more than one connection that inasmuch as all action is a transition from potency to actuality, it is totally impossible that it can take place without the continuous agency of a cause exernal to the immediate agent, that otherwise we should be driven to admit that a being can confer on itself a new reality which it does not possess, giving to itself that which it has not got to give. The principle that the transition from potency to actuality presupposes the operation of a cause which itself possesses the perfection actualized, is, we maintain, self-evident—though, of course, the perfection may exist in the cause in a higher manner, and not in the manner in which it is found in the effect. It follows that the operations of a finite agent can only take place in virtue of a premotion ultimately referable to the First Cause. The finite cause is instrumental in regard to the First Mover; and apart from a "previous" concurrence, its efficient powers lack their final complement.

In every case of purely instrumental causality, although the action is one, proceeding from both agents acting together, we may distinguish in the effect produced that which is proper to the principal cause, and that which appertains to the instrument. Thus, in the written page we discriminate between what is due to the pen and what to the directing mind. The same holds good in the case of all finite activity. There is an element referable to the First Cause: an element proper to the finite agent. In so far as the result, be it substance or accidents, is being, it is due to the First Cause, Subsistent Being. The particular character of the being—its determination to this or that kind—is the part to be assigned to the immediate agent, the finite cause.

Yet here a word of caution is necessary. The causality of creatures in regard to the First Cause is not absolutely similar to instrumental causality in the usual acceptance of the term. The points of difference should be noted as well as the points of resemblance. Created causes, even such as are styled principal, resemble instruments properly so called, inasmuch as they can only operate in virtue of the action of a higher cause; while the action emanating from them is due to the common efficiency of both, the lower acting in subordination to the higher. Moreover, just as a human agent uses different instruments according to the end to be attained—the carpenter, for example, selecting a particular tool for a particular kind of work—so the First Cause produces the variety of effects which the created order displays, through causes which correspond in each case to the result intended. Yet there is a radical difference between the two. Where instrumental causation in the usual acceptance of the term is in question, the work achieved does not resemble the instrument but the principal cause. The statue resembles the conception in the mind of the sculptor; for the idea is the formal principle determining the principal cause. It does not resemble the chisel. The function of the instrument is to enable the material to receive the form communicated by the principal cause. Finite principal causes are not instruments in that sense. The effects which they produce resemble, not God, but themselves. The oak-tree produces an oak-tree; man a man; the sculptor, as we have just noted, a statue modelled on the idea which he has conceived (St. Thomas, Sent. IV, d. 19, q. 1, ar. 2 sol. 1).

This point is of the first importance. Since the form which the instrument aids in producing has no stable inherence in the latter, it follows that an instrument cannot be a cause endowed with free will, producing its effect when it chooses. It depends absolutely on the cause which employs it, and which gives to it a transient elevation, transmitting through it the form in question. It is otherwise as regards finite principal causes. The forms which they produce have a stable inherence in them, either permanent as in the case of their specific nature, or temporary as in the instance of the statue. Hence their instrumental relation to the First Cause is not of such a kind as to exclude the very possibility of their being endowed with free will (St. Thomas, De Veritate, q. 24, ar. 1, ad. 5).

St. Thomas, in a well known and much commented passage, enquires regarding the measure in which the actions of finite beings depend on God. He sums up his discussion by enumerating four distinct ways in which the operation of every subordinate cause is due to the First Cause. God, he tells us, (1) confers the capacity for action,—the active powers; (2) He conserves them; (3) He calls them into activity (applicat actioni); and finally (4) it is through His assistance that all created powers operate. The distinction between these last two modes of dependence interests us here. Just as conservation is requisite as the continuance of creation, so, too, where the operation of a creature is in question, God must not only by an initial premotion call the agent from potentiality to act, but must throughout sustain the action by a continuous influx of causal efficiency. The conclusion follows directly from the principles of St. Thomas' philosophy, nor would any other solution be consistent with them. He goes on to remind us that God's active power is one and the same with the Divine Essence; and, further, that God in virtue of His immensity is present within every finite agent, conferring on it the gift of existence. These considerations make it yet more manifest how intimate is the influence of the First Cause on all created activities, whether they belong to the material order or proceed from spiritual faculties such as the intellect and will (De Potentia, q. 3, art. 7).

We cited above a passage from Martineau, in which he supports his view that there are limits to the Divine prescience by contending that there are events in which the Divine causality plays no part. "Lending us a portion of His causation," he says, "He refrains from covering all with His omniscience." It will appear from what we have said that we regard this supposition as wholly inadmissible. For efficient activity of any kind to operate apart from the premoving influence of the First Cause would seem as repugnant to reason as for finite being to exist without the creative and conserving action of the Creator.

2. THEORY OF SIMULTANEOUS CONCURRENCE

We have mentioned above the theory of simultaneous concurrence taught by Molina and Suarez. Although we regard it as erroneous, it is necessary to give a brief exposition of it, since during the last three centuries it has been defended by many Scholastic writers, including the majority of those belonging to the Society of Jesus. Convinced that the Thomistic theory of the predetermination of the human will was both false and pernicious, they felt unable to accept a doctrine which apparently was so closely allied to it. In their anxiety to avoid a most dangerous error they went to the opposite extreme. According to this system, as we have already noted, a created cause needs no premotion to pass from potency to act. It requires, indeed, Divine concurrence to enable it to produce any effect. For every effect is being under some form or other, and there can be no production of being without the exercise of Divine causality; since being, as such, is always and everywhere due to the operation of Subsistent Being, viz. God. But there is no subordination of the created cause to the Divine causality; the former is not instrumental in regard of the latter. It must not, however, be imagined that there are two distinct actions which combine to produce a single result, very much as two men might unite to draw a load too heavy for one of them alone. There is but one action, which proceeds alike from the created cause and from God, yet so that priority belongs to neither of them (Suarez, *Disp. Metaph.*, XXI, sect. 3, nn. 8, 10). That the created cause stands in no need of premotion, may, Suarez holds, be easily shown. Secondary causes are not incomplete in their respective kinds, but complete. To suppose that they may need a Divine premotion to determine them to their action is to affirm that they are incomplete, and are not of themselves adequate principles of the result which they produce. But if it be admitted that they are, apart from any complement, true principles of the effect attained, then nothing is demanded of the First Cause save a concurrence with their action; premotion is unnecessary.

. . . In this explanation, the question at once arises, how the correspondence between the Divine and human contribution is to be explained. As regards necessary causes there is no difficulty. God from all eternity has foreseen the mode of action connatural to each creature at each moment of its existence according to the circumstances in which it will be placed, and has decreed to afford it the concurrence requisite for the exercise of its powers. Where, however, the acts of free agents are concerned the case is different; for the Divine decree must be such as to allow for liberty of choice. Here recourse is had to *scientia media*. God foresees the alternatives presented to the created will in each individual contingency, and foresees likewise which alternative the creature will freely choose, provided the choice be rendered possible by the concurrence requisite for its realization. That particular concurrence, and not another, He has decreed from all eternity to give. He would have decreed otherwise, had his foreknowledge shown Him that the created agent's choice would take another direction. The future free volition of the creature determines which shall be the concurrence destined for it. Yet we may say with truth that when the moment for action comes, God offers to the will a concurrence for any one of the various possible alternatives. Did He not do so, it would not be really capable of taking any other course than that which it actually chooses (*D. Met.*, XXII, sect. 4, n. 21).

Such is the system of simultaneous concurrence. Without attempting to deal with it at length it will suffice to indicate two points which in our judgment are fatal to it considered as an explanation of the activity exercised by secondary causes. In the first place, it involves the rejection of the principle *Quidquid movetur ab alio movetur*—the self-evident truth that the transition from potency to act can only take place through the operation of an efficient cause other than the agent in question. The Suarezian theory is based on the supposition that secondary causes, whether necessary or free, if placed in suitable conditions, can exercise their causal powers without any impulse from without. Were it not so, he holds, as we have seen, that the cause would be incomplete. He fails to see that it would be only incomplete in the sense that it lacked something which no secondary cause can possibly possess; nothing would be wanting to its perfection viewed as a secondary cause (St. Thomas, *De Pot.*, q. 3, ar. 7, ad. 7). Thus he is led to explain away a principle of vital importance in the Scholastic metaphysics, and even to contend that neither Aristotle nor St. Thomas Aquinas really meant what they said in their appeal to this axiomatic verity (*Disp. Metaph.*, XXII, sec. 2, nn. 20 seq.; 47 seq.).

Equally decisive is another argument against this theory. Suarez is emphatic that the concurrence is with the action as such (*Dis. Metaph.*, XXII, sect. 3, n. 4). Otherwise we should, as he clearly saw, have to admit that a new reality could arise in no way dependent on the source of all reality, Subsistent Being. Hence the action must be attributed to both agents simultaneously, the created and the uncreated. Now it is true that one and the same work may be accomplished by a plurality of agents, acting together, provided that the work in question be divisible into quantitative parts, so that the several agents may contribute each a share.

Thus, to employ an illustration already given, a number of men might combine to haul a heavy tree. But here we are concerned, not with the work (*operatum*), but with the action (*operatio*). And we need only consider what is essentially involved in the very notion of action to see that an action due to two agents is a contradiction in terms. An action is not an effect viewed in abstraction from the source from which it proceeds. It is a change considered precisely as proceeding from the active powers of the agent to which it is attributed. Or, as viewed from the side of the agent, it is the determination of its active powers to the production of the change in question. In creatures it is necessarily an accidental determination. In God, no accidental determination is possible; but His action *ad extra* is none the less the change produced, viewed precisely as issuing from Him as cause. It follows that if a given change is due to two agents not subordinated the one to the other, but acting independently, we have not one action but two. If then the action of the creature is but one; and if it must, in so far as it is something real—a new determination of the finite agent—be due to a causal influx of the First Cause, the source of being, this can only be because the secondary cause operates instrumentally as regards the First. In no other way is it possible for one and the same operation to be referred to more than one agent (*Summa Theol.* I, qu. 105, ar. 5, ad. 2).

3. CONCURRENCE AND FREE WILL

It remains for us to consider the bearing of the doctrine of previous concurrence which we are engaged in defending, on the question of the free volitions of the human agent. Can the two be reconciled? Is it possible to hold that divine premotion is requisite for every action, and that nevertheless the elective acts of the will are not predetermined by the First Cause? The Thomist school, as we have seen, deny the possibility. The transition from potentiality to actuality involved in every election cannot, they maintain, be initiated by the secondary cause. It lacks altogether any power of such initiation; it is simply indeterminate save in so far as determined to one course or another by the efficiency of the First Cause. Yet God so predetermines it, that it follows the path which He has marked out, not by constraint, but freely. We have already shown that we find ourselves unable to accept this view of the case. To us it appears far more manifest that predetermination and free will are mutually repugnant, than that there is a metaphysical impossibility in an election in which the will so determines its own course that the choice is in no sense predetermined for it. Nor does this self-determining power of the will seem to us incapable of reasonable defence.

We have seen that the object of the will is the good known as such by the intellect. Whenever the intellect recognizes an object as good— whether its goodness lie in its intrinsic excellence, or be relative to ourselves, consisting simply in its power to satisfy some desire felt by us—

the rational appetite is at once, in a greater or a less degree, attracted to it. There arises forthwith in the will an indeliberate movement towards the object. The force of this impulse varies very greatly. On the one hand it may be so strong as to render resistance a matter of extreme difficulty; on the other, so slight as to be hardly perceptible. This indeliberate act, we contend, proceeds from the operation of the First Cause, and is in fact an initial premotion. It does not constrain us. We are free to cooperate with it, and so to act instrumentally in its regard. But we may, if we will, refuse our correspondence, and turning to some other object which attracts us, pursue that instead. Or, we may, as we shall shortly point out, simply desist from action. The choice which we make is our own. But in so far as we act at all, the whole motion of the will is due to the First Cause as *causa principalis*. The action of the secondary agent is instrumental, in the sense in which we have explained the term above. For the finite agent lacks all power to initiate movement in its own right; it operates in every case in virtue of an impulse conferred by the Prime Mover. It will be observed that, according to the account just given, there is an exact correspondence between the final and the efficient causation to which an action is due. The efficient premotion of the First Cause is not arbitrarily given. God does not premove the will to desire this or that particular object, while in regard to other objects equally attractive in themselves, the will receives no such premotion. Whenever an object is such as to exert upon the will the attraction proper to final causality, the initial premotion of the efficient cause is conferred. It thus appears that the action of the Prime Mover on the free agent is analogous to that exercised upon inanimate substances, and, on a different plane, upon the brute creation. These are premoved in accordance with fixed laws. Inanimate substances have, each of them, certain specific characteristics which determine what their activities shall be; and they are premoved to such action as these inherent "forms" require. Thus, to take a simple example, iron, water, mercury, receive respectively the premotion which corresponds to their natures. Similar, though, as we have said, of a higher kind, is the premotion directing the activities of brutes in accordance with their natural appetites and instincts. Nor is it otherwise with the premotion of the will. This, too, is ruled by law. In so far as the mind views an object as good—as a final cause—the will is premoved towards the thing in question. Just as in inanimate things premotion is conditioned by an inherent "form," so in the rational will it depends upon a "form" temporarily inherent in the intellect. But many objects offer satisfaction to our physical appetite from which the law of right reason would bid us abstain. To allow them to exert their final causality on us—to make them an end of action—would involve a breach of moral obligation. Yet the mind cannot help being aware of their attractive force; and in so far as it gives its attention to any one of them, and regards it as adapted to the satisfaction of some desire, does the will experience an initial premotion towards that object. We are not speaking here of the final practical judgment which is the final determinant of the free act. We are concerned to explain what at first sight is calculated to cause surprise, that the will receives initial premotion to acts which are wrong, as well as to acts which are right. And we say that this is explained by the law which rules the activity of the faculty, viz., that in so far as the intellect views an object as capable of satisfying some desire, an indeliberate movement towards that object always takes place in the will.

We have already pointed out that there is one object in regard to which the will is not free, but necessitated. We cannot look on beatitude—full and complete happiness—as undesirable, and hold it in aversion. If we contemplate it at all, we must desire it. But in regard to all the other things we are at liberty to will them or to reject them; for these come before us as partial and incomplete realizations of the good. If the will yields to the attraction of such an object and desires it, it does so freely. For we only need to bid the intellect contemplate it, not in its attractive qualities, but in its limitations, and we are no longer under any constraint to desire it. Just as there arose an indeliberate movement towards the object in virtue of what in it was good, so by reason of the disadvantages attached to it there springs up a movement in the contrary direction—a premotion to its rejection: for in this case rejection appears as a good. The two movements will, doubtless, be of unequal intensity. But the will is not obliged to follow the stronger. We may deliberately adopt what we know to be a lesser good if we choose to exclude the thought of that in which it is defective and consider solely the gratification to be obtained. Or, without a positive act of rejection, the mere contemplation of the deficiency and incompleteness of the object may lead to a cessation of desire. If, indeed, a man's mind should become so absorbed by some particular object that he can neither take note of its limitations, nor compare it with other ends, he is no longer capable of elective choice in its regard. This actually occurs from time to time when a man is suddenly mastered by an excess of anger, fear or some other passion. But the case is exceptional; and in such circumstances man ceases for the moment to be a rational agent at all. He is no more responsible for his action than one of the lower animals. Normally, man is master in his own house. Thus, if we have received an injury, the remembrance of the wrong will probably arouse in the will an indeliberate desire to pay off old scores. But we know perfectly well that if we consent to this desire we do so as free agents, and become responsible for an act which it is in our power to avoid. We can, if we choose, consider revenge under a very different aspect. We can view it as a violation of God's moral law, and seeing it thus, can turn away from it.

Thus, though human volition depends absolutely on the divine premotion, and in this, as in every other form of activity, there can be no transition from potency to act except through the efficient action of the First Cause, the will is not predetermined. Freedom, we maintain, consists essentially in the power of self-determination. And to assert that the choices of the will are predetermined by a higher cause appears to us wholly irreconcilable with freedom and consequently with moral responsibility in man. Even as regards beatitude, though it is impossible for the will, if it act at all, to do other than desire it, yet it is free either to act or not to act. It remains *libertas exercitii*. For though the object contemplated is happiness in its fullness, yet the subjective act of desire is a finite and, therefore, a partial good. We may turn the mind to some other object of consideration, and thus banish the thought of beatitude; or we may find an object of desire in the mere exercise of liberty—*stat pro ratione voluntas* (*De Malo*, q. 6, art. 1).

But how is it that man determines himself to abstain from corresponding with one premotion, and to admit another? Here is the mystery of free will, and of this we have no explanation to offer. We can describe the conditions of the faculty's exercise, but cannot explain the act itself. Yet it will not escape notice that to abstain from correspondence is a very different thing from the initiation of motion on the part of the finite agent. We do not claim for the creature any power to originate reality apart from the First Cause. What is claimed in this regard is negative, not positive—not a power of independent action, but of abstinence from action. Where the creature acts positively, it acts instrumentally; and the action, so far as real, proceeds from the First Cause.

49

GOD'S DOMINION AND MAN'S FREEDOM *

THERE is a group of questions which occurs and re-occurs in Christian thinking. The questions run somewhat as follows: If God knows everything, He knows the future and what man will do; how, then, can man be free? If God is the cause of everything, and all that happens is His work, how can man be a cause? If God is good, desires the good, and is able to accomplish what He desires, how is evil possible? Can there be such a thing as evil, and to the frightful degree which our experience often forces us to believe? Is God really all-powerful, and if so, to what extent does He participate in evil-doing? Can He really be good? Is He not, rather, a frightful being? . . . These questions are difficult and depressing. Many times in history, notably during the Renaissance, they have been asked very insistently. Moreover, certain serious-minded, over-sensitive people fall easily under their sway. Clergymen and physicians know well what power these questions can exercise

* Romano Guardini, *The Faith and Modern Man*, trans. by Charlotte E. Forsyth (New York: Pantheon Books, 1952), ch. III.

over the life of such people, a power sometimes so great as to render their victims unfit for useful living. They know, too, how hard, if not impossible, it is to set such people straight.

Let us examine the questions now—as far as the limits of this essay permit—for it would be a positive gain to find an answer to them, or even a clear position in their regard. Aside from this, we have another purpose in view. We need to be clear in our minds not only concerning the subject matter of such problems, but also their nature, not only about the truth of them, but how these difficult, even dangerous questions must be approached if we are to derive any useful results.

First of all we must reduce this tangled web of questions to a simple form. To do so would be a great gain, for (we shall return to this point later) much of the difficulty in questions of this kind arises from the confusion caused by the intermingling of points of view, of thoughts with feeling, of concepts with inner unrest. Let us express what lies at the root of the matter by this question: If God is all-knowing and all-powerful, how can there be any genuine human freedom?

We can now isolate this question and discuss it. We can examine how, in man's actions, God's will and man's will stand in relation to one another; what part each plays in the act; how, if the expression be allowed, the responsibility is shared. The task will be difficult, and even if some good were to come of it, the final result will be disappointing. But should a so-called solution be found, and reason feel satisfied, this would indeed be a cause for misgivings. Actually, something would have gone awry. Either the human will would have been repressed and the answer given in terms of the pure, perfect efficacy of the divine will—which would altogether eliminate human freedom—or human freedom would have been given its due, but in a way that would limit the divine will, which, in turn, eliminates the divine character of that will. And a "solution" satisfactory to every aspect of the problem might well correspond to the old saying, "God does not cause evil, He merely permits it," which, on closer examination, reveals itself as meaningless, a mere sedative for our emotions. The question remains as before—awaiting an answer.

Such a line of argument gets us nowhere. To avoid wasting our intellectual efforts and the ever-ready danger of falling into the wrangling and dogmatizing which, alas, runs through the whole course of Christian thought, we must try another approach. A prize was once offered for the solution of equations of a highly complicated character. A talented young mathematician answered the question by giving the reasons for its insolubility. Something similar must apply here. For whenever we approach the problem directly, we find ourselves baffled. We must therefore try to find where the special difficulty lies and see whether it is at all possible to overcome it. At the instant we find ourselves faced with a task utterly beyond our powers. For in order to understand how the human will can subsist along with the divine will, we should have to place both "quantities" on the same plane under a common denominator, and this cannot possibly be done. Thus we are unable to "solve" this or any similar problem directly. The only honest answer consists in admitting this fact and explaining why it is so. Any other answer either evades the problem, or the alleged solution covers up the difficulty without mastering it. Our question concerns the nature of man's finite existence before God, the way the created subsists as created. It is unanswerable because our human reason is unable to grasp the relationship between the glorious self-subsisting of God and the finite human creature. Recognition of this fact is part of the truth of existence. We must accept the insolubility, make of it a confession of humility and a form of adoration. In so doing the problem is "solved," not intellectually, but in the form of a vital act.

But what if someone were to reply that this "insolubility" was sheer nonsense. That a faith which expected acceptance of such a thing would insult honor and reason, and that a man would have the right, indeed, the duty, to break with it. And what if the objector would go on to show that at the root of these age-old questions lurked a deep-seated denial of life, the causes of which had been worked out by psychologists. Also, that a person disturbed by these questions has no more urgent duty than to rid himself of them, to realize their essentially unreal character, and to spend the strength hitherto wasted upon them upon things more real, more rewarding. The psychological argument is impressive, especially when it can be shown that concern over such questions is often associated with certain grave manifestations—scruples, violent forms of impatience, fanaticism and religious depression. But is it true? Are there not phenomena in our daily lives which, while they cannot answer our question, do at least indicate that the puzzle which they present is not caused by lack of reason—more than that, that it rests upon a genuine reason? There are such. Let us now look closely at one of them.

Whenever a physical force acts upon an inanimate object as, for instance, when pressure is exerted by a lever on a stone, necessity enters in. The lever will raise the stone to a height which is in exact proportion to the power applied to it. Thus it invariably acts, at all times, in all places. What, on the other hand, is the relation between the sun and a grain of wheat buried in the earth? Warmth and light affect the seed so that it opens and, in the course of time, sends roots downward and shoots upward. Would you say that warmth and light act upon the seed in exactly the same way that the lever acts upon the stone? Obviously not. We express the difference in our everyday speech by saying that the lever "lifts" the stone; the sun "awakens" the seed. In the latter case, the light is directed toward the property of life inherent in the organism. The sun arouses the grain's initiative. The processes of growth, now set in motion, proceed from the organism's own living center. What then happens is not an immediate transformation of the object by the operating power, but a gradual response on the part of the object's own life principle.

How does mind act upon mind? When a man wants to win another to his point of view, he can influence him psychologically by making threats or promises, by exercising the power of sympathy, by arousing his pride and thereby guiding the other's judgment. He does not really overcome the other's objections but talks him out of them, and by continually repeating his own point of view, acts upon his emotions and imagination until the other gives in and simply agrees. The operation resembles the lifting of the stone by the lever, or even the skillful manipulation of his plants by a gardener. It is not an intellectual but a psychic influence. It is suggestion, the application of mental force.

The intellectual influence is altogether different. It consists in setting forth the truth so clearly, so profoundly, so effectively relying so entirely on reason, that the hearer is affected inwardly, and genuinely convinced. Here no force has been exerted, but rather the depths of the other man's mind have been moved in such a way that he recognizes the truth and responds to it. Truth is the life of the intellect. Through words the mind's natural relation to truth is touched, and the mind responds naturally. The speaker must curb his enthusiasm and his persuasiveness out of respect for the hearer, out of the obligation not to influence him directly, but rather to awaken him to himself. The influence of light on the grain of wheat releases an innate power; here the same happens, to an even greater degree, and differently; genuine intellectual influence is possible only through acting freely upon a comprehending, creative center.

And now a final illustration. The love which one person bestows upon another exercises a powerful influence in the life of the one loved. There are different ways of loving. Love of an immediate, instinctive kind seeks physical gratification. Another kind, not physical in origin, seeks ultimately to make the loved one dependent and to dominate him. An observer of human relationship will grant that this latter way of loving is the most common. Fundamentally selfish, it is a devious way of securing the upper hand; it forces, makes dependent, subjugates. But there is such a thing as genuine love which is always considerate. Its distinguishing characteristic is, in fact, regard for personal dignity. Its effect is to stimulate self-respect in the other person. Its concern is to help the one loved to become his true self. It seeks him for his own sake. In a mysterious way such love finds its best realization in its power to stimulate the other to attain his highest self-realization. Thus its effect is to draw the other out into freedom. And if the loved one were called upon to give an account of what love had meant to him, he would say: "I owe everything to it, most of all the fact that through it, alone, I became my real self." A marvelous paradox! Truly, life's ultimate mystery!

What have we just been doing? We have been going from one form of influence to another, from the lower to the higher. In each case there has been a decisive difference. Each time an effect has been produced. Step by step the influence has become stronger, more essential, more radical. For the effect of light on the grain of wheat is greater than that of the lever on the stone; greater still the effect of mind on mind; greatest of all the power of love in the life of the one loved. At the same time the influence has more and more assumed the attitude of reserve. More and more strongly has it seemed to be directed toward some property inherent in the object—toward freedom. Not as if it were directly intending to effect freedom for the object, but as if it were by nature related to freedom and concerned with awakening it.

Does this process end with man? In the human sphere alone there are innumerable degrees. From this point of view how greatly men vary in their behavior—in respect for others, in magnanimity, in unselfishness, in creative mental ability, in the generative power of love. The list is endlessly long and runs through the whole of creation, why not beyond creation? Why should it not have significance for God Himself? And not because He is involved in, and is part of, world processes, but because what we have been observing seems to be but a reflection of something essentially and perfectly in Him alone. Is it not in this direction that the "insolubility" of our problem points? God is pure power. Not a power like that exercised by the lever, not like that of instinctual urges, but intellectual power; and not simply undifferentiated power of knowledge and will, but individual, personal power. Our use of the words "I" and "you" is but a reflection of God's being. Holy Scripture tells us that God is love. Not merely that He is loving, which might imply that He loves as we love, only more and better; not even that He is the embodiment of love, the fountainhead of that which is evident whenever one being turns lovingly to another. It means more than all that. It means that Love is God Himself, that what a man does when he loves is but a reflection of what God is. And whenever a man speaks simply of "Love," he means God, whether he realizes the fact or not. If this be true—and that it is true constitutes a mystery of the Christian faith—must not freedom emerge in fullest measure under the dominion of divine love? No, not simply in fullest measure, but actually there alone, so that the earthly phenomena which we have been observing will serve as hints and preparation for what can exist essentially only in the relationship between God and His creature.

In this must be found the true source of that paradox of love of which we have been speaking. For God's power is love. God's will is love. By directing His love toward man, God enables man to become what he essentially was meant to be—a free person. The more actually a man is led by God's love, the more fully he realizes his true self; the more completely a man's acts spring from love, the more completely they become his own.

But though this is the mystic's blessed answer, let us not misunderstand it. Such an answer cannot be a "solution" to the problem we are considering, it can only give us a hint that the word "insolubility" is a term for a mystery of profound reality.

But truth must be tested in living. And if this doctrine is true, what will its effects be in our lives?

Chesterton, in a brilliant passage, says: "The sun is the one created thing which one cannot look at; it is the one thing in the light of which one looks at everything else; like the sun at noon-day, mystery explains everything by its own invisibility. Detached intellectualism is (in the exact sense of a popular phrase) all moonshine, for it is light without heat; it is secondary light reflected from a dead world." *

Dogma is a mystery into which we cannot look directly. If it is taken as a starting point from which to approach the world, if it is, so to speak, behind us so that its light can fall upon the objects before us, these objects will stand out clearly, and we can make our way among them. If the light itself could be looked at, it would lack the illuminating quality necessary for seeing things properly. The world is rightly seen only in the light that comes from above, and that light must itself be invisible to human sight.

The problem we are considering involves the dogma of grace. Whatever a man does, he does through God's power; whatever of eternal worth he is able to achieve, he achieves by God's help. Everything, therefore, is a gift—everything, even our work. It is our work, indeed, because it is a gift. Man is a creature, his essence and being are given to him, he exists by receiving them continually from God. He can effect something real only through something received, that is to say, through grace. God working in man enables man to work, and to be responsible to Him for that work. Proprietorship and responsibility come not by limitation of God's dominion, not by what might be called a counterplay to the divine will, but as the fruits of that will. This is the doctrine of grace. How does it affect the life of one who believes?

Let us review the question of God's dominion and man's freedom in reverse order. It is a mystery. It transcends the power of human comprehension. We may try to dispense with the mystery by suppressing the one or the other side of the paradox. Then, apparently, the problem clears up. We may argue, for example, as the proponents of the sole, absolute dominion of God, the so-called Predestinationists, have done, that God effects everything, and that man is but His tool. The mind can take hold of this statement. But as soon as man tries to apply the teaching to his life, he loses the powers which make for courageous Christian action. He becomes a fatalist, that is, a slave. And his sons, or at any rate his grandsons, will consider his views untenable and unworthy, they will rebel against the "enslaving God" and rely wholly upon their own reason and natural impulses.

* *Orthodoxy*, "The Maniac," p. 50.

We may adduce the enlightenment on the other side, as the so-called Pelagians and other defenders of human autonomy have done, and declare that man is his own master, that he acts merely by his own means, and that what he achieves is exclusively his own work. This statement also is clear and applicable, only on the opposite side. God is now relegated to the outer edge of existence; man has a free hand. But if man adopts this view in earnest, he will overstrain himself. He will forget about reverence and moderation and become superficial and self-seeking. He will no longer try to live as a man, but as some kind of god. And that mystery which he has betrayed will eventually penetrate into his life. He will become a pantheist, one who sees man merely as a fleeting manifestation of the divine; or a biologist who sees man merely as an organ, a cell or a pulsebeat of the universal life; or a materialist who regards man merely as an accidental form of matter—unless he falls prey to superstition and puts his faith in things which a religious man would be ashamed to believe.

However, if a man will accept the mystery and allow it to become a living influence in his life, he will be enabled to do the hardest things of all, namely, to live in the truth, to make his way along that narrow ridge assigned to mankind. He will achieve that inner balance which will enable him to act with confidence, yet to take everything as coming from God. This, in turn, will give him a sense of responsibility and help him to realize that he lives by grace. It will also safeguard that soundness of the emotions which is more important, even, than soundness of body—soundness of mind, of heart, of being.

In the course of these reflections there has been sketched, if only roughly, a way of tackling our question. First, we reduced what is indefinite and confused in it to a clear form. Then, we saw how the problem really stood. Next, we went into it, and had to admit in honesty that we could come to no conclusion. We asked ourselves why this should be so and perceived the cause of the insolubility. This brought up the further question as to whether this insolubility was an indication that the question had no meaning, or whether it rested on an ultimate, if inscrutable, reason; a comparison with natural phenomena pointed to the validity of the second assumption. Finally, we reviewed the points and asked ourselves what effect this acceptance of the incomprehensibility would have upon life, and saw that this was the only way by which life can be mastered.

Now a final thing. Questions are of various kinds. Some exist that they may be answered. If one approaches them with reason and mental vigor, they are solved and dissolved. Others must be answered by being lived. They cannot be answered otherwise, not because one's personal intellectual effort or the preliminary scientific research are insufficient, but because they wholly transcend the power of the human mind. In them is revealed the nature of our creaturely, finite existence which signifies that we are what we are because God made us so. Such questions can only be recognized for what they are, accepted, and lived through.

Asking serious questions and making an effort to answer them goes on profitably for a while, but there may come a turning point. Up to this point, the questions have given depth to life, earnestness to character, breadth to the mind—but here they become burdensome, hampering, and cause life to get snarled up. What has happened? A foreign element has entered into the pure question. For the question itself seeks only truth, truth for its own sake, and all truth makes for freedom. Now another motive is at work, one so hampering that it hinders the proper mental effort needed to find the answer. This condition reveals that the man is no longer seeking truth sincerely, but that something within him is using the question as a pretense for indolence, cowardice, indecision. An unhealthy element is using the question for its own ends. As we have said, physicians and clergymen are familiar with the fact that such questions can inflict endless self-torture, destruction of self-confidence in action, of all joy in living, and of the unity of the inner self.

In depression, more than in any other state, such questions are used destructively. The same applies to religious scruples, themselves but preliminary or subsidiary forms of depression. Certain violent mental disorders are attributable to the same cause. The experiences of the saints teach that the Tempter makes use of these questions to disturb the mind, to upset the faith, to confuse good intentions, and thus to divert from obedience to God. Therefore, from a certain point on, the questions become temptations.

And not these questions only, but kindred ones which have their source in that same deep mystery, of the relationship between God and man, for example, the problems of predestination, forgiveness and rejection, responsibility for another's sin. Here a man must keep a clear head, and know what he is doing. One does not withstand temptation simply by thinking about it and investigating it, but by facing it squarely. Temptation is not a problem to be solved, but an enemy to be overcome. It is easier to see these things in another than in one's self, but one must see them in one's self, when the problem begins to cast its spell and threatens one's peace of mind. The discriminating power of the Christian conscience must get to work. A problem may be difficult, it may call for great effort, the greater as one sees more and more deeply into things, and as one's perception sharpens. Then, even though the struggle may grow wearisome, it will remain good and wholesome. However, when a sinister unrest gets in, when the heart is depressed without apparent reason, when the same question repeats itself monotonously, tormentingly, when it undermines all one's courage, all one's joy, the time has come to take a firm stand against it. One must stop thinking because one's temptation now is to follow one thought until it loses all meaning. One must act, one must draw a line, break the spell. One must recognize what lurks behind the question—a trick on the part of nature, something unhealthy in one's temperament, some hidden insincerity or cowardice, some concealed desire to find an excuse for giving up one's faith, or whatever else it may be. When one is ready to face the facts, one will see at a glance what the truth is, and the false question, to call it by its right name, vanishes like a ghost.

50

ITS MYSTERY *

WE FIND in this doctrine a *chiaro-oscuro* incomparably more beautiful than that we admire in the works of the greatest painters. It is perfectly clear, on the one hand, that *God cannot will evil,* nor can in any way, directly or indirectly, be the *cause of sin.* We have even a greater certainty of the absolute rectitude of God's intentions than we have of that of our purest ones. It is equally certain that God *never commands an impossible action;* it would be contrary to His justice and goodness. Therefore He wills to make possible to all obedience to His precepts and salvation.

On the other hand, it is absolutely beyond contest that *God is the source of all good,* that His love is the cause of all created good, even of the goodness of our good resolve to work for our salvation; otherwise what is best in the created order would not issue from His creative power. It follows, in the words of St. Thomas echoing St. Augustine, that *no one would be better than another, did not God love him more.* That universal law applies to the state of innocence as well as to the present state, and to every good action, whether it is natural or supernatural, easy or difficult, in its origin or its progress. That law of predilection which stands over all problems implies the whole doctrine of predestination and of the efficacy of grace to which Our Lord refers when He says of the elect that "no one can snatch them out of the hands of my Father" (John 10:29).

How do these two principles harmonize, which are so certain when taken separately, that of salvation open to all, and that of predestination? St. Paul gives us the answer: *O altitudo divitiarum sapientiae Dei* (Rom. 11:33). We must always return to them; no created intelligence, man or angel, can grasp the intimate harmony of those two principles until it has entered beatific vision. To perceive this harmony would mean to see how infinite justice, infinite mercy and sovereign freedom become one without losing their identity, in the transcendence of Divin-

---

* Reginald Garrigou-Lagrange, O.P., "Prémotion physique" in *Dictionnaire de Theologie Catholique* (Paris: Letouzey, 1936), Vol. XIII, conclusion, col. 76-77.

ity, in the inner life of God, in what in God is absolutely inaccessible and ineffable.

Even more, the more these two principles we want to harmonize become evident to us, the greater, on the contrary, is the transluminous obscurity of the Divine transcendence in which they become one. In the superior *chiaro-oscuro*, we must be on our guard not to deny the clarity, on account of the darkness as this would mean replacing the mystery with contradiction; we must also leave in their places the clear and the dark, as they set each other off admirably. If we leave the mystery in its place, we shall grasp better and better its position above all reasoning and theological speculation, as only an object of supernatural contemplation, of that contemplation which springs from a faith enlightened with the gifts of wisdom and intelligence. Thus we shall begin to see that what is highest in God is precisely what remains most obscure to us, and even beyond our reach owing to the weakness of our vision. In that contemplation grace, by a sort of secret instinct imparts peace to us regarding the way to harmonize infinite justice, infinite mercy, and sovereign freedom; and grace gives that peace precisely because it is itself a participation in the nature and the intimate life of God. It is to that contemplation, that theological speculation about divine motion must lead us, if it is not to lose to a great extent its very *raison d'être*. At this point everything becomes simple and we come to see that the darkness we meet is not the darkness of inconsistency, or absurdity, but the darkness which is produced in our weak vision by an excess of light.

II. Providence and Government

51

AQUINAS: SELECTED PASSAGES *

Q. 22, art. 1: It is necessary to attribute Providence to God.

For all the good that is in created things has been created by God, as was shown above (qu. 6). In created things good is found not only as regards their substance, but also as regards their order towards an end, and especially their last end, which, as was said above, is the Divine Goodness (qu. 21). This good of order existing in things created, is itself created by God. Since, however, God is the cause of things by His Intellect, and thus it behooves that the idea of every effect should pre-exist in

* *Summa Theol.*, I, q. 22, art. 1, 2, 3; q. 103, art. 5, 7.

Him, as is clear from what has gone before; it is necessary that the reason of the order of things towards their end should pre-exist in the Divine Mind. The reason of things ordered towards and end, however, is, properly speaking, *Providence*. For it is the chief part of *Prudence*, in which the other two parts are subjected—namely, remembrance of the past, and intelligence of the present; inasmuch as from the remembrance of what is past and the understanding of what is present, we gather how to provide for the future. It belongs to prudence, according to the Philosopher, to order other things towards an end, whether in regard to oneself—as, for instance, a man is said to be prudent, who orders well his acts towards the end of life—or in regard to others subject to him, in a family, city, or kingdom; in this way he is said to be a "faithful and wise servant, whom his Lord has placed over his family." In this way Prudence or Providence may suitably be attributed to God. For in God Himself there can be nothing ordered towards an end, since He is the last end of all. This reason of order in things towards an end is therefore in God called *Providence*. Whence Boethius says that *Providence is the Divine reason itself, seated in the Supreme Ruler; which disposeth all things*. Disposition may be said to be both the reason of the order of things towards an end, and the reason of the order of parts in the whole.

Q. 22, art. 2: Everything is subject to the Providence of God.

Certain persons totally denied the existence of Providence, as Democritus and the Epicureans; laying down that the world was made by chance. Others taught that incorruptible things only were subject to Providence, but corruptible things not in their individual selves, but only according to their species, for in this respect they are incorruptible. These views are thus expressed in the Book of Job (22:14): "The clouds are His covert; and he doth not consider our things; and He walketh about the poles of heaven." Rabbi Moses (Maimonides), however, excluded men from among things corruptible, on account of the excellence of the intellect which they possess, but in reference to all else that suffers corruption he adhered to the opinion of the others.

We must say, however, that all things are subject to Divine Providence; not only in general, but even in their own individual selves. This is clear: for since every agent acts for an end, the arrangement of effects towards that end extends as far as the causality of the first agent extends. Whence it happens that in the effects of an agent something takes place which has no reference towards the end, because the effect comes from a cause other than, and outside the intention of the agent. But the causality of God, who is the first agent, extends to all being, not only as to the constituent principles of species, but also as to the individualizing principles; not only of things subject to corruption, but also of things not so subject. Hence all things that exist in whatsoever manner are necessarily directed by God towards some end; as the Apostle says:

Those that are, are ordained of God (Rom. 13:1). Since, therefore, as the Providence of God is nothing less than the reason of the order of things towards an end, as we have said; it necessarily follows that all things, inasmuch as they participate existence, must likewise be subject to Divine Providence. It has also been shown (qu. 14), that God knows all things; both universal and particular. Since His Knowledge must be compared to the things themselves, as the knowledge of art to the objects of art, all things must of necessity come under His plan as all things wrought by art are subject to the rule of that art.

Q. 22, art. 3: God has immediate providence over everything.

Two things belong to Providence; namely the plan of the order of things foreordained towards an end; and the execution of this order, which is called government. . . .

Q. 103, art. 5: All things are subject to the Divine government.

Augustine says (De Civ. Dei, V): "Not only heaven and earth, not only man and angel, even the bowels of the lowest animal, even the wings of the bird, the flower of the plant, the leaf of the tree, hath God endowed with every fitting detail of their nature." Therefore all things are subject to His government.

For the same reason is God the ruler of things as He is their cause, because the cause gives existence as it gives perfection; and this belongs to government. Now God is the cause not indeed only of some particular kind of being, but of the whole universal being, as proved above (qu. 44, ar. 1, 2). Wherefore, as there can be nothing which is not created by God, so there can be nothing which is not subject to His government. This can also be proved from the nature of the end of government. For a man's government extends over all those things which come under the end of his government. Now the end of the Divine government is the Divine goodness; as we have shown (ar. 2). Wherefore, as there can be nothing that is not ordered to the Divine goodness as its end, as is clear from what we have said above (qu. 44, ar. 4; qu. 65, ar. 2), so it is impossible for anything to escape from the Divine government.

Foolish therefore was the opinion of those who said that the corruptible world, or individual things, or that even human affairs, were not subject to the Divine government. These are represented as saying, "God hath abandoned the earth" (Ezech. 9:9).

Q. 103, art. 7: Nothing can happen outside the order of the Divine government.

It is possible for an effect to result outside the order of some particular cause; but not outside the order of the universal cause. The reason of this is that no effect results outside the order of a particular cause, except through some other impeding cause; which other cause must be reduced to the first universal cause; as indigestion may occur outside the order of the nutritive power by some such impediment as the coarseness of the food, which again is to be ascribed to some other cause, and so on till we come to the first universal cause. Therefore, as God is the first universal cause, not of one genus only, but of all being in general, it is impossible for anything to occur outside of the order of the Divine government; but from the very fact that from one point of view something seems to evade the order of Divine providence considered in regard to one particular cause, it must necessarily come back to that order as regards some other cause.

52

ALL MUST BE REFERRED TO DIVINE PROVIDENCE *

REMEMBER, my Lord, that the long sequence of particular causes which make and unmake empires, must be traced to the secret decrees of Divine Providence. In the heights of heaven God holds the reins of all kingdoms; He has all hearts in His hand; now He checks passions, now He gives them free way, and thus stirs all mankind. If He wants to raise conquerors, He sows fright in front of them, and animates them and their soldiers with an unconquerable boldness. If He wants to create lawgivers, he instills in them a spirit of wisdom and foresight; He enables them to prevent the evils that threaten States, and to lay the foundation of public peace. He knows how human wisdom is ever short in some direction; He enlightens it, He broadens its views, and then He leaves it to its ignorance; He blinds it, He breaks it, and confounds it with its own mistakes; left to itself, it rolls and gets entangled in its own subtleties and finds a snare in its very precautions. In this way God carries out His formidable designs, in keeping with the rules of His ever infallible justice. Egypt, once so wise, now pursues an intoxicated, stunned and staggering course; the reason is that the Lord has cast a spirit of vertigo on her deliberations, and therefore she no longer knows what she is doing; she is lost. But let no man be mistaken about it; When He pleases, God makes straight the stray reason; and he who taunted the blindness of others is apt to fall into thicker darkness, often without anything more being needed to upset his mind than his long prosperity.

This is the way God rules over all nations. We should no longer speak of chance or fortune, or if we use the name, let it be merely to cover our ignorance. What is chance in regard to our uncertain plans

* Jacques Bénigne Bossuet (1627-1704), conclusion of "Discours sur l'Histoire universelle." *Oeuvres*, ed. Lachat (Paris: Vives, 1862), Vol. 24, pp. 653-655.

is a design contrived by a higher intelligence, viz., that intelligence which includes in one great plan all causes and all effects. Thus all works for the same end, and it is because we do not know all that we find chance and irregularity in particular events.

Thus is verified the word of the Apostle "God is the Blessed and the only Mighty, King of kings and Lord of lords" (1 Tim. 6:15). The Blessed Whose rest or repose is unalterable, Who watches all things changing without Himself undergoing a change, Whose immutable design is the source of all changes; Who confers and withdraws power; Who transfers that power from one man to another, from one dynasty to another, from one nation to another, to make clear that none has it but on borrowed terms, and that in Him alone it dwells by nature.

That is why all those in authority feel subject to a higher power. They accomplish more or less than they imagine, and their plans have never failed to bring unforeseen effects. Neither are they masters of the arrangements that past ages have brought about in human affairs, nor can they foresee the course the future will take, far from their being able to determine it. He alone holds everything in His hands, Who knows the name of everything that exists, and of what is not yet, who presides over all ages and anticipates all plans.

Alexander did not think that by his conquests he was working for his captains and preparing the ruin of his family. When Brutus enkindled an immense love of freedom in the Roman people, he did not dream he was casting into their minds the seed of that unbridled license, through which the tyranny he wanted to destroy would one day be restored harder than under the Tarquins. When the Caesars pampered their soldiers, they did not intend to give masters to their successors and to the empire. In one word, there is no human power that does not in spite of itself serve other purposes than its own. God alone knows how to bring everything under His will. That is the reason why we are surprised at everything so long as we think only of particular causes, and yet everything proceeds according to rule. This Discourse makes it plain to you; and, not to mention the other empires, you see through how many unforeseen and yet logical designs, the fate of Rome was disposed from Romulus to Charlemagne. . . .

53

THE TWOFOLD PROVIDENCE *

FROM all these things we must conclude that there exists a *twofold*
Providence, the universal and the particular; and that each of
these follows a law of its own.

Universal Providence follows the law of supreme goodness, which, if
considered as to its mode of operation, receives the denomination of
"the Law of the Least Means," treated at length in this book.

The law, however, which is followed by the *particular Providence* is
that of supreme justice, equity, congruity, and conformity with the other
divine attributes, of which we have just spoken.

The conciliation and *harmonizing of these two Providences* and of
their two laws, is what constitutes the perfection of the government of
the world.

The two Providences and the two laws by which they are governed
appear sometimes in opposition to one another; it seems as if the *particular* good were in conflict with the *universal*. The perfection of the
divine government of the world consists, therefore, in maintaining all
that justice, congruity, and the divine attributes demand in providing
for each individual creature in particular, and at the same time, in disposing all things with such due measure and proportion and correspondence, that the good of individuals and the regard with which they
are treated, far from impeding, shall provide in effect most useful means
and necessary elements for attaining the maximum of universal good.
The universal good remains, therefore, the supreme object of all the
divine government, and all things serve to this end.

Now, admitting the two Providences, and the two different laws which
guide them, we may affirm of Divine Providence by which the Supreme
Being disposes of men, propositions that seem contradictory, whereas in
truth they are in marvelous agreement; so that the divine government,
which in its operations brings the two laws into harmony one with the
other, verifies in an unexpected and wonderful manner, each of the two
series of propositions.

Of the Universal Providence it is written: "Shall the thing formed say
to Him that formed it, why hast Thou made me thus? Hath not the
potter power over the clay, of the same lump to make one vessel into
honour, and another into dishonour?" (Rom. 9:20-21). To it we may

* Antonio Rosmini-Serbati (1797-1885), *Theodicy: Essays on Divine Providence*
(London: Longmans, Green, 1912), Vol. II, pp. 437-440.

apply all those innumerable passages in which the Scripture speaks of the supreme predestination of men, which is nothing else than the grand decree of the maximum of the universal good.

But of the Particular Providence it is written: "Tribulation and anguish upon every soul of man that worketh evil, of the Jew first, and also of the Greek; but glory and honour and peace to every one that worketh good, to the Jew first and also to the Greek. For there is no respect of persons with God" (Rom. 2:9-11), and again, "Behold, all souls are mine; as the soul of the father, so also the soul of the son is mine; the soul that sinneth, the same shall die" (Ezech. 18:4), and we may apply to it all those passages in which God describes Himself as a just and equitable judge, nay, even as one that treats with reverence all and each of His creatures.

The means adopted for bringing the two orders of Providence into full harmony and agreement were, as has been said, the permission of wilful sin. By thus sinning, men deliberately renounce the benefit of God's particular Providence over them, and so leave His Infinite goodness the fullest freedom to dispose of individuals whether in mercy or in justice, in such a way as shall best conduce to the greatest general good. St. Paul seems to say this in these words: "For God hath concluded all in unbelief, that He may have mercy on all. O the depth of the riches of the wisdom and of the knowledge of God! How incomprehensible are His judgments, and how unsearchable His ways! For who hath known the mind of the Lord? . . . For of Him and by Him and in Him are all things: to Him be glory for ever. Amen" (Rom. 11:32-36).

With these words I am fain to conclude my work. Far from having been so bold as to venture to search into the deep secrets of God, it has rather been my purpose to show that they are unsearchable. With this object I have called attention to those sublime laws which He observes most faithfully in the government of the universe, laws of which He alone comprehends the infinite breadth and vastness, and which He alone is able to apply. It has been my desire in doing so and my hope that I might thus aid men to refrain from all censure and complaint against the supremely good and wise Providence of God, and rather, hushed in silent contemplation before it, to render every day new love and praise and blessing to

> The Providence, that governeth the world,
> In depth of counsel by created ken
> Unfathomable
>
> (Dante, *Paradise*, XI, 28-30).

54

THE FREE EXISTENT AND THE FREE ETERNAL PURPOSE *

G OD's plan is eternal, as is the creative act itself, though it have its effect in time. But eternity is not a kind of divine time which precedes time. It is a limitless instant which indivisibly embraces the whole succession of time. All the moments of that succession are physically present in it. If all things are naked and open to the eyes of God it is because they are seen by His divine "science of vision" in their presentness. "To foresee" is an improper word to use when speaking of God. We employ it because we project into His eternity the anteriority (in relation to future events) of the knowledge which *we would have* of these events if *we* knew them *before* they happened. They are known to Him "already," which is to say, always. He sees them as actually taking place at a given temporal instant which is present in His eternity. All things and all events in nature are known to Him at their first coming forth and in the eternal morning of His vision because they are willed by Him, beyond all time, in the eternal instant with which their whole succession coexists.

But when we deal with the world of freedom, and not only with that of nature, when we deal with the free existents, creatures endowed with freedom of choice (a freedom inevitably fallible), we must go still farther. We must say that in a certain fashion those creatures have their part in the very establishment of the eternal plan, not indeed, by virtue of their power to act (here all they have they hold from God) but by virtue of their power to nihilate, to make the thing that is nothing, where they themselves are first causes. Free existents have their part in the establishment of God's plan, because in establishing that plan, He takes account of their initiatives of nihilating.

The divine plan was always willed. Assuming that God willed it at all, it cannot be but that He willed it always. Yet conversely, assuming that He had not willed it, it would necessarily have to be that He had *never* willed it. He freely willed it always, for all its contingency is on the side of *that which* is directed and ordained, not on the side of the act that directs and ordains it. And I say that, since the spectacle of created existents ordained and directed (i.e. the term, or matter, of the divine plan) is essentially and radically contingent; and since this contingency in no way affects the divine plan itself or the divine act that

* Jacques Maritain, *Existence and the Existent*, trans. by Lewis Galantiere and Gerald Phelan (New York: Pantheon Books, 1948), pp. 113-122.

established it, there is nothing to prevent the free nihilating of the creature from intervening in this contingency of the spectacle immutably ordained and directed by God. For that nihilating is itself eternally and immutably seen by God, without for that reason introducing a shadow of contingency into His knowledge. And since the spectacle of created beings is ordained and directed from all eternity—not *in advance* (as if eternity were itself in time and the eternal act a thing of the past), but in the eternal *today* in which all the successive moments of existence are indivisibly present; since this is so, the effect which ensues from that nihilating is eternally and immutably permitted or non-permitted by God without for this reason introducing a shadow of contingency or of conditioning into His will.

The divine plan is not a scenario prepared in advance, in which free subjects would play parts and act as performers. We must purge our thought of any idea of a play written in advance, at a time prior to time —a play in which time unfolds, and the characters of time read the parts. On the contrary, everything is improvised under the eternal and immutable direction of the almighty Stage Manager. The divine plan is the ordination of the infinite multiplicity of things, and of their becoming, by the absolutely simple gaze of the creative knowledge and the will of God. It is eternal and immutable, but it could have been otherwise (since it could not have been had there not been things). *Once fixed* from all eternity, once *assumed* as fixed in such and such a way from all eternity, it is immutable. And it is by virtue of the eternal presence of time in eternity (even before time was), by virtue of the embrace, by the eternal instant, of history in the making (perpetually fresh in its newness and indeed—as regards free acts—in the unforeseeability) that the divine plan is immutably fixed in heaven from all eternity, directing history towards the ends willed by God and disposing towards those ends all the actors in the drama, on behalf of those ends, of the evil itself of which they are the nihilating first cause and which God permits without having caused it. •

By reason of this free nihilating, the creature has a portion of free initiative in the drama. Unless the free existent has received at one stroke an unshatterable impetus to good, it depends solely upon him whether he will or will not take the initiative of nihilating or of non-consideration of the rule, under the motions and activations which bear him towards the good. Will he or will he not nihilate under the hand of the potter? As concerns his good or evil act, and the repercussions it may have upon what follows in the drama, it is at that instant in time, known from all eternity, that the immutable plan is simultaneously established from all eternity. Let us suppose that the free creature has not, in that instant, the initiative of the thing that is nothing. The initiative of nihilating not being seen (from all eternity) in the free existent by the "science of vision," from all eternity, the primordial will of God (which willed the good act of this creature in the direction of the particular end towards which it ordained him) is confirmed by the definitive or circumstanced will. Thus from all eternity the accomplishment of this good act by this creature is immutably fixed in the eternal plan. Let us suppose, on the contrary, that at that instant the free creature has the initiative of the thing that is nothing. Then, this is seen from all eternity in the free existent by the "science of vision"; and from all eternity God's definitive or circumstanced will (if it does not will to prevent the natural effect of this nihilating) permits the evil act of which this creature has the first initiative; and from all eternity the permission of this evil act, ordained to a better good (itself willed either determinately or indeterminately), is immutably fixed in the eternal plan. Thus we can conceive, by the aid of the moments of reason which our human mode of conceiving is forced to distinguish in the divine will, that the variegated drama of history and humanity, with its infinite interweavings, is immutably fixed from all eternity by the perfectly and infinitely simple dominating act of the divine knowledge and free will, account being taken of all free existents and of all the free nihilations of which these existents have or have not the initiative, throughout the whole succession of time whose every moment is present in eternity. Let no one say that man alters the divine plan. Man does not alter it. He enters into its very composition and its eternal fixity by his power of saying No.

To tell the truth, I do not see how things could be conceived otherwise. Suppose that the eternal plan were a scenario prepared in advance. Suppose that in that scenario it was written that Brutus was to assassinate Caesar. Then, when Brutus steps forth upon the stage of the world, either the Stage Manager will leave him truly free to have or not have the first initiative of sin, in which case Brutus might not murder Caesar and might thus frustrate the eternal plan—which is absurd; or else the Stage Manager will arrange in one way or another, with antecedent permissive decrees or supercomprehension of causes, that Brutus really assassinates Caesar but still commits the murder freely. How then and by what subtleties, can one avoid the conclusion that God had the first initiative of the sin, and, were it merely by slackening His hand, caused the creature to fall into it?

It was Brutus who had the first initiative of the free nihilating by which, God permitting, the decision of murder entered into his will and into the history of the world. If, at that instant in time, eternally present in the eternal instant, he had not had that initiative of nihilating, the immutable plan would have fixed things in another way from all eternity. Caesar's fall would have been led up to by other ways, as would also the accomplishment of God's designs with regard to Rome and to the world to which that fall was related and for which it was willed.

I have said that in God there is no idea of evil. He invented Behemoth and Leviathan and all the terrifying forms which people nature and the world of life—the ferocious fishes, the destroying insects. He did not invent moral evil and sin. It was not He who had the idea of all the defilements and abominations and contempts that are spat upon His Face, the betrayals, lecheries, cruelties, cowardices, bestial wickednesses, refined perversions, depravities of mind which it is given to His creatures to contemplate. Those were born solely of nihilation by human liberty. They came forth from that abyss. God permits them as a creation of our power to make the thing which is nothing.

He permits them because He is strong enough, as St. Augustine says, to turn all the evil we choose to introduce into the world, into a greater good—hidden in the mystery of transcendence, and such that nothing in nature allows us to conjecture what it may consist in. The man of faith who is to have a suspicion of the greatness of that good, and marvel at it, measures the greatness of the evil for which a good will supercompensate.

Our misfortune is precisely that there is no scenario written by God in advance (it would be less sinister); and that the ill-omened element of the drama comes from created existents, ourselves; and from the fact that God plays fair. Since the evil of the free act is our creation, it is in letting our monsters proliferate to the very end, and allowing the infinite resources of our power of nihilating to develop all forms of degradation and corruption of being, that divine liberty manifests the sublimity of its omnipotence by drawing *from that itself* the higher good which God designs, not for Himself but for us. Meanwhile, despite all the energies of goodness at work in man, nature, and history, which cause them by rising above their ruins, "the whole world is seated in wickedness" (1 John, 5:19), and the terrible, the incorruptible, divine fair play leaves us to flounder in the mire. Such at least is the way in which it is allowable for a philosopher to look upon the order of nature. Fortunately, there is also the order of grace, and the virtue of the blood of Christ, the sufferings and prayers of the saints, and the hidden operations of mercy. All these, without infringing the laws of divine fair play, introduce into the most secret recesses of the plot factors which transfigure it. They manifest the heavenly ordering according to which souls are deputed to eternal life, bodies to resurrection, and the wickedness of the free creatures becomes the price paid for glory. On this very earth, they make love prevail over sin (if, at least, we have eyes to see); and they come invisibly to help each one to reach the hereafter even while the sad, ordinary laws and the miseries of the herebefore are at work upon all. For those who serve God they cause all things to cooperate in goodness, and to cover with His wings those who have given all to Him. They strengthen the springs and the resources of nature by offering, in spite of everything, some respite to peoples and to nations; and, in spite of everything, by guiding history towards its accomplishment. A more than human grandeur is dissembled in our creeping destinies. A sense is given to our wretched condition; and this is probably what matters most to us. It remains a wretched condition—but the existent who vegetates in it is cut out to become God by participation.

III. The Problem of Evil

55

AQUINAS: SELECTED PASSAGES *

As APPEARS from what was said (ar. 1), the evil which consists in the defect of action, or which is caused by defect of the agent, is not reduced to God as to its cause.

But the evil which consists in the corruption of some things is reduced to God as the cause. And this appears as regards both natural and voluntary things. For it was said (ar. 1) that some agent inasmuch as it produces by its power a form to which follows corruption and defect, causes by its power that corruption and defect. But it is manifest that the form which God chiefly intends in things created is the good of the order of the universe. Now, the order of nature requires, as was said above (q. 22, art. 2 ad 2um; q. 48, art. 2), that there should be some things that can, and do sometimes, fail. And thus God, by causing in things the order of the universe, consequently and as it were by accident, causes the corruptions of things, according to 1 Kings, 2:6: "The Lord killeth and maketh alive." But when we read that God hath not made death (Wis. 1:13), the sense is that God does not will death for its own sake. Nevertheless the order of justice belongs to the order of the universe; and this requires that penalty should be dealt out to sinners. And so God is the author of the evil which is penalty, but not of the evil which is fault, by reason of what was said above.

* *Summa Theol.*, I, q. 49, art. 2.

56

THE PROBLEM OF EVIL IN ST. AUGUSTINE

Providence and Evil *

Book I, ch. 1: Apparent conflict between the notion of Divine Providence and the existence of evil.

To perceive and to grasp the order of reality proper to each thing, and then to see or to explain the order of the entire universe by which the world is truly held together and governed—that, Zenobius, is a very difficult and rare achievement for men. Moreover, even if one had this power, he is not thereby enabled to find an audience fitted for such divine and hidden things, either by personal worth or by an acquired habit of learning. And yet there is nothing that the most gifted minds search out more eagerly, nothing that those who, with heads uplifted as much as they may, still see the rocks and storms of this life below—there is nothing that these are more desirous of hearing and learning than how it is that God has a care for human affairs, and nevertheless perversity is so serious and widespread that it must seem unattributable not only to God's governance, but even to a hireling's management, if indeed such management could be entrusted to a hireling.

Wherefore, those who ponder these matters are seemingly forced to believe either that Divine Providence does not reach to these outer limits of things or that surely all evils are committed by the will of God. Both horns of this dilemma are impious, but particularly the latter. For, although it is unsound and most perilous to the soul to hold that anything is beyond God's control, yet even among men no one is blamed for what he could not do or prevent. The imputing of negligence is indeed much more pardonable than the charge of ill will or cruelty. Reason, therefore, not unmindful of piety, is in a manner forced to hold that they are governed by powers divine or that they are neglected and unnoticed, rather than to hold that they are governed in such wise that all complaining about God is inoffensive and blameless.

But who is there so dull of mind that he will hesitate to attribute to divine power and divine government whatever there is of order in corporal operations, apart from human arrangement and will? Unless, perhaps, by some play of nonsense we shall have the hardihood to hold one

* St. Augustine, De Ordine, trans. by Robert P. Russell, O.S.A, Fathers of the Church (New York, 1948), vol. V, pp. 239-241; 286-289.

of three hypotheses: (1) that the most accurately measured and fitted organic parts of the smallest animals are the result of chance; (2) that what one admits to be not the work of chance can in any way not be the effect of design; or (3) that what we find marvelous in every single thing throughout the universe, arranged in a manner surpassing the utmost efficiency of human power, belongs not to the hidden control of divine majesty.

Yet, here is a point suggestive of even more questioning: that the organic parts of a flea are marvelously fitted and framed, while human life is surrounded and made restless by the inconsistency of countless disorders. On this line of reasoning, if one were examining the details in an inlaid pavement, and if his searching eye could grasp no more than the outline of one little cube, he might censure the artificer for lacking skill of arrangement and order. On this account he might think the uniformity of the little stones disarranged, just because the drawn lines, harmonizing into one integral form of beauty could not be seen and examined all at once. Something very similar to this is found in the case of uninstructed men, who, on account of their feeble mentality, are unable to grasp and to study the integral fittingness of things. They think that the whole universe is disarranged if something is displeasing to them, just because that thing is magnified in their perception.

The chief cause of this error is that man does not know himself. Now, for acquiring this self-knowledge, he needs a constant habit of withdrawing from things of the senses and of concentrating his thought within himself and holding it there. This they alone succeed in doing who definitely mark out in solitude the impressions of opinion which the course of daily life has made, or correct them by means of the liberal branches of learning.

Book II, ch. 4: Evils not opposed to the harmony of the universe.

But let us get back to order, for Licentius may at any moment be returned to us. For the present, I ask you the question: Does it seem to you that the unwise man acts according to order, no matter what he does? But, mark what snares the question contains. If you say that he acts according to order, what will become of that definition: *Order is that by which God governs all things that are?* And, if there is no order in the things that are done by the unwise man, then there will be something which order does not embrace. But you are not willing to accept either alternative. See to it, I beg you, lest in your defense of order you throw everything into disorder.

At this point Trygetius answered again, for the other boy was still absent.

"It is easy," he said, "to reply to this dilemma of yours. For the moment, however, I cannot call to mind an analogy by which my opinion ought, I know, to be declared and illustrated. I shall simply state my impression, for you will do what you did a little while ago. Certainly that mention of the darkness has brought us a great deal of light on what has been put forward very obscurely by me. Indeed, the entire life of the unwise, although it is by no means consistent and by no means well regulated by themselves, is, nevertheless, necessarily included in the order of things by Divine Providence. And, certain places having been arranged, so to speak, by that ineffable and eternal law, it is by no means permitted to be where it ought not to be. Thus it happens that whoever narrow-mindedly considers this life by itself alone is repelled by its enormous foulness, and turns away in sheer disgust. But, if he raises the eyes of the mind and broadens his field of vision and surveys all things as a whole, then he will find nothing unarranged, unclassed, or unassigned to its own place."

What great and wonderful response does not God Himself—and, as I am more and more led to believe, also that unfathomable order of things—send to me through you. Verily, you speak things of such import that I cannot understand either how you discern them or how they can be spoken unless they are discerned. And for that reason I believe that they are both true and from on high. Now, you were looking just for one or two illustrations for that opinion of yours. To me there already occur countless illustrations which bring me to complete agreement. What more hideous than a hangman? What more cruel and ferocious than his character? Yet he holds a necessary post in the order of a well-regulated state; himself criminal in character, he is nevertheless, by others' arrangement, the penalty of evildoers. What can be mentioned more sordid or more full of turpitude than prostitutes, procurers, and the other pests of that sort? Remove prostitutes from human affairs, and you will unsettle everything because of lusts; place them in the position of matrons, and you will dishonor these latter by disgrace and ignominy. This class of people is, therefore, by its own mode of life most unchaste in its morals; by the law of order, it is most vile in social condition.

And is it not true that in the bodies of animals there are certain members which you could not bear to look at, if you should view them by themselves alone? But the order of nature has designed that because they are needful they shall not be lacking, and because they are uncomely they shall not be prominent. And these ugly members, by keeping their proper places, have provided a better position for the more comely ones. What more agreeable to us—because it was quite an appropriate sight for field and farmyard—than that contest and conflict of the barnyard cock, which we have related in the preceding book? But, what have we ever seen more abject than the deformity of the vanquished one? And yet, by that very deformity was the more perfect beauty of the contest in evidence.

So it is, I think, with all things, but they have to be seen. Poets have found delight in what they call solecisms and barbarisms. But, by a mere change of name, they chose to call them tropes and metaplasms, rather than refrain altogether from the use of such manifest blunders. Remove these from poems: we shall be wanting their delightful relish. Crowd a great many of them into one passage; I shall loathe the whole passage as sour, malodorous, and rancid. Carry them over into familiar and forensic speech: who will not bid them flee and retreat from the theater? Because order directs and restrains them, it does not suffer them to be in excess of their proper place, or to be anywhere out of place. Unpretentious and seemingly inelegant diction, interspersed in a discourse brings into bolder relief the fancy flights and the ornate passages. If it is ever by itself alone, you throw it out as worthless. On the other hand, wherever it is lacking, those adornments are not conspicuous—they are not dominant, so to speak, in their provinces and realms; they are a hindrance to themselves by their own brilliance, and they confuse the whole design.

Evil and Free Will According to St. Augustine *

The rôle of grace is only understood in terms of the evils it is to cure. There is a radical deficiency in man as well as a disorder made possible by that very deficiency; in a word, evil exists. The existence of evil raises a problem over which Augustine worried for a long time even before his conversion. If the word 'God' has any meaning, it can only signify a perfect being who is the author responsible for all things. But to say that there is evil in man is to admit the imperfection of the universe. How are we to reconcile the work's imperfection with the workman's perfection? And how are we to find a remedy for it?

The problem belongs essentially to metaphysics, in that the human will is but a fragment of the universal order. To solve it, therefore, we have to begin with a consideration of being.

By definition and in keeping with the proofs establishing His existence, God is the sovereign good. Now in as much as He is the supreme good, no good exists above or apart from Him. God, then, cannot change; not having any good to acquire, He has nothing to gain or lose. This is what is meant by saying that God is immutable and eternal. Creatures, on the other hand, only exist *through* Him, but they are not *of* Him. If they were, they would be identical with Him, i.e. they would no longer be creatures. Their origin is, as we know, quite different: they have been created and so were brought out of nothingness by Him. Now a thing which comes from nothing participates not only in being but in non-being as well; hence, there is a kind of fundamental deficiency in a creature which in turn gives birth to the necessity of acquiring and, con-

* Etienne Gilson, *The Christian Philosophy of Saint Augustine*, trans. by L. E. M. Lynch (New York: Random House, 1960). Copyright, 1960 by Etienne Gilson.

sequently, of changing as well. This is the metaphysical root of their mutability. Plato's philosophy sought to express this by saying that things cannot in any absolute sense be said either to be or not be (*nec omnino esse nec omnino non esse*). The difficulty is to specify the relation of being to non-being in each separate case.

To overcome this difficulty we have but to consider the universal attributes which make created things good. No matter what kind of substance we consider, whether spiritual or corporeal, God has bestowed on it measure, form and order (*modus, species, ordo*). If these three perfections are of high degree, the creature possessing them will be a great good; if they are mediocre, the creature will be only a mediocre good; if none of them are there, the creature will be no good at all. Nature, however, is in proportion to the good. Hence, higher measure, form and order imply a higher nature; lower measure, form and order imply a lower nature; no measure, form or order at all mean no nature at all Now *nulla natura* means either "a worthless nature" or "no nature at all," as you prefer. In any case, it is nothing. Since, then, every nature is made up of three perfections, by definition every nature is good.

If this is goodness, evil can only be the corruption of one or other of these perfections in the nature possessing them. An evil nature is one in which measure, form or order is vitiated, and it is only evil in exact proportion to the degree in which they are vitiated. If the nature were not vitiated, it would be all order, form and measure, i.e. it would be good; even when vitiated, as nature it is still good, and evil only in so far as it is vitiated. This relation between the evil and good in a subject we express by calling evil a *privation*. Evil is the privation of a good which the subject should possess, a failure to be what it should be and hence, a pure nothingness.

In keeping with this doctrine, it is not enough merely to admit that the Manichaeans are wrong in considering evil a being, because it is a pure absence of being; we have to go further and say that, since by definition evil is nothing, it could not even be considered apart from some good. For evil to exist, there must be a privation; hence, there must be a thing which is deprived of something. Now the thing as such is good, and it is only in so far as it is deprived of something that it is evil. What does not exist has no deficiencies. Thus, whenever we speak of evil, we implicitly assume the presence of some good which is not all that it should be and is therefore evil. Evil is not merely a privation: it is a privation residing in some good as in its subject.

Augustine was not satisfied to state this thesis in general terms; he applied it specifically to the voluntary evil which is sin. The voluntary, free act may be compared to any substance endowed with measure, form and order. If these perfections are not what they should be in a determined act, that act is thereby imperfect and therefore, bad. But in this case also the malice of the act is to be found only in that of which the act is deprived. If the act were nothing, it would not be deprived of anything;

hence, an evil will is one which is good as will, but falls short of being quite the thing it should be. In this case as in others, evil cannot exist apart from some good.

Once these principles have been set down, it becomes possible to account for the presence of evil in the world. These principles reveal the purely privative nature of evil and by so doing free God from the reproach of having created it, because what is nothing cannot have been created; they even prove that since God did create, evil was inevitable, because to create means to bring out of nothingness, and a thing which comes from nothing is corruptible; and lastly, they enable us to settle this knotty problem: if creation *ex nihilo* was necessarily accompanied by evil, would it not have been better to create nothing at all? In discussing this question, it is advisable to distinguish between natural and moral evil; consequently, the question falls into two: why create corruptible natures? Why create fallible wills?

As regards natural evil, it will be enough to recall that, in so far as things exist, they can only be considered good. It is true that they are born, corrupt and die; the universe is the scene of constant destruction and, in the case of living things and of man in particular, this is accompanied by the cruelest suffering, anguish and sorrow. We must not forget, however, that all of the beings which replace one another in this way are themselves good, so that it is always good things which follow one another endlessly on the stage of the universe. Moreover, there is a certain beauty and perfection even in their succession, and one may find a satisfactory reason for the violent destruction of many of them. However insignificant the perfection of each thing may be, it only exists because of the good it has, and it is to God that it owes the possession of it. He has so disposed all things that the weak give way to the strong, the less strong to the strongest, and earthly things to the heavenly bodies superior to them. In fact, in following one another as they disappear only to be replaced by others, things display a kind of beauty different from the beauty our eyes behold in space. It is, so to speak, a beauty which unfolds in time. A thing which dies or ceases to be what it was, neither mars nor impairs the order or balance of the universe. Quite the contrary; for just as a well-ordered speech is beautiful even though the syllables and sounds of which it consists slip by and die away, as though each dies to allow the next to be born, so too does the universe roll on, like a poem whose very movement makes it a thing of beauty.

As for moral evil, the problem seems more difficult to solve. If man's actions are not always what they should be, his will is responsible for it. He makes his decisions freely and it is in virtue of this freedom that he is capable of doing evil. The question, then, is this: how could a perfect God endow us with free choice, i.e. with a will capable of doing evil?

When the problem is stated in these terms, it amounts to determining whether and to what extent free will may be numbered among the things which are good. The answer cannot be other than that given in the case of corporeal things. In the world of bodies, there are many things which we can put to bad use, but this is no reason for saying that they are evil and that God should not have given them to us, because, considered in themselves, they are good. Now why could there not be good things like this in the soul, i.e. things of which we can make evil use but which, being good, could only have been given us by the author of every good? Being deprived of its hands is a serious loss to the human body, so hands are good and useful things; but the man who commits criminal or shameful acts with them makes bad use of them. A human body without feet would obviously be very imperfect, but a person who uses his feet to go and injure another or to disgrace himself makes bad use of them. What is true of these members is true of all the other parts as well, of the eyes, for example; and this is the reason why the same may be said of the will. In itself, the will is good, because without it no one could lead an upright life. It comes to us, therefore, from God, and we should find fault with those who use it badly, not with Him Who gives it to us.

Perhaps some will be inclined to object to this conclusion as being purely dialectical and abstract. Furthermore, by giving us a will capable of doing evil, did God not give us something so dangerous that, of itself, it constituted a real evil? It is true that in all liberty there lurks a danger; nevertheless, our liberty is the indispensable condition for the greatest good which can fall to our lot, namely our happiness. In itself, free will cannot be an evil; nor is it an absolute good like fortitude, temperance or justice, things we cannot use for evil without destroying them in the process. Free will is an intermediate good: its nature is good, but its effect can be good or bad according to the way man uses it. Now the use to be made of free choice is under the control of free choice itself. Reason, the source of all knowledge, knows itself; memory, the storehouse of all recollections, remembers itself; free will, the master of everything else—for it is all at its free disposal—is also master of itself. Hence, it rests with free will, and free will alone, to put to evil use the good that it is.

On the other hand, the possibility of the evil use of free will was the necessary condition for the goodness and happiness brought about by its good use. When our will clings to that immutable and universal good, truth, in order to find its joy in it, it possesses the happy life, which is man's supreme good. Now, that happiness is not identical with Truth; it is only the individual possession of it. It is by adherence to one and the same Truth, to one and the same Wisdom, both common to us all, that all men become happy and wise; but one person cannot be happy with another's happiness any more than he can be prudent, just or courageous through another's prudence, justice or fortitude. This is the reason why man must have a will that is personal and free; and since the will itself is an intermediate good, it remains free to turn towards the supreme good and to possess it in happiness, or to turn away from it to enjoy itself and lower things, which act constitutes moral evil and sin.

Turning away from the Sovereign Good, turning to secondary goods: these are, in brief, the two free acts which decide our eternal happiness or misery.

Agreed, you will say, but how does it happen that the will chooses sin? God is the cause of everything; hence, He is the cause of the act whereby free choice turns away from the supreme good to fasten on lower goods, and since that act is unquestionably a sin, God is therefore the cause of sin itself. Or, if that act does not come from God, where does it come from? The only honest answer that can be made to this question is that we do not know anything about it; not, to be sure, that we do not know where the real responsibility lies, but rather, because we cannot know a thing which is nothing (*Sciri enim non potest quod nihil est*). What is the metaphysical significance of this reply?

Every good comes from God; every nature is a certain good; therefore, every nature comes from God. This strict conclusion applies to sensible as well as to intelligible things. Whenever we see a being in which measure, order and number are to be found, let us not hesitate to acknowledge that God is its author. But if we strip that being of the order, measure and number it has, and remove them altogether, absolutely nothing will remain. As long as a rudiment of form remains, however crude and imperfect it may be, there is still a seed of goodness, and like a kind of matter, it can be brought to its perfection step by step. If an adumbration of being is a certain good, the complete deprivation of good is by definition equivalent to an utter destruction of being. Consequently, it becomes quite inconsistent to imagine a positive cause like God at the origin of the act whereby free will turns away from Him. It is true that He has made the will master of itself and capable of adhering to the sovereign good or of turning away from it; but once so made by God, it was in its *power* to separate itself from God, it was its *duty* not to do so. Its fall—for that is what it was—was not the natural and necessary fall of a falling stone, but rather the free fall of a will letting itself go. And since it was a deficiency, a lack of order, and consequently a lack of being, the original fall had no other source but nothingness, i.e. non-being. But if sin is nothing, how could it have an efficient cause? Here we can only speak of a deficiency in the cause. To look for the cause of a deficiency or of a lack of being, is like looking for a positive cause for silence or darkness. Silence is merely an absence of sound; darkness is simply an absence of light; in the same way we might say that sin in our will is merely an absence of the love for God. Our will is changeable because it was created from nothing, and is therefore imperfect; it had only to sink from Creator to creatures to introduce the initial disorder of sin into itself and the universe. But, let us add, God helps us bring order out of the disorder for which He is in no way responsible; He extends His hand to fallen man to raise him from his fall and, through grace, restores the original order destroyed by sin.

57

EVIL IN THE LIFE OF MAN AND ITS FINALITY *

I. EVIL IN THE LIFE OF MAN

I T IS not without reason that we have waited so long to describe the Good in itself. This idea is for us of great importance. In its light we can measure the vast horizons of the empire of Evil. It is, indeed, in the man capable of perceiving Good in itself that Evil attains its zenith.

The plant, while suffering from Evil, has no idea of it. The animal knows it, but only in an imperfect way; only physical, material pain (pain exclusively related to touch) affects it. And again, it can only feel it at the moment when it occurs; it cannot hasten or retard it by one second; with the cessation of the feeling of touch it infallibly disappears. Limited in duration, it is also limited in space. It is localized in the organ that receives the excitation from outside, or, at most (by virtue of the law of "irradiation" of sensations in the organism), in those that are tied to that organ by the sensitive nerves.

Man, on the contrary, is subject to every kind of Evil. He suffers not only from physical evils but also from moral; not only from the Evil which attacks him at the present moment but also from that which threatens him in the future, whether that future be near or far or even in eternity. He suffers from past evil as well as from present evil. For once Evil has reached the spiritual faculties, it takes root there and continues in the form of regret or remorse. Man is subject to individual and to social evil. He feels as much the evil that strikes his family, his nation, his country as that which affects him personally. Some men bear their own sorrows with more courage than those that befall their near relatives. Man is subject to fictitious evil as well as to real. The difference between the two is merely exterior; it only depends on the object; from the subjective viewpoint, none exists; fictitious evil is still a true evil. It is sometimes even more painful than what is called "real."

Man can suffer not only from tactile sensations, as can the animal, but through all his senses, without exception. Grief can reach his imagination and his memory, for these two faculties do not always work at man's will. And that is what makes him suffer. Even intelligence, the

* Paul Siwek, S.J. (1893-   ), *The Philosophy of Evil* (New York: The Ronald Press, 1951), chs. v, VIII.

noblest and highest faculty of man, is not free from suffering. Like the magnetic needle that turns constantly towards the North, the intelligence orientates itself towards truth. This tendency is in its nature, and one can do nothing against nature. Now, how often is our mind plunged into ignorance, into doubt, into perplexity? Intelligence tends desperately towards the clear light of day that only the immediate evidence procured by intuition could give it. Now very often it must be content with a twilight glimmer of partial or desultory knowledge and with faith.

Thus all the wealth of man, all his faculties, are subject to suffering and to evil. And this suffering is rendered more acute by the consciousness that he has of it; he knows that he suffers, he knows that he is unhappy. The animal also suffers, but it does not say to itself: "I suffer, I am going to die." It does not know the "I." The suffering of the animal is therefore less penetrating, less profound, less immanent, and only affects the surface, so to speak, of its being. It is impersonal and evaporates quickly. Man, on the contrary, reflecting on his "ego," accentuates the weight of the evil that oppresses him; he even has the sad faculty of being able to foresee Evil before it reaches him and so to intensify his grief. In the abyss that he creates around his Evil, nonentity sometimes appears to him as the only way of escape, as a good thing. He comes to desire it. . . . Man alone is capable of suicide.

And here is a remarkable fact; the more a being rises in the hierarchy of life, the more he is subject to Evil. Evil increases in proportion to the nobility and dignity of the creature. It is the noblest creature, the one rightly or wrongly called *primogenita creaturarum*, it is Man who suffers the most. "When, in order to know my individual place in my species, I consider the diverse ranks and men who hold them, what a spectacle," J. J. Rousseau said. "The picture of Nature showed me only harmony and proportion, that of humanity only confusion and disorder. Concord exists between the elements, and men are in chaos. O Wisdom, where are your laws? O Providence, is it thus that you govern the world? Beneficent Being, what has become of your power? I see Evil on the earth."

Since we are concerned with Man in general, we ought to add that all men are not equally sensitive to suffering. Egoists, for example, are scarcely touched by any suffering that does not affect them personally. They practically ignore the sufferings of their neighbours. Those persons whose mental development has been arrested show much resemblance to primitives and to children when they reach adult age. Like them, they are engrossed in the present and consequently do not suffer from anticipation of pain in the future nor from pain that they have suffered in the past; they live in the present, they suffer in the present. Those persons whom we speak of in current language as "hardened to evil" (and who are generally rather rough individuals) have less fine nerves, less delicate sensibility. To make them suffer, they must be shaken somewhat severely; ordinary stimulants will leave them un-moved. Ed. v. Hartmann said "It is the coarse and primitive people who are the most satisfied, and among the cultivated people the least instructed classes are so. With the progress of instruction of a people, its discontent increases, as has been well established. Manufactures, steamers, railways and telegraphs have not yet done anything for the felicity of humanity." With the progressive development of humanity, not only an increase of needs is produced . . . but also that of the sensi-bility of the nervous system and of the culture of the mind. Conse-quently, there also appears an excess of pain felt with regard to pleas-ure experienced and the demolition of the illusion, that is to say, the consciousness of the misery of life, of the vanity of most pleasures.

But why multiply examples? One suffers less because one is a little less of a man. Suffering increases in direct ratio to the perfection of man. The more an individual realizes the "measure" of a man, the more susceptible he is to suffering. In rising towards the ideal, one dis-covers always new, always unexpected prospects of suffering, horizons al-ways vaster, always wider open to Evil. The scruples of the saints are a striking example of this; the "little" imperfections, the peccadillos they were always discovering because of their own moral elevation, caused them extreme torment. In the same way, whoever thoroughly studies science discovers more and more reasons for doubt, for painful perplexity: he sees new problems always rising that seem to hide new mysteries, and the perpetual anxiety is also painful.

The Hierarchy of living beings, the Hierarchy of Evil—there is a strange parallelism in Nature. It is pure chance, perhaps. But this chance would then enjoy singular prerogatives; it would be steady, uni-versal; it would allow of general and sure foreknowledge and by that might serve as the foundation of a science. Now such prerogatives, we can clearly see, are incompatible with the idea we have of chance. Chance is always something that cannot be foreseen; it has no rules; there is nothing stable, permanent in it. Chance is an exception to the normal course of things.

No. The parallelism we have just made clear is not the effect of chance. It is a law of Nature. Let us remember this conclusion, for it will help us to understand the finality of Evil and to discover its origin.

II. THE FINALITY OF EVIL IN THE REALM OF MAN

As to the finality of Evil with regard to the kingdom of Man, we can make a distinction between several aspects of importance. First of all, Evil recalls to man his immortal destiny.

The Good proportioned to man, his end, is the Good in itself. This Good considered relatively is—we can say—still the man but conceived abstractly, having reached the complete realization of his purpose, in a word, "ideal man."

It is hardly necessary to add that such a man has never existed; even in the God-Man there was sorrow, suffering, and death. Now none of these should touch the "ideal man" as our intelligence conceives of him, as our will strives to realize him.

Let us consider this ideal of man.

The ideal man represents the consummation of all our natural tendencies taken together. It does not depend on us to create this ideal at our pleasure or to abstain from doing so. Man is born with this ideal, as he is born with a certain nature that is especially his own, and his effort in this sense is self-imposed just as his natural inclinations are. This aspiration that cannot be coerced comes then from the Author of all things; it is the will of God. It is God who unceasingly incites man to the pursuit of the ideal of perfection.

But it would be impossible for God to direct man towards nonentity, so the ideal of man is certainly not a fiction. It is a positive and true possibility. On what is it founded? Its foundation is of the same nature as that of the "possibles," the "essences," and the "universals." It is in God Himself.

All ideals are not equivalent. For example, that of the plant does not contain knowledge nor the sensation of pleasure; on the contrary, it excludes them; for a plant that possessed the faculty of knowing, and of feeling pleasure, would by that very faculty deprive itself of its own essence and therefore cease to exist.

The ideal of the animal involves knowledge and the search for pleasure. But this knowledge and this pleasure are purely "sensitive"; they are only a matter of a faculty essentially organic and, consequently, corruptible and mortal. The ideal of the animal does not include immortality. Such an outlook would no doubt be repulsive to it. Indeed, as it possesses no immortal faculty, what sense could an eternally inactive, sterile, and stupid existence have for it?

Man's ideal does include the idea of immortality. How could it fail to do so, since his soul is immortal?

It is true that man is not pure spirit; he also possesses a body. He is then a composite thing. On principle, that which is composed can be decomposed; man is then corruptible, mortal, and, as a matter of fact, he dies. However, this death cannot be final. Man, thanks to his natural intelligence, conceives immortality and desires it for his whole being and not for a part of himself. It is a wish for complete resurrection that animates him; he wants to live again in his body. This resurrection is not an impossibility in principle, since all things are possible with God. Besides, this would not be, strictly speaking, a miracle, because this divine intervention would not be "exceptional" but would be the rule. It would be the fulfilment of the natural desires that God has placed in human nature, and therefore not a question of a voluntary favor nor of a true "grace." (We are speaking from the philosophical viewpoint.)

But whatever one may say of the resurrection of the body in the natural order, it is certain that the soul of man is immortal and that in it and by it man lives eternally. His existence on earth is in view of a future life that is its natural and necessary "complement." That is the true destiny of man, the reason for his existence and his purpose in life.

Life on earth is but a "movement" towards this end, a "means" towards this purpose. That is why one should never allow oneself to be engrossed in the present. Each must live for the future and work, thinking of eternity.

But man, because he is not pure spirit, is also an animal by his very nature. The animal in him never renounces sensible good. When it loses it, it considers itself lost forever, as it knows that it will not find it again in eternity; and then it thinks no more of eternity and does not look so high but lives absorbed in the present moment. That is the origin of the conflict that troubles the conscience of man, a conflict very embarrassing for all thinkers, the more so as it arises from the depths of man's being. This conflict is the source of many of the ills that afflict man. It is the terrible "law of the members" of which the Apostle complains; it is the slavery that weighs down the heathen: *video meliora proboque, deteriora sequor.*

It is very obvious to the human being that there is a disproportion between him and the universe. The world is not made to his measure; it is undoubtedly not made for him, it is not an end for him.

Such is the finality of Evil for man; it recalls him to his higher destiny. The part that suffering plays is somewhat like that of the miracles, which also apply to our eternal destiny. A miracle is a means in the hands of God to attract the attention of man to His words and to His will. God speaks to man constantly, and constantly reveals to him His will, which is expressed in the natural laws that are binding on all creatures and by that essential order which is for us a true moral rule (*ordo essentialis rerum*). But just because of the persistence and the monotony of these laws, man sometimes becomes a little indifferent to their immense murmur, just as a miller becomes accustomed to the sound of his mill: so long as the everlasting tick-tock continues, our miller sleeps peacefully. If the lulling music stops, he awakes suddenly. So when the normal course of things is suspended, the attention of man is awakened; anguish seizes him, he tries to discover the cause of such trouble. And it is then that the will of God is revealed to him.

We have said that there is an analogy between suffering and what is called "miracle." Suffering disturbs a regular rhythm, upsets an established order, suspends continuity, breaks up equilibrium. And in so doing it also awakens Man and makes him feel the disproportion that exists between himself and the world he lives in, gives him the impression that he is a stranger there, that he is only beginning to acclimatize himself to it; that he might in the long run be contented there, and sleep there in a gentle torpor. It shakes him, jostles him, and detaches him from the perishable to draw him to that which is eternal, towards his high destiny. Daily experience confirms this; conversions, religious or moral, very often take place when sorrow appears. Yes, suffering recalls us to the eternity of our destiny as men. That is one of its purposes.*

. . . .

Lastly, let us consider the fourth finality of Evil in the life of Man. To realize his end, the living being must act. The end for the living being is its own perfection; this can be accomplished only by its immanent actions; it could not be the result of a simple exchange of encounters with the surrounding world. It must come from within, as the fruit from the blossom.

We have seen how pain contributes to the perfection of the animal. In itself it is not good. It affects the organism like intoxication; it slows down or checks certain secretions; it limits appetite and causes emaciation, it weakens the organism and lessens its power of resistance in the struggle for life. Spinoza had good reason for saying that suffering "diminishes" the being. It is not then that pain can per se procure any good for the animal. It is a cause *per accidens,* in that it awakes in it the desire to protect itself or to fly from the approaching evil. It is always the effort of the living being, that action that it uses on this occasion, that is the creator of good. And that is also true where man is concerned. It is not that Evil could ever help him in his struggle towards the ideal, but the action that he is forced to use to protect himself from it does help him.

However, let us notice here a detail of great importance. For Evil, in the form of physical pain, to change into good for the animal, it has only to be perceived by the animal. The result is inevitable. The perception of the Evil gives birth in the animal to certain affections automatically, so to speak. They are shown by its movements. In this respect one might look upon the animal as a "psychic automaton"; it carries out promptly, faithfully, and completely, the suggestions received; it never resists them. It is, moreover, incapable of doing so because it is not free.

The situation of man is very different. He is free. Thanks to his liberty, he can reply or not to the invitation that comes to him from Evil. For suffering to do a man good, it is not sufficient for it to be perceived, it must also be accepted. In other words, suffering must be ennobled by consent to the sacrifice; man must consent to submit to an evil because he has in view a good of a higher order.

Sacrifice is not, then, of a passive nature. It is an action, and one that justly shows the nobility of man, his dignity, and his greatness. To un-

---

* For brevity's sake we omit the pages in which the author points out two other purposes of suffering: a) it turns man away from Evil, and b) it may be an abundant source of merit gained for eternity; and we quote the last pages of this chapter.

derstand this we need only compare the attitude of an animal with that of a man in the face of the same danger. The animal flees from it; it has not the strength to cope with it—it yields—it thinks itself beaten without having put up a fight. Man, on the contrary, looks Evil in the face, accepts the challenge, he fights it and overthrows it. Man is thus the victor. The victory increases his strength, exalts his whole being. He is thereafter in some way more than man: his faculties are widened, deepened, amplified.

Let us consider one of his faculties—his intelligence, for example. Naturally it finds complete satisfaction in the direct vision of Truth, for it is always towards Truth that it tends. But how poor and miserable it would be if it held as truth only that of which it had itself experience. It would then know only that which happened in the neighborhood, that to which his senses could bear testimony. Its provinces would be limited to the place that man inhabited, to the time that he spent on earth. All that had gone before him, all that would happen after him, would remain wrapped in the clouds of ignorance and man would resemble the animal. He would not even know the place nor the date of his birth, for we have no direct immediate knowledge of these things. He would have neither parents, nor country, nor genealogy, nor traditions, for how could he possess all that? By faith. Now faith is a sacrifice on the part of intelligence in renouncing any claim of admitting only that which fully satisfies the mind, Faith contents itself heroically with truth in the glimmer of twilight; with the simple testimony of a man or of God. Intelligence will never be satisfied with that; it will suffer. But this sacrifice on the part of intelligence will enrich man in his intelligence.

Let us pass on to the will of Man. That is free. Nature has not wished to determine it; the things that it meets on its way, the particular goods, are not strong enough to determine it. Only the Good in Itself can do that. But that good resides in the sphere of the ideal and man lives in the real world. Now the ideal is always the same, its action is immutable, and Man must act in a world that changes unceasingly and flows on like a torrent. Man must decide for himself according to circumstances.

Liberty is the instrument of man's greatness. It is liberty that gives him the noblest empire of all, empire over himself. A transcendent but terrible privilege. For liberty may easily degenerate into license and cause the waste of precious strength and the dispersal of treasures. To save himself from such disaster, man must use his liberty with prudence; to the physical liberty which gives him the power to do what he will he must add the moral liberty that gives him the power to do what is right. Physical liberty is a gift of Nature; moral liberty must be the work of man. How is he going to acquire it? By imposing upon his physical activity certain regulating principles, by always directing it towards his ideal. We must add to our inborn character, the gift of

Nature, another character that will be our own creation. That will be what we call our "virtues"; acquired forces that man establishes by the power of his will and which in a continuous and vigorous manner direct him towards God and send him forward towards the ideal.

Now how can one acquire these virtues? They are only "good habits." And good habits are the result of repeated efforts, thanks to which the moral being wins the finest victories, victories over himself. And this victory over self involves a struggle against self, a struggle always hard, always painful. Virtues are the fruit of sacrifice, the fruit of suffering.

We might without exaggeration say that all there is of beauty and of greatness in the life of man is due to suffering and the result of sacrifice. For the farmer to be able to reap an abundant harvest he must have sacrificed some of his grain; he must have thrown it into the ground and allowed it to die. It is the same law for Man. It is by fighting, by suffering, by sacrifice, that he builds character. Education would be an impossibility without a continuous struggle against self, without suffering, without sacrifice. The pedagogic methods that claim to spare the child all effort produce very mediocre subjects. But Man has to continue the work of education all through his life; he must never cease the fight against self.

We said before that even the purely passive progress of the animal kingdom implies some pain, some suffering. But this automatic progress is no more than a shadow of true progress, of active progress. In reality, passive progress only gives what its surroundings have supplied to the animal. The fact could be interpreted by a kind of equation if it could ever be expressed in mathematical terms. All true progress creates a new reality, and such progress involves sustained effort, hard work, many sacrifices.

In the same way, every invention involves some sacrifice. We imagine sometimes that inventions spring ready made from the brain, like the helmeted Minerva from the head of Jupiter. Let us not forget that the goddess whom we call Minerva or Pallas Athena is only a myth. Even when inventions come into man's consciousness unexpectedly they are still the fruit of a long, secret work of incubation, a result of thought and efforts of attention that had as their object a single group of very special problems. They also required sacrifices.

It is by suffering, by the acceptance of Evil, by sacrifice, that man arrives at his full realization, that he approaches his ideal and draws nearer to perfection.

59

EVIL: SCANDAL AND MYSTERY *

This is the last of sixteen essays which deal with the most important truths of the Christian religion. The author begins by defining the dimensions of the problem and showing where it lies; he then considers evil as a philosophical problem and as a religious mystery. We content ourselves with giving the introduction and the conclusion of the essay.

A SOLUTION at last? Hardly: we are under no delusion that any arguments of ours will succeed in answering all the difficulties; but at least we can explain why no such solution is to be expected, or even possible. On the problem of evil—on the question, that is, in so far as it admits a solution—much that is cogent has already been said; probably everything. Like others before us, we shall bring forward arguments which are not without force. But it is not so much the problem itself we propose to deal with—or rather, not the metaphysical problem—as the problem in its human aspect, as man actually encounters it; and more particularly as he encounters it when he takes it into his head to reflect on his own destiny, on the meaning of himself and of everything else. For it is then he runs up against evil as an obstacle masking the face of God. When we take unto consideration the dimensions of the problem, and where it really lies, we shall see that fundamentally what man needs most is to perceive in a true light the *meaning* of evil and of the scandal it presents.

. . . .

The metaphysical problem is not to be ignored, nor is the light that metaphysics is capable of shedding; but the decisive question about God is that of His existence as First Cause and eternal Axiom. The latter is an important truth, the recognition of which is invaluable for all else; but it is one which men are little concerned with and very few deny. No: the decisive issue is that of God's dealings with the world, his design, the intention he has of drawing all our destinies in himself.

That is why the question of evil is profoundly existential; epistemologically it belongs to apologetics rather than to philosophy pure and simple. Or so it seems in the matter of these three characteristic points:

* Yves M. J. Congar, O.P. (1904-   ), in *God, Man and the Universe: A Christian Answer to Modern Materialism,* edited with an introduction by Jacques de Bivort de la Saudée (New York: P. J. Kenedy, 1954).

(1) There is an apologetic of demonstration and argument, another of what we might call "monstration," revealing the values of existence; and in leading people to faith the second is more decisive than the first. In just the same way there is a treatment of evil as a problem, at the level of explanations, and a treatment of it as mystery, at the level of choice of destiny, and values of existence. But they are not alien to one another, these two different ways of tackling the question. We have seen this above, where in the first part of the chapter we already had to anticipate religious considerations; and in a sense these considerations, as Father Sertillanges has already pointed out, have apologetic value only when combined with a satisfactory metaphysical solution.

(2) As in apologetics, what really counts is the totality of the answer. Firstly, because any partial difficulty puts in question (so to speak) God's indivisible honour. But chiefly because we are not concerned with this or that explanation so much as with a view of the total design; indeed without this view of a total design no particular explanation can be completely valid. Evil exists in the world, and it is chiefly a matter of providing a view of things in which the existence of evil is seen to harmonize with the wisdom and goodness of God. Such a view is provided in Christianity. Of course a man can reject that view *en bloc*. But if he ignores this view put forward by Christians—a view that embraces their God and the world and the evil that exists in the world—he cannot argue that the existence of evil in any way implicates the Christian God.

And here one might insert a general remark worth bearing in mind. Christianity is to be taken as a whole, and it is only within that whole that the solutions it has to offer are valid. Take, for instance, the subject of purity. What it has to say about this is true and practicable; but not if isolated from prayer, from faith and the sacraments. Its social doctrine is also true and applicable; but it is bound up with its whole conception of man and of the means it offers for putting it in effect. So Christianity justifies God in regard to evil; but not without providing a complete theology, and the concrete means of passing from a state of hostility or indifference to a filial attitude of communion with God. The vestibule of Christianity stands wide open, and there are plenty of doors to give access to it; but its vision of things is to be seen only from within.

(3) If we take the problem of evil as a whole—and this is also the concrete problem—we have to recognize that its law of light and obscurity is like that which governs the order of faith. Pascal defined it unforgettably: "It was not fitting," he says, "that Jesus Christ should appear in a divine fashion, carrying total conviction; but neither was it fitting that he should come in a manner so hidden that he could pass unrecognized by those who honestly sought him. He willed to be perfectly recognizable to these. And so, willing to appear openly to those who sought him with all their hearts, he tempered man's knowledge

of him in such a way that the signs he gave of who he was, were visible enough to those who sought him, but invisible to those who did not. *There is enough light for those whose only desire is to see, enough obscurity for those who have such desire.*" What touches God and our destiny is always a mingling of light and shadow. It is the field of self-realization, of the paradoxical play of freedom and grace.

One might say that here, if the justifications in themselves are stronger, the difficulties are more acutely realized. They derive from all that is most sensitive in us, all that is most immediate. The lights, on the other hand, come from the metaphysical relation of the created to the Uncreated, from the nature of God or his design. But this last is also a mystery; when revealed to us, it is known only by faith, and even then much more in its general lines than in the details of its working. Unlike the soldier in battle, Stendhahl's Fabrice at Waterloo, the faithful know the general's broad plan of campaign, they are certain of the issue, but the detail escapes them; and it is in the matter of detail that so many of the evils occur that they experience most cruelly.

Moreover, as so often happens in apologetics, the objection is very much easier than the answer. To present a difficulty in all its force, all I need is a short sentence and half a minute's experience. But to work out the answer and perceive all its bearings calls for a lengthy discourse, mental poise and years of preparation. After all, it is easier to knock a man down than to lift him up; a few ounces of lead are enough to lay him out.

It depends on the heart: by which we mean something entirely different from a mere sentimental choice, made more or less blindly. "Heart" must be understood here in the Biblical sense, which is near enough to the Pascalian sense. It means man in so far as he adopts with his whole self, and primarily with his mind, a standpoint that is primarily one of refusal or acceptance. It is there that we begin to be either carnal or spiritual again in the Biblical sense, in which it is possible to be spiritually carnal, and in one's bodily life spiritual. How closely Pascal's thought is here in line with Scripture can be seen in texts like the following: "Good men see a light down in darkness" (Ps. 111:4); "The man whose life is true comes to the light" (John 3:21). Those whose hearts are inclined towards God recognize—beneath his dealings with the world, so mysterious to us—a wisdom comparable to that which is revealed in nature, where so many processes, equally impenetrable to us, work out ultimately for good. Even in the midst of great suffering, such souls have no difficulty in justifying Providence.

Occasionally they are criticized. They seem to some to have a kind of arrested animist mentality, seeing intentions everywhere, explaining everything that occurs by the direct intervention of some higher spirit. Or again those who do not look at things in such a light of loving confidence may perhaps discern a kind of will to be deceived in the imperturbable calmness with which such souls resolve beforehand to see an admirable Providence wherever they turn, find always some means of detecting good in evil.

Such criticism raises the question of every good founded on faith. It would be possible to answer it by reasons and explanations: the whole of this chapter provides the elements of such an answer. After all, if we ourselves put so much intention into what we do, why should not infinite Intelligence, the Creator and Governor of the universe, put an infinite amount of intention into his work? But fundamentally, here again, the objection lies at an existential level, where we choose the highest values of our life. It introduces no new intellectual arguments; it simply challenges the application of a principle that is dependent entirely on the Christian choice. It is to be hoped that the foregoing pages have furnished some serious motives for this choice. But at such a level what is really worth most of all is testimony. Such a testimony is provided, for those whose hearts are inclined towards God, by the experience they have had of the total truth of St. Paul's words: "We are all assured that everything helps to secure the good of those who love God" (Rom. 8:28).

Since we are all, even the most religious of us, carnal as well as spiritual, and since both believer and unbeliever, alternately or simultaneously, take possession of our hearts, for us evil is always both a scandal and a mystery we are bound to revere in faith. The very mingling of the two things is typical of this ambiguous world of freedom where the question of evil is practically encountered. The believer, when he has silenced the voices that prompt him to refuse and is in the very act of adoring, cannot but say: "Lord, I believe. Succour my unbelief . . . " (Mark 9:23).

A NOTE ON THE TYPE
IN WHICH THIS BOOK IS SET

This book is set in Baskerville, a Linotype face, created from the original types used by John Baskerville, the eighteenth-century typefounder and printer. This type has long been considered one of the finest book types ever developed. The letters are wide and open and have a businesslike approach. The finer hairlines give exquisite delicacy. The heavier strokes give color and strength. The relation of the two in combination gives a brilliant effect and makes for easy reading. The book was composed, printed and bound by the Wickersham Printing Company of Lancaster, Pa. The typography and design are by Howard N. King.